The Founding
of English America

The Founding of English America

An Introduction to the Lost Colony and Jamestown

JOHN MAY

McFarland & Company, Inc., Publishers
Jefferson, North Carolina

LIBRARY OF CONGRESS CATALOGING-IN-PUBLICATION DATA

Names: May, John, 1942– author.
Title: The founding of English America : an introduction to the Lost colony and Jamestown / John May.
Other titles: Introduction to the Lost colony and Jamestown
Description: Jefferson, North Carolina : McFarland & Company, Inc., Publishers, 2024 | Includes bibliographical references and index.
Identifiers: LCCN 2024010701 | ISBN 9781476695242 (paperback : acid free paper) ∞ ISBN 9781476652610 (ebook)
Subjects: LCSH: Jamestown (Va.)—History—17th century. | Roanoke Colony. | Great Britain—Colonies—America—History—17th century. | Virginia—Colonization—History—17th century. | Roanoke Island (N.C.)—History—17th century.
Classification: LCC F229 .M44 2024 | DDC 973.2/1—dc23/eng/20240306
LC record available at https://lccn.loc.gov/2024010701

BRITISH LIBRARY CATALOGUING DATA ARE AVAILABLE

ISBN (print) 978-1-4766-9524-2
ISBN (ebook) 978-1-4766-5261-0

© 2024 John May, Jr. All rights reserved

No part of this book may be reproduced or transmitted in any form or by any means, electronic or mechanical, including photocopying or recording, or by any information storage and retrieval system, without permission in writing from the publisher.

Front cover image: "Colonists Leaving England for Jamestown," 1907 World's Fair Collection postcard, Jamestown Amusement & Vending Co. Inc., Norfolk, Virginia, 8.8 cm. × 14.0 cm. (Donald G. Larson Collection on International Fairs and Exhibitions, Special Collections Research Center, California State University, Fresno)

Printed in the United States of America

McFarland & Company, Inc., Publishers
  Box 611, Jefferson, North Carolina 28640
    www.mcfarlandpub.com

To Alice

Table of Contents

Tudor Family Tree	viii
Dramatis Personae	1
Introduction	11
1. The Virgin Queen	17
2. The Sea Dogs	33
3. The Lost Colony	50
4. The End of an Era	73
5. Jamestown	90
6. Pocahontas and John Smith	110
7. The Wreck of the *Sea Venture*	134
8. The Starving Time	151
9. Redemption	166
Epilogue	181
Chapter Notes	195
Bibliography	243
Index	249

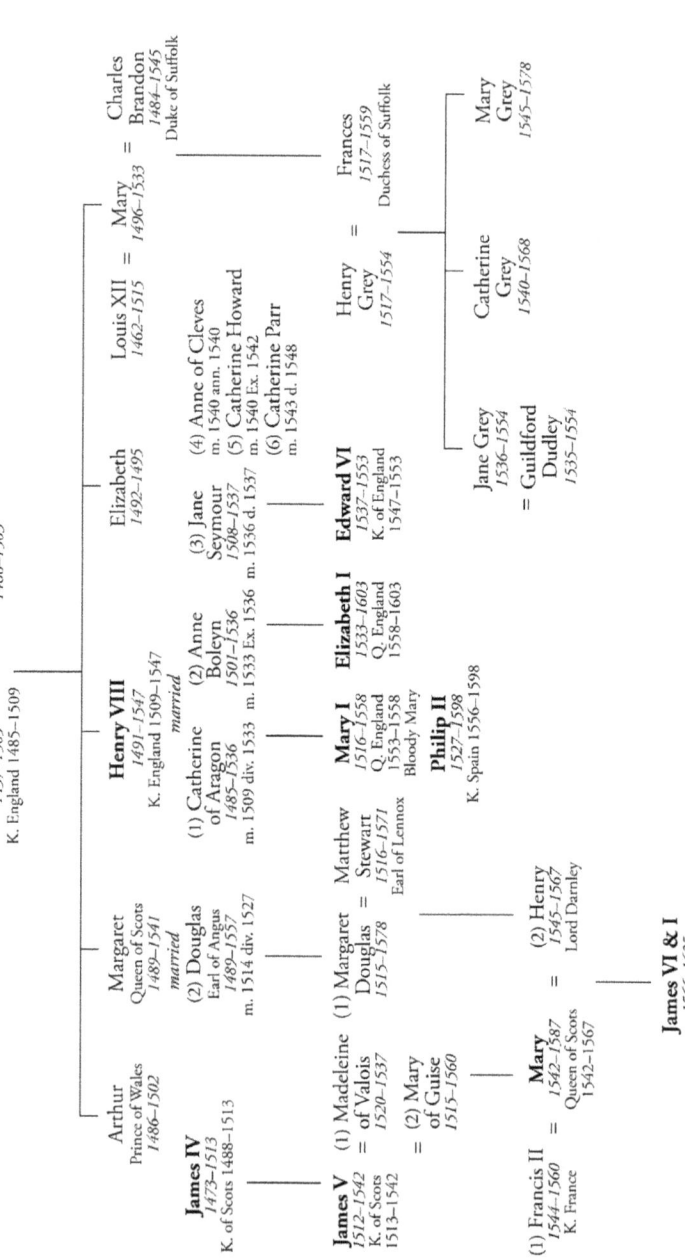

Dramatis Personae

Royalty

Anne Boleyn (ca. 1507–1536), **Queen of England** as second wife of Henry VIII and mother of Queen Elizabeth I of England. Anne Boleyn had beautiful, black almond-shaped eyes that captivated Henry when she returned from serving at the French court in 1522. He ultimately married her and made her his queen, but when she failed to produce a male heir, he trumped up charges of infidelity. She was convicted and beheaded. Henry proceeded to marry three more times, but he never fathered a legitimate male heir who would survive to adulthood.

Charles V (1500–1558), **Holy Roman Emperor**, born in Flanders, inherited the Hapsburg Netherlands encompassing modern-day Belgium, Luxembourg, and the Netherlands. Father of Philip II. He claimed to "speak Spanish to God, Italian to women, French to men, and German to my horse."

Edward VI, King of England (1537–1553), son of Henry VIII and Jane Seymour. Died of tuberculosis.

Elizabeth I, Queen of England (1533–1603), daughter of Henry VIII and Anne Boleyn.

Francis, Duke of Alençon and Anjou (1555–1584), younger son of Henry II of France and Catherine de' Medici. Though twenty-two years younger than Elizabeth, he came close to marrying her in the early 1580s. Later, he died of a fever in Château-Thierry in France. He was "very small and very ugly; but he was also most entertaining and disarmingly eager."

Henry VIII, King of England (1491–1547). Died of a surfeit of food, drink, and wives.

Henry Frederick, Prince of Wales (1594–1612), eldest son of James I of England. Lobbied for the release of Sir Walter Raleigh from imprisonment in the Tower of London, and died of typhoid at age eighteen, reputedly after swimming in the Thames.

James I, King of England (1566–1625), son of Mary, Queen of Scots and Henry Stuart, Lord Darnley. He was also King James VI of Scotland.

Mary I, Queen of England (1516–1558), son of Henry VIII and Catherine of Aragon. Also known as "Bloody Mary."

Mary, Queen of Scots (1542–1587), daughter of James V of Scotland and Mary of Guise. Executed.

Philip II, King of Spain (1527–1598), married Mary I of England and by right of his wife, was King of England from 1554 until 1558.

English Officials

Robert Cecil (1563–1912), **Earl of Salisbury**, son of William Cecil, and Secretary of State under Elizabeth I and James I. He attended St. John's College, Cambridge, and Gray's Inn. Short and hunchbacked, he was solemn and businesslike. He is credited with the smooth transition of power after the queen's death in 1603. He feigned friendship with the Raleighs, but quietly made sure James kept Raleigh imprisoned in the Tower of London.

William Cecil (1520–1598), 1st **Baron Burghley**, secretary of state and lord high treasurer to Elizabeth I. Called by the Spanish ambassador "prudent and virtuous," he had attended St. John's College, Cambridge and Gray's Inn and was thirty-eight when Elizabeth came to the throne.

John Dee (1527–ca. 1608), English mathematician, Greek scholar, astronomer, astrologer, necromancer, writer, and advisor to Elizabeth I. He was educated at Trinity College, Cambridge and had a notorious reputation as a necromancer. He was tall, thin, handsome with a long beard "as white as milk."

Robert Devereux (1565–1601), **Earl of Essex**; and royal favorite. Neale says of him "All the qualities for a brilliant career were his, save judgment, an equable temper, and discretion." He was the stepson of Robert Dudley, and he was executed for treason. Hibbert tells us he had "shining auburn hair and striking black eyes" but that he was "reckless and vain, heedlessly extravagant."

Robert Dudley (1532–1588), **Earl of Leicester**, soldier, politician, courtier, and royal favorite. Tall and extremely handsome with well-shaped legs, he was considered the finest horseman in England and was a perennial winner in jousting tournaments. Considered something of a radical, his power as the queen's favorite became a counterpoise to that of William Cecil, creating the team of rivals that characterized Elizabeth's privy council. Despite Dudley's perversity—he was called unreliable and arrogant—he was the queen's supreme favorite, perhaps even the love of her life.

Sir Christopher Hatton (1540–1591), knight, Lord Chancellor of England, Captain of the Yeomen Guard, and royal favorite. Educated at Oxford, he ultimately became Chancellor of Oxford University. He was a fine dancer; in fact, it was said "he danced his way into favor." With Leicester, Burghley, and Walsingham, he was one of the four most influential men in government." Industrious and fiercely loyal to the queen, he was a tall, agreeable man and a skillful horseman. He never married but had several secret paramours.

Charles Howard (1536–1624), 1st **Earl of Nottingham**, 2nd Baron Howard of Effingham, and Lord High Admiral. With Drake, Howard was admiral of the English fleet that defeated the Spanish Armada.

Sir Francis Walsingham (ca. 1532–1590), principal secretary to Queen Elizabeth I. Educated at Cambridge and Gray's Inn—the ideal path for political advancement—he became responsible for foreign affairs. He was considered intelligent, wily, and astute. He became Elizabeth's "spy master," and his evidence proving unequivocally that Mary, Queen of Scots, was plotting to bring down the monarch led to Mary's execution. He paid many of his spies out of his own pocket and died in debt.

Sea Dogs and Explorers

John Cabot (ca. 1450–ca. 1500), Italian, born Giovanni Caboto possibly in Genoa, navigator, explorer, discover of Newfoundland and father of **Sebastian Cabot** (ca. 1474–ca. 1557), Italian, born in Venice, navigator, explorer.

Thomas Cavendish (1560–1592), explorer, privateer, soldier, circumnavigator. Cavendish was from Suffolk from a wealthy family. A member of the Durham House coterie, he was second in command of the 1585 English fleet carrying the original Roanoke Island colonists to America. He remained with the colony over the winter. In 1587, he sailed into the Pacific via the Straits of Magellan in his own ship and captured a Spanish galleon with a cargo worth 2 million pesos. He circumnavigated the globe on his return to England, only the third to have done so. The Dutch would be fourth in 1598–1601.

Sir Francis Drake (ca. 1540–1596), English privateer, circumnavigator, vice-admiral of the English fleet in the defeat of the Spanish Armada in 1588. A Devonshire native, he grew up nearer London where he was apprenticed to a ship's captain. He was said to have a lively spirit and was resolute, quick, affable and easy of access. His circumnavigation was second only to Magellan, and he brought home loot worth millions in today's currency.

Sir Martin Frobisher (ca. 1535–1594), English explorer, privateer, naval commander. Frobisher made three voyages to find a northwest passage, in 1576, 1577, and 1578. All failed to find an open sea lane, but he collected 1,136 tons of ore believed to contain gold. It proved worthless and was used to pave London streets. Later he served as commander of one of England's four squadrons that defeated the Spanish Armada, the others being John Hawkins, Francis Drake, and Charles Howard, Lord High Admiral.

Sir Humphrey Gilbert (ca. 1539–1583), explorer, adventurer, soldier, and member of Parliament for Plymouth. Half-brother of Walter Ralegh. It was said of him that he had symptoms of a disturbed personality. He was passionate, impulsive, violent, and cruel, but also an intellectual and visionary with great personal magnetism.

Sir John Hawkins (1532–1595), English privateer, naval officer, Treasurer of the Navy from 1578 until his death. A very ambitious man, Hawkins was said to be slow, jealous, and inclined to 'malice with dissimulation." He was mentor to his younger distant cousin, Francis Drake.

Roanoke Island and the Lost Colony

Philip Amadas (d.1618), ship's captain, explorer. A native of Plymouth in Devonshire, Amadas may have been a distant relative of Walter Raleigh and was employed by Raleigh at Durham House. One writer claims he was a member of Middle Temple, implying he was a gentleman. He was said to be small in stature but headstrong and hot tempered. He was a veteran of Irish wars in 1580–81. According to one source, he was in his early twenties when he captained one of the ships in the reconnaissance voyage to Virginia in 1584, but another source has his date of birth as 1550. He returned to Roanoke the following year and is charged with responsibility for the unfortunate retaliatory attack on Algonquins living in the Secotan village of Aquascogoc, burning their homes and crops. After this, he disappears from Raleigh's employ.

Arthur Barlowe (1550–1620), ship's captain. Barlowe served with Raleigh in Ireland in 1580–81. He was captain of one of the ships in the reconnaissance voyage in 1584 then returned again the following year. He was said to have a steadying influence on his companion, Philip Amadas. His journal is an excellent primary source for these voyages, and his powers of observation were quite good.

Simon Fernandez (ca. 1538–ca. 1590), navigator, privateer, born in Terciera in the Azores—a Portuguese possession at the time. He was trained in Portugal and claimed to have served on a Spanish expedition that coasted the North Carolina Outer Banks. Fernandez was captured off the coast of England and charged with piracy, then pardoned in return for service to the crown. He served under Sir Francis Drake in the West Indies in 1577. He was Sir Humphrey Gilbert's pilot on at least one of his voyages to America and later served Walter Raleigh as his chief navigator.

Sir Richard Grenville (1542–1591), English soldier, privateer, politician, and captain of the *Revenge* immortalized in a poem of that name by Alfred, Lord Tennyson. A native of Bideford in Devonshire, he was the son of gentry whose father owned considerable land in Cornwall. A man of action, young Richard killed a man in a duel with his sword, was pardoned, became a soldier, and fought in Ireland. He was admiral of Walter Raleigh's first fleet to establish a colony on Roanoke Island in 1585. In the Azores in 1591, Grenville's ship, the *Revenge*, took on the Spanish fleet almost by itself. His ship dismasted and sinking, he refused to surrender until, fatally wounded, he was begged to do so by his crew. He died aboard the Spanish flagship two or three days later.

Richard Hakluyt (1553–1616), ("*HAK-let*"), English cleric, writer, geographer. A longtime advocate for colonization in the New World, Hakluyt wrote essays and compiled voyage of discovery narratives that remain in print to this day. He was engaged by Walter Raleigh to write a monograph for Queen Elizabeth I, urging her to lend her support to Raleigh's efforts to found England's first colony.

Thomas Harriot (ca. 1560–1621), English mathematician, scientist; astronomer. Born in Oxfordshire and educated at Oxford where he may have met Walter Raleigh through Richard Hakluyt. Hired by Raleigh in 1584, he composed a navigational manual while living at Durham House, Raleigh's headquarters for his planned colony in Virginia. His accomplishments in mathematics made him one of the seminal scientists of his time.

Ralph Lane (ca. 1528–1603), English soldier and explorer. He was engaged by Walter Raleigh to command the first English colony in America that settled on Roanoke Island, North Carolina. Lane oversaw the exploration of the region and personally led an exploration of the Albemarle Sound and the Chowan and Roanoke rivers. He ultimately battled the local Algonquin tribe in which the tribe's chief was beheaded after which he decided to abandon the colony.

Christopher Marlowe (1564–1593), English playwright and poet. He was born in Canterbury and died in a bar fight in Deptford. Accused of homosexuality and atheism, he would have been right at home among the freethinkers that gathered at Durham House with Walter Raleigh's coterie.

Elizabeth Throckmorton Ralegh (1565–1647), wife of Walter Ralegh, Gentlewoman of the Privy Chamber.

Sir Walter Ralegh (ca. 1552–1618), knight and captain of the Queen's Bodyguard, founder of the Roanoke Colony, and royal favorite. He never once spelled his name "Raleigh," although that is the spelling customarily used, including in this book.

William Sanderson (ca. 1548–1638), London merchant and sometime business manager for Sir Walter Raleigh. He was married to Margaret Snedale, Raleigh's niece.

John White (ca. 1539–ca. 1593), English artist, colonist, 2nd governor of the Roanoke Colony. White led the second colony to Roanoke Island with the backing of Walter Raleigh, the colony that became known as the Lost Colony. His attempts to return to America to rescue his colony were thwarted by war with Spain and England's battle against the Spanish Armada.

Jamestown

Gabriel Archer (ca. 1574–ca. 1610), explorer, Jamestown colonist. Archer attended Cambridge with Bartholomew Gosnold and was a member of Gray's Inn. He had sailed with Gosnold when Cape Cod and Martha's Vineyard were discovered in 1602. Archer may have had Catholic sympathies. He died during the starving time and his grave in the chancel of the old church in Jamestown has been discovered by archeologists.

Samuel Argall (ca. 1572 or 1580–1626), adventurer, naval officer, Jamestown official. Argall was the first captain to attempt a more direct crossing of the Atlantic to Jamestown, saving precious time and supplies. A capable soldier and seafarer, he orchestrated the kidnapping of Pocahontas in 1613 and later had success trading for badly needed corn with the Potomac River Algonquins. He served as governor of Virginia from 1617 to 1619. Argall was later instrumental in chasing the French out of North America. He was a cousin by marriage to Thomas Smythe.

Sir Thomas Dale (ca. 1570–1619), career soldier with twenty-three years' experience. He served as marshal and no-nonsense governor of the Virginia Colony from 1611 to 1616. Dale had served with Thomas Gates in the Netherlands. A stern taskmaster, he decreed martial law for the colony and meted out severe and, on occasion, deadly punishment for violations. He approved the marriage of John Rolfe to Pocahontas, and their son, Thomas, was named for him.

Dramatis Personae

Bartholomew Gosnold (1571–1607), mariner, explorer, privateer, co-founder of the Virginia Company of London and member of the original governing council of Jamestown. In 1602 he discovered and named Martha's Vineyard for his deceased daughter and the grapes that grew wild on the island. He died of unknown causes shortly after arriving in Jamestown.

The Reverend Robert Hunt (1569–1608), Jamestown's first minister. Migrated there after being forced to leave his parish in Sussex for several indiscretions. He worked to free Captain John Smith from imprisonment and to keep the peace among fractious Jamestown councilors in the early days of the colony. He was buried in the church in Jamestown, and his grave was found by archeologists. He died in the spring of 1608 shortly after all his personal possession had been destroyed by fire.

George Kendall (ca. 1570–1608), an original Jamestown councilman. He conspired with Wingfield to abandon the colony and return to England. He was tried and executed apparently by firing squad in December 1608. He was also accused of being Catholic, a Spanish spy, and a double agent working for William Cecil.

Captain John Martin (ca. 1560–1632), an original Jamestown councilman. Martin had sailed with Sir Francis Drake to Roanoke Island in 1586 and was with Bartholomew Gosnold when he discovered Cape Cod and Martha's Vineyard in 1602. Later, he developed Martin's Brandon Plantation on the south bank of the James River from a land grant of 7,000 acres. It was still in operation in 2020.

Christopher Newport (1560 or 1561–1617), sea captain, privateer, explorer. Born in Limehouse in greater London, Newport is reported to have crossed the Atlantic nearly forty times. He participated in Francis Drake's highly successful raid on Cadiz in 1587. Newport lost a portion of his right arm in a sword fight while trying to capture a Spanish vessel in 1590. He was selected to command the immensely rich Spanish prize, the *Madre de Dios,* back to England in 1592, having made a fortune in plunder. His wealth bought him a comfortable house and garden on Tower Hill. In 1605, he captured two young crocodiles and a wild boar in Hispaniola and personally presented them to King James. Newport had two sons and a daughter. He captained fleets carrying colonists to Jamestown, Virginia five times.

George Percy (1580–1632), seventh son of the eighth Earl of Northumberland, soldier, president of the Jamestown Council from September 1609 until May 1610. He attended Eton College, Oxford University and the Middle Temple. At age sixteen, he inherited an annuity from his mother of £60 per year, enough for a comfortable though not lavish lifestyle. One historian called him "a horrible snob."

John Ratcliffe (1549–1609), also known as John Sicklemore, having changed his surname as a result of his mother's remarriage. He was an original Jamestown councilman and later president of the colony from September 1607 until September 1608, killed by Algonquins in December 1609. Oldest of the original council members, Ratcliffe allied with John Martin and Gabriel Archer against John Smith.

Captain John Smith (1580–1631), soldier, explorer, president of the Jamestown colony. He earned the rank of captain while serving in the army of the Holy Roman Empire prior to migrating to Virginia. According to Haile, Smith "had a reputation for being difficult and he earned it. We call him a leader, an adventurer, an explorer, map maker, soldier, writer, scholar, and more, but most of all he is doer of 'high deeds in Hungary,' a fascinating character, one larger than anybody but Powhatan."

Sir Thomas Smythe (ca. 1558–1625), merchant, politician, first governor of the East India Company and chief executive of the Virginia Company whose father **Thomas "Customer" Smythe** (1522–1591) was a customs official and member of Parliament.

Francis West (1586–1633/34), Jamestown colonist, brother of Thomas West, Baron De La Warr. Sent to the Potomac River by Governor Percy in 1609 to trade for corn, he committed atrocities there, loaded his ship with stolen corn, then—instead of returning to Jamestown—he sailed to England, abandoning the colony he had been charged to save. He later returned to Jamestown and, despite his shameful past, served as Deputy Governor of Virginia from 1627 to 1629.

Thomas West (1577–1618), third **Baron De La Warr**, soldier, politician, governor of Jamestown. Attended Oxford and served in the English army under Robert Devereaux, Earl of Essex, who knighted him in Ireland in 1599. West joined Essex's insurrection conspiracy against Queen Elizabeth I and was briefly imprisoned before being acquitted. He later became one of James I's privy councilors. In Jamestown in 1610, he was taken ill and abandoned the colony after only a few months to return to England to recover his health. He died aboard ship returning to Jamestown in 1618 at the age of forty-one.

The Reverend Alexander Whitaker (1585–1616), Anglican clergyman educated at Cambridge. A closet Puritan, he traveled to Virginia in 1611 and established a church at Henrico. Thomas Dale placed the kidnapped Pocahontas in Whitaker's care, and he instructed her in English and Christianity and baptized her. He drowned in 1616 while crossing the James River.

Edward Maria Wingfield (1550–1631), soldier, president of the first governing council of Jamestown. He was a veteran of military action in Ireland and the Low Countries. His leadership was undermined by his arrogance, and his tenure as president of the first Jamestown colony was thereby short lived.

Sir Francis Wyatt (1588–1644), politician, twice governor of Virginia, grandson of Thomas Wyatt, the leader of Wyatt's rebellion against Queen Mary Tudor.

Sea Venture

Richard Buck (1582–1623), graduate of Oxford, chaplain of the Anglican Church at Jamestown from 1610 until his death, sailed on the *Sea Venture* with his wife and two daughters. He also presided at the marriage of John Rolfe and Pocahontas on April 5, 1614.

Sir Thomas Gates (ca. 1560–1622), soldier, interim governor and, later, governor of Jamestown. Born in Colyford, Devon, he completed a residency at Gray's Inn. Gates went out to Jamestown aboard the *Sea Venture* as interim governor of the colony until the arrival of Lord De La Warr. He was marooned on Bermuda with other survivors for ten months.

John Rolfe (1585–1622), Jamestown colonist, pioneer tobacco farmer, member of Jamestown governing council, married Pocahontas in 1614. His first wife was Sarah Hacker Rolfe (d. 1610), who died either en route from Bermuda to Jamestown or shortly after arriving in Jamestown.

Sir George Somers (1554–1610), privateer, politician, admiral, founding father of Bermuda. A native of Lyme Regis, Dorset, the son of a prosperous merchant. Became a privateer and sailed to the West Indies in the 1590s and the early years of 1600, and he also served in Ireland. He became mayor of Lyme Regis and a member of Parliament in 1604. Became admiral of an eight-ship fleet sailing for Jamestown when his ship, *Sea Venture*, crashed upon the reefs of Bermuda where he and the other passengers and crew were marooned for ten months.

William Strachey (1572–1621), writer, poet, London theater owner, and secretary of the Jamestown colony from June 1610 until September 1611. Born in Safron Walden, the grandson of a prosperous local landowner. Strachey was educated at Cambridge, enrolled in Gray's Inn, and became a part owner of a troupe of boy actors who performed at Blackfriars Theatre. He served as secretary for the English ambassador to the Levant for a short time before being dismissed. Returning to London, he invested in the Virginia Company and migrated there in hopes of employment.

Sir George Yeardley (1587–1627), soldier, Jamestown colonist. Yeardley served under Gates and was marooned with him and other *Sea Venture* survivors on Bermuda for ten months. He served several terms as deputy governor and governor of Virginia between 1616 and his death in 1627, became a large landowner, developed tobacco plantations, and owned slaves.

Introduction

The history of English America begins with a phrase coined in 1577 by a mathematician and cosmographer named John Dee. Born in 1527, Dee attended Trinity College, Cambridge, where he embraced its Renaissance-inspired secular humanism. At age twenty he sailed to Flanders to study under Europe's leading geographers, a group that included Gerardus Mercator.[1] A keen practitioner of astrology, Dee was arrested in 1551, charged with the treasonable offense of casting the horoscope of Queen Mary and her husband, Philip of Spain.[2] He also dabbled in astronomy, alchemy, and the occult, and his library became one of the largest in England. In a contemporary portrait he looks to be the quintessential wizard.[3] During Elizabeth's reign, he made his home in the Arthurian-sounding village of Mortlake, ten miles upriver from Whitehall Palace, to which he was occasionally summoned to give advice to the queen. A work composed by him for her in 1576, *General and Rare Memorials Pertaining to the Perfect Art of Navigation*, advocated for the expansion of her realm by the construction of a larger and more powerful navy and the creation of colonies in the New World.[4] The phrase he coined in 1577 was "Brytish Impire."[5]

It is at this exact moment in time that the clock starts ticking on the history of English America.[6] The work before you tells the story of the thirty-odd-year struggle to turn Dee's vision into reality and of the men and women who brought it to fruition. The founding of the first enduring English American colony was one continuous effort interrupted by war with Spain. The Roanoke Island and Jamestown colonies constitute the selfsame history in all meaningful respects. Think of Jamestown as the second act of a two-act play but under new direction and with an all-new cast of characters—all new, that is, save one: Richard Hakluyt.

English America is the lengthened shadow of many people, but first among them is Richard Hakluyt. Of Welsh descent—his surname was pronounced "HAK-let"—he was born in London between 1551 and 1553 into a middle-class family originally from Herefordshire.[7] His parents died when he was a boy, so he became the ward of his uncle, also Richard Hakluyt. The younger Richard attended the prestigious Westminster School after which he enrolled at Christ Church, one of the colleges that comprise Oxford University.[8] Founded in 1546 by King Henry VIII, Christ Church had just over one hundred undergraduates when Hakluyt attended between 1571 and 1577. During part of this time, Walter Raleigh, son of Devonshire gentry, was enrolled in the older but smaller Oriel College, also a part of Oxford University located just across King Edward Street.[9] Raleigh's date of birth is not known, but was sometime between 1552 and 1554, so the two were near in age. Though there is no record, these two foremost pillars of English imperialism likely met as students in college.

Young Richard developed a passion for geography and exploration that was nurtured by his guardian who was considered an authority on these subjects by Francis Walsingham, the queen's Secretary of State. Walsingham sought the elder Hakluyt's advice on behalf of Humphrey Gilbert, who was granted a royal patent in 1578 to settle a colony in Newfoundland as a base for discovering a northwest passage to the Orient.[10] As Raleigh was Gilbert's younger half-brother and captain of one of his ships, he would have been involved in the planning, as was the younger Hakluyt.[11] Here we see the two eager youngbloods—both in their mid-twenties—in talks to create an English America.

Fascinated by voyages of exploration and trade, the younger Hakluyt had searched out and interviewed merchants involved in foreign commerce, ships' captains, and even common sailors while still at Oxford.[12] The focus of his studies, however, was the ministry, and he became an ordained Anglican cleric.[13] In his spare time, he collected voyage of discovery narratives with the goal of someday publishing a compendium of such narratives to engender in English citizens a greater awareness of their nation's rich history of seafaring and foreign trade and of the many benefits to be gained by expanding such activities. In the course of his studies at Oxford, he had mastered six languages in addition to English, essential for translating the discovery narratives of other nations.[14] In 1582 he published his first work, *Divers Voyages Touching the Discoverie of America and the Ilands Adjacent unto the Same*. With this, Richard Hakluyt the younger succeeded John Dee as England's most vociferous and trenchant advocate for the establishment of a colony in the New World.

After Gilbert's venture failed and his homeward bound ship disappeared beneath the waves, Raleigh inherited his patent.[15] He then persuaded his friend Hakluyt to write a prospectus for the queen, outlining the potential advantages of a colony located in that part of North America Raleigh chose to name Virginia in honor of England's Virgin Queen. Raleigh's Virginia encompassed all of North America between thirty degrees and sixty-nine degrees north latitude, that is between today's St. Augustine, Florida, and the Arctic Circle.

At this time, Hakluyt was living in Paris, serving as chaplain and secretary to the English ambassador to France.[16] This notwithstanding, he produced a monograph entitled *A Particuler Discourse Concerninge the Greate Necessitie and Manifolde Commodyties That Are Like to Growe to This Realme of Englande by the Westerne Discoueries Lately Attempted, Written in the Yere 1584.* The title was later shortened to *A Discourse on Western Planting.* Hakluyt placed the handwritten document in the queen's hands in September or October 1584.[17] It was for her eyes only.[18] Its purpose was to entice her to underwrite the colony Raleigh envisioned, but it succeeded only in obtaining the surreptitious loan of a ship, the *Tyger*, and £400 worth of gunpowder.[19] We do not know Elizabeth's private opinion of Raleigh's venture, but a good guess is that she was as keen on the idea as her three most trusted privy councilors, William Cecil, Robert Dudley, and Francis Walsingham. But to invade what King Philip II of Spain considered Nueva España was so blatantly hostile that Elizabeth needed plausible deniability, crucial in avoiding all-out war. Raleigh would have to find seed money elsewhere, and in time he did, by means both fair and foul.[20]

The significance of Hakluyt's *Discourse* is that it highlighted the benefits that he and Raleigh believed would accrue to England by the settlement of a colony in North America.[21] From this document we can deduce the venture's objectives, but with no firsthand experience in exploring the New World, their ideas and perceptions were often naïve, impractical, or wildly optimistic.[22] Be that as it may, these objectives remained unchanged for next twenty-five years. But in all those years of trial-and-error—of one heartbreaking failure after another—the one constant and central presence in the effort was Richard Hakluyt.

Walter Raleigh's interest in Virginia flamed out for several reasons, foremost among them being the lack of profitability.[23] In the 1590s, his head was turned by rumors of El Dorado, a city of gold hidden deep in the Amazon rain forest.[24] This says much about the man that disappoints, but Raleigh had a short attention span and a lust for wealth. Others were not discouraged. A powerful cohort emerged to assume his leadership role, the same men who had been at the forefront of English foreign trade since long before John Dee. This group consisted of two factions—West Country seafaring gentry and wealthy London merchants: men of the sea from Cornwall and Devon and men of money from London. The former included no-nonsense, ship-owning tradesmen who had learned privateering from John Hawkins and Francis Drake. The latter included men like England's merchant prince, Thomas Smythe, and William Sanderson, Raleigh's chief financier.[25] All were eager to take up the baton and see what profits could be squeezed from the great unknown of North America about which Hakluyt promised so much.[26]

The lynchpin of this coalition of West Country seadogs and wealthy London merchants was Hakluyt. As a man of the cloth *and* the foremost authority on English overseas trade and exploration, he became the spiritual and secular center of gravity for the cause of English imperialism. He kept the pot stirred with advocacy and with publication after publication in the ensuing years of war with Spain, drought and economic depression, and the long but inexorable decline and demise of Queen Elizabeth I that kept her fleet close to home, thus precluding New World exploration and settlement.

When this cohort convened in 1606 to restart colonial efforts, Hakluyt was there to provide counsel. Following Raleigh's precedent, they named their new enterprise The Virginia Company.[27] Their overarching motive was also the same as Raleigh's—profit—although Hakluyt insisted on emphasizing their goal of converting Native Americans to Christianity in order to embellish their initiative with a more appealing and virtuous facade. But make no mistake, The Virginia Company was a for-profit corporation in which the state had no ownership interest.[28] And the means to the financial gains they sought—that is, the objectives necessary to achieve profitability—were identical to those Hakluyt had outlined in his *Discourse* twenty years earlier, with one humane addition: that those charged with governing the new colony seek to find survivors of Raleigh's Roanoke Island Colony, who had been forsaken by the threatened onslaught of the Spanish Armada.[29]

The plan was to settle on the Chesapeake Bay, just as Raleigh's so-called Lost Colony had intended, but had failed to do.[30] Raleigh's 1585 colony found no deep-water harbor in the vicinity of Roanoke Island that could accommodate a fleet of ships, necessary for the privateering base he envisioned.[31] In the course of the colonists' exploration of the region that winter, however, they discovered the Chesapeake Bay, and plans were soon afoot to relocate the colony there.[32] In the words of one historian, "Roanoke had shown the way to Jamestown."[33] The latter colony was, therefore, a continuation of the former, but with a new name to honor a new monarch, James I.

Roanoke and Jamestown colonists encountered members of the same Native American language group, Algonquin. The Algonquin peoples then residing on Roanoke Island could communicate with those residing on the shores of the Chesapeake Bay, though dialects may have differed somewhat.[34] For this reason, Jamestown colonists had some notion of the Native Americans they were about to encounter. They even had an Algonquin/

English dictionary that had been compiled by Roanoke colonist, Thomas Harriot.[35] They had access to the journals and publications of Roanoke colonists and advice from the principals involved in Raleigh's organization, including Raleigh himself, who was still very much alive, albeit incarcerated in the Tower of London.[36]

The English who immigrated to Jamestown in 1607 resembled those who had settled Roanoke Island in 1585. They came principally from two cohorts: the younger sons of aristocratic families, many of whom were soldiers, and England's jobless rogues and vagabonds. By the English law of primogeniture, the former group—the so-called "junior cadets"—would receive little or no inheritance and had few prospects.[37] The latter group consisted of the refuse of English society—its so-called "masterless men."[38] As will be seen, these two groups of mostly layabouts explain in large part why the two colonies committed the same errors and suffered the same privations and calamities.[39]

The two colonies had the same objectives, the same two cohorts of supporters, the same destination—the Chesapeake Bay—where colonists, who came from the same two pools of candidates, confronted the same Native American nation, having been persuaded to emigrate from England primarily by the same crusader—Richard Hakluyt. The two colonies are so inextricably linked that they constitute one discrete historical turn of events, and they should, therefore, be presented in one chronological unity.

Many students of United States history are unaware of important elements of our founding: the tragedy of the Lost Colony, the remarkable wreck of the *Sea Venture* that inspired William Shakespeare's *The Tempest*, and the clever, albeit doomed stratagem of the Algonquin chief Wahunsenacawh that brought together his daughter, Pocahontas, and the English Captain John Smith. I am a writer, not an historian. I undertook this project because the founding of English America is fascinating—devastating for those whose land was invaded and whose culture was destroyed, brutally oppressive for those doomed to forced labor in its creation, yet, ironically, in a few centuries time, for freedom-seeking peoples the world over, one of the most fortuitous events in all human history.

◆ 1 ◆

The Virgin Queen

At the dawn of the fifteenth century, trade in exotic spices from the Far East was the most lucrative commercial activity in all of Europe. Such commerce was made possible by Arabs of the Middle East, who purchased pepper, cinnamon, cloves, nutmeg and other rarities in India and transported their cargoes by boat via the Persian Gulf or Red Sea or by camel caravan across the Arabian Desert to ports on the Mediterranean—Alexandria, Aleppo, and Constantinople. There the precious cargoes were purchased by merchants from Italian principalities like Venice and Genoa to be sold throughout the Mediterranean and up and down the Atlantic coast. Cinnamon, cloves, and nutmeg were highly valued as flavorings for food. In Europe it was said that nutmeg was worth its weight in gold, cloves were a form of currency, and the peppercorn contained a natural preservative that kept meat palatable into the winter months.[1] Pepper sold in Lisbon at forty times the price paid in Calicut.[2] Any European nation that could circumvent this trade would become immensely rich and powerful.[3]

Portugal was first to accomplish this tour de force. Its efforts began in the early 1400s with a less grandiose scheme: to find the source of gold mined in central Africa and transported by Arab Berbers across the Sahara by caravan to ports on the southern Mediterranean. Europe needed gold to coin its currency, and its best source was Sub-Saharan Africa.[4]

Portuguese prince Dom Henrique, Duke of Viseu, an ambitious younger son of the king, was a latter-day crusader whose purpose in life was to defeat the infidel. After battling the Islamic Sultanate in North Africa to a standstill, Henry realized that if he could circumvent the gold caravan trade, he could rob the sultan of his profits and, thereby, his means of waging war.[5] By pursuing these activities, Henry believed he would be doing God's work, and the profits derived thereby were thus justified. To accomplish this, however, it was necessary for his ships to venture beyond what was then believed to be the point of no return—Cape Bojador on the "hump" of West Africa. The fear was that beyond this cape, the fierce northeast trade winds that blow year-round and the relentless currents driven by these winds would make a return to Portugal impossible.[6] By challenging his captains to venture beyond Cape Bojador, he became known as Henry the Navigator, father of the Age of Exploration.

To volunteer for a such a mission, Portuguese sailors required assurances that their ships could bring them home. After years of innovation and experimentation with sails and hull design, this problem was overcome by a new class of oceangoing vessel, the lateen-rigged, two- and three-masted caravel. The fore-and-aft sails and narrow hulls of these ships enabled them to sail much closer to the direction of the wind than the big-bellied, square-rigged, single-masted trading craft then prevalent in the North Atlantic and North Sea. The caravel gave Portuguese sailors the needed confidence.[7] Though it was slow going, these ships were able to tack or "beat" their way back to Portugal against the wind. The narrower hulls put a limit on cargo space, but Henry was seeking to trade for gold, so hull capacity was not initially viewed as an obstacle.[8] With such ships Madeira was discovered in 1420, then the Azores and Cape Verde Islands in quick succession. Cape Bojador was rounded in 1434. Henry's captains reached the Senegal River in 1444, which divided the Muslim-controlled Sahel to the north from Guinea to the south. The long-sought African gold coast had finally been reached.[9]

Henry soon learned, however, that the commodities most valued by his African warlord customers were horses, for which caravel carrying capacity was deficient.[10] He also learned that for his ventures to yield a profit, he must accept slaves in return for his trade goods. In Henry's mind slaves were converts to Christianity, so once again, he was doing God's work. In time, captured Africans—even while chained together on the beach—were being baptized in a language they could not understand before being loaded onto ships that would carry them into forced servitude in a strange land. Darker-skinned Africans were favored, because they had no hope of escaping captivity in Europe.[11] The normal exchange rate was seven slaves for one horse.[12]

As fortune would have it, just as the need for ships with greater cargo capacity became evident, so did a speedier route for returning to Portugal. By trial and error, Henry's captains learned that they could sail northwest from the coast of Africa far out into the Atlantic, blown by the northeast trades until they reached the prevailing westerlies in the latitude of the Azores that would blow them due east to Portugal. This course, called the "Guinea Track," was faster, and it obviated the need to sail upwind.[13] This discovery marks the beginning of a veritable sea change in world history. The Portuguese had discovered that ocean currents are driven by winds that blow in dependable patterns and that if they could learn these patterns, they could sail anywhere in the world with confidence they could find winds to bring them home.

Following this revelation, Portugal's shipwrights created a new hybrid, the carrack, with square sails on the fore and mainmast and a lateen sail on the aft or mizzen mast.[14] The forerunner of the European galleon, this new ship could carry more sail with a smaller crew.[15] It performed better running before the wind and was more stable under sail than lateen-rigged ships that leaned or "heeled" to leeward when sailing upwind.[16] The new design also allowed for construction of above-deck superstructures or "castles" fore and aft. Best of all, it greatly increased cargo capacity.[17] As this new ship evolved in tandem with Portugal's growing knowledge of ocean wind patterns, so too did the idea of rounding the southern tip of Africa to reach India. By so doing, they could circumvent the Arab spice trade, just as Henry had circumvented the African gold trade.[18]

Henry the Navigator died in 1460, but by then exploration and discovery were part of the Portuguese psyche, and this condition was infectious.[19] French and Spanish ships were soon poaching on Portugal's African trade contacts, and Spain launched its own oceanic attempt at a coup de maître. The 1492 fleet of Christopher Columbus was never intended to discover a New World. It was a trade mission that failed because heretofore unknown continents obstructed the way to the Orient. This new discovery would change everything, of course, but the full manifestation of this did not become apparent for another two centuries.

More impactful at the time was the successful achievement of Portugal's Vasco da Gama, who reached India in 1497 by rounding the Cape of Good Hope, the southernmost point of Africa. Tiny though the peppercorn is, its lure was irresistible. By 1511 the Portuguese had a trading base in the East Indies, followed by one in China in 1549 and another in Japan in 1571. Their efforts proved successful, and the Portuguese enjoyed a monopoly on European seaborne trade with the Orient until the end of the sixteenth century. Being first comers, they were entrenched and fortified by the time competition arrived.

During the Middle Ages, the pope had become the arbiter of disputes in the Catholic world in the struggle to unite the fractious countries of Europe in crusades to recapture the Holy Land.[20] With the discoveries of Columbus and da Gama, Spain and Portugal emerged as the only countries in the world to possess the requisite technology in navigation and ship construction to cross oceans. To forestall the inevitable conflict that was certain to arise between the two, Pope Alexander VI stepped into the breach and divided the non–Christian world into two halves, awarding the east to Portugal and the west to Spain.[21] The pope was Rodrigo Borgia, a native of Spain. Borgia's dividing line, codified by the Treaty of Tordesillas in 1494, was in the middle of the Atlantic at 42° 30′ West longitude—1,110 nautical miles west of the Cape Verde Islands. The French, English, and Dutch, however, spurned such a presumptuous arrangement. They had also caught the discovery bug and were fast catching up with their Iberian rivals.[22]

Charts and other navigational aids were called "rutters." They became closely guarded state secrets.[23] Henry's captains never included sailing directions in their reports and smuggling a rutter out of the country was a crime punishable by death.[24] But the five European monarchies with Atlantic Ocean coastlines—England, France, Holland, Portugal, and Spain—were always at sword's point over religion or territorial claims, like siblings fighting over the family silver. Many of their battles were fought at sea. Ships were captured and brought home as prizes. Any innovations in their construction, rigging, or sails were noted and adopted if deemed beneficial. Captains and pilots were captured and held for ransom while their rutters were seized, copied, and shared with friends. Navigators were kidnapped and forced to serve their captors. Others did so voluntarily. A native of Genoa in Italy, Christopher Columbus discovered the Americas in the service of Spain. Other Italians explorers served foreign masters: Giovanni Caboto for England, Amerigo Vespucci for Portugal and Spain, and Giovanni da Verazzano for France. The Portuguese, Ferdinand Magellan, also served Spain as admiral of the first fleet to circumnavigate the globe.

The result of this cross-pollination was that all five nations made advances more or less in unison. They built on one another's ideas, constructed bigger and faster ships and invented bigger and better artillery with which to arm their ships.[25] In this same manner, they gained knowledge of prevailing trade winds and ocean currents and their seasonal patterns. Without these advances, crossing oceans and returning home was impossible.[26] The maritime activities and innovations of this quasi-cartel were so closely guarded that these five alone gained worldwide dominion over the high seas. Together—despite their internecine warfare—they maintained global maritime supremacy—a thalassocracy if you will—until the end of the nineteenth century, a development that upended the concentration of world power. It enabled European colonialism and imperialism.

At the dawn of the sixteenth century, the world's economic powerhouses were China and India. India's population was twelve times that of Spain and Portugal combined, China's nearly twenty. India's textile industry—largest in the world—dwarfed that of England, a country that prided itself on its output of wool. And India was the land of the peppercorn. China had a monopoly on porcelain and guarded the secrets of its production, and China's output of silk and cotton textiles was enormous. But five Western European monarchies were now on the cusp of dominating the world's oceans, and by virtue of this, they had the wherewithal to eliminate the middleman and dominate world trade.[27]

Spain and Portugal observed the pope's decree, which explains why Portuguese became the official language of such far-flung nations as Brazil, Angola, and Mozambique. It also explains why the Philippines are named for King Philip II of Spain. By virtue of their head start, Portugal and Spain explored, colonized, and feasted on the low-hanging fruit of their respective pontifical bequests for the next one hundred years. The opportunities, however, were so rich, so vast, and so far distant that these two Iberian kingdoms could not prevent the English, French, and Dutch from encroaching on their activities and invading their newfound possessions.

The discovery of gold and silver in the New World focused Spain's full attention on what they called New Spain. Meanwhile, the English, French, and Dutch began searching for alternative routes to the Orient—northeast and northwest. In 1496, Henry VII of England underwrote a voyage by John Cabot, the anglicized Giovanni Caboto of Italy, to go in search of a navigable seaway to the Orient north of the American continents. Cabot and his son Sebastian discovered Newfoundland and Baffin Island and ventured as far as the entrance to Hudson Bay. A huge body of salt water, the bay served to perpetuate two myths: a passage northwest of Labrador leading to the Pacific Ocean and an old and persistent fairy tale of a large inland sea within North America that fed west-flowing rivers that emptied into the Pacific.[28] It was on the basis of Cabot's 1497 landfall in the New World that Hakluyt would claim possession for England of all of North America north of Florida, and, absurd as it may seem, England ultimately made good on it. The Cabots failed to find an ice-free seaway to the Pacific, but they did discover the rich fishing grounds off the east coast of Newfoundland known as the Grand Banks. Thereafter fleets from all five of Europe's Atlantic Coast countries came annually to fish for cod, haddock, herring, and mackerel. They dried and salted their catch on shore during the late spring and summer months and returned home fully laden in early August.[29]

Jacques Cartier, sailing for France, resumed the search for a northwest passage on two voyages in 1534 and 1541. He failed to find the desired seaway but discovered the Gulf of St. Lawrence and sailed far up the St. Lawrence River before giving up. Even the Portuguese sought a northwest passage, knowing it would be a faster route to the Orient than by way of the Cape of Good Hope.[30] The Spanish considered attempting one also, but there is no record that they actually did.[31] All attempts failed due to mutiny, lack of food, or ice blocking the way.

The idea of a Northwest Passage gave rise to the notion of a Northeast Passage. It was postulated that by sailing north of Scandinavia and Russia, one might reach the Pacific and, thereby, the Orient. In pursuit of this, Sebastian Cabot and others founded the Company of Merchant Adventurers to New Lands in 1555. This marked an important capitalist innovation, the joint-stock company—an entity apart from its owners—with an independent de jure existence.[32] Heretofore, companies were single proprietorships or partnerships whose owners were liable for their debts. In a joint-stock company or corporation, liability was limited to the entity itself, a limitation that made possible ventures of such inordinate risk they might not otherwise be undertaken. Investors purchased shares, each with a vote, and elected a board of directors to oversee management. Shares could be bought and sold to other individuals or entities independent of company operations.[33]

On the Merchant Adventurers' maiden voyage, one of its ships chanced upon a Russian fishing village six hundred miles north of Moscow. The ship's captain traveled overland to Moscow at the invitation of Czar Ivan the Terrible where they agreed on a trade pact—English woolens for Russian furs. The company enjoyed modest success trading with Russia but never reached the Orient, so its name was changed to the Muscovy Company. A Dutch explorer, Willem Barentsz, for whom the Barents Sea is named, sought the northeast passage on three later occasions, but as with the northwest passage, ice inevitably blocked the way.

Spain's exploration of Mexico, Central, and South America proved that there was no navigable access to the Pacific except by way of the Straits of Magellan. As no northwest passage proved viable either, attention naturally shifted to the North American continent, which by mid-century was still largely unknown. The Spanish had explored the southern mainland to a limited extent but found no opportunity sufficiently promising to divert their attention from the rich pickings of Mexico and Peru.[34] Spain's human resources were stretched to the limit as were those of Portugal, which had its hands full with its Far East operations.[35] This left the English, French, and Dutch to consider the possibilities of this neglected wilderness of, as yet, unknown proportions. The race was now on for North America.[36]

The well-informed Englishman of this period pictured a map of the world through a European prism. Western Europe was distinct, Africa and Asia much less so. America consisted of numerous tropical islands surrounded by an arc-shaped mass of mainland encircling them. Even less well-defined were Newfoundland far to the north and Brazil and Peru far to the south. Near the southern pole—separated from America by the Straits of Magellan—was an amorphous, possibly continental-sized landmass called Tierra del Fuego on some maps, Terra Australis on others.[37] To the average English bloke, therefore, the world was still vast, mysterious, and probably flat.

On the far side of the Isthmus of Panama was the Southern Sea, *Mar del Sur*—discovered by the Spanish explorer Vasco Núñez de Balboa in 1513.[38] There is a plausible explanation for this misnomer. At the point where Balboa was standing when he first sighted the Pacific Ocean, the coast of Panama runs east-west. Therefore, he was facing due south. He rightly concluded that across this Southern Sea lay Cathay and India. Had Balboa known that little more than a hundred miles to his west, the coastline trends north for six thousand miles, he might have chosen a different name. As it was, the name Southern Sea led cartographers to the mistaken conclusion that Asia extended eastward to connect with the northern part of America, and for this reason the term "Indian"—as in a resident of India—was applied to the aboriginal inhabitants of the newly discovered lands.[39] The Southern Sea was assumed to be south of this northern connector. This theory was soon disproven, but the understanding was yet to come that North and South America were separate continents. For years, America remained one large nebulous blob, changing shape with each new mapping. And of the thousands of miles of coastline between Florida and Newfoundland, almost nothing was known.[40] It remained terra incognita.

At this time England was a backwater—a land of sheep and shepherds.[41] As a small island kingdom off the outer rim of a continent that dwarfed it in area and people, it suffered from a sense of inferiority that fostered a growing and aggressive nationalism.[42] The population of England, which then included Wales but not Scotland or Ireland, was four million.[43] By contrast, Spain and Portugal combined were more than double that, and there were twenty million French.[44] The Holy Roman Empire—which encompassed today's Germany, Austria, Hungary, Bohemia, and Moravia—contained in excess of twenty-five million people. But England's insularity would become her greatest asset.

When Henry VIII broke with the Roman Catholic Church in 1533, then had his marriage to Catherine of Aragon annulled and married his lover, Anne Boleyn, he did so because he wanted a male heir. But Anne gave birth to a girl. The child Elizabeth became a symbol of England's break with Rome, ending an alliance that had lasted a thousand years.[45] It is not surprising, therefore, that when Elizabeth became queen in 1558, those with the wisdom and leisure to ponder weighty matters viewed their country through new eyes—singular, unique, independent. They sensed that Elizabeth's reign marked the beginning of a new era and speculated as to what this nascent age might bring. In 1577, a much-venerated Cambridge professor of mathematics, John Dee, an adviser and astrologer to the queen, published a book in which he envisioned a "Brytish Impire."[46]

For *this* country at *this* time to propose *this* as a national aspiration was the very pinnacle of arrogance and audacity. But ego is a powerful force for change.

In 1577 when Dee made his prognostication, Elizabeth was forty-four. She had ruled England for nineteen years. The only surviving child of Henry VIII, she had been a precocious youth—bright, energetic, eager to learn. Her tutors were among England's finest scholars—all from Cambridge, all humanists, all Protestants. She became fluent in French, Italian, Latin, and Spanish. She was proficient in Greek and acquired a familiarity with Welsh, Flemish, and German. She read Plato, Aristotle, Cicero, and other classical authors and for fun translated Sophocles and Demosthenes from Latin into English then back again into Latin. She spent hours each day reading history. She enjoyed as fine an education as anyone in Europe or, for that matter, the entire world.[47]

She had endured a tumultuous upbringing. She was thirteen when Henry VIII died, old enough to remember much about her father's final tempestuous years. At the impressionable age of fourteen, she was sexually abused by her guardian, a man twenty-five years her senior.[48] He planned to marry her and put himself in the line of succession. His impudence cost him his head and came close to bringing Elizabeth down also, innocent and chaste though she doubtless was. She escaped accusation, if not suspicion.[49] Following Henry's death, his ten-year-old son—Elizabeth's half-brother—inherited the throne. He died of tuberculosis six years later and was followed by Elizabeth's half-sister, Mary Tudor, daughter of Henry VIII and his Spanish queen, Catherine of Aragon.[50]

Mary restored Catholicism and married Philip, heir to the Spanish throne. The idea of a Spanish king and Mary's persecution of Protestants, however, seeded rebellion, and one of the insurgents, Thomas Wyatt, conspired to prevent Mary from marrying Philip and insure that Elizabeth remained in the succession.[51] Wyatt was caught and hanged, but Elizabeth had been implicated in his plot and was imprisoned in the Tower of London. Mary was advised to put her to death.[52] Convictions for a charge of treason could be arranged if the monarch wished it so, and a trial would have given her execution the stamp of legitimacy. Wiser heads prevailed, however, and she was released on the very same day that, eighteen years earlier, her mother had been executed for infidelity. But Elizabeth was not free. She remained under virtual house arrest for the next four years.[53] Having twice escaped the executioner proved edifying, and thereafter, she modeled an image of innocence, modesty, and simplicity—an affectation necessary for survival.[54]

Elizabeth bore the scars of these traumas. Denied a mother and disinherited by her father, she grew up mistrusting people when so many around her were spies. At times frightened, at other times angry or lonely, she likely succumbed to poor self-esteem and bouts of depression. We know she suffered illnesses and doubtless loss of appetite in times of stress; she was thin throughout her life.[55] And a preoccupation with death would follow when so many around her were suffering execution.

Had it gone the other way—had Elizabeth been beheaded for her part in Wyatt's Rebellion—then upon Mary's death in 1558 the crown would have been claimed by rival forces sympathetic to either Mary, Queen of Scots (Catholic), or Lady Katherine Grey (Protestant). Either way, England would have suffered more religious conflict, perhaps even civil war, in which case there may have been no English Renaissance and the conception of an English America may have miscarried.[56] As it was, Mary died in November of 1558 at the age of forty-two, probably of cancer, and Elizabeth became queen.

Her first act addressed the religious question. She was well aware of developments on the Continent. There, Holy Roman Emperor Charles V had acceded to the demands of his German princes and accepted the policy of *cuius regio, eius religio*—"who rules, his religion."[57] Here was precedent. For order and stability, Elizabeth believed England had to adhere to a single creed and that she—not the pope—must be its head.[58] She was raised a Protestant, and her education had convinced her of the corruption of the Roman Catholic Church. By act of Parliament in May 1559— just six months after Mary's death—Protestantism was restored, as was the Act of Supremacy making Elizabeth head of the church. Her actions did not arise from heavenly inspiration but from pragmatic, down-the-middle compromise—something in between Catholicism and the Protestantism being practiced on the Continent—something kinder, less fanatic, less dogmatic.[59] In time, English esteem for their Virgin Queen became suffused with the immaculate aura of the Virgin Mary as in, for example, the belief that her royal touch cured the King's Evil (i.e., scrofula).[60] This subtle transference proved a balm to the more superstitious among her countrymen who might have been nostalgic for the accoutrements of the old religion.

The Elizabethan Religious Settlement was not motivated by righteous fervor on Elizabeth's part as much as by genuine fear of religious civil war. And the Reformation was not achieved with consummate skill, though the outcome won praise from the Protestant majority in the south of England. Wary of religious conflict, the Catholic majority in the north acquiesced, but not without qualms and not for long. Though devout in her own religious faith, Elizabeth had no wish to invade the intimacy of her people's relationship with God.[61] Outward conformity was deemed sufficient.[62] Regardless, by the same settlement, church attendance remained obligatory.

One might argue that Elizabeth Tudor was the first thoroughly modern woman in history. But in one respect, she was still medieval, for she assumed without question the absolute power and divine right of kings.[63] Her youthful scars became manifest in the tenacity with which she clung to power and opposed change. Her motto was *semper eadem*, "always the same."[64] She appointed trusted family to key posts and basked in the adoration of power-seeking courtiers and of a genuinely loving people.[65] She had little desire for a private life divorced from her public persona, therefore it is fruitless to try to separate the woman from the sovereign. After having been unwanted flotsam in the ebbs and flows of her predecessors' reigns, Elizabeth discovered that being queen was most agreeable.

When she inherited the throne in 1558, England was decades behind Spain, Portugal, and France in ship construction, navigational capability, and oceangoing experience.[66] An island kingdom, England was naturally a seagoing country, but not an oceangoing one.[67] England's mariners were expert at coastal piloting, but few could compute their position at sea using celestial navigation and mathematics. Elizabeth's predecessors had maintained the Royal Navy so as to retain mastery of the English Channel, but the focus was defense, not conquest or exploration. There were exceptions—the voyages of the Cabots, for instance, and isolated outliers who had pushed the envelope by crossing the Atlantic—but these were few, and most of them involved fishing for cod on the Grand Banks.[68]

England's interest in the New World had languished during the reign of Henry VIII, and Elizabeth was not of a mind to revive it, at least as a state-sponsored endeavor.[69] She lacked the resources to fund exploration and colonization. Insofar as expanding the boundaries of her realm was concerned, she had her hands full with Ireland. The English crown had long sought to extend its hegemony over Ireland and the island's disparate feudal warlords. Burdened with the expense of this military quagmire so close to home, Elizabeth and her privy council had little interest in more foreign adventurism.[70]

Indeed, the foremost issue of concern to her privy council was her marriage. William Cecil, her tight-lipped chief minister, was devoted to his new queen, but his service came with the expectation that for the sake of her kingdom, she marry and bear sons—an heir and a spare.[71] Upon her marriage, she was expected to leave affairs of state to her husband. Any other arrangement defied the Laws of Nature and the teachings of the Bible.[72] Until a consort arrived to share her bed and burden of responsibility, Cecil saw his role as managing affairs much like a regent. It followed, therefore, that privy council members would make suggestions as to whom she should marry and press her to do so as soon as possible. Charles, archduke of Austria, was a popular choice. It would take time for

Elizabeth's councilors to come to realize that being England's broodmare was not her style.[73] Not in the least.

Educated at Cambridge, Cecil had survived Mary's reign by outwardly converting to Catholicism, as had Elizabeth herself—indeed as had most prominent English Protestants who did not flee into Marian exile on the Continent.[74] Cecil's quiet, patient, and circumspect manner concealed the immense power he now wielded and relished.[75] Viewed by others as "prudent and virtuous," he was far too conventional to accept that his queen should *not* have a husband, but Cecil was no power behind the throne.[76] Elizabeth was her own man.

She had little interest in the archduke of Austria or anyone else deemed suitable. Perhaps Cecil and her other councilors dismissed her obvious affection for Robert Dudley, her master of the horse, as a passing infatuation. It was not. Dudley was handsome, athletic, and entertaining in a louche sort of way that Elizabeth found irresistible. She was learning that as queen, she could relax and be herself. Gone was innocence, modesty, and simplicity. Elizabeth was a sensual woman with every right to love whomever she wished.[77] But her master of the horse and would-be King Robert came saddled with an impediment. He had a wife.

Most women of Elizabeth's age were long married, and she might have been had her brother lived. Now she relished the company of men, and Dudley in particular, for whom she chose the affectionate sobriquet "Robin." She threw caution to the wind and let her willful, independent nature come to the fore. She delighted in courtship and would for the rest of her life. Courtly love with Elizabeth as the supreme yet unattainable prize would become a feature of her reign, inspiring her courtiers to new heights in art, literature, and science as a means of winning her favor and growing rich in the process. She became their muse—their Helen of Troy, their Diana, their Cleopatra, their Cynthia, their Gloriana.[78]

With Elizabeth on the throne, all was topsy-turvy. Traditional roles were reversed. The king was an attractive unmarried woman, fond of being wooed, for as a child, she had had too little love. With a king on the throne, the men around him were sycophants, careful not to outshine and risk displeasure. But with Elizabeth, men were free to be as extravagant and conspicuous as their judgment and purse allowed. And rather than be jealous, she was flattered and entertained by their exuberance and braggadocio. She loved nothing more than a vainglorious rake dressed in sartorial splendor who could dance, compose treacly sonnets, amuse her with the latest court gossip, or captivate her with clever ideas for singeing the beard of the king of Spain.[79] Here was an all-new dynamic.

Dudley was the first of four supreme favorites, and, despite his being egotistical and perverse, she remained loyal to him, as she did to two who came later—Christopher Hatton and Walter Raleigh.[80] The fourth, Robert Devereux, whose lèse-majesté she could not forgive, ended up losing his head. Playing favorites had a depressing effect on court morale, however, and led to bribery, deception, and duplicity—the hallmarks of Elizabethan court modus vivendi. It was an atmosphere in which backstabbing was almost de rigueur.[81]

To what degree was Elizabeth promiscuous? We shall never know.[82] Was she truly *virgo intacta*? It is quite possible.

She might have married Dudley had his wife not died under mysterious circumstances just when his affair with Elizabeth had reached its most erotic intensity. On a Wednesday morning, Amy Dudley—living a discreet distance from court near Oxford—sent her servants away for the day. That evening she was found at the foot of the stairs, dead of a broken neck.[83] Her death was ruled accidental. An investigation determined she had fallen down the stairs, but this failed to quell rumors that Robert Dudley had his wife killed to free himself to marry the queen. It was even bruited about that Elizabeth was complicit.[84]

The appearance of a plot to kill Amy Dudley made it impossible for Elizabeth to marry her Robin.[85] Amid all the brouhaha that ensued, she may have decided that ceding power to a husband was not something she wished to do. But keeping the petulant Dudley lurking about kept foreign suitors at bay and her councilors guessing. From now on, Elizabeth played her cards close to her breast.[86] Her councilors' demands that she marry would continue, and she would parry them with ambiguous ripostes and bon mots. Indeed, she learned to use the prospect of her marriage as a negotiating tool. She was not being mendacious, she was being politic.

As time passed, Elizabeth found her stride and self-confidence, and her councilors gained respect for her prudence and perspicacity.[87] She beguiled them with digression, dissimulation, and circumlocution, and subjected them to a "hellish torment" of indecision.[88] She blathered like a magpie, but her indecisiveness was rooted in shrewd intuition.[89] Her mutability served to fend off foreign entanglements that might lead to war, which she viewed as a dreadful waste of lives and money, not to mention a threat to internal stability.[90] Whereas in the past, the principal business of monarchy was waging war, Elizabeth proved that the maintenance of peace was a more worthwhile royal endeavor. She discovered that equivocation served well in matters of state *and* in matters of the heart. She remained high-spirited, loved to flirt, dance, party, play games, and with rising self-assurance, she became arrogant, something of a snob, and ever more resistant to the notion of being ruled by a man.[91]

At this time London had a population of two hundred thousand, making it second only to Paris in size among all cities of Europe.[92] Male citizens of sixteenth-century England owed allegiance to overlapping spheres of authority. In this way, every man was accounted for and expected to muster for military service or pay tax assessments levied in times of war. Women belonged to their husbands and children to their fathers. When a daughter married, she became the property of her husband. In this way, control of the adult male of the species was de facto control of his wife and children—his human property—and he could cane them if they misbehaved. The rule of thumb applied.[93]

London contained over one hundred Anglican parishes.[94] The church was the foundation of societal accountability, and the parish was the basic unit of authority, ecclesiastical and civil. In addition to its sacerdotal duties, the church provided the state with a control apparatus, this in return for its religious monopoly. Recusants were sought out, reprimanded, forced to pay their tithes, and fined for nonattendance. Parish ministers were charged with maintaining records of christenings, marriages, and burials and otherwise keeping close tabs on their flocks.[95]

London contained twenty-six municipal wards, each encompassing as many as a dozen parishes. Working in concert, these temporal and spiritual authorities provided a mechanism for preventing anyone from falling between the cracks. Each ward had its alderman and his staff of constables, beadles, and watchmen who patrolled the streets day and night and kept track of who lived where. Interlopers could thereby be identified and incarcerated or banished as was deemed appropriate.[96]

In addition, there were England's livery companies, so named because each had its own identifying uniform or badge. In 1570 there were a hundred such trade organizations, the oldest dating to the twelfth century.[97] The Worshipful Company of Mercers, the Worshipful Companies of Grocers, Drapers, Fishmongers, Haberdashers, and the rest were outgrowths of medieval occupational guilds formed to control product quality and guard against charlatans and swindlers.[98] The Worshipful Company of Carpenters, as one example, accepted fifty new apprentices each year. Over time, these companies became large bureaucratic organizations that recruited and trained apprentices, founded schools, funded charities and university scholarships, provided for aging and disabled members, supported members' candidacies in local governmental elections, purchased land, built impressive halls, and became social centers for their members' enjoyment. The Merchant Taylors' Hall, for example, dates to the first half of the fourteenth century. It was and is the venue for banquets that rival anything a nobleman could boast of.[99] Upon completion of his seven-year apprenticeship, a member gained the Freedom of the City of London, status leading to the right to buy property, vote in elections for parliament and city government, social advancement, and the accumulation of wealth.[100]

A majority of London youth became apprenticed to a livery company member, and at the time of Elizabeth, three-quarters of London's male citizens belonged to one. The trades were well regulated. Prices and wages were fixed by the companies in coordination with the lord mayor and his counselors.[101]

Those who did not belong to a livery company answered to someone of higher rank. England's elite had their retainers and bodyguards, and in some cases, a private army. Such men were also benefactors who supported artists, writers, musicians, and actors. A nobleman was a patron, protector, and master—in a word, an overlord. Those in his charge were his to promote, his to debase.

The vast majority of London males were answerable to one or more of these higher authorities. Each parish, ward, livery company, and aristocrat was responsible for the deportment of those within their jurisdiction. When England was threatened, each was required to furnish men and arms.[102] As an adjunct to England's Royal Navy, this protective carapace of civilian militia was meant to safeguard the homeland, and each of its units was also responsible for collecting imposts necessary to pay for this defense. Each maintained an armory of military equipment, each provided the necessary military training, and each answered ultimately to the queen.[103] To evade this interconnected web of authority took no small effort, and anyone who tried might find his ear nailed to the pillory.

Two categories of male citizens formed exceptions to this authoritarian network. They were the younger sons of nobles or landed gentry excluded from inheritance by the law of male primogeniture and—at the other end of the pecking order—so-called "masterless men," society's ignoble debris.[104] An infestation of scoundrels and homeless outcasts plagued England.[105] Punishment for misdeeds was harsh. In Devon alone—one of England's twenty-nine counties—there were seventy-four hangings in a single year.[106] Unemployment was high due to many factors, including the ripple effect of the dissolution of the monasteries and a growing trend of fencing open fields that denied access to pasture for subsistence farmers. The unemployed were an ever-present burden.[107] It was from these two incompatible and unsuitable pools of candidates—younger sons of the upper crust and masterless men—that English America would draw most of its colonists, the former tending to be indolent, and the latter, amoral.

The English Religious Settlement of 1559 put Elizabeth in direct conflict with Philip II of Spain, her erstwhile brother-in-law. A humorless man, Philip had inherited the thrones of Spain and the Netherlands, and principalities in Italy: Milan, Naples, Sicily, and Siena. Later, he added Portugal to his collection of crowns.[108] One consequence of all these thrones was that at almost any given time in his forty-two-year reign, Philip was waging war on two or more fronts against the French, the Dutch, other Italian Principalities, the Turks, or the English.[109] His attention was so divided that he commanded those reporting to him to keep their correspondence brief. Complicating matters was his tendency to micromanage.[110] His purpose in life was as clear and dear to him as the image of Jesus on the Cross: *defend the Catholic faith*. He never lost sight of that purpose but often got bogged down in operational minutiae. Regardless the consequences, regardless the costs, regardless the deaths, Philip's mission was to extirpate the infidel and disseminate the Catholic faith to the benighted inhabitants of the world. Pope Pius V may have been Christ's Vicar on Earth, but Philip II of Spain was His Commander in Chief.[111]

Resolved to eradicate Protestantism within his domains, Philip ordered the Netherlands' branch of the Spanish Inquisition to attack insurgent Dutch-speaking Protestant communities in the country's northern provinces. Commercial activities were disrupted, including England's long-standing export of woolen fabrics through the major European trading entrepôt of Antwerp.[112] Philip had started a trade war. But a development in 1568 focused his full attention on England. At odds with Scottish nobles, Mary, the Catholic Queen of Scots, was forced to abdicate her crown to her infant son James. After a losing battle against those same nobles to restore her rights, she fled to England to become Elizabeth's unwelcome guest.[113] Granted sanctuary in one of Elizabeth's castles, her movements and communications were restricted, and her person closely watched, but her presence in England became a clarion call for Catholics everywhere and for Philip in particular.[114]

In February 1570, Pope Pius excommunicated Elizabeth. By so doing, he released English citizens from their allegiance to their queen and exhorted them to dethrone her by any means possible. In addition, he put English nobles on notice that further obedience to her commands would be considered anathema. The papal bull inspired a plot conceived by a Florentine banker living in London, Roberto Ridolfi, a Roman Catholic who had important English connections. After securing secret commitments from Mary, Queen of Scots and the Duke of Norfolk—Elizabeth's second cousin—to marry and raise support from English Catholics in the north of England, Ridolfi traveled to the Vatican.[115] There, having informed Pope Pius of his progress, he obtained the pontiff's written instructions, ordering Philip to invade England with a Spanish army launched from the Spanish Netherlands with the goal of joining forces with an English Catholic insurgency under Norfolk. The combined forces would then assassinate Elizabeth, place Mary and Norfolk on the throne, and restore Catholicism in England.

There was little chance of keeping secret such a grandiose scheme even if Ridolfi had been discreet. In fact, he was so indiscreet that Philip suspected him of being an English double agent.[116] Ridolfi underestimated the patriotism of English Catholics and vastly overestimated their desire to risk their necks in an armed rebellion.[117] Be that as it may, Philip needed his army in the Netherlands to fight Dutch rebels. What is more, he had opposed the pope's excommunication of Elizabeth for fear of reprisals against English Catholics. He may have applauded Ridolfi's initiative, but he refused to provide support, financial or military.

The plot was discovered. Ridolfi escaped to Rome, but the foolish Norfolk lost his head. Elizabeth refused to execute Mary despite the demands of many of her nobles to do so, but even so, the lines were now clearly drawn. What began as a trade dispute had escalated into a deadly religious conflict.[118] England and Spain were on a collision course. At the time, Spain's military pike-and-shot formations were the most formidable fighting forces in all of Europe, and the Spanish navy was the largest and most powerful in the world.[119] This grim fact plus Elizabeth's natural aversion to war and England's geographic isolation kept things at a simmer for the time being, but England had been invaded in the past, and Philip would soon resolve to try it again.[120] Despite the threat, Elizabeth knew—as did every man, woman, and child in England—that there is more than one way to shear a sheep.

◆ 2 ◆

The Sea Dogs

On instructions from Philip, English ships trading in Spanish ports began encountering punitive regulations, harsher penalties, and harassment by the Inquisition. This on top of disruptions in Antwerp caused by the Dutch Rebellion put the English in an untenable position.[1] Elizabeth and the always cautious Cecil decided to send Philip a message but to do surreptitiously.

The messenger was thirty-year-old John Hawkins, a native of Plymouth, a seaport in Devonshire on England's southwest coast. Unlike other ship-owning tradesmen who plied the English Channel, Hawkins's father had thrice led trading expeditions to Brazil, proving that crossing the Atlantic required no great feats of navigational skill.[2] A corked bottle tossed overboard off the Iberian coast will eventually wash up on Caribbean sands. It is just a matter of time. For young Hawkins, the tricky bit was getting where he wanted to go once he got there.

As noted earlier, the new breed of oceangoing ships was square-rigged, meaning the sails generating most of the power were square or rectangular, intended to catch the wind and be pushed forward by it. Since ships could not sail into the wind, the desired destination had to be downwind. Hawkins knew he could get to the Caribbean simply by being blown there by the trades, and he was not too concerned about where he landed.

At sea, an Elizabethan ship was a floating kingdom. The ship's captain ruled supreme—so long as he held sway over his sometimes-mutinous crew.[3] Ashore, he was among his town's most honorable citizens. With a wife and children at home, he served on boards, paid his taxes, and lived at the foot of the cross. When times were good, he was a merchant, transporting woolens to the continent to exchange for French, German, and Italian wines, wheat from eastern Europe's breadbasket, sugar from Brazil, nutmeg and pepper from the Spice Islands. When times were hard, he could revert to piracy to feed his family.

Elizabethan era pirates were in no way romantic figures, despite Herculean efforts to turn barbarous philistines into picaresque Robin Hoods.

Captain and crew had to fulfill the duties of sailor and soldier with equal facility and ferocity. In times of war, piracy became legal, in which case the captain became a privateer, though his actions and methods were indistinguishable from those of a pirate.

Like his father, John Hawkins had gained experience trading in the Canaries and on the African Guinea coast for sugar, gold, indigo, and ivory to be sold in Spanish and English ports. Since such trade with Spain was now disrupted by Philip's new bellicose policy, Hawkins sought to demonstrate to the Spanish king an unintended consequence of his lack of hospitality. His plan was a triangular venture—to Africa with cloth and other manufactured goods to trade for slaves, from there to the Caribbean to sell his human cargo to Spanish plantation owners, then back home with a cargo of sugar, cacao, indigo, and tobacco.[4] Despite sailing with Elizabeth's furtive blessing, he carried no official license. In the eyes of Spain, therefore, Hawkins was a pirate violating Spain's monopoly on trade with its New World possessions. If asked, Elizabeth could deny knowledge of the whole affair.

His first venture with three ships left Plymouth in October 1562. His transaction appears to have been prearranged and facilitated by bribes on both sides of the Atlantic.[5] Hawkins and his crew purchased or captured three to four hundred Africans and transported them to Hispaniola, where he exchanged them for hides and plantation crops—at the point of a gun, or so claimed Spanish authorities there who were willing to trade but needed cover to do so.[6] Hawkins's caper was so profitable that he repeated it two years later with one of the Royal Navy's largest ships, thus exposing the queen's complicity. The second venture was as lucrative as the first.

The English were not the first to poach on Portugal's African slave monopoly. The Dutch and French had been at it for decades. Following their lead, Hawkins made a tidy profit, and—as the queen's cat's-paw—he tested Philip's resolve. Hawkins would continue to lead and invest in such ventures, but the success of his first two made him a wealthy man. He married the daughter of the treasurer of the navy and in 1571 was elected to represent Plymouth in Parliament. This called for a residence in London, and his new status earned him a coat of arms. Despite Elizabeth's denials, Philip and his ambassador in London suspected Hawkins had been guided by her all along.

Philip may have grasped Elizabeth's irritation over disruption of trade in Antwerp, but he considered Hawkins's forced-trade retaliation a trivial consequence of a larger problem—the Dutch Protestant rebellion that had escalated into all-out war. The Protestant Reformation had found fertile soil in the Dutch provinces of the Spanish Netherlands, and

Philip was determined to eradicate it root and branch. Compared to this, an illicit trading venture by an English corsair was of little consequence.

John Hawkins's slave-trading ventures failed to persuade Philip to cease his ill treatment of English shipping in Spanish ports. To curtail further escalation, Elizabeth forbade Hawkins to go again. He obeyed but sent a surrogate instead. When this venture failed, he embarked on yet another in 1568, this time going himself with a larger fleet, including a ship captained by his young cousin Francis Drake. The mission ended badly when one hundred English crew were abandoned to the mercy of the Spanish. To deflect criticism, Hawkins blamed Drake, but conflicting reports of the ugly incident point to Hawkins as acting in his own selfish interests.[7] It is unclear if the one hundred volunteered to be left behind due to the loss of the flagship or were intentionally deserted because they were threatening mutiny. Regardless, the Spanish put some to death and sentenced others to serve as galley slaves.[8] The incident—the first deadly clash between the two countries—incited fierce Hispanophobia in England. Hawkins later threatened the Spanish ambassador, warning him that many English sea captains now knew their way to New Spain and would go with or without him.[9]

The religious standoff between Elizabeth and Philip thrust England into a proxy war in the Low Countries. Like the English, the Dutch were a seagoing people, and to advance their Protestant rebellion, Prince William of Orange issued letters of reprisal to shipowners, giving them license to attack Spanish shipping in the English Channel. Such letters constituted official permission to plunder any ship of a nation at war with the issuing authority. The Dutch were then joined by Huguenot privateers, their Protestant allies in France. Inevitably, Dutch and Huguenot ships began seeking refuge in English ports to rest and refit. Elizabeth had little choice but to allow the practice, which served to further escalate tensions with Spain.[10]

At home, however, England was to all appearances at peace. The two decades—1570 to 1590—were the halcyon years of Elizabeth's reign.[11] The economy thrived thanks to capitalist-friendly governmental policies, the influx of continental artisans fleeing religious persecutions, a welcoming business environment due to fewer regulations and trade restrictions, and the growing industrialization that resulted. Farm wages and productivity were increasing due to the continuing effect of the dissolution of the monasteries, which had put one-fifth of England's arable land into the hands of the profit-minded. Indeed, the dissolution of church properties and the increase in money supply brought about by the influx of precious metals from the New World fed a growing prosperity. Population and optimism rose thanks to this pro-business climate, better nutrition, and a lower rate of infant mortality. In contrast to their aversion to Mary Tudor, the English populace began viewing their new queen with increasing admiration and affection. The St. Bartholomew's Day Massacre in France in 1572 that killed thousands reminded the English of the perils of religious conflict and gave them a greater appreciation for their queen's tolerant attitude.[12] She became immensely popular. Her annual summer progresses into the countryside were occasions for celebration and provided her opportunities to mingle with her subjects and demonstrate her genuine affection for them.

In the fall of 1568, a convoy of Spanish ships sought refuge in English ports, chased there by French Huguenot privateers. The Spanish ships were carrying gold and silver worth £85,000 borrowed from Genoese bankers and bound for the Netherlands to pay Philip's army.[13] Here was a windfall Elizabeth could not resist. She kept the money, and when Spanish soldiers went unpaid, they rebelled—a win-win for England. In retaliation, Philip seized all English ships in Spanish ports, and Elizabeth followed suit by doing the same to Spanish shipping in English ports.[14] Taking advantage of the cover produced by this tit for tat, Francis Drake returned to the Caribbean, not for trade this time, but to raid Spanish settlements.

From Huguenot pirates cruising the West Indies, Drake learned how the Spanish transported the gold and silver mined in Peru.[15] The treasure traveled by ship fifteen hundred miles from Lima to Panamá (now Panama City) then forty miles across the isthmus by mule train to Nombre de Dios on the Caribbean side, there to be collected by the annual Spanish flotilla for transport to Spain.[16] Drake and the Huguenots agreed to a joint venture, and guided by Cimarrons—escaped African slaves hiding in the Panamanian highlands—they bushwhacked their way through rain forest to the treasure trail high in the cordillera. While awaiting the mule train, the Cimarrons led Drake to a tree from the top branches of which he could see both shores—the Caribbean to the north and the Southern Sea to the south. As he clung to the branches—enthralled by a magnificent view of the Pacific Ocean—Drake implored God for a chance to captain an English galleon in the Mar del Sur.[17]

After a brief skirmish, the combined English, French, and Cimarron forces chased the Spanish guards away and captured the gold and thirty tons of silver carried by the two hundred mules. It was far too much to shoulder through jungle, so they buried the silver to be recovered later and returned to their boats with eighty to one hundred thousand pesos worth of gold.[18] Before parting company, Drake and his Huguenot allies vowed further collaboration and Protestant colonization in America. While Drake's reasons for wanting an English American colony may have differed from those of Richard Hakluyt, the potential benefits of a New World possession were becoming clear to everyone.

Though the Spanish recovered the silver buried by Drake, his success sent shivers down Philip's spine. His flow of treasure from America was only as strong as its weakest link. Drake arrived back in Plymouth in August 1573 just as news of his raid reached Spain. Relations between the two countries had become so volatile that both Elizabeth and Philip blinked.

By an accord signed in August 1574, Elizabeth agreed to stop all raids on Spanish settlements and shipping in the New World. In addition, she settled with Spain's Genoese bankers, repaying the £85,000, and she agreed to cease granting sanctuary to Dutch and Huguenot privateers. All merchants were compensated for their loses. Philip responded in kind and made concessions in the Netherlands that reduced tensions there. He had little choice since the value of Spanish goods impounded by England far exceeded the value of English goods impounded by Spain.[19] In addition, diplomatic relations were restored. But this détente served only to delay the inevitable.[20]

Elizabeth was not often pinned down into signing something that might return to haunt her. She was dancing a dangerous quadrille.[21] Her dancing partners were Spain, which wanted her dead, the Dutch, who were only after her money, and France, a majority–Catholic country, cross-channel rival, and sometime archenemy. A misstep could mean war, and war meant invasion.

She did not trust the Dutch. True, they were Protestant, but they were also rebelling against their anointed sovereign, Philip, and by the principle of "who rules, his religion"—which served Elizabeth's purposes well enough—it was Philip's right to choose the creed.[22] She loaned money to Dutch rebels, which they never repaid. The most she got from the alliance was a training ground for English soldiers who volunteered to fight under a Dutch flag. But providing aid to the Dutch kept Philip bogged down in the Low Countries. By keeping all her dancing partners distracted and off balance, Elizabeth avoided having her toes crushed.

Thinking long term, however, Philip became resolved to what would soon be known as "The Enterprise of England," an invasion to restore Catholicism regardless the cost. The pope was demanding it.[23] France had been distracted by its own religious conflict, but as the Huguenots were marginalized after the St. Bartholomew's Day Massacre, France could not be counted as neutral should Spain invade England.

Elizabeth was pragmatic enough to view the conflict in geopolitical terms without the muddling effect of a religious overlay.[24] In her mind, Philip had to be denied victory in the Netherlands, and she found the means to enlist French aid by courtship with the Duke of Anjou, brother of the French king, who was single and casting about for a kingdom of his own.[25] At the time Dutch Protestants happened to be looking for a prince, and Anjou fit the bill, especially if he were to wed the queen of England.[26] His religious convictions were a slave to his political aspirations, so his Catholic upbringing posed no impediment. Philip feared an English-French alliance, but having never learned to live within his income, there was little at present he could do to prevent it. Spain declared bankruptcy in 1575, and its working capital remained constrained for years thereafter by disputes with creditors.[27] Since Philip was unable to pay an army in the Netherlands, calm prevailed for the present.[28]

In this atmosphere, the Duke of Anjou came courting and found Elizabeth amenable to his overtures. At about this same time, she invested in another Drake venture to raid Spanish shipping, this time in the Pacific.[29] She understood the venture would be a provocation and, if successful, another blow to Philip's financial woes, all of which would keep him dancing to her tune. Drake left Plymouth in December 1577 with four ships and one hundred and sixty-four men. His success depended to a large extent on a ruthlessness that became the model for English privateers—Elizabeth's "sea dogs"—men on whom she would later rely to defend England and to whom England would turn to establish and support English colonies in America. To better understand their methods, consider Drake's actions in Puerto San Julián.

On a Friday in June, he led his fleet into a secluded inlet at 49° south latitude on the coast of Patagonia in southern Argentina.[30] The inlet was discovered and named by Magellan in 1520. Located fifteen hundred miles south of Buenos Aires, Puerto San Julián is three hundred miles north of the entrance to the Straits of Magellan through which Drake intended to sail in order to reach the Pacific. Early European explorers found Patagonia to be sparsely populated by hostile humans known as the Tehuelche people, aboriginal nomads who were later hunted to near extinction.

Drake was looking for a place to wait out the southern-hemisphere winter before entering the tempestuous straits, the most inhospitable waterway in the world. He also needed to "bream" his ships—scrape the hulls clean of the barnacles, weeds, and shipworms that had accumulated in the six months since leaving England. Drake carried an account of Magellan's circumnavigation odyssey of 1519–1522. It may have been that of Antonio Pigafetta, *Report of the First Voyage Around the World*, which had been translated into English by this time. Pigafetta was one of only eighteen of Magellan's original crew of two hundred and forty who survived. He described the mutiny of two of Magellan's captains who resented his being Portuguese and who were critical of his seamanship. While anchored in Puerto San Julián, Magellan ordered one of the mutinous captains put to death, after which his body was quartered, the parts hung on gibbets as a warning to any like-minded members of their crews. The other captain and a priest were marooned there and never heard of again.[31]

Drake had been dealing with his own recalcitrant captain. His old friend Thomas Doughty had become critical of the admiral at the very time Drake—a true martinet—came to believe that absolute obedience from his crew was essential in view of the difficult challenges ahead.[32] Thinking this, he may have recalled Magellan's similar troubles and referred to Pigafetta's book for the relevant passages. Perhaps it served some droll sense of justice within the man to confront mutiny there, just as Magellan had fifty-eight years earlier.

But there was an important difference. Magellan had sailed with the authority of the Spanish king, whereas Drake had no official government backing. Ostensibly, his was a private trading venture to the Mediterranean.[33] Spanish spies in London saw through this jiggery-pokery and warned Philip that Drake planned to prey on Spanish settlements and shipping in the Caribbean. This is precisely what Drake and his investors—the queen included—expected the Spanish would surmise. If captured, therefore, Elizabeth would disavow knowledge of his venture, and Drake would hang like a common pirate.[34]

Drake had long sought respectability. His cousin and mentor John Hawkins was now treasurer of the Royal Navy, and Drake envisioned similar aggrandizement. A profitable venture backed by the queen would be his calling card. In Puerto San Julián, as he contemplated the perils ahead, he resolved to rid himself of all dissension. As military commander of the venture, Doughty considered himself Drake's equal.[35] But Francis Drake was not disposed to sharing command with someone he viewed as inferior in ability.[36]

Two weeks after arriving in Puerto San Julián, Drake ordered all hands ashore. The desolate, rocky beach was an ominous setting for Drake's crew to witness a court of inquiry to decide if Thomas Doughty was guilty of mutiny. Doughty questioned Drake's authority and asked to see his commission. In deft obfuscation, Drake produced official parchments with impressive seals and signatures, but there was no royal commission among them. He then professed to have left it in his cabin by mistake, but the copious display of official documents presented served to persuade illiterate and tractable sailors that Drake had the necessary authority.[37]

Assured by Drake that a guilty verdict would not result in execution, the jury humored their captain and returned a verdict of guilty.[38] Drake then insisted that Doughty, having been convicted of mutiny, could not continue with the fleet, that his presence would inflame discord and division. He then digressed, promising his crew that if they obeyed his orders, the lowest among them would return to England with riches beyond his wildest dreams.[39] With this as his lure, Drake then led his crew to his way of thinking that Thomas Doughty must die—that for the success of the venture, execution was the safest course of action. On a cold July Sunday morning, the beleaguered Doughty was beheaded in the presence of all hands. His friends remained silent, fearful now for their own lives.[40]

Before leaving Puerto San Julián, Drake took the last steps necessary to consolidate power. He declared no one exempt from work regardless of their status, and in the presence of all, he relieved his officers of their authority—all of them.[41] He did this despite many of them being employed by their ships' owners and despite the indignity most must have felt of being demoted. Drake would no longer tolerate divided loyalty. This done, he reinstated most of them and appointed others whom he trusted to the vacancies with the unmistakable understanding that they now served at the pleasure of and by the authority of Francis Drake and Francis Drake alone.

Of just such brass as this were the English sea dogs forged.[42]

Embarking on a privateering venture, the common sixteenth-century sailor had only a fifty-fifty chance of seeing home again. Often the dregs of society, they were layabouts and scofflaws looking for a free meal, a dry place to sleep, and a share of the spoils of a captured vessel. Many were serving time or were kidnapped by press gangs, having been found drunk in the gutter of some seaport town.

Crewing on tall ships was difficult and dangerous work. Sailors slept in cramped, airless quarters either between decks or in a fusty, windowless miasma known as the forecastle or fo'c'sle. The diet was monotonous and unhealthy—ships' biscuits called hardtack or "molar breakers," salt-cured meat and fish, and, on occasion, peas and moldy cheese. Mouth fungus from salted meat was common. Sailors died of scurvy, dysentery, or typhus, commonly called "ship fever" and carried by rats, which thrived aboard ships. Scurvy, caused by a vitamin C deficiency, led to anemia, exhaustion, pain in the limbs, and ulcers in the mouth that led to loss of teeth. At this time, ships' captains were discovering the healthful benefits of fresh fruit. Some required their crews to take a daily dose of lime juice, hence the slang "limey."

On long voyages, kegs of water became contaminated with algae and bacterial growth, causing diarrhea and vomiting. Instead, sailors drank ale and were mildly intoxicated much of the day.[43] To defecate, they used the "head" at the beakhead of the ship—the protruding part of the bow—so that excrement dropped directly into the sea. In heavy seas, therefore, a bowel movement included a saltwater soaking.

Sailors washed overboard or fell from yardarms during storms into raging seas or were killed in attacks on enemy ships or in tropical settlements, where they were just as apt to catch malaria or yellow fever as a musket ball in the chest. If they were insubordinate, they could be flogged or marooned on a hostile shore thousands of miles from home. The pay was bad, and their lives were miserable and expendable.

Drake's ships navigated the Straits of Magellan and sailed on to capture Spanish ships in the Pacific freighting gold and silver from Peru to Panama.[44] He then ventured up the coast of North America searching for a passage leading back into the Atlantic. When none was found, he had no choice but to circle the globe via the Pacific and Indian oceans, and he arrived back in England in September 1580 with plunder worth hundreds of millions in today's currency.[45] By virtue of his purchase of a grand estate, Buckland Abbey, he achieved landed gentry status and the cachet of respectability he so desired.[46] Drake and his fellow sea dogs enabled England to become a great sea power, and his circumnavigation was second only to that of Magellan.[47]

During Drake's absence, another Devonshire sea dog, Humphrey Gilbert, won a patent from the queen to discover the fabled Northwest Passage. Gilbert's aunt, Katherine Ashley (née Champernowne), had been Elizabeth's governess from her early childhood until Ashley's death in 1565. Through this connection, Gilbert came at age fifteen to serve as a page to twenty-one-year-old Princess Elizabeth during the reign of Mary Tudor.[48] Later, after being educated at Eton and Oxford, he entered the military and served in Ireland during the 1560s. Tall, domineering, and irascible, he gained a reputation for brutality, lining the path to his tent with the severed heads and limbs of Irish rebels, their wives and children, as a reminder of the cost of rebellion.[49] But Gilbert's passion was the New World, and he authored an essay, *A Discourse of a Discoverie to Prove a New Passage to Catay*, presented to the queen upon his return to England.[50]

Elizabeth's fondness for Gilbert and his belief in the existence of a Northwest Passage won him her moral support if not her financial backing. His patent included the right to settle a colony in North America to serve as a way station on the passage to the Orient.[51] Also stipulated was the queen's one-fifth share of all precious metals found or taken.[52] His first venture with ten ships—purported to be a voyage of discovery—left England in November 1578. It may well have been a privateering expedition in disguise. One ship, captained by his younger half-brother Walter Raleigh, and piloted by Portuguese navigator Simon Fernandez, ventured into the Bay of Biscay. It was overwhelmed by Spanish warships and limped home with many killed.[53] Others were beset by adverse winds. The whole thing ended in failure, and there is no evidence that the first attempt to settle an English colony in America ever reached its destination.[54]

The following summer, the Duke of Anjou arrived in London to court the queen, and by force of his personality, won her favor. As a boy, Anjou had smallpox, and his face and nose were deeply pitted. In addition, a congenital spinal defect spoiled his posture, but to his credit, he was a bright, affable, and lusty lad of twenty-four. Elizabeth was forty-six. Despite the age difference, she fell for her "frog," as she dubbed him, and he rose to the occasion, pretending it was love—not money—that aroused his passion. He was next in line to the French throne, and Philip was apoplectic at the idea of such a union. The courtship continued on and off for two years until the farcical duet devolved into political gamesmanship, and it became clear to Elizabeth that her fawning frog was more interested in her purse than her person. She then realized that he would not leave without being bribed to do so.

Anjou was desperate for funds with which to pay his troops fighting in the Netherlands. Elizabeth held out to keep Philip at bay with the notion of an Anglo-French alliance, but in February 1582 she relented, gave Anjou £10,000 with a promise of more to come, and waved goodbye as he set sail across the Channel, never to return.[55] With him went England's last hope for a French alliance to forestall Spain's growing hostility.[56] Her sorrow was heartfelt, but more for herself than for Anjou, though she was clearly fond of him.[57] The insincerity of his courtship forced Elizabeth to face the fact that she would soon turn fifty. Visions of marital love and children could no longer be indulged with real conviction. She was alone and growing old, and all the trappings of majesty offered little recompense.

While Elizabeth languished in self-pity, the glitter of new tinsel caught her eye.[58] Legend has it she was walking in the gardens at Greenwich Palace when she met with a muddy patch, and a heretofore little-noticed courtier sacrificed his expensive cape for the sake of her satin skirts and slippers.[59] Such a chivalrous gesture fit to a tee Walter Raleigh's flair for the dramatic. His sudden appearance in the queen's company is best explained by the fact that Humphrey Gilbert's patent for finding the Northwest Passage was due to expire in another year, and Gilbert returned to court seeking another try at finding it.[60] With him came his ambitious younger half-brother, cape and all.

Raleigh brought Elizabeth out of her melancholy. By year's end, he was her constant companion. His stunning rise gives evidence of his power to charm. He was young—twenty-eight—and more mature than Anjou. At six feet, he was tall for his time. He had bluish-grey eyes, dark curly brown hair, and a soldier's posture and physique.[61] In addition to his native tongue, he knew French, Spanish, Italian, and Latin.[62] His West Country accent delighted Elizabeth, and she mimicked it, calling him "Warter," eliding the "L" and trilling the "Rs." His wit—quick and apt—matched her own, and it was thus that he seduced her, not with kisses as from her Robin or fawning flattery as from the unctuous Christopher Hatton.[63] She once asked when he would cease being a beggar, to which Raleigh replied, "When your gracious Majesty ceases to be a benefactor."[64] She reveled in clever badinage of this sort. And he wrote poetry. What was not to love?[65]

Few records exist of their conversations, but she did accuse him of begging. For what did Raleigh beg? To start, he begged permission for Gilbert to have another go at discovering the Northwest Passage.[66] She granted this request but with reluctance, as she seems to have had a prescient foreboding of Gilbert's fate at sea.[67] As a parting gift, she had Raleigh convey a present, a bejeweled anchor pin, and asked Gilbert's portrait miniature in return. But she refused Raleigh permission to sail with him, as her new favorite's presence had become indispensable.[68] Indeed, Walter Raleigh never set foot on North American soil.

Raleigh looked up to Gilbert, who was fourteen years older. They were men cut from the same Devonshire worsted as Hawkins and Drake, and it should be noted that West Country folk were resolutely anti–Catholic and anti–Spain. Gilbert's patent gave him imperial rights to the vast colony he was to establish, and he made gifts of huge tracts of land to those willing to invest.[69] He had a creative mind and grandiose plans. From April through July, the Grand Banks attracted scores of fishing vessels—Dutch, English, French, Spanish, Portuguese.[70] Gilbert sought to force them all to submit to English hegemony and pay for the use of the mainland where they processed their catch and dried their nets.[71] In this way, he envisioned a self-sustaining commercial foothold overseen by Englishmen to serve as a way station en route to the Northwest Passage.

Nothing went as planned. Outward bound, one of Gilbert's ships, carrying supplies for a year, turned back mid-ocean due to an outbreak of contagious disease.[72] Probing the coast of Nova Scotia, a second ship ran aground in thick fog and sank with the loss of more supplies and eighty men.[73] Undaunted, Gilbert took possession of the land then went exploring in the *Squirrel*, a small, shallow-draft pinnace.[74] In his absence, his remaining crew became mutinous, and many sought passage home on one of the Grand Banks fishing vessels.[75] By summer's end, low on food, Gilbert ordered what remained of his fleet and crew to head for home, insisting he sail aboard the *Squirrel*. In heavy seas north of the Azores, the flagship pulled alongside, and its captain implored Gilbert to come aboard for his safety. He refused, citing the nearness of heaven.[76] That night the tiny *Squirrel* disappeared.[77]

Raleigh was doubtless saddened by the loss of the brother he idolized.

But he had been infected by Gilbert's passion, and, building on his ideas, Raleigh created his own unique vision and called it Virginia, a name coined to honor the Virgin Elizabeth and endear her to the project.[78] The English were resolved to claim as theirs any land not ruled by a Christian prince, hence Raleigh's presumption that he had naming rights. The gesture helped him win Gilbert's patent. Thereafter he and the queen must have spoken often of an English America. We know that on one outing—riding together on horseback from Richmond to Greenwich—they passed the Mortlake home of John Dee, and Raleigh persuaded Elizabeth to pay a call on the noted savant who had first promoted the idea of a "Brytish Impire."[79]

Born in Devonshire not two miles from the Channel coast, Walter Raleigh was Humphrey Gilbert's brother by a different father. Their mother, Catherine Champernowne, had been widowed in 1547, after which she married the senior Walter Raleigh. Their family was of that resolute Tudor strain, middle-class gentry, but with connections leading to upward mobility for someone with young Walter's talents. Their Champernowne lineage had strong French ties, and, after elementary school, Raleigh followed relatives to France and served on the Huguenot side of the French religious conflict.[80] A voracious and indefatigable reader, he furthered his studies at Oxford after soldering in France for several years as a young teen.[81] While at Oxford, it is probable that he befriended Richard Hakluyt with whom he would soon be closely associated. After Oxford Raleigh matriculated at Middle Temple, after which he joined the military and served as an officer in Ireland.[82] A born leader, he possessed that unique medley of traits that propels certain individuals to the fore—intellect, ambition, confidence, courage, imagination, good looks, panache, and a large ego.[83] But in a word *what* was Walter Raleigh? Soldier, explorer, entrepreneur, historian, intellectual, litterateur, politician, scientist, visionary, courtier? All these but courtier foremost, for this role enabled the rest.

If need be, Elizabeth granted those in her service a sinecure to cover their expenses.[84] As the youngest of nine sons from his parents' four marriages, Raleigh had little inheritance or income, but he was soon the recipient of significant royal largess, notably a monopoly on fees charged to vintners and tavern keepers for their annual licenses and import permits.[85] This produced an income of several hundred thousand pounds per year in today's money. Almost overnight, he became influential and rich, a rise that mystified and irritated the peerage. Though a few tolerated Raleigh as a counterpoise to the unpopular Robert Dudley, in short time Raleigh was the most hated man at court.[86] Despite this, more royal gifts would come his way, but of greatest value to the parvenu was the near presence of the queen's ear. Raleigh had ideas, lots of them—more than his monopoly could pay for.

In 1582 Richard Hakluyt published *Divers Voyages Touching the Discoverie of America*, a collection of voyage-of-discovery narratives. Citing John Cabot's discovery of Newfoundland in 1497, he asserted England's right of possession of North America. His widely acclaimed book reinforced John Dee's earlier exhortations for English expansion.[87] As noted, Hakluyt went to Paris in 1583 as chaplain and secretary to the English ambassador. While there, at Raleigh's request, he wrote a monograph enumerating the advantages that would accrue to England by the settlement of a colony in North America. He listed as benefits the conversion of indigenous inhabitants to Christianity, the sourcing of commodities that the English now obtained at high cost by trade with Europe, employment for the thousands of masterless men that currently plagued England, a share of the riches the New World had to offer evidenced by Spain's experience, and the salvation of the unsuspecting natives of North America from the ravages that Spain had inflicted on the aboriginal inhabitants of New Spain. On a visit to England the following year, he presented his manuscript to the queen.

Hakluyt's monograph also hinted at the opportunities that could arise from a privateering base in the New World should relations with Spain warrant it.[88] As expected, Francis Drake's privateering venture-cum-circumnavigation exacerbated tensions with Spain, and he and other sea dogs—seeking more such remunerative opportunities—recognized the potential benefit of a permanent North American outpost where ships and their crews could recuperate, refit, and revictual. Being a West Countryman like Drake and Hawkins, Walter Raleigh was steeped in the seafaring traditions of Devon and Cornwall. Whether for the development of plantations and trade and the spread of Protestantism as Hakluyt advised, or for war with Spain as many believed inevitable, a fortified base in the New World made sense, and, by virtue of his abilities and the queen's affection, Raleigh became the movement's new champion—the "especial man," as John Hawkins dubbed him.[89]

Though disliked by most of Elizabeth's court, Raleigh's venture had considerable support. Her most trusted advisors—William Cecil, Robert Dudley, and Francis Walsingham—believed that Hawkins and Drake had proven that Spain's New World possessions were lightly defended. It was from those same possessions, however, that Spain's source of wealth derived. Having the wherewithal to attack Spain by preying on her homeward bound plate fleet was viewed as the most efficacious strategy for combatting the much more powerful continental rival. This necessitated a North American colony. There was a second reason explaining the support for Raleigh of these three powerful members of Elizabeth's privy council. They were all secretly sympathetic to the Protestant nonconformist elements arising in England. A Virginia colony could also become a haven for a growing and dangerous fringe of heterodox religious sects.[90]

To accomplish his goal, Elizabeth granted Raleigh the use of Durham House, a palatial residence on the Thames near Whitehall Palace, the queen's principal residence.[91] It had belonged to the Catholic Diocese of Durham until Henry VIII broke with Rome. Indeed, what need did the bishop of Durham have for such stately accommodations in London, two hundred miles from his episcopate? The imposing riverside residence "with lofty marble pillars" came with accommodations for forty servants, stables along the Strand for twenty horses, a garden, an orchard, and a water gate.[92] Unmarried and childless, Raleigh had little need for such capacious digs, and Elizabeth would have preferred that he remain in his own suite of rooms in Whitehall Palace, available for late-night chats or a game of cards or backgammon. But Raleigh and Hakluyt needed a headquarters to serve as the locus for planning the colony they envisioned. Durham House was an agreeable solution but an affront to the nobility, who considered the impressive row of West End riverfront palaces the exclusive club of dukes and earls.[93]

With the queen's official patent good for seven years, Raleigh set about assembling a team to advance plans for the Virginia colony.[94] First came Thomas Harriot, an Oxford-educated mathematician in his early twenties who would become Raleigh's lifelong adviser and friend and one of Europe's seminal sixteenth-century scientists.[95] Others were soldiers Arthur Barlowe and Philip Amadas, and the aforementioned navigator Simon Fernandez. Barlowe had soldiered in Ireland, where he and Raleigh likely met. Little is known of Amadas, but his later actions lead one to conclude that he, too, was a military veteran.[96] A pilot, Fernandez was a native of the Portuguese Azores and a former pirate with experience in American waters. These men lived and worked at Durham House, all in the pay of Walter Raleigh.

There were, in addition, adjunct members of the team, including soldier Richard Grenville (Raleigh's cousin and a native of Cornwall), future circumnavigator Thomas Cavendish, and Oxford-educated scientists Robert Hues and Walter Warner.[97] In addition there were ad hoc advisers including Dee, mathematicians and scientists Thomas Allen, Thomas Diggs, Thomas Hood, Emery Molyneux, and Nathaniel Torporley, plus writers Edmund Spenser, George Chapman, Ben Jonson, and possibly the mercurial Christopher Marlowe.[98] It is believed that Spenser completed the third book of *The Faerie Queene* while residing at Durham House.[99] Here was a coterie of intellectuals and freethinkers who would soon court trouble with the nobility, the clergy, and the public.

Raleigh insisted that his team deliberate even the most minute detail and prepare for every contingency. Harriot initially focused on improving navigation by perfecting the technique for determining latitude.[100] Assisted by Hues and Warner, he spearheaded an effort to better pinpoint latitude by refining the method for determining magnetic variation and creating tables to reduce the number of necessary steps. This work required thousands of discrete calculations that resulted in the revelation that existing data were inaccurate. The length of a degree of latitude is sixty nautical miles, and a typical English galleon averaged only about four nautical miles per hour, therefore a minor miscalculation of one's position could result in significant delays and the waste of precious supplies.[101]

At this time, ascertaining longitude while at sea could only be done by estimating distance and direction travelled, so-called "dead reckoning."

Eager to tackle the challenges Raleigh assigned, Harriot's inquisitive mind always sought a deeper understanding. A born scientist, he ventured beyond contemplation to hands-on, experimental research. Years later he responded to a question about the nature of his work by saying he sought only to be free to pursue knowledge wherever it led for the pure joy of learning, a statement that served to revive old accusations of atheism against Raleigh's Durham House coven of freethinkers.[102] But insofar as a predilection for free inquiry was concerned, Harriot and Raleigh were well paired.[103]

Harriot's work on latitude led him to tackle the loxodrome, the result of a constant compass heading that will spiral toward the poles without a change of course due to the curvature of the Earth. Plotting a long-distance course of successive arcs on a sphere was a challenge for navigators. To solve this, Harriot discovered the formula for computing the area of a spherical triangle formed by three intersecting arcs.[104] He put off publishing this and all his findings until others eclipsed him, but his spherical triangle solution predated by forty years official discovery of the formula by René Descartes.[105]

As a byproduct of his efforts on Raleigh's behalf and his later work, Harriot created many of the algebraic symbols we use today, a shorthand that simplified this branch of mathematics.[106] But the work of Raleigh's scientists was not limited to navigation. At his behest, they grappled with every relevant issue imaginable—from the amount of food necessary to support a given population for a given time to computing the most space-efficient way to store cannonballs.[107]

Hakluyt returned to London from Paris to consult with Raleigh on the critical question of how colonists in a remote, exotic, and potentially hostile environment could best govern themselves.[108] Both men favored befriending the native American inhabitants, a policy calculated to help win the queen's financial support.[109] This was in stark contrast to the brutal treatment of the indigene by Spanish conquistadores in their conquest of the New World. The writings of Bartolomé de las Casas, Gonzalo Fernández de Oviedo, and Peter Martyr d'Anghera recounting these atrocities were well known throughout Europe, this despite Spanish Inquisition efforts to suppress publication of firsthand accounts that came later—works by Pedro de Cieza de León and Bernal Díaz.[110]

Raleigh may have been instrumental in the publication of Las Casas's work in England, and at his own expense, Hakluyt translated Martyr's *De Orbe Novo* into English and saw to its publication.[111] We know that Raleigh read the portion of Cieza de León's description of the invasion of Peru that was published before censorship was imposed by the Inquisition. Rape and genocide in Spain's New World colonies had given rise to the "Spanish Black Legend" promulgated by Protestant evangelists in northern Europe.[112] It held Spain and the Roman Catholic Church responsible for the millions of deaths.

On the pretense of bringing knowledge of Christ to unenlightened New World infidels, Spanish adventurers plundered, murdered, and raped their way through Hispaniola (1493), Cuba (1511), the Spanish Main (1514), Mexico (1517), Guatemala (1519), Honduras (1524), the Yucatán (1526), Peru (1531), and New Granada (1539). The Spanish crown viewed the conquest of the New World as a Christian crusade, but the Spanish hidalgos who volunteered to go were enticed by reports of nuggets of gold large as loaves of bread, of sapphires and emeralds the size of goose eggs, and of pearls by the hundredweight.[113] They went to find their fortune and have their way with Native American girls.

Peter Martyr told tales of gold on almost every page—so plentiful it was of little value to the indigene—and of females who gave themselves willingly.[114] He described appalling treatment of the Amerindians in lurid detail and justified such treatment on the basis of their ignorance, nakedness, and brutality.[115] He condemned their idolatry, sodomy, human sacrifices, and cannibalism and claimed they had no respect for the truth. Las Casas painted an altogether different picture and decried the cruelty of his countrymen. He returned to Spain in 1515 to inform King Ferdinand that the Amerindians were being enslaved to dig for gold and silver and that they were dying from overwork while their wives and daughters were forced to suffer the lust of the Spanish invader. He told horrendous tales—of the practice of cutting off the head of a dead slave rather than unfasten the iron collar around his neck that enchained him to fellow slaves—of a small child wrenched from his mother and butchered to feed a conquistador's dogs. Las Casas's appeal for reform fell on deaf ears.[116] The Spanish crown was too addicted to its one-fifth share of the gold and silver to reform its heinous practices. Spanish enslavement of Amerindians was not abolished until 1542, by which time millions had been killed.[117] To take their place, enslaved Africans were shipped in, a traffic in humans that would continue for three hundred years.[118]

Raleigh and Hakluyt believed that, as allies, Amerindians and English colonists could assist each other, including, if necessary, joining forces against Spain. We cannot know Raleigh's private thoughts, but his future actions and writings reveal a less humane and more mercenary mindset.[119] It appears that the benevolent strategy was a means of achieving desired ends, not an expression of genuine altruism. No stranger to violence, Raleigh had commanded the 1580 massacre at Smerwick in Ireland of six hundred disarmed Catholic soldiers—Spanish, Italian, and Basque—all put to the sword, a slaughter of human life that shocked Europe.[120] That he was following orders does little to mitigate the atrocity. In a book on Guyana written years later, Raleigh likened the fabled El Dorado—the land of gold hidden in the interior of South America—to a virgin's maidenhead in that its palaces, temples, and graves had never been violated, the implication being that they awaited plundering by a latter-day English conquistador.[121] No doubt the sexual innuendo was calculated to titillate a virgin queen.[122]

The term "noble savage" was yet to be coined, but inspired by the writings of Las Casas, this romantic perspective was popularized at this time by French philosopher Michel de Montaigne.[123] In 1562 in Rouen, Montaigne met with three Native Americans who had been brought to France, and though taken aback by their nakedness, he was impressed with their innate sense of justice. Public sentiment for the naïve notion of innocent and virtuous aborigines living in a Golden Age—unrealistic though it was—gained currency in England.[124] The maidenhead analogy would seem to belie Raleigh's professed regard for the native peoples of the New World.[125] Or perhaps his humanism calcified over time in like measure with a rising tide of frustration and his eclipse as the queen's favorite? We cannot know. Regardless, at this still young age, intoxicated as he was by newfound wealth and power, Raleigh's idealism was incandescent, and with Hakluyt—a man of similar passions and a fellow Oxonian—suffused with boundless enthusiasm and optimism.

◆ 3 ◆

The Lost Colony

Raleigh received the queen's patent in March 1584, and a reconnaissance mission sailed in April—two ships commanded by Philip Amadas and Arthur Barlowe, with Simon Fernandez as navigator. On the 4th of July, they sighted the North American coast and followed it north one hundred and twenty miles to an inlet. With some difficulty, the ships crossed the bar and came to an anchor off the north end of an uninhabited barrier island between thirty-five- and thirty-six-degrees north latitude. It became known as Hatarask Island, and the inlet was named Port Ferdinando in honor of Fernandez.[1] In the next two days, a party went ashore to explore and climbed to the top of tall dunes from which they could see the extent of the long narrow island and the inland sea between Hatarask and the mainland. This body of water became known as Pamlico Sound. On the third day, they espied canoes carrying three Algonquins, the native inhabitants of the area, and one of them approached the English ships and was invited aboard. After being entertained with food and wine, he returned to his canoe and fished for the newcomers, his catch ample to feed the entire crew. In the days that followed other Algonquins appeared, and friendly colloquy and trade commenced—European geegaws and metal tools for animal skins and hides. Among the visitors was Granganimeo, brother of the local chief, who brought his wife and children, and they were entertained aboard ship and given gifts. Thereafter Granganimeo sent daily supplies of wild game, fowl, fish, and fruits for the crew. After a week or two of such fellowship, a party of eight English led by Barlowe took the ship's boat twenty miles north to an island the Algonquins called Roanoke at the north end of which was Granganimeo's village. Here the English were entertained by his wife, Granganimeo being away, and they remained overnight anchored just offshore. They returned to the ships anchored at Port Ferdinando the following day. Their stay lasted six weeks, and they returned to England with enthusiastic reports and two guests—Wanchese of the Secotan Tribe and Manteo, a Croatoan (*CRO-ah-TOE-uhn*).[2]

3. The Lost Colony

In London, the Algonquins were dressed like English gentlemen, given room and board at Durham House, and embraced as members of the team.³ Thomas Harriot taught them English and learned and recorded the Algonquian dialect spoken by the two, a language he called Virginian. He invented a system of phonetics and created a rudimentary English-Virginian dictionary for future use by colonists.⁴ As a result, Roanoke Island was chosen as the site for England's first New World colony.

By this time, the vital tasks of recruiting colonists and raising needed funds were well advanced. John White now joined the Durham House team. A middle-aged artist and illustrator, White had accompanied Martin Frobisher in 1577 on one of his three failed attempts to find a Northwest Passage.⁵ White's watercolors of the Algonquins of coastal North Carolina, showing their abodes and activities, would become famous throughout Europe. He is also recognized in history as the maternal grandfather of Virginia Dare—the first child of English parents born in America.

In January 1585 Raleigh was knighted by the queen and given important administrative responsibilities for Cornwall.⁶ He was also elected a member of Parliament for Devonshire. This marks the pinnacle of his favor with Queen Elizabeth, who soon became less interested in her pet's New World project and more concerned with the threat of Spanish invasion.

A month before, Spain and France—the latter having subdued the Huguenots—agreed to a pact that appeared to Protestants throughout Europe as a blatant Catholic threat.⁷ A frightened Elizabeth responded by sending an army under Robert Dudley to reinforce the Dutch in their struggle against Philip, and she issued letters of reprisal to anyone with a ship and a crew willing to attack Spanish shipping.⁸ This storm had been gathering since her excommunication fifteen years earlier, and these developments marked the beginning of open warfare against Spain, a conflict that would continue until her death.

The licensing of privateers portended a potential windfall for Raleigh. Unable to raise sufficient funds to cover the cost of his colony, he would rely on privateering to offset the shortfall.⁹ Just as his brother Humphrey Gilbert had hoped his Newfoundland colony would profit him as a trading entrepôt, Raleigh envisioned his Virginia colony as a for-profit privateering base for ships operating in the West Indies, selling ship's stores and victuals and providing maintenance services and perhaps even crew if Algonquins could be taught the necessary skills.¹⁰ Such an operation would enable the pursuit of other objectives outlined by Hakluyt in his *Discourse on Western Planting*: finding a passage to the Pacific, locating sources of precious metals and minerals, opening new markets for English products, relieving England of its idle population, and, above all, bringing the native inhabitants to Christ and propagating Protestantism in an English America to countervail the Catholicism of New Spain.[11]

It seems almost certain that insofar as Walter Raleigh was concerned, a North American privateering base was a red herring. It made for good propaganda, and Hakluyt trumpeted it relentlessly, but it lacked practicality. By 1585, the pattern of Spanish shipping to and from the West Indies was well known. The homeward bound Spanish treasure fleet passed through the Azores archipelago in late summer or autumn every year, therefore English privateers either followed it across the Atlantic or laid in wait for it in the Azores, hoping to capture a prize.[12] Once the season was over, it made no sense to return to North America. England was nearer, crews wanted to go home, and there were better facilities there for repairing ships and resupplying them for the next season. Raleigh must have realized from the outset that a Virginia privateering base was not viable, a fact that begs the question, what was his true motive for establishing a Virginia colony?[13] It was not for nothing that Raleigh was called "The Fox." Judging from his later interest in El Dorado, one might speculate that his real motive was finding a hidden New World empire like the Aztecs or Incas filled with gold and silver. In a word, plunder. And failing that, his fallback was selling land no one had ever seen that belonged to someone else. As one historian observed, "religion supplied the pretext and gold was the motive."[14]

Raleigh coveted a private dream: a dominion of his own. Elizabeth's patent gave him imperial power over a vast expanse of North America. Land was the true measure of wealth in Elizabethan England. Raleigh had seven years to establish a permanent colony and thus fulfill his dream. Otherwise, visions of a Cortés-like empire would vanish. Such was also the dream of many adventurers who imagined a primeval civilization pregnant with plunder hidden in the misty interior of an unknown vastness. It was apparent from the reconnaissance mission that nothing of the sort existed on the coast, but the hope was that it thrived in the interior, just as it had in Mexico and Peru.[15] There was one problem—the reconnaissance mission failed to find a deep-water harbor that could accommodate a fleet of tall ships, essential for a privateering base *or* an invasion.[16] With visions of conquest in mind, it would soon become evident that amity with the Native Americans was a hopeless fantasy.

In April, five ships departed Plymouth bound for Roanoke Island under the command of Richard Grenville. Simon Fernandez served as navigator. On board were six hundred men with provisions to sustain a colony of two hundred for a year.[17] The colony's governor, Ralph Lane, was a fifty-three-year-old soldier recruited for the post from the English counterinsurgency force in Ireland. Families were to come later, since the initial colony was only intended to establish a temporary redoubt—military with a scientific auxiliary—from which to search for a deep-water port.[18] To assist Lane in implementing the Durham House plans were Harriot, White, and Thomas Cavendish. The Algonquins Manteo and Wanchese were also aboard, but once again, the queen forbade Raleigh from going.

The coast of North Carolina was an inauspicious choice for a first colony. From the seashore inland for up to fifty miles, the land is swampy or so low-lying it often floods, and much of it in the sixteenth century was thick forested wetlands that were all but impenetrable. English galleons had an average draft of twelve feet, but inlets into the Pamlico Sound—through which Roanoke Island is accessed—are blocked to such ships by shallow sandbars that shift with every major storm. Dangerous offshore shallows— Wimble, Diamond, and Frying Pan Shoals—extend miles out into the Atlantic, and seas off the Outer Banks are subject to riptides and crosscurrents caused by the conflux of the Gulf Stream and the Labrador Current. These hazards have caused countless shipwrecks and given this region of the North American coast the baleful epithet "Graveyard of the Atlantic."[19]

Two large bodies of water separate the barrier islands from the mainland: Pamlico and Albemarle Sounds. They are ringed by land that was occupied in 1585 by Amerindians numbering between eight and ten thousand.[20] They lived in small villages of one to three hundred individuals each of which on average one-third were men of fighting age.[21] They subsisted on fishing, hunting, foraging, and horticulture—farming a small package of domesticated crops: corn (maize), beans, and squash.[22] Except for dogs, they had no domesticated animals, no beasts of burden.[23] Though the area of land occupied was large—over five thousand square miles— its carrying capacity augmented by the fishable waters could support only a limited number of people, considering the Algonquins' quasi-neolithic existence.[24] At this time population density was not more than two individuals per square mile, which must be considered at or near optimum for the catchment area. It is not surprising, therefore, that the English wrongly concluded that most of the land was not utilized.[25]

The Algonquins of Tidewater North Carolina were a moral people with an ancient, rich, and complex culture.[26] They were devout in their religious beliefs and obedient and deferential to authority. Referring to them, Arthur Barlowe wrote, "a more kind and loving people, there cannot be found in the world."[27] Their calendar was rich in celebration and ritual, and they revered their gods, loved and nurtured their children, and honored their dead. They were a communal society and would defend to the death the territory on which their lives depended. They thought of their wealth as manifest in their women and children, and they possessed little of value to Europeans except for their sometimes-meager supply of food.

They called their land Ossomocomuck (*os-sah-MO-ca-muk*), and it was home to nine autonomous or semi-autonomous tribes made up of alliances of villages sharing some commonality.[28] Ossomocomuck stretched from today's North Carolina-Virginia border one hundred and twenty-five-miles south to Bogue Sound and inland up to fifty miles. The Great Dismal Swamp created a natural demarcation wilderness separating Ossomocomuck from the Algonquin-speaking tribes of Tidewater Virginia. Farther inland were the Siouan-speaking Mandoag to the west and the Iroquoian-speaking Tuscarora to the south. The word "Mandoag" meant "enemy" in Algonquin, the most prominent and perhaps only language spoken in Ossomocomuck.[29] All Algonquins lived in villages, none lived in the forests. Tribes consisted of as few as three villages to as many as eighteen, the former being the Croatoan of the Outer Banks, the latter, the Chowanoc (*CHOW-a-noc*) Tribe situated on the north bank of the Albemarle Sound.[30] Each village and tribe had its own chief, called a weroance (*WAYR-uh-ance*), whose power and autonomy depended on the strength of neighbors. Village and tribal conflicts were common, and alliances shifted from time to time. No paramount weroance ruled over all of Ossomocomuck.

The Algonquin village of Roanoke was one of the eight to ten villages that made up the Secotan Tribe, numbering two to three thousand people.[31] The Secotan inhabited Roanoke Island and the mainland between the Alligator and Pamlico Rivers, which encompassed Lake Mattamuskeet, a shallow freshwater lake, now a wildlife preserve. South of the Secotan lived the Pomoiok (*pah-MOW-ee-ock*) Tribe, situated on the Pamlico-Neuse River Peninsula, and south of the Neuse River were their allies, the Neusiok (*nee-YOU-see-ock*), and another tribe, the Coree. It is not known if these three tribes were Algonquin- or Iroquois-speaking peoples.[32] Just before the English arrived, the Secotan were attacked at a banquet by their Pomoiok guests, resulting in serious injury to Wingina, weroance of the Secotan.[33]

North of Roanoke Island was the large Albemarle Sound, on the northern shore of which lived the Weapemeoc (*way-yah-PEH-meh-ock*) with ten villages and perhaps two thousand people.[34] Their northern frontier was the Great Dismal Swamp. West of the Weapemeoc was the Chawanoc Tribe of three to four thousand people, largest and most powerful of the Ossomocomuck tribes, and opposite the Chawanoc on the south bank of the Albemarle Sound—between the Alligator and Roanoke Rivers—lived the smaller, semi-autonomous Moratuc Tribe. The Croatoan, smallest of Ossomocomuck tribes with three to five hundred people, lived on the Outer Banks. The Croatoan were under the sway of the Secotan, but being accessible only by boat, they appear to have enjoyed a degree of autonomy.[35]

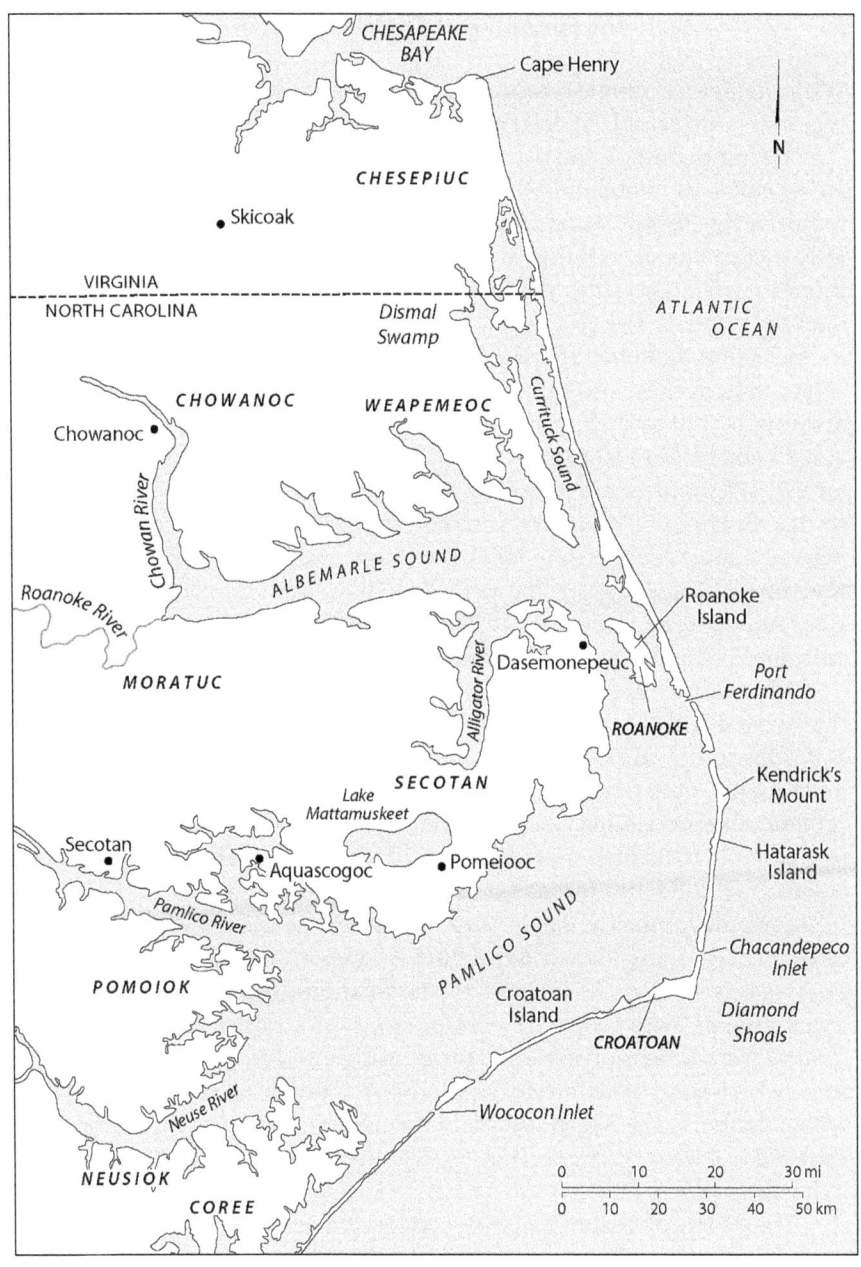

Ossomocomuck

In 1585 Ossomocomuck was a pristine coastal biome. It was home to numerous ecosystems: saltwater and freshwater marshes, cypress and mixed hardwood swamps, low-lying pine and hardwood forests, and extensive peat bogs called pocosins, the Algonquin word for swamp.[36]

With a temperate climate, rainfall was ample, but, being near sea level, the region was vulnerable to destructive nor'easters and hurricanes.

Ossomocuck hosted over a thousand plant species that were either edible or medicinal.[37] Learning their names, preparation, and uses required significant training. The sounds, estuaries, rivers, and streams were a cornucopia, yielding not just fish and shellfish, but also seasonal migratory fish (herring, shad, sturgeon, striped bass), many species of ducks plus geese, swans, cranes, egrets, and other migratory birds, some in flocks that darkened the sky. The estuaries teemed with oysters, crabs, clams, eels, snakes, and tortoises, plus grasses and hemp for baskets and bedding as well as shells for tools, weapons, and jewelry. The forests provided habitat for turkey, quail, and other wildfowl that supplied feathers for fletching arrows and adorning headdresses in addition to being a food source. Beaver, fox, opossum, raccoon, rabbit, bobcat, and bear provided pelts and meat for the stewpot.[38] The most coveted prey of all, however, was the white-tailed deer that provided food, hides for clothing, moccasins, and bedding, bone and antlers for sewing needles, tools, weapons, and glue, and sinew for fishnets and fishing weirs.[39]

Woodlands provided saplings and bark for constructing houses that were durable, dry, and warm thanks to a superabundance of peat and firewood. And the marshes, meadows, and forests were a source for mushrooms, nuts (walnuts, chestnuts, hickory nuts, chinquapins), fruits (grapes, blueberries, blackberries, crabapples, persimmons, strawberries), roots (onion, tuckahoe, snakeroot, sassafras), dyestuffs (bloodroot, sumac, pokeberry), and herbs for medicines.[40]

Ossomocuck villages were located on navigable waters. Algonquins traveled and fished by dugout canoe; a village's most valuable possessions were its cedar and cypress canoes, some large enough to accommodate forty people.[41] Fields for crops were adjacent to villages, and beyond were forests or wetlands for hunting and foraging, the boundaries of which were ill-defined and, therefore, a potential source of conflict with neighbors. The Algonquins had no metals except for trinkets of copper used as currency and decoration, obtained in trade from Amerindians living farther inland.

The people of Ossomocuck had black hair and light skin darkened by sun exposure and often painted and tattooed. In warm weather, adults wore a loincloth of deerskin. Women went bare-breasted and children, naked until puberty.[42] When not defending territory or raiding a neighbor, men fished or hunted, and women tended crops, cured meat and fish, foraged for tubers, roots, herbs, nuts, and fruit.[43] In the absence of suitable stone, the Algonquin's spears and arrows were tipped with antler, mussel shell, turkey spurs, or birds' beaks, and a single arrow seldom inflicted

3. The Lost Colony

a lethal wound.[44] Shields and bucklers were made of bark or a weave of fibrous plant bast, somewhat effective against arrows and truncheons but useless against European firearms.[45]

Having been carried by trade winds to the West Indies then up the strait between Florida and the Bahamas, the English fleet reached the coast of North Carolina in late June 1585. In an attempt to enter Pamlico Sound through an inlet near today's Portsmouth Island, Grenville's flagship, the *Tyger*, ran aground.[46] John White blamed the mishap on the carelessness of Simon Fernandez, but the charge may be unfair.[47] At the time, there were no reliable charts of the coast or of the submerged offshore shoals that bedevil shipping to this day. With difficulty, the *Tyger* was refloated but not before foodstuffs had been ruined.[48]

The *Tyger* accident was the first of many mishaps that led to a suspicion of sabotage directed against Walter Raleigh.[49] Arrogant by nature, Raleigh invited antipathy because of his temperament and nouveau riche status. He has been described as narcissistic, histrionic, indiscreet, impatient, insensitive, insolent, overbearing, vain, tactless, and ruthless, as he doubtless was. But this complex figure was also brilliant, charming, creative, curious, fearless, generous, imaginative, proud, resilient, and loyal.[50] His followers were devoted, his enemies hostile and vindictive. But it was not sabotage in the New World that dealt the first blow to amity with the native Americans. It was the same patronizing hauteur on display when the entitled censure the needy, or the literate the illiterate, the refined the unrefined. And it was doubtless modeled at the top by Raleigh himself.

The shallow continental shelf forced Grenville's fleet to anchor a mile or more offshore, vulnerable to foul weather.[51] This was the only option for tall ships and the principal reason for seeking a more suitable harbor elsewhere.[52] While repairs were made to the *Tyger*, a delegation was sent to Roanoke Island to inform the Secotan of their arrival. Once they returned, a reconnaissance party of three boats crossed Pamlico Sound to explore the mainland. Grenville led the expedition that included Amadas, Harriot, and John White. They visited three villages, all in Secotan territory.[53] At Aquascogoc, the second village, White painted a watercolor of a Secotan mother and daughter, the daughter clutching an English doll, one of the gifts being handed out as tokens of friendship.

Moving on to a third village, the explorers realized a silver cup had gone missing. Suspecting theft, they returned to Aquascogoc and demanded its return. When it was not forthcoming as promised, Amadas ordered the town and crops burned, and terrified Secotan men, women, and children fled.[54] The English then returned to their fleet, weighed anchor, and sailed north to an anchorage nearer the inlet leading to Roanoke Island. In his narrative, Grenville expresses neither regret nor remorse for the brutality of his retaliation, which was out of all proportion to the trivial nature of the crime. The incident poisoned relations with the Secotan, though Wingina feigned friendship for as long as it took to get what he wanted from the English. Before the colonists ever reached Roanoke Island, the mere loss of a silver cup may have scuppered any hope for amity with the indigenous inhabitants and, by extension, their conversion to Christianity.

But hostility was not the only consequence of this cruel reprisal. The time was early July. Three crops of corn would have been in the fields—one planted in April, one in May, one in June—with vines of beans climbing the cornstalks, and squashes and melons trailing on the ground.[55] The April crop would have ripened and been ready for harvest in a matter of weeks, prompting the annual green corn celebration.[56] It appears neither Grenville nor Amadas paused to consider that the loss of victuals aboard the *Tyger* would necessitate reliance on the Secotan for food the following winter and spring. Impulsive English hubris proved so myopic as to burn the very crops they would be desperate for ten months later.

The Secotan village of Roanoke was ruled by Granganimeo, Wingina's brother. He, his wife, and his father, Ensenor, welcomed the English, some of whom they had met the previous year. In Algonquin culture, sovereignty passed matrilineally from one generation to the next, so Wingina may have inherited his chiefdom from his mother. This would explain why Ensenor was not the tribe's weroance. It is likely Granganimeo was expecting the visitors and the return of native sons Wanchese and Manteo.

No Englishman alive relished a fight more than Richard Grenville, and by this time he and Ralph Lane were at loggerheads.[57] The torching of houses and crops at Aquascogoc likely caused further alienation. Lane would later accuse the admiral of intolerable pride and insatiable ambition.[58] As governor, Lane had to contend with the Secotan going forward, whereas Grenville was about to return to England.

The English negotiated for land on which to build a fort. They may have given the Secotan something in return—there is no record of a payment—but to Algonquins the transaction would not have constituted a transfer of ownership.[59] Beyond clothes, tools, and weapons, they had no personal possessions.[60] To them the idea of owning land was as incomprehensible as owning water.[61] More likely, any payment was considered recompense for short-term occupation since the English viewed the Roanoke Island base as temporary until a deep-water harbor could be found.[62]

Granganimeo would have been eager for a trading monopoly with the English. Anything metal, especially copper but also iron hatchets, shovels, and spades, was highly prized by the Algonquins. It is easy to imagine the labor-saving value of a simple iron hatchet for a people who used the trees of the forest for so much—tools, weapons, houses, warmth, canoes, cleared land for crops, and constructing fishing weirs and palisades. These and other trade goods brought by the English—colorful glass beads, jewelry, toys, mirrors, and brass and copper pots—would bring a high price from other Ossomocomuck tribes. But having need of a sheltered anchorage for tall ships, the English would not be contained. While some colonists worked at constructing houses and defensive earthworks, others went exploring.

In early August, Amadas and others sailed north across the Albemarle Sound to explore Weapemeoc territory. A report of violence on this excursion lacks corroboration and plausibility but is the only existing detail of what occurred.[63] As they crossed the sound, Amadas would have discerned one or more inlets into the sound from the Atlantic. They would have been shallow and variable like those of the Pamlico, but they have since silted up.[64] Though there are twelve to twenty feet of depth mid-channel in the Albemarle and Pamlico Sounds, the shallows that support and, therefore, skirt the barrier islands block access to this deeper water. By taking soundings, Amadas would have come to the conclusion that both the Pamlico and the Albemarle Sounds were inaccessible to oceangoing English ships. To find a suitable harbor, therefore, Lane and company would have to explore farther afield.

With the English becoming entrenched, Wingina moved to Roanoke Island. Though far from the geographic center of his territory, the presence of the English had the potential to upset alliances, and he wished to control the situation. Being paramount weroance of the Secotan, Wingina had great power, but his power was not absolute.[65] By Algonquin tradition, tribes were governed by their weroance and shaman alike, assisted by lesser weroances called cockarouse and lesser shamans.[66] Political etiquette dictated that the weroance build consensus among the tribe's officials.[67] Shamans had great influence in Algonquin polity, and their blessing was vital in any undertaking.[68] Wingina was likely enraged by the burning of Aquascogoc, but his anger was tempered by his brother's and father's beliefs that the English had extraordinary powers and trade goods advantageous to the Secotan and that their presence should be tolerated, at least for the present.

The English considered a fortification to be a precaution against attack by unfriendly Native Americans or by the Spanish, who would not tolerate an English colony in what they considered Florida territory.[69] Construction of a defensive earthwork was completed in mid–August, and cannon were brought ashore and mounted on platforms at key positions.[70] A demonstration of English cannon fire would have frightened and intimidated the Algonquins and must have occurred. An English sword would have fetched a high price but keeping deadly weapons out of the hands of Native Americans was paramount.[71]

Grenville and Fernandez returned to England aboard the *Tyger*, followed in early September by the last of the tall ships, leaving just over one hundred colonists. About half were soldiers.[72] With the fort nearing completion, Harriot led an exploration into the interior. As his party departed each village it visited, Algonquins began dying. Illness and death resulted so soon after the English departed that the villagers attributed the cause to the dark powers of the newcomer, but the English were as dismayed by the phenomenon as the Algonquins. Harriot reported that many died—in some towns twenty, in some forty, in one over one hundred, the total constituting a significant number of the inhabitants.[73] Considering the rapid onset of disease and death, the likely cause was influenza or measles, maladies for which the Algonquins had no inherited immunity.[74]

It did not go unnoticed that there were no women among the English. And it appeared to the Algonquins that the interlopers had no interest in Algonquin women.[75] Abstention from the pursuit of carnal pleasures is not characteristic of English soldiers now or at any time in history. They were apparently under orders from Raleigh to refrain from intimacy with the Algonquin women.[76] Such prohibitions are never observed for long. Boys will be boys, but Governor Lane proved a stern disciplinarian. By keeping his men in line, he kept them alive—more than can be said for the future governors of Jamestown.[77] The Algonquins' superstitious assumptions regarding the newcomers accrued to the advantage of the English, since many Native Americans concluded that their uninvited guests were not born of women and must, therefore, be immortal.[78]

Sometime in October or November, an exploring party traveled north to the Chesapeake Bay.[79] The English had only secondhand knowledge of the immense estuary discovered and named Bahia de Santa Maria by the Spanish. It is not known who led the expedition. Lane did not, but Harriot and White were among those who went.[80] The only firsthand reports are three sentences from Ralph Lane's narrative that pose more questions than answers and a map painted by White showing the south shore of the bay and location of two Algonquin towns.[81] The territory was that of the Chesepioc (*ches-ah-PEE-ock*) Tribe of the Tidewater Virginia Algonquins, now the area encompassing Norfolk and Virginia Beach.[82]

The expeditionary force sailed up Currituck Sound, which separates the barrier islands from the mainland, then out into the Atlantic through an inlet that no longer exists.[83] From there it was only twenty miles north to the entrance to the bay at today's Cape Henry.[84] Once within the bay itself, the explorers realized they had found the holy grail—a deep-water harbor vast enough to shelter every ship in England. The third largest estuary in the world, Chesapeake Bay is fed by one hundred and fifty rivers.

3. The Lost Colony

Hugging the southern shoreline, the expedition anchored first in Lynnhaven Bay and then continued along the coast to the Elizabeth River eighteen miles west of Cape Henry. Proceeding upriver from there, the men made camp near the Chesepioc village of Skicóac and spent the winter in apparent harmony with their hosts.[85]

It is evident from the paucity of firsthand accounts of this venture that the Durham House team decided to relocate their colony to the Chesapeake Bay and hide all evidence of their intent.[86] After returning to England, Harriot wrote a treatise on his New World experience but says nothing of this expedition except a telling comment about sleeping on the ground in the open air in the middle of winter.[87] Had he wintered on Roanoke Island, he would have slept in a house built for him, with wattle and daub or mud-and-stud walls and a thatched roof, one of the structures that the Secotan later threatened to burn.[88] This is the only evidence suggesting Harriot was on the expedition.

There are no surviving paintings by John White of the Chesapeake Bay area or its inhabitants except for his map of the coastline, which includes the southern shore of the bay and the location of the village of Skicóac.[89] It may be that others were lost during the colonists' hasty departure from Roanoke Island the following June when trunks belonging to Harriot and White were thrown overboard to lighten a pinnace that kept running aground while rushing to ferry colonists and their belongings to the tall ships waiting offshore. The loss of a significant portion of a year's work was much lamented by both men.[90] It is evident, however, that reports of the Chesapeake Bay signaled a turning point in the thinking of Raleigh, Hakluyt, and the Durham House regulars.

The superstitions of Granganimeo and Ensenor regarding English omnipotence gave Wingina pause. The chief would have questioned Wanchese, however, whose winter in London taught him much, not the least that England was peopled by both men and women, all of them mortal. We know nothing of Wanchese's experience while in England, but he returned to Ossomocomuck antagonistic toward the English and thereafter led Secotan efforts to destroy them.[91] Over the winter, Wingina's attitude also hardened, but the newcomers' rich trove of trade goods kept the English safe from harm for the time being.[92]

Harriot and White returned from the Chesapeake Bay in late February. In early March, Granganimeo died. At once, Wingina changed his name to Pemisapan. It was tradition in Algonquin culture for an individual to change his or her name to signal profound transformation.[93] Twenty-eight years later almost to the day, eighteen-year-old Pocahontas changed her name to Rebecca upon marrying the Englishman John Rolfe in Jamestown.[94] Wingina's name change was an important signal to his people, a signal lost on the English. Unbeknownst to Governor Lane, Pemisapan began plotting the destruction of his colony.[95]

Later that month, Lane led an expedition across the Albemarle Sound to establish contact with the powerful Chowanoc. His task force traveled by pinnace up the Chowan River to the chief's village where he met Menatonon, the most powerful weroance in Ossomocomuck. After receiving the usual English gifts, Menatonon answered Lane's questions regarding the region and its people. With Manteo interpreting, Lane learned of the land of Chaunis Temoatan, twenty days' journey to the west, the source of wassador, as copper was called in Algonquin.[96] Menatonon's description of a "whiter" metal hinted at gold and silver also.[97] The cherished wassador was obtained by barter at an important Amerindian trading center located on an island in the Moratuc River—today's Roanoke River—called Occaneechee, where the river intersected the Great Trading Path.[98] With this revelation, Lane sensed the treasure his employer had sent him to find. Absent precious metals or a viable route to the Pacific, Lane had already concluded that Raleigh's Virginia was not worth the effort and expense.[99]

Reports of Chaunis Temoatan did not suggest a citadel filled with golden idols hidden in the interior like the Aztecs' Tenochtitlan or the Incas' Cuzco. But one can imagine such images flooded Lane's imagination. Two hundred years later, copper and gold were discovered by European settlers in the Carolina Slate Belt, two hundred miles southwest of the Chowanoc capital. Modern names in this auriferous region—Eldorado, Gold Hill, Goldston, Richfield, Silver Hill, Silver Valley—suggest that the area may have been the source of Algonquin copper.[100] Harriot claimed to have learned also that the Roanoke River had its headwaters in the Gulf of Mexico, doubtless an Amerindian fable embellished to encourage the English to move on.[101] The prospect of finding both a source of precious metals *and* a means of traversing North America persuaded Lane to venture up the Roanoke River to Occaneechee.[102] To ensure the safety of his crew, he took Menatonon's son Skiko as a hostage. An exchange of hostages as a guarantee of goodwill would become common practice in future English-Algonquin dealings.[103]

Lane and his party descended the Chowan River, crossed the Albemarle Sound, and began the difficult task of rowing against the strong discharge of the Roanoke River.[104] Low on food, they expected with every meander in the river to encounter Algonquins of the Moratuc Tribe, or the fearsome Mandoags, whose territory they were nearing the farther west they traveled. On the verge of starvation, Lane put to a vote the question of retreat, but his crew urged him on. To survive, they killed and cooked the two mastiffs on board. Algonquins feared these English dogs, largest in the world. Finally, Amerindians hidden in the forest began calling out to

3. The Lost Colony

Manteo. When he responded, they began a cacophonous chant, the meaning of which prompted Manteo to reach for a musket and warn others. A hail of arrows followed, doing little harm, and the attackers fled as the English fired their muskets.[105] Out of food and worried for their safety, Lane postponed the search for Occaneechee, and he and his crew returned to Roanoke.

Pemisapan had not been idle. Resolved to rid Ossomocumuck of the English, he cobbled together an attack force that included Chowanoc warriors plus Mandoag mercenaries bribed with metal objects bartered from the English.[106] On April 20, Ensenor died, leaving only Manteo to plead the English cause, but by this time, Manteo had become persona non grata except to his Croatoan relatives.[107] Lane used his hostage, Skiko, as leverage to force Pemisapan to plant corn and build a fishing weir for the English, but privately Pemisapan, assisted by Wanchese, was appealing to his allies to assemble in the Secotan village of Dasemunkepeuc (*DAY-sah-mun-ke-puc*) on the mainland just across the water from the English fort.[108]

In late May, the English—starving and desperate for resupply from England—found their recently planted corn crop destroyed and their new fishing weir broken beyond repair. Suspicious, Lane got wind of Pemisapan's plot and on the first of June launched a preemptive strike on Dasemunkepeuc. Several Secotan warriors were killed in the skirmish, and Pemisapan was shot in the buttocks but escaped, fleeing with his warriors into the forest.[109] One of Lane's troops pursued the Secotan weroance and returned with his severed head. Lane mounted it on a pike to display at the entrance to the fort as a warning.[110]

Within a week a large fleet of English ships anchored off Hatteras Island. In command was Francis Drake, returning to England from a successful raid on Spain's colonies on the Spanish Main and in Florida.[111] His raid had been devastating to New Spain and would further inflamed hostilities.[112] Drake came to offer reinforcements, food, munitions, and additional shallow-draft boats for the colony's use, much of it Spanish plunder. The windfall was timely, but before these supplies could be brought ashore, a storm struck that forced the fleet to hoist sail so as to avoid being trapped against a lee shore.[113] The storm, which may have been an early hurricane, raged for several days, leaving some ship's captains no alternative but to continue on to England rather than beat back against Gulf Stream trade winds. Once the storm abated, Drake returned to fulfill his pledge, but a discouraged Lane and his besieged colonists decided to throw in the towel and return home.[114] With them went Manteo, his life in danger.[115] Now considered a turncoat by Wanchese and the Secotan, had he returned to his native Croatoan Island, he may have invited an attack on his birth tribe.

The beheading of Pemisapan demanded retaliation by the Secotan and in consequence, English urgency to be gone. As noted earlier, trunks containing White's paintings and Harriot's scientific notes and samples were thrown overboard in the haste, and three men were left behind. Speculation has it they were upcountry in Chowanoc territory returning the hostage Skiko to his father. The three were never seen again. With so many veteran soldiers among the colonists, was anyone surprised by the outcome? It must be said that for want of amity with the Native Americans, the first Roanoke Colony was abandoned one week shy of its first anniversary.

Within days of their departure, a ship sent by Raleigh arrived with emergency supplies to replace those lost when the *Tyger* ran aground a year earlier. Finding no one and the fort and dwellings in disarray, the unnamed captain of the unnamed ship concluded the colony had been abandoned and returned to England. A few weeks later Richard Grenville arrived with the long awaited second supply—a half dozen ships carrying two hundred new colonists—all male—with supplies for a year.[116] They, too, found Roanoke Island deserted except for the lifeless bodies of two men—one Algonquin, one English—both hanged by the neck and in a state of decay.[117] A hurried search of the mainland nearby resulted in the capture of three Secotan. It is possible the arrival of an English fleet induced most Secotan living there to flee into the interior. Two of the captives escaped. The third confessed to Grenville that Lane's colony had sailed away with Drake.[118]

No doubt, the ruthless Richard Grenville extracted more from his Secotan captive. He would have learned of Pemisapan's plot to attack the colony, of Lane's preemptive assault on Dasemunkepeuc, and of the beheading of Pemisapan. Despite all, Grenville wished to maintain an English presence in Virginia to protect Raleigh's patent and to maintain the foothold in America he now viewed as vital to England in light of growing tensions with Spain. He left fifteen men with a pinnace, ample provisions, and armaments.[119] Considering the ominous signs—the grisly specter of decaying bodies, the disorder that indicated an ignominious exodus, and the absence of Algonquins in a region that was once well-peopled—did Grenville truly believe a garrison of only fifteen could hold out? Their vulnerability notwithstanding, at the end of two weeks, he gave orders to weigh anchor, eager to spend what remained of the season cruising the Azores for Spanish prizes.

The return to England of the entire Roanoke Island colony must have discouraged Walter Raleigh. Reports of conditions there were so grim as to require censorship. Surveying the situation, he might have decided to give up on Virginia. Raleigh had important obligations and a new, more promising opportunity. Regarding the former, he had pressing administrative responsibilities for Cornwall and Devon. As to the latter, a month before Drake and Lane returned, Raleigh was among the lucky few granted parcels of the attainted lands of recently captured Irish rebel leader, the Earl of Desmond. Raleigh received twelve thousand acres in the counties of Cork and Waterford and, by additional transactions, parlayed his grant to forty-two thousand acres—not a kingdom perhaps but a very respectable principality.[120] Why spend good money chasing bad in Virginia when he had a better option just across St. George's Channel? There, land was already cleared of troublesome native inhabitants, and fields for agriculture or grazing were already cleared of rocks and trees. Being nearer England, Ireland was more appealing to English colonists reluctant to leave family so far behind, and there was a castle with a view that needed only renovation to earn Raleigh landed gentry status, perhaps, even, a barony.[121]

What made Ireland even more appealing was the backing and protection of the crown.[122] As conflict with Spain grew more heated, Elizabeth sought to fortify and populate southern Ireland with English soldiers and farmers to prevent Spain from using Catholic Ireland as a military base from which to invade England. With such a promising opportunity plus the protection of the Royal Navy, Raleigh might well have abandoned Virginia altogether were it not for the fifteen men left by Grenville and a new initiative involving John White.[123]

White envisioned a Virginia settled by families, including his own.[124] He imagined farms, not a privateering base. And those who volunteered to join him were not soldiers but working-class citizens, eager to invest their own sweat equity, furnish their own supplies, and be self-sufficient once there. In return for passage and weapons, White would preserve Raleigh's patent by establishing the "Citie of Raleigh" in Virginia.[125] Why a new name if not to indicate a new location? The intent was to create the Citie of Raleigh on the Chesapeake Bay but to reveal nothing of this plan, for if Spain were to find out, the new settlement would be in danger of attack.[126] White had no illusions about where things stood with the Algonquins. He would not have wanted to return to Roanoke Island if land for farming was his intent. Considering relations with the Secotan, White would have needed a small army.

A few months before Lane's colonists arrived back in England, Mary, Queen of Scots, was executed. After nineteen years as Elizabeth's prisoner, Mary had given her blessings to a plot to assassinate Elizabeth, this one led by Anthony Babington with a promise of support from the Spanish ambassador. It was only the latest in a series of such plots, and Francis Walsingham, Elizabeth's spymaster, caught Mary red-handed. With this, the gloves came off. Now, there would be no more scheming by the Queen of Scots and no more proxy war in the Netherlands or West Indies. The time had come to confront Philip where he lived. Elizabeth's advisers hatched a plan to attack Spanish ships in Spanish harbors—to destroy Spain's navy before Philip had time to launch his "Enterprise of England." Francis Drake—now infamous in Spain as *El Draque*, "the dragon"—was given command. With this development, the need for a privateering base in the New World evaporated.[127] Almost overnight, Raleigh's Virginia was a dead letter.

Despite these headwinds, White formalized arrangements in November 1586 with plans to sail in the spring. In January, Raleigh signed the necessary documents and secured coats of arms for the twelve members of White's governing council, an honor that cost Raleigh nothing.[128] Amid Drake's preparations to attack Spain, White's colonists assembled in London. It is quite possible they were Puritans seeking religious freedom.[129] A libertine in such matters, Raleigh would have voiced no objection, but nor would he have advertised the fact.[130] The association had all the earmarks of a cooperative enterprise with a religious foundation. Raleigh provided shipping and weaponry, but he could ill afford even this limited assistance. Already the queen was distracted by a new arrival at court—the handsome and temperamental twenty-one-year-old Robert Devereux, Earl of Essex. With his salad days behind him, Raleigh's tenure as Elizabeth's supreme favorite was coming to an end.[131]

Three ships departed Plymouth in May with one hundred and eighteen colonists led by John White, captain and governor. With him went his pregnant daughter Eleanor and her husband, Ananias Dare. Simon Fernandez was chief navigator. White wrote the only firsthand account of this venture, and he was critical of Fernandez from the start. He complained of mishaps on the voyage over—the intentional loss of one of the ships, two missed rendezvous (one for salt needed to cure meat and fish), drinking contaminated water, eating poisonous fruit, and the desertion of two members of the crew—most of which White blamed on Fernandez.[132] Portuguese by birth, Fernandez may have had Catholic sympathies, a possible bone of contention were White, indeed, a crypto–Puritan. Other than this and typical English xenophobia, there is no explaining White's animosity, if such it was.[133]

The fleet anchored off Hatteras Island on July 22 and was joined two days later by the "lost" ship. Writing of these events a year later, White states that he intended to plant his colony on the Chesapeake Bay.[134] We must assume that during the winter of 1585–86 when he, Harriot, and others trekked north to the bay and spent the winter there in close proximity to the friendly Chesepioc Tribe, they found the deep-water bay so hospitable they decided to settle a colony there—either the one then residing on Roanoke Island under Lane or some future colony. It has been noted that so little was reported of that episode as to indicate an effort to conceal it.

White wrote that once at anchor off Hatteras Island, he launched one of the ship's boats with forty of his "best men" to go to Roanoke Island. His purpose was to find the fifteen men left by Grenville the previous summer and "to have conference concerning the state of the country and savages."[135] After so doing, he intended to return to the ship and sail up the coast to the Chesapeake Bay, there to build a fort as directed "in writing" by Walter Raleigh.[136] By "best men" one supposes he meant those best able to fight should the need arise, an indication White anticipated the possibility of trouble.

What is perplexing about this is that it implies he did not intend to rescue the fifteen left by Grenville. Surely there was no intention to leave them there. Why not bring them aboard and debrief them on the way to the Chesapeake? And why would White care how things stood with "the country and savages" if he had no intention of staying?

He then states that as the boat pulled away from the ship, one of Fernandez's petty officers called down orders to the oarsmen to leave all the colonists on Roanoke Island except White and two or three of his chosen subalterns.[137] The petty officer went on to say the summer was far spent, and that Fernandez would land them on Roanoke Island and "in no other place." White adds that Fernandez and his crew were so adamant in their determination that it was useless—perhaps dangerous—to argue with them.[138]

Recall that White was an artist by training and Simon Fernandez, a former pirate. Possible religious differences aside, they could not have been more dissimilar. White was the designated captain of the venture, but it is apparent Fernandez was in charge. Fernandez had been in Raleigh's service for eight years. Presumably, he had earned his employer's trust, and there is no record of Raleigh being upset with Fernandez for not delivering White and his fellow colonists to the Chesapeake Bay. The following summer, Fernandez served with the English Navy in defeating the Spanish Armada.[139] There is nothing to suggest he was in disfavor. White's puzzling statement about Grenville's fifteen men and his jaundiced portrayal of Fernandez renders his narrative suspect. And there is no basis to suspect Fernandez failed to follow orders other than White's puzzling accusation.

Doubtless Raleigh instructed Fernandez to settle the colony on the Chesapeake Bay. But considering the manifest dangers, he would also have cautioned Fernandez to follow his best judgment. Furthermore, he would have ordered Fernandez to arrive in the Azores in time to capture a homeward-bound Spanish prize before returning to England. This may explain the comment, "the Summer was farre spent." Raleigh never sent ships to the New World without orders to plunder Spanish shipping, this to pay the cost of the venture, each of which had to be self-sustaining.[140] Despite lavish favors from the queen, Raleigh could not afford the immense costs of leasing, manning, and outfitting a fleet of ships for the better part of a year. On the other hand, it made no sense—financial or otherwise—to imperil the colonists for the sake of Spanish booty.

What is most likely is that Fernandez decided the Chesapeake Bay was too dangerous.[141] The execution of Mary, Queen of Scots had added yet another poison pill to the already toxic relations with Spain.[142] On the voyage over, a member of the crew had deserted in Spanish-occupied Puerto Rico.[143] The sailor—an Irishman named Darbie Glaven—had also crewed in the fleet carrying Ralph Lane's colony in 1585, so Glaven knew the location of Roanoke Island and possibly also White's intention to build the Citie of Raleigh on the Chesapeake Bay. Given his origins, Glaven may have had no love for the English. Fernandez concluded, therefore, that Spanish authorities would capture and interrogate him—using torture if necessary to obtain information—then search for and destroy the colony.[144]

Fernandez would have recalled the fate of Fort Caroline, a French settlement near present-day Jacksonville, Florida.[145] In 1564 explorer Jean Ribault established a colony there as a refuge for French Huguenots seeking freedom to practice their religion. A Spanish army attacked the fort a year later, slaughtered several hundred French soldiers and colonists, and took prisoner fifty women and children.[146] Philip of Spain demanded Spanish hegemony in the New World, and Fernandez feared a similar fate were the English colonists' whereabouts to become known. We know that the Spanish ambassador in London wrote repeatedly to Philip urging him to destroy the English colony.[147] Indeed, the following summer the Spanish launched a search party as a result of intelligence obtained from Darbie Glaven. They cruised the Chesapeake, finding no sign of an English colony, then they sailed south along the coast and discovered the Roanoke Island fort, though they found no one there.[148]

It appears that the Spanish threat compelled a change of plans.[149] But Secotan hostility made Roanoke Island as untenable as the Chesapeake Bay. White states that the colonists decided "to remove fifty miles further up into the main."[150] This quote leaves so much open to interpretation that one suspects White was either purposefully vague or that the destination had not yet been determined. It does not rule out the Chesapeake, though the bay is seventy-five miles north of Roanoke Island, not fifty. Perhaps White misjudged the distance. It seems more likely, however, that "into the main" meant "into the interior," not "up the coast." It is probable, therefore, that this change of plans was made *after* Glaven's desertion in Puerto Rico but *before* the fleet anchored off Hatteras Island. Logic would lead us to believe that the decision was made by Fernandez over White's objections and that they argued about it all the way up the coast.

On landing at Roanoke Island, White and his forty "best men" found it deserted save for the bleached bones of a human male. He wrote that the fort was "rased down," referring most likely to a structure—an armory or blockhouse (we are never told)—inside the fort probably destroyed by fire. The fort itself was a triangular earthen embankment with a ditch on the exterior perimeter and elevated reinforced platforms for cannon at key points. This enclosure would have remained, though by now overgrown with weeds. Houses outside the fort were still standing though covered inside and out with vines. Deer nibbled on melons growing inside one of the dwellings. White and others began clearing the debris and commenced repairs as more colonists—men and women—arrived from the tall ships to begin the process of settling in.

A week later, colonist George Howe wandered away from camp while gigging for crabs in the shallows. Two miles from the fort, he was attacked and beaten to death by Algonquins using their wooden cudgels.[151] Alarmed by this, White sent Manteo with twenty of his men to Croatoan Island to learn what they could. On seeing the English approaching, the Croatoan began fleeing until lured back by Manteo. Frightened, they begged the English not to steal their corn, for their supply was low. It is telling that this was their most immediate concern since it was nearing time to harvest their first corn crop. Manteo promised not to take their corn and reassured them that the English desired friendship, and after much discussion, the Croatoan agreed to be emissaries of friendship to the Secotan villages across Pamlico Sound, instructing the weroance of each village to meet with White at the Roanoke Island fort within seven days to conclude a pact of friendship.[152]

From the Croatoan, the English learned that the fifteen men left by Grenville had been attacked by Secotan warriors. They set fire to the fort to smoke the English out. A Secotan warrior and two Englishmen were killed in the fray, and the surviving English escaped in their pinnace to one of the small, uninhabited barrier islands north of Roanoke Island.[153] Soon after, they disappeared altogether. Had they remained, they would have starved to death or been killed. Most historians have assumed that they set sail for Newfoundland for rescue by the annual English fishing fleet. In a small open boat, such an undertaking would have been utter desperation.[154] Another theory posits that they sailed up Currituck Sound and were given refuge by the Chesepioc tribe residing in today's Norfolk/

Virginia Beach area with whom Thomas Harriot and John White had wintered in 1584–85 and that they were slaughtered by Algonquins of the Powhatan nation of Tidewater Virginia twenty-one years later, just before or just after the Jamestown colonists arrived.[155]

When no Secotan weroance appeared at Roanoke in the seven days specified, White assumed the worst. He resolved to avenge the deaths of Howe and the two Englishmen marooned by Grenville with a surprise attack on Dasemunkepeuc, the Secotan village on the mainland where he suspected Howe's attackers lived, Wanchese among them.[156] On the pre-dawn morning of August 8, his force attacked and, in the darkness, could not see that their victims were not Secotan, but Croatoan. The Secotan had fled after the murder of George Howe, and the Croatoan were there harvesting the abandoned crops that would otherwise be consumed by animals and birds. Among the foragers was a mother with her newborn baby in a sling on her back.[157] She and her child survived the attack, but a Croatoan warrior was killed. Realizing their error, White and Manteo begged forgiveness, but the incident served to further isolate White's colony.[158]

In a ceremony on the thirteenth of August, Manteo was christened and made Lord of Roanoke and Dasemunkepeuc.[159] The title was an empty and cruel gesture for someone who had served the English well. The affection of Raleigh, Harriot, and White for Manteo was doubtless genuine, but with no intention of remaining on Roanoke Island, the English were putting him in harm's way. By then, he had no friends among the Secotan, and the disastrous attack on Dasemunkepeuc suggests a distance had developed between Manteo and his birth tribe. Absent the English, Manteo was a chief without a tribe.[160]

A week later the two ships returning to England were ready to depart. The third, a pinnace, would remain with the colony. White's narrative implies that his council decided at the last minute that someone must return to England to obtain supplies—he does not specify what supplies. More likely, the colonists had started a list of needs since deciding to resettle somewhere "further up into the main." It is evident they did not trust Fernandez with the responsibility. The change of plan must have forced them to reassess their ordnance, further proof that they had no intention of going to the Chesapeake Bay for which—we must assume—they were adequately equipped. Having to portage possessions fifty miles distant would have necessitated smaller, more portable artillery instead of the heavy cannon earmarked for the Citie of Raleigh fort with which they were doubtless supplied.[161] Had they planned to trade with the Algonquins for food for the winter, the enmity they now encountered precluded that option, leaving them perhaps also short of rations. All tribes were short of corn due to the drought that was parching crops in the region.[162] Whatever additional supplies were deemed necessary, some trustworthy envoy with influence and the power of persuasion had to return to England to obtain them.[163]

After some discussion, one of White's councilors volunteered, then changed his mind the following morning. All eyes turned to White. He refused, citing, first, the infamy he would suffer in England for abandoning his leadership responsibility to people he, himself, had recruited and, second, the risk of loss of his personal property. White had left his life in England behind, so he would have come with all his portable possessions, some of which—we later find—were packed in three trunks. A curious and disturbing omission is any mention of his daughter and new grandchild, Virginia Dare, who had been born just four days earlier.[164] Add to this the troubling implication that some of his property had already been pilfered.[165] (See note for White's exact words.)

As noted, White wrote his narrative after returning to England, so it was not composed in the feverish upheaval of the moment. Regardless, this does not excuse his self-absorption and apparent insensitivity to his family's plight, and, once again, we are left to wonder about White's mental and emotional state. At any rate, he insisted he would not go. The colonists persisted—the entire company this time—both men and women—citing his close relationship with Walter Raleigh and his status as governor. Again, he refused and again they persisted, agreeing to provide an affidavit stating their demand that he go despite it being against his will. In the end, he relented and agreed.[166]

It bears mentioning that of the one hundred and eighteen colonists, only White and two others had been to America before, James Lacie and John Wright.[167] One or both—boys, most likely—may have been White's personal servants, for neither was a member of the governing council of twelve, and White was known to have servants accompany him. It follows, therefore, that neither was a candidate to assume White's leadership position. Given his experience and close association with Thomas Harriot, White may have spoken some Algonquin, making him perhaps the only colonist with a passing understanding of the language.[168] His experience in the New World was invaluable to the colony, so by sending him back to England, the colonists were either desperate for the unspecified supplies or—as more than one writer has suggested—eager to be rid of John White.

With his departure, the colony had no one on the governing council with New World experience. White never named a successor, a curious omission that points to someone whose name he may have decided not to reveal for obvious reasons. Were the colonists devout in their adherence to a creed, as seems likely, they would have put their trust in God to see them through the dangers ahead, but not in God alone. To find a place to settle required negotiating with the weroance, elders, and shamans of the territory chosen, and for this the colonists needed a guide and a translator. This would have dictated that they put their trust in Manteo. Logic leads us to conclude that with White's departure, Manteo became the "especial man."

To ascertain where the colonists went, all we can do is follow the breadcrumbs left in the incomplete and often ambiguous narrative of a man whose abilities and stability are suspect. Nevertheless, this single clue regarding Manteo is vital to that quest.

On August 27, White boarded the smaller of the two ships returning to England. He left Virginia with the understanding that the colonists would soon relocate. No doubt he was thinking it would take him the better part of a year to return, but he was much mistaken. The colonists agreed to leave a sign on Roanoke Island indicating their whereabouts and to carve a cross above the destination if forced to leave under threat of violence.

White chose not to sail on the flagship with Fernandez. It appears he blamed the Portuguese navigator for the overthrow of his plans for the Citie of Raleigh, for his forced return to England, and for having to leave his daughter and grandchild in harm's way. His plans thwarted, White assuaged his frustrations by blaming his misfortune on Fernandez, and he gave vent to his anger by contriving the calumny that Fernandez refused to take the colonists to the Chesapeake Bay. White let enmity cloud his narrative and, as a consequence, our understanding of what happened.

In mid–September the two ships sighted the Azores. They made for the island of Terceira, the rendezvous point for Spanish treasure ships returning from the West Indies and warships sent out from Spain to escort them home. The island was also Fernandez's birthplace. On this occasion, luck was not on their side. He and White returned to England empty handed.

A month before their November arrival, Elizabeth ordered all ships confined to port as England prepared to defend itself against invasion by the Spanish Armada expected to sail the following summer.[169]

• 4 •

The End of an Era

Before White's colony departed for Roanoke Island in May 1587, he and Fernandez may have learned of Francis Drake's successful raid on the Spanish port of Cadiz in April. Moored within the Spanish harbor were ships being readied to attack England. In the raid, Drake's fleet destroyed over two dozen Spanish warships and vast quantities of provisions.[1] The destruction set Spain back a full year. Were he aware of this, White left England knowing the Spanish would be merciless should they discover his colony. This may have further contributed to Fernandez's decision to refuse to deliver White and his colonists to the Chesapeake Bay.

When White returned to England that November for the unspecified supplies, he found his country preparing for invasion. Despite a ban on shipping, Raleigh begged the queen's permission for White to resupply his colony.[2] Over the winter, the two arranged for two small privateers to ferry White, his supplies, and fifteen new colonists back across the Atlantic. The ships were too small to serve in the defense of England, so their captains eagerly agreed, knowing they were free to attack Spanish shipping with impunity.

They sailed in April 1588 and, nearing Madeira two weeks later, were overtaken by two French ships. Overpowered and outmanned, the English were attacked and boarded. In the hand-to-hand fighting that ensued, White and his new recruits were forced to fight for their lives. Several combatants were killed and many injured. The English yielded and were robbed of all supplies intended for the Roanoke Colony.[3] As the two ships limped back to England, White nursed wounds from a musket shot in his buttocks and blows to his head—one from a sword, one from a pike. Lucky to be alive, he arrived back home in May.[4] His colony would have to hold out for another year.

Still committed to the Enterprise of England, Philip rebuilt his navy. In late May 1588—six days after White's return—he launched a 120-ship armada with thirty thousand soldiers and crew.[5] His orders were for his commander, the Duke of Medina Sidonia, to rendezvous off Calais with a

Spanish army of sixteen thousand based in the Netherlands commanded by the Duke of Parma. The combined armies were to then invade England. Philip believed his armada to be so invincible, he leaked its specifications, hoping to strike fear into the hearts of English Protestants and to motivate English Catholics to rebel against Elizabeth and join his cause.[6]

The English navy, commanded by Charles Howard, Earl of Nottingham, and Francis Drake, was well prepared. The cocksure Drake was so confident of victory that, when news came that the armada had reached the English Channel, he insisted on finishing a game of boules he was enjoying on Plymouth Hoe.[7] His confidence was well founded. Years earlier, Elizabeth had the good sense to put John Hawkins in charge of her navy. Spanish naval warfare strategy was to grapple an enemy ship, board, and fight hand to hand.[8] Drawing on the recent success of English sea dogs, Hawkins believed a better strategy was to fire a broadside at close range—but not too close as to allow boarding—slip away to windward out of range of enemy cannon, reload while coming about, make another pass, and fire another broadside.[9] This strategy compensated for the fact that England was outmanned, but it necessitated superior speed. Spanish ships were built for cargo—gold and silver mined in the Americas. They were wide, deep-draft, big-bellied leviathans with castles fore and aft that robbed sails of their power source.[10] The largest of these immense carracks had seven decks. To prepare the English Navy for warfare, Hawkins lowered the castles and increased the ratio of length to breadth from three-to-one to four-to-one. In other words, he built vessels shaped more like fish.[11] They were galleons—men-of-war—smaller, faster, and more maneuverable thanks to less resistance to wind and water. In this way John Hawkins revolutionized naval architecture.[12]

The Spanish Armada lumbered into view on July 21. In the following days, a running battle raged as Spain's fleet turned northeast toward Calais and its rendezvous with Parma. Spanish ships could not get close enough to board English vessels, but the English cannonade inflicted little damage on the reinforced oak hulls of the Spanish galleons.[13] On the evening of the twenty-seventh, the armada dropped anchor four miles short of Calais, there being no deep-water port nearer Dunkirk, twenty-four miles away, where Parma's army was mobilized.[14] With only a cordon of smaller ships protecting his rear, Medina Sidonia waited for Parma's army to come out. Unbeknownst to the admiral, however, Parma's orders from Philip had been either ambiguous or misconstrued, and he wanted cover and more time to ferry his troops out to the waiting ships because of a Dutch blockade off the Flemish coast.[15]

With the incoming tide that night, the English launched eight fireships loaded with explosives and directed them into the heart of the

4. The End of an Era

Spanish fleet. In a panic, Spanish ships severed anchor cables and fled in disarray, carried northeast by the wind.[16] The next day, threatened by a lee shore, low on shot and powder, and with winds that opposed a return to the rendezvous point, the armada entered the North Sea.[17] The English pursued until, low on ammunition themselves, they returned to port. With strong winds blowing out of the southwest, the armada had no choice but to continue hundreds of miles north around Scotland and Ireland in order to return to Spain. No ordinary sou'wester, the storm blew weathercocks off rooftops all over England.[18]

In seas unknown to Spanish pilots and winds still southwest, many Spanish ships were wrecked on the rocky west coast of Ireland. As sick and starving survivors washed ashore, they were put to the sword by English and Irish alike.[19] One observer counted eleven hundred bloated corpses on one single beach.[20] Of the one-hundred-and-thirty-ship armada, only half made it back to Spain.[21] Of the thirty thousand soldiers and sailors on board, twenty thousand were killed, drowned, or died of starvation or disease, victims of a perfect storm of poor planning, poor execution, and the force majeure of Mother Nature.[22]

Credit Elizabeth with the wisdom to leave strategic planning to her sea dogs—Hawkins, Drake, and Martin Frobisher prominent among them. For command of land forces, she chose her "Robin"—Robert Dudley, now the aging Earl of Leicester. Despite being in debt and suffering stomach pains, Dudley accepted with enthusiasm and implored the queen to review his seventeen thousand troops at Tilbury near the mouth of the Thames, a hastily constructed stronghold for the defense of England.[23] At ebb tide on Sunday morning, August 7, Elizabeth sailed down the Thames in her royal barge, leading a flotilla of craft bearing her trumpeters, guards, ladies-in-waiting, and members of her privy council. Believing that her navy's ten-day battle with the Spanish Armada had ended indecisively, Elizabeth and her councilors still feared a land invasion by Parma's army.

Her home guard was small, ill-trained, and poorly armed—as many longbows as muskets, but insufficient powder for the latter.[24] An attempt to blockade the Thames with derelict ships chained together had failed when the barrier sank during construction. In the event of invasion, Dudley's plan was token resistance followed by a retreat toward London to join forces with an army quartered at St. James Palace just west of London proper. Elizabeth had been advised to flee farther west to Hampton Court or an even more remote refuge, but she refused.

She came ashore at Tilbury resplendent in white velvet.[25] She was bareheaded save for her *postiche*—a wig, red as a radish, bedizened with pearls and a jewel-encrusted diadem. With pomp and ceremony, she was greeted at the water's edge by Dudley and his principal adjutants. Among them was the flamboyant and handsome Robert Devereux, the young Earl of Essex, a man of prodigious ego and volatile temperament, so like Shakespeare's Hamlet, for whom he may have been the inspiration.[26] To demonstrate his army's readiness and resolve, Dudley had prepared a mock battle for the queen. Following this demonstration, she donned a silver cuirass—breastplate and backplate armor—and mounted a white gelding. Holding a silver field marshal's baton, she was led forward by a page holding her silver helmet on a white cushion.

"God bless you all," she called again and again, all smiles as she acknowledged her soldiers' salutations. She circled the encampment to the sound of drums, fifes, and cheers until late in the day, when she retired to a nearby manor house prepared for her and her ladies.

The next morning Dudley greeted her with a report that Parma's army would sail with the tide. Despite the danger, she again donned her armor and mounted her horse. With Dudley and Lord Gray, marshal of the camp, leading the procession, she rode amid phalanxes of soldiers armed with bows, muskets, and pikes followed by her ladies and councilors.[27] Again, ebullient shouts of approbation came from the mass of soldiers as they pressed toward her procession to get a better view of their sovereign. She had been warned of possible violence. Assassins had made attempts on her life in the past. These thoughts must have flashed through her mind as she gazed at the multitude of armed men. Summer sunlight reflected in their armor and steel-tipped pikes. Beyond was the Thames estuary, placid and radiant. It was from that direction Parma's invasion would come, but as yet no ships were seen, only dayboats out fishing, oblivious to their parlous situation. Elizabeth reined in her horse and emboldened by the vision of so many, delivered her speech.

"My loving people," she began, "for fear of treachery, we have been persuaded by those careful for our safety, to take heed how we commit ourselves to armed multitudes. But I assure you, I do not desire to live to distrust my faithful and loving people. Let tyrants fear. I am come amongst you not for my recreation and disport but being resolved—in the midst and heat of the battle—to live and die amongst you all; to lay down for my God, and for my kingdom, and my people, my honor and my blood, even in the dust. I know I have the body but of a weak and feeble woman; but I have the heart and stomach of a king, and of a king of England too. I myself will be your general, judge, and rewarder of every one of your virtues in the field, and we shall have a famous victory over those enemies of my God, of my kingdom, and of my people."

Without doubt Elizabeth's words brought forth cheers, but only those nearest her would have heard clearly. For most, she was a distant image, and perhaps she took solace in knowing that those who could not get close would not see the wrinkles her Venetian face paint failed to hide. At noon she dined with Dudley in his tent, and late that afternoon word came that Parma had not sailed after all. Indeed, he would not—not in 1588—not without Philip's navy. The season for fighting was over.

In 1590 Edmund Spenser published the first three books of a poetic panegyric, *The Faerie Queene*, in which Elizabeth is represented as Faerie Queen Gloriana. The name evokes what the French prized as *La Belle Gloire*. Glory in this regard encompassed courage, fortitude, honor, pride, splendor, and valor, and it could only be won in battle. The defeat of the Spanish Armada was the pièce de résistance of Elizabeth's reign. England had forced the most powerful kingdom in Europe to its knees. Elizabeth was now viewed not only as the defender of the faith in England but the defender of Protestantism throughout Europe.[28] The pope who once demanded her death now expressed admiration.[29] She was Gloriana indeed.

Lost in England's euphoria at home, however, was concern for its fugitive colony in America. After returning from Roanoke Island, Thomas Harriot composed *A Briefe & True Report of the New Found Land of Virginia*. Published the year of the armada, the essay was a response to rumors spread by disgruntled returning colonists of the hardships experienced during their year on Roanoke Island.[30] Lane's colonists had had unrealistic expectations of what awaited them in the New World, a serious flaw in Durham House planning. Harriot's *Briefe Report* rebutted the rumors with exotic portrayals of the native peoples and idyllic descriptions of the land. He condemned the rumors as the slanders of a spiteful few who had transgressed while in America and been punished for their misdeeds.

One item of significant value in Harriot's essay failed to garner the attention it deserved. He stated that the "New Found Land" extended "some ways many *hundreds* of leagues" and that there were mountains in the interior, knowledge he must have acquired through interviews with Algonquins. A league being three miles meant a landmass that stretched a thousand or more miles in several directions.[31] Until then, no Englishman had conceived of the North American continent as so vast, and none heeded this valuable morsel of intelligence.[32]

Harriot ends by expressing confidence that with time the native inhabitants could be brought to "honour, obey, feare, and love us" despite the fact that toward the end, some of the soldiers were "too fierce in slaying some of the people, upon causes that on our part, might easily have been borne withal."[33] Leaving aside the cavalier disregard for human life, the impression is one of docile creatures imbued with a prelapsarian innocence.[34] The *Briefe Report* was pure propaganda designed to attract investors, blatant in its omissions.[35]

Implicit in Harriot's essay was a grant of five hundred acres of land from Walter Raleigh to anyone willing to venture and settle.[36] Harriot describes a land with many people living in many small villages, so where was land for Englishmen to come from if not from people already in possession of it—people who were not now kindly disposed toward the English? This proposition could not pass the scrutiny of anyone thoughtful enough to consider the implications. Even as the *Briefe Report* reached booksellers, Raleigh, Harriot, and others of the Durham House ménage must have realized that despite noble intentions, one way or another the Algonquins—like the Irish—would have to bear an English yoke or get out of the way. The viability of the enterprise depended on the lure of land, for there was nothing else of sufficient value to entice prospective colonists. Did Raleigh's team discuss this sinister consequence? One suspects they did and dismissed it as inevitable. Perhaps it is for this reason that Raleigh has been called "the ominous prophet of imperialism."[37]

One wonders if Raleigh's soldiering in France and Ireland had inured him to human suffering. Beneath all the noble declared intentions was there scant regard for the less civilized peoples of the world, making this an easy tradeoff? Or did he have sincere misgivings about their fate? We cannot know, but in England the prevailing attitude was xenophobic topped with an ethnocentric arrogance.[38] Knowing the fate of Native Americans as we do, we must accept that their ill treatment was not an unintended and tragic consequence of imperialism or manifest destiny. To the contrary, it was a conscious and sober decision made by intelligent and well-educated people. An enticement of free land and lots of it was enough to turn most men into prostitutes. Sadly, humans are innately selfish creatures who—in defense of their self-interests—can be cruel and pitiless.

Following the defeat of the Spanish Armada, Raleigh sailed to Ireland to oversee his estates and remained there until spring. With his patron gone, John White's hands were tied. The Roanoke colonists had been on their own now for the better part of two years, but Elizabeth's prohibition on ships leaving England remained in effect. As soon as Raleigh returned to London in March 1589, White begged for assistance, but English ships were being mobilized for another Cadiz-like raid on Spanish shipping, this time in Portuguese ports.

Desperate to relieve his Virginia colony, Raleigh entered into an agreement with a consortium of London merchants, giving them the right to tax-free trade with Virginia in return for help in financing a relief expedition as soon as possible.[39] Among the directors were Richard Hakluyt, William Sanderson, and Thomas Smythe, the thirty-year-old son of London's chief customs official, Thomas "Customer" Smythe.[40] With this, Hakluyt became an investor and director as well as a consultant. The

4. The End of an Era 79

younger Smythe would soon become the city's leading merchant. Nothing became of this arrangement, but Hakluyt and Smythe would spearhead colonization efforts eighteen years later in Jamestown, Virginia, using a similar pooling of interests to ameliorate risk. London merchants had long been involved in international trading companies, but this marks the beginning of their investment in colonization.

Again in 1590, Elizabeth imposed an embargo on English ships for fear of another Spanish invasion.[41] By dint of his influence, however, Raleigh obtained her permission to assist John White in rejoining his Virginia colony. Raleigh arranged for a small ship, the *Moonlight*, to ferry White and newly recruited colonists plus their supplies and equipment across the Atlantic. The ship's captain, Edward Spicer, had commanded one of the ships that sailed with White and Fernandez in 1587. To escort the *Moonlight*, Raleigh brokered a deal with London privateering merchant John Watts, securing for him letters of reprisal and permission to sail on condition that his ships deliver White and the others on their return to England.[42] Watts was a man of about Raleigh's age, a shipowner and successful entrepreneur.[43] His flagship, the *Hopewell*, was captained by Abraham Cocke, and her escorts were the *John Evangelist* and the *Little John*, the latter captained by Christopher Newport, a twenty-nine-year-old veteran English sea dog and a man destined to play an important role in helping establish Jamestown.[44] The *Little John* was Newport's first command.

White wrote that when he and fellow colonists went to board the *Hopewell*, Cocke refused admittance to all but White. And despite his protestations, White was only permitted one chest of personal belongings. As the ships' captains were ready and eager to depart, White had no time to appeal to Raleigh for help.[45] Watts's three ships sailed from London around to Plymouth from which they departed in late March. A month later they arrived off Dominica in the Antilles, and for the next three months prowled the coasts of Hispaniola and Cuba chasing and capturing Spanish prizes.[46]

In early July the fleet was joined by the *Moonlight*. The rendezvous point off the Tiburon Peninsula of Hispaniola had obviously been prearranged. White now claimed Captain Spicer had been "left in England," implying he and his ship were part of the fleet all along but had been delayed for some reason. The *Moonlight* carried the unspecified supplies White had been sent back to England in 1587 to obtain plus the new colonists, so White's earlier insinuation that he was traveling alone and with no supplies was not the truth.[47]

In late July the *Hopewell* and the *Moonlight* left the Caribbean and their consort ships and headed north. According to White, on Monday, August 9 they anchored within a mile of Wococon Inlet, about ten miles south of Croatoan Island.[48] This was where Richard Grenville's *Tyger* ran aground in 1585, so White had been there before.[49] For reasons that will become obvious, Croatoan was his destination, not Roanoke Island.

It is evident throughout White's 1590 narrative that he did not tell all. He had two excellent reasons for concealing the whole truth. For one, the seven-year patent of Walter Raleigh—White's patron—was due to expire in 1591. Evidence that his Virginia colony was still alive gave Raleigh the right to claim possession of a land so vast its limits were as yet unknown. No doubt it was White's fervent hope to provide such evidence. Secondly, White would not have wanted Spain to learn the whereabouts of his colony for fear they would destroy it, so when asked by Richard Hakluyt upon his return to England to write about his 1590 rescue mission for publication, White chose omission, misdirection, and outright prevarication. The lives of his daughter and granddaughter depended upon his discretion.

Before White left Roanoke Island in 1587 on his mission to England for the unspecified supplies, there must have been considerable discussion about where the colonists would go. They had already decided to leave Roanoke Island and, as White stated, "remove fifty miles further up into the main." A final landing place, of course, depended on negotiations for a plot of land with one or more of the Algonquin tribes, so the question of where could not be settled before White left for England. In light of the colonists' dependence on Manteo, however, it would have been logical and sensible to settle some of the colonists on Croatoan Island with his birth tribe.[50] Though Croatoan territory was too small to absorb and feed all one hundred and eighteen colonists, it was the safest and most convenient place for some of them to await White's return.[51] From there, they could guide him to the permanent settlement, wherever that might be.[52] It is reasonable to conclude, therefore, that a Croatoan Island observation outpost was agreed to before White left for England in 1587. Assuming this was the case, the sole purpose of the sign the colonists were to leave on Roanoke Island indicating their whereabouts was to either confirm or alter this plan.

Wococon was the widest and deepest inlet into the Pamlico Sound, and it was the inlet closest to Croatoan Island known to be navigable. It goes without saying that ships sailing north from the West Indies arrived there first, making it more convenient than Roanoke Island as a place to rendezvous. With this understanding, White had no need to return to Roanoke Island in 1590, and, in fact, he never claimed Roanoke Island was his destination.

This makes sense when one considers the colonists' options. The Secotan would stop at nothing to avenge the beheading of Pemisapan and be rid of the English. Lane had alienated the Chowanoc by kidnapping Menatonon's son and threatening to kill him. The Weapemeocs and the Moratucs were subservient to their more powerful neighbors—the Secotan and Chowanoc—and the Spanish would be searching for the colony on the Chesapeake Bay. With this in mind, and having common cause with any enemy of the Secotan, Manteo and the colonists would have looked south instead of north for a safe place to settle.[53] This meant the territories of the Pomoiok and Neusiok, the former a known enemy of the Secotan.

White wrote that the *Hopewell* and *Moonlight* remained anchored off Wococon for three nights during which time they spent two days ashore, fishing and fetching fresh water.[54] This defies belief. White had now been separated from his colony and family for three years almost to the day. He nearly lost his life in one desperate attempt to rescue them. But we are supposed to believe he spent two days fishing when he could have been searching for them? Something is amiss. It appears White omitted from his narrative an attempt to land on Croatoan Island by sailing into and up Pamlico Sound in one of the ships' boats and going ashore from the sound side. This entailed sailing past uninhabited, fifteen-mile-long Wococon Island on the way north to Croatoan Island, the two islands being separated by a narrow impenetrable breach then called Port Grenville.

White's attempt to land proved impossible. He could not have known that access to Croatoan Island from within Pamlico Sound was blocked by thickets of cordgrass, clam shoals, oyster beds, and mudflats that extended two miles or more from shore—much of it exposed at low tide—too shallow for even the ship's boat. Recall that in 1587 White sent Manteo and others to Croatoan after George Howe's killing. That group had approached Croatoan from the north with Manteo on board—someone with local knowledge of navigable channels. This latest attempt to land there failed, however, forcing White to try an alternative.

On the morning of the twelfth, the *Hopewell* and *Moonlight* weighed anchor and sailed thirty-five miles up the coast of Croatoan Island to an anchorage at its north end, just off Chacandepeco Inlet, a breach into Pamlico Sound that was not navigable.[55] White omitted from his narrative any mention of his observations during this daylong sail—eight to ten hours from anchorage to anchorage.[56] There was ample depth to sail within a mile of shore for most of the way. Did he see signs of life—perhaps smoke rising from Croatoan cook fires? Did he see anyone on the beach, beckoning to the ships? One would expect White would have recorded sightings of this sort, or—if he saw nothing—that, indeed, he saw nothing. The absence of signs of habitation would have been considered noteworthy, whether White thought his colonists lived there or not.

At the time, Chacandepeco Inlet separated Croatoan Island from Hatoraske Island. This inlet has since silted up.[57] On the following morning, August 13, with the tall ships at anchor, White and others rowed toward the inlet in one of the ships' boats. As they went, they took depth soundings with a plumbline attached to a lead weight. White went into exacting detail regarding this activity, giving depth in fathoms for ten different positions between the ships at anchor and the inlet. The readings indicate a deeper bottom than elsewhere along the coast, never less than three fathoms or eighteen feet. Although the inlet is now closed, depths just offshore of its former position are very consistent with the measurements White recorded. Most sixteenth-century ships, therefore, could have approached to within five hundred yards of the inlet without running aground, though in 1590 the bar itself and the sound beyond for at least a mile were not more than a foot deep. A ship's boat could have easily come ashore on the beach at the north end of Croatoan Island.

In his narrative White gave no explanation for why this survey of the inlet was undertaken, but the only reason that makes any sense is that he came ashore.

According to his narrative, that same afternoon the *Hopewell* and *Moonlight* weighed anchor and sailed north to a new anchorage off the north end of Hatoraske Island, arriving there on the evening of August 15. This would have been Port Ferdinando—named for Simon Fernandez—the inlet the English always used to access Roanoke Island. By White's timeline, therefore, it took two full days to sail the forty miles from the north end of Croatoan Island to Port Ferdinando—a distance the average English galleon could ordinarily cover in a mere eight to ten hours.[58]

White's narrative asserts, therefore, that from the ninth to the fifteenth of August—six nights and five days—the fleet did little more than fish, fetch fresh water, measure the depths of an inlet that even if navigable would serve no useful purpose, and travel eighty miles. It makes no sense that White—having been gone three years and, no doubt, desperate to find his family—would spend so much time accomplishing so little.

Croatoan Island was narrow and only twenty miles long. It had contained three Algonquin villages, the largest of which was on the island's north end—just inside Chacandepeco Inlet.[59] Doubtless White went ashore there sometime during this five-day period and later decided to say nothing of it. It defies logic to think otherwise, and the only reason he had to suppress this information was that Croatoan Island was deserted. It seems almost certain that White knew this before he ever set foot on Roanoke Island. His narrative bears the traces of a piece of writing based on a journal but with omissions made for the purpose of concealing this vital fact.

Recent research in Spanish archives has uncovered evidence that a destructive hurricane hit the Atlantic seaboard in September 1589, the

4. The End of an Era

year before White's rescue mission.⁶⁰ The storm caused the sinking of ten Spanish ships, including four large galleons, in the Florida Straits. Such storms often track north along the coast then back out to sea. Saltwater storm surge from this hurricane may have inundated the low-lying barrier islands, including Croatoan, leaving their soil infertile. An event of this magnitude at this time in history could have rendered these islands uninhabitable until rainfall leached salinity from the soil—a process that might take years.⁶¹

Had this been the case, White would have found the former Croatoan villages in shambles and their fields overgrown with invasive salt-tolerant weeds. He and the new colonists—some of whom may have been relatives of the 1587 colonists—would have searched the debris for evidence of English presence. White would have suspected an attack by the Secotan and concluded the worst—that his family and the other colonists were either captives or dead.

When the fleet dropped anchor off Port Ferdinando on the evening of August 15, smoke was seen rising from the direction of Roanoke Island. This revived hopes. The next morning as crew prepared to launch the two ships' boats, cannon were fired at regular intervals to draw the attention of anyone within hearing range—ten miles or more depending on wind direction. Halfway to the inlet, smoke was again seen, this time to the south, rising from a cluster of tall dunes known as Kendrick's Mounts on uninhabited Hatoraske Island. These dunes have since washed away but then they marked the location of offshore shallows known today as Wimble Shoals, in the vicinity of present-day Rodanthe.⁶² Deciding to go there first and thinking it not far distant, both crews led by White and Captains Cocke and Spicer walked what turned out to be twelve miles of beach in midday August sun with no fresh water. They found the smoldering remains of a brushfire but no sign of human presence. By the time they got back to their boats—tired, thirsty, and disappointed—it was late in the day, so they returned to the tall ships anchored offshore.⁶³

Seas were rough the next morning. Gale-force winds from the northeast blew directly into the inlet. At about ten, both ships' boats were launched, and Captain Cocke's boat led the way in. Dangerous waves were breaking over the bar, and, once within the inlet, a wave broke over the stern of Cocke's boat, filling it half full, but by bailing and adroit helmsmanship the vessel was safely beached. Captain Spicer was not so fortunate. His boat entered the inlet with its mast still erect and was at once overturned by a following wave. Pounded again and again, it was tossed and tumbled like flotsam. Several crewmen were trapped beneath the upturned hull. Others who tried to cling to the sides or wade ashore were continually battered and forced under by crashing waves. At this time few

English sailors knew how to swim. Cocke and other strong swimmers from the first boat swam out with ropes to try to rescue Spicer and his crew, but only four were saved. Six crewmen drowned along with their captain, Edward Spicer.[64]

We must assume that bodies washed ashore or were retrieved and buried. By the time this work was done, it was late afternoon. Spicer's boat was retrieved, still in one piece, but the surviving sailors, depressed by the loss of shipmates, were in no mood to renew a search for lost colonists. White states that, by commandment and persuasion, he and Cocke succeeded in cajoling the seventeen to finish the job. They then rowed toward Roanoke Island, approaching it from the south, and it was dark by the time they reached the northern end where the colony had been situated. In the darkness, they missed the landing place, but up ahead saw a fire burning deep in the forest, so they continued on until just offshore they dropped anchor and sounded a trumpet. When no response came, they began calling and singing English songs late into the night, all to no avail.[65]

White would not have risked going ashore in the darkness. He must have suspected they were being watched. The Algonquins were masters of stealth, and the English did little that went unnoticed.

The next morning, they went ashore to find the smoldering remains of a fire and fresh footprints in the sand.[66] From there, they hiked on around the north end to the place White had taken leave of his family three years earlier. Carved in a tree trunk above the riverbank were the letters "CRO." Farther on, at the site of the former village, they found the houses "taken down" but the area enclosed with a palisade made of tree trunks.[67] On one of the timbers in a space where bark had been removed was carved the word, "CROATOAN," but without the designated cross above it that would have indicated that the colonists left under threat of harm. There had been no palisade in 1587 when White left, and the houses had been dismantled, not destroyed. The colonists' pinnace and other small boats were gone.[68] The evacuation appeared to have been orderly, with hardware removed from houses for reuse elsewhere—hinges, bolts, locks.[69] As White studied the scene, knowing the palisade would have taken time to erect, he must have wondered how long they had remained and where they might have gone?

They found other things strewn about—metal bars for making musket shot and pieces of artillery, all too heavy to carry without difficulty. They found five chests that had been buried in a trench by the colonists and later dug up by Algonquins. Three belonged to White. Many of his personal belongings were scattered about—books with covers ripped off, ruined pictures and broken frames, a rusted suit of armor. White wrote that he grieved at seeing his things thus ruined but was overjoyed by the "certaine token of their safe being at Croatoan ... the Iland of our friends."[70]

Though the message on the pale was clear—that at least some of the colonists had gone to Croatoan Island—there was no sign of them there now.[71] Most of them must have gone elsewhere, perhaps followed later by those who initially went to Croatoan or who stayed behind at Roanoke if they had migrated in stages, which now seemed a reasonable assumption. But something had intervened, something that could only be construed as catastrophic.

When they returned to the tall ships that night, a storm was brewing, packing winds of such force they feared the anchors would not hold. The next morning—ostensibly with the intention of returning to Croatoan Island—the captains ordered anchors raised. In the process the *Hopewell*'s cable broke, and the ship was blown astern toward Kendrick's Mounts. To prevent grounding on Wimble Shoals, another anchor was dropped, and it held just in time. Taking stock of opposing winds, scant supplies, and the loss of three of the *Hopewell*'s four anchors, White stated that he and Cocke decided to return to the Caribbean for the winter, there to prepare for another season of privateering followed by a renewed search for the lost colonists.[72] With the *Moonlight* in need of repair, her former master and now captain, John Bedford, gave orders to return to England. Two days later, heading southwest, the *Hopewell* encountered a change in wind direction from northeast to west by northwest. With adverse winds *and* an opposing current, the only alternative was to sail for England by way of the Azores. The *Hopewell* arrived back in Plymouth in late October.[73]

Richard Hakluyt published John White's 1590 narrative—written at Hakluyt's request—in a compendium of voyage of discovery narratives ten years later in 1600, seven years after White's death.[74] No one published a rebuttal disputing White's version, so we must assume it was accepted as factual. The Spanish would have read it. Hakluyt must have been a rich source of intelligence on English doings in the New World, augmenting Spain's capable spy network. Logic would have us believe that White claimed his colonists were where they were not in order to throw Spain off the scent. The subterfuge failed to keep Raleigh's patent alive, but the misdirection worked.[75] Spanish ships went looking for Croatoan Island but could not find it. And for reasons that are pregnant with suggestion, no Englishman bothered to return to Croatoan Island for over a hundred years. It is apparent that those in the know—including those who settled Jamestown sixteen years later—believed the island had been abandoned. In the years that followed, the English searched for their Lost Colony north, west, and south of Croatoan Island, but, despite the message on the pale, no one thought it worth their time to look there again.

John White's half-truths and omissions have confounded historians ever since. One wonders if he exaggerated the adversities he encountered to ameliorate a sense of failure. Raleigh would try again to find his Lost Colony, but John White was done. He had made five voyages to the New World. He spent the equivalent of years at sea, often in harm's way. He had been attacked, he had been wounded, he spent whatever fortune he possessed and lost much—if not all of it—in desperate attempts to relieve his colonists and reunite with his family. For him, the unknown must have been agonizing.[76] History owes much to John White. He left us priceless paintings of a world that is lost. He retired to Ireland to live on Raleigh's estates and died in Newtown, County Cork, in 1593.[77] From what we can glean from future English efforts to find the lost colonists, we can assume White went to his grave with no clue as to their whereabouts.[78]

Those who write history usually have an agenda that can be—as in White's case—a noble one that forces them to misrepresent it in some small way. White wished to publicize the plight of the Lost Colony to inspire his fellow countrymen to continue the search for his family, but if he told the whole truth, he would have imperiled their lives by giving the enemy information regarding their whereabouts. We cannot blame him for doing what any father would do. In just this way the whole truth often eludes the grasp of the reader. History is light refracted by the human prism through which its rays must pass to reach us.

Walter Raleigh did his best to fulfill his obligation to White.[79] He may have suffered the queen's displeasure by begging permission for White's 1590 rescue mission, and the failure of the Roanoke Colony must have disheartened him. Though Hakluyt urged him not to give up, Raleigh had spent the better part of a decade and most of his income on an unrealistic vision of limitless personal wealth and power that in hindsight seemed more vainglorious delusion.[80] The colony and his fortune had disappeared in the swampy pocosin wetlands of an inhospitable unknown. But Raleigh had little time to dwell on misfortune. His attention was diverted by other matters: his responsibilities for Cornwall and Devon, his new duties as captain of the Queen's Guard, and—his diversion of choice—an affair of the heart.

With Elizabeth drawn to her new favorite, Robert Devereux, Raleigh's gaze drifted to one of her attendants, Elizabeth Throckmorton. Life at court was fraught with intrigue—political, social, sexual. The queen was cocooned within a gynaeceum of eligible young women made up of royal ladies-in-waiting, ladies of the Privy Chamber, ladies of the Bed Chamber.[81] Selected by her, they were the daughters of aristocrats for whom court was a finishing school where young maidens had an opportunity to meet eligible bachelors with promising prospects.[82] It improved their chances of being chosen by the queen if they could dance, sing, or play

4. The End of an Era

a musical instrument, but anything above an elementary education was pointless.

The queen was responsible for her attendants. Flawless behavior was demanded and enforced, as was, for good reason, permission to marry.[83] Marriages involving the children of important families were the equivalent of strategic alliances that could alter delicate balances of power within the realm, and for someone of royal blood to marry without the queen's permission was an act of treason.[84] When one of the queen's attendants became pregnant—as Bess Throckmorton did in July 1591—things could get dicey.[85] Bess's condition went unnoticed for months thanks to the exaggerated bouffant of the farthingale skirts then in fashion.[86] Later, however, her condition forced her to contrive excuses and leave court. She and Raleigh were married in secret in November, and she went into seclusion for her accouchement. A son was born in late March 1592 but did not survive. Soon after, the queen learned all, and she was livid. By June the newlyweds were confined to separate cells in the Tower of London. Now middle-aged and out of favor, Raleigh's dreams of an English America were bankrupt and all but abandoned.

Raleigh and Bess were released from the Tower, and in time he regained the queen's trust, if not her supreme favor.[87] Whipsawed by failure and by scathing invective at court, he endured the humility of seeing his Durham House coterie drift to greener pastures.[88] His lack of popularity was such that his fall from grace had been universally acclaimed, and his prospects for the future dimmed. He sought solace in a vision of El Dorado.[89] New to him, perhaps, the legend had been around since 1542 when a Spanish conquistador returned to Spain after traversing the full length of the Amazon River with news of a land of gold hidden deep within the Brazilian rainforest.[90] It told of a kingdom so rich that its cacique often doused himself with gold dust for his own delectation.[91] Raleigh became obsessed with the chimera of this undiscovered honeypot called Guyana—in his imagination commensurate in wealth to the realms of the Aztecs and Incas.[92] Virginia and its tick-infested swamps lost all appeal.

The war with Spain dragged on. Robert Dudley died—Elizabeth's "Robin." Walsingham died. Drake and Hawkins died. William Cecil, old and infirm, retired in favor of his son Robert. Beginning in 1590 England suffered a decade of crop failures, plague, and a faltering economy. Amid war and depression, the disgruntled English began to feel that old Queen Bess was overstaying her welcome. As the old guard met its demise, the younger generation that followed—usually their sons and nephews—grew impatient with their monarch.[93] Her ladies-in-waiting ridiculed her, snickering at her vanity behind her back.[94] What was once dismissed as charming now appeared arrogant and narcissistic. What was once admired as careful frugality now came across as greed.[95] Instead of cunning, she was calculating and unscrupulous. Once seen as a sage and able leader, she had ossified into a deceitful and vituperative shrew. Even her toleration of Catholics and Protestant nonconformists had given way to persecutions.[96] No longer a model of purity and decorum, she was vulgar and undignified, so immodest that at age sixty-five in a meeting with a new ambassador from France, she allowed the front of her gown to gap open, exposing her naked, "wrinkled" breasts. She appeared as unfazed by the faux pas as she was by her court's disdain.[97]

Her final years were marked by an uneasy exhaustion. Her people—forgetful of her golden age and stressed by war, disease, and famine—waited for her to die.[98] Behind her back, her councilors hastened to ingratiate themselves with James VI of Scotland, her default successor, who was likewise impatient. He had considered an invitation to shortcut the waiting, viewing the English crown as the godsend that would rid him of his penury and piddling domestic problems.[99] He had long been in communication with Robert Cecil, William's son, now Secretary of State, and other court lapdogs who sought favor from the soon-to-be king. Cecil's was the hand that guided the ship of state to and through the interregnum.

The queen died in the early hours of March 24, 1603, slipping away in her sleep as rain beat against the windowpanes of Richmond Palace. Though surrounded by onlookers, she died alone. Riders hastened to Edinburgh. Now James I of England, the new king rode south, joined at intervals by nobles, knights, and gentlemen seeking preferments such that when he reached the purlieus of London he was thronged by well-wishers. He conferred knighthoods on three hundred of these lickspittles and gadflies for nothing more than having ridden out to welcome him.[100] He was paunchy, unkempt, effeminate, and feckless but with the incurable self-conceit that comes with a middling intellect and a surfeit of power.[101] He was easily led but impossible to manage, a steadfast devotee of the royal prerogative and the infallibility of kings.[102]

His coming marked the end of an era that would come to be viewed as the cultural rebirth we call the English Renaissance. In Elizabeth's time, bold new ideas like those of John Dee were pollinated by the patronage of men like Cecil, Dudley, Hatton, Raleigh, and a battalion of noblemen and lesser favorites. With their wealth, these men encouraged architects, artists, philosophers, scientists, and writers by providing them the wherewithal to bring their ideas to fruition. It was the age of Shakespeare, Spenser, and Marlowe, of Drake, Hawkins, and the English sea dogs. It was the age of Raleigh. Elizabeth's unbridled self-assuredness had combined with England's success on the high seas to instill in the nation's collective consciousness confidence and optimism. Though perhaps indifferent to the English Renaissance herself, her role in it was that of providing the means for those with the vision to innovate and effect positive change.[103] In her reign, we get an early, fleeting glimpse of what the enterprise of a free people will someday look like.[104]

♦ 5 ♦

Jamestown

King James I was willing to think ill of Walter Raleigh without questioning the veracity of what he was told.[1] On this subject, his mind was settled before he ever left Edinburgh.[2] On his journey south, accompanied by a gaggle of obsequious Scottish lairds, James met Raleigh at Burghley House, the estate of the late William Cecil. James greeted him by boasting that he would have taken the English crown by force had it proved necessary. To this Raleigh responded that had James tried, he would have been able to tell his friends from his foes. The new king was not so appreciative of a nimble rejoinder as his predecessor. He had heard that Raleigh was an advocate for replacing the monarchy with a commonwealth ruled by Parliament.[3] The rumor was an exaggeration, if not entirely false, but it added to the accretion of obloquy against Raleigh in James's mind.[4] It speaks to Raleigh's character that he did not stoop to adulation at a moment when arrogance was inappropriate. He contributed to his own downfall.

James wasted no time in dismissing Raleigh as captain of the Guard, evicting him from Durham House, and arresting him on a charge of treason.[5] Though Raleigh had no claim to sainthood, he was no traitor. Regardless, he spent the rest of his life—fifteen years—imprisoned in the Tower of London except for one last quixotic quest for gold in the hinterlands of the Orinoco River Basin. Success would have earned his freedom and given James the wherewithal to settle mounting debts, but the mission was an utter failure and cost the life of Raleigh's son Wat. There were no temples filled with golden idols, but in the late nineteenth century, the site of El Callao in Venezuela near where Raleigh searched became for a time the richest goldfield in the world.[6]

To Raleigh's credit, he had backed two more attempts to find his Lost Colony before Elizabeth died—both captained by Samuel Mace, one in 1602 and one in 1603.[7] The first got no farther than the mouth of the Cape Fear River.[8] The second sought in vain to find the colonists in the Chesapeake Bay and in the process became enmeshed in a dustup with the indigenous inhabitants, costing the lives of five Englishmen. Revenge was taken against an Algonquin tribe on either the Pamunkey or Rappahannock River in which a weroance was killed and several captured warriors were hanged from one of the ship's spars.[9] By the time Mace returned to England, Elizabeth was dead and Raleigh was imprisoned.

James sought peace with Spain regardless the cost. On August 18, 1604—Virginia Dare's seventeenth birthday were she still alive—he signed the Treaty of London, ending war with Spain. The treaty called a halt to English privateering and to Spain's efforts to restore Catholicism in England. James had little interest in the New World, and an end to privateering eliminated the need for English ships to cross the Atlantic except to fish for cod on the Grand Banks.

But England had a long and storied history of New World exploration, and interest in the fate of Raleigh's lost colonists remained keen. In 1606 Richard Hakluyt and others petitioned the king to grant a patent for renewed colonization efforts, and James complied with a charter for a joint stock enterprise called The Virginia Company.[10] James was motivated by a wish to counterbalance for Protestantism the growing power of Catholic Spain.[11] The new entity contained two subsidiary colonies. The London Company subsidiary was awarded the southern grant—from the mouth of the Cape Fear River to the mouth of what would become the Hudson River.[12] The second became the responsibility of the Plymouth Company subsidiary that received the northern grant from Delaware Bay to the Bay of Fundy—today's Canadian border. The following August, the Plymouth Company planted a colony on the Kennebec River in Maine, but it was abandoned within a year, and thereafter the Plymouth subsidiary became dormant for a time.

The London Company's charter named as principals Thomas Gates, George Somers, Richard Hakluyt, and Edward Maria Wingfield. Among the investors were London's wealthiest citizens, including Thomas Smythe, who would serve the company as chief executive. Hakluyt's name is no surprise. He now served as clergy at Westminster Abbey.[13] His name on the petition added gravitas.[14] Somers, a former West-Country privateer, was spending time in London as a member of Parliament for Lyme Regis. A soldier, Thomas Gates would later serve as governor of Jamestown. Another West Countryman, he was born in Devonshire, less than two miles from the Channel coast and six miles from Lyme Regis, Somers's birthplace.[15] Gates may have accompanied Francis Drake on his raid of the Spanish Main in 1586. If so, he was with Drake's fleet when Ralph Lane's Roanoke Colony was rescued.

The fourth London Company principal, Edward Maria Wingfield, was also a soldier. Born in 1550 with bright red hair in a former priory in Cambridgeshire, he was the grandson of Sir Richard Wingfield, a man of prominence during the reign of Henry VIII. Wingfield's middle name honored his father's godmother, Queen Mary Tudor. Wingfield was reported to have served in Ireland in the 1570s after which he entered Lincoln's Inn for a time, then he resumed military service in the Netherlands. He was commended for bravery at the Battle of Zutphen in 1586, and it was then that he likely met Gates. In 1588 Wingfield was taken prisoner by Spain, and he remained a captive for over a year. Later he served in Ireland again, this time with Ralph Lane, former governor of Raleigh's Roanoke Colony. Wingfield retired from the military in 1600, and soon after began recruiting efforts for a colony in Virginia. This work brought him to London.[16]

Though his name appeared last on the charter, Wingfield was perhaps the prime mover in establishing the London Company and—with his younger cousin Bartholomew Gosnold—in recruiting colonists.[17] He would have learned much from Ralph Lane about the obstacles facing an inchoate New World settlement, and he may have been responsible for bringing Gates on board. The four men—Gates, Somers, Hakluyt, and Wingfield—are listed, and others are not, for reasons that invite speculation. Perhaps they were the largest investors, but it is more likely they were the ones who doggedly pursued the project, the most determined, forceful, and passionate. Only Wingfield planned to be an active participant. Despite his age—fifty-six when the charter was granted, oldest of the four—he was unmarried and sufficiently fit to take on such a challenge.

These four—Gates, Somers, Hakluyt, and Wingfield—would have met to begin formulating plans. We can picture them in the autumn of 1606 huddled around a table spread with maps and nautical charts. Not a man jack among them had ever set foot on North American soil, yet there they were planning no less than the invasion of a continent and the resurgence of English America.[18]

It would be unfair to fault London Company officials for their planning. They had no successful model of colonization to emulate, only failed attempts. But the company was to blame for many of the ills that would torment the colony, particularly insofar as the quality of recruits was concerned. Sadly, London Company minutes for the first decade of its existence are lost, but from other sources, an accurate distillation of its objectives emerges.[19] In the near term, there were five—first and foremost, the establishment of an enduring settlement. Others were forging amicable relations with the Algonquins, discovering a viable route across North America to the Pacific, locating sources of precious metals and minerals, and finding survivors of Raleigh's Lost Colony.[20] Regarding this last objective, it was in the best interests of the Virginia Company to perpetuate the belief that Roanoke colonists survived somewhere in the American wilderness, this

for the sake of recruitment. But it was admirable, nonetheless, that twenty years on, the English were still hoping to find their fellow countrymen and women who had been abandoned on the far side of the Atlantic.

There were longer-term goals also. Of utmost importance to Hakluyt was bringing the Algonquins into the Anglican faith, but he recognized that this work should wait until the colony was on secure footing.[21] With religious conversion came the notion of helping Native Americans achieve a higher standard of living by the introduction of the advancements and modes of behavior of a civilized society such as the English enjoyed. One example would be teaching the nearly naked Native Americans the comfort of wearing English woolens, this perhaps in exchange for their gold and silver, or so it was hoped. Such a metamorphosis in Algonquin culture would naturally accrue to the honor and profit of the English people. These more noble goals served to mitigate the concerns of those who objected to taking Algonquin land without provocation.[22] Though this moral uncertainty existed, it was nowhere evident in the final outcome.[23]

Finding an inland route to the Pacific and the search for gold and silver were compatible in that both required exploration. Both could be pursued by the same expeditionary force on the same reconnaissance mission. London Company investors viewed the discovery of gold or silver as the masterstroke scenario. The company was, after all, a for-profit enterprise, and neither Algonquin conversion to Christianity nor Roanoke colony survivors would yield a spendable dividend for shareholders.

Yet another objective was to rid England of the expense and aggravation of its burgeoning vagrant and prison population. This would be implemented to the gratification of a few but to the detriment of the proposed settlement, which would end up being little better than a penal colony for all but the gentlemen and officers. Be it reputable volunteer or forced conscript, neither went with the understanding that once there, they would not be permitted to return.

The determination to win the goodwill of the Algonquins was not surprising. The lessons of Roanoke Island were clear at least in this regard. The directors were adamant that the colonists take "care not to offend the naturals."[24] But contravening this from the outset was the need for land. Indeed, company instructions warned that trade with the Algonquins for food should be concluded *before* they realized that the English meant to settle permanently.[25] This was not just unrealistic, it was ludicrous. It goes without saying that investors intended for the colony to grow and in time subdivide into additional settlements.[26] Migration was open-ended. After all, there were ten thousand vagrants in England, each a candidate for deportation. No limit on number of colonists was ever envisioned, a predilection that was certain to cause conflict sooner or later.

But once again, the need for land was not viewed as problematic. The prevailing perception remained that possession came by right of discovery by a Christian nation. Furthermore, North America was viewed as wilderness, vast and all but unpeopled. By necessity, land was the ultimate payoff for volunteers as well as for vagrants and inmates released from incarceration in Bridewell and the Clink, the latter given a pardon, ship's passage, and fifty acres.[27] London Company investors were assured that the Algonquins would be paid for their land if such proved necessary, but this was avowed in private hope that Native Americans could be enticed to part with their land in exchange for protection against the Spanish or against an enemy tribe, or, failing that, for hatchets, copper pots, and colorful glass beads. And these assumptions came with the expectation that the Algonquin language contained words for "buy" and "sell," backed by comprehension of what these words meant to an Englishman.

Of perhaps greatest importance to company officials, however, was one last objective—and, in truth, the most delusional of all—that the colonists achieve "an early self-sufficiency" and thereby pose no further burden to the company, financial or otherwise.[28]

One week before Christmas 1606, three ships pushed away from the Blackwell docks, east of London, and fell with the tide to the mouth of the Thames. Upon entering the North Sea, the fleet was opposed by fierce southwest winds, the same winds that had doomed the Spanish Armada. Admiral Christopher Newport ordered the fleet to anchor in the shelter of the Downs to await favorable conditions.

By reason of his privateering experience and knowledge of Atlantic waters, Newport had been hired at the munificent rate of £100 per year to shepherd the company's ships to and from Virginia.[29] Now forty-five, Newport had captained one of the ships that escorted John White in 1590. On that venture, after separating from the *Hopewell* and the *Moonlight* off the coast of Hispaniola, Newport's *Little John* and his consort ship attacked a Spanish galleon south of Cuba. During the fighting, Newport's right arm was severed in a swordfight.[30] Not one to be mollycoddled, he was back in action in the Azores later that same summer. Newport and his handicap may have been the inspiration for the hook-handed pirate of popular fiction.[31]

The flagship, the *Susan Constant*, carried seventy colonists and crew. Riding at anchor beside her in the Downs was *Godspeed* with something over fifty and *Discovery* with twenty-five, the last, a purpose-built vessel for the colonists to use in riverine waters.[32] In all, there were one hundred and five adventurers—all male, including four boys—and fifty-six crew jammed aboard the three small ships.[33]

The *Susan Constant* measured one hundred and sixteen feet from stem to sternpost and had a cargo capacity of one hundred and twenty tons. Its hull capacity was one-fourth that of the *Ark Raleigh*—a ship built by Walter Raleigh that had served as flagship for the English fleet that confronted the Spanish Armada.[34] Fifty men were shoehorned into a space the size of two tennis courts—one atop the other—with under six feet of headroom, along with firewood, coal, candles, barrels containing food, flour, cooking oil, vinegar, water, spirits, pitch, and tar, trunks containing personal belongings, furniture, canvas tents, hardware and building materials, crockery, tools, grindstones, cannon, muskets, pikes, swords, armor, ammunition, trade goods, seeds for planting, spare ropes, sails and tackle, several spare anchors, a galley that included a brick hearth for cooking, and a fully-constructed but disassembled barge able to carry twenty-five men in shallow water, all with little ventilation and the stench of putrid bilgewater wafting up from the hold.

Opposing winds kept the fleet anchored in the Downs for six weeks. Perhaps the most miserable in a ship full of malcontents was the Rev. Robert Hunt who, though only a dozen miles from his family and snug fireside in nearby Kent, was hopelessly seasick.[35] Hunt endured without complaint, but others did not. Every ship has its grumblers and growlers, and they skulked about during this seemingly endless delay. By the time Newport ordered sails unfurled, there was seditious talk in dark corners below deck and in the fo'c'sle where crew slept.

By order of the directors, each ship carried sealed instructions to be opened upon arrival in Virginia.[36] The document named the seven chosen to serve on the colony's governing council, one of whom was to be elected president. Each councilor was to have one vote, the president, two votes. Why London Company directors decided to keep secret the identities until arrival in America is difficult to fathom. For reasons of security, top candidates would have been dispersed among the three ships, but the fleet kept together and often stopped at an island to refresh. Much might have been accomplished in building esprit de corps, delegating responsibilities, and learning to work as a team during the four and a half months it took to reach Virginia. This opportunity was lost, and instead, rival candidates eyed one another with suspicion, divided into factions, and plotted against each other. It may have been a foregone conclusion that Wingfield would become president. He and Gosnold had taken the lead in recruiting, and, at fifty-seven and well connected, Wingfield likely felt he had a right to the top job.[37] But at sea, Newport ruled supreme.

Of the one hundred and five colonists, fifty-nine were gentlemen.[38] Many of these were recruited by Wingfield and Gosnold who sought the younger sons of aristocratic families.[39] Some were soldiers, others, ne'er-do-well idlers, but most were beguiled by dreams of a fortune to be made in the New World. They would have been familiar with the Spanish conquest histories of Las Casas, Oviedo, and Peter Martyr and fancied themselves Elizabethan conquistadors venturing for the gold the indigenous inhabitants scorned because of its abundance and for the bare-breasted aboriginal girls who would comfort their nights.[40] The disdain with which English gentlemen viewed hard labor surpassed even that of the unemployed and intemperate conscripts dragooned into the enterprise from London's workhouses and prisons.[41] One is left to wonder who London Company officials thought would supply the actual labor required to build the colony's defenses and plant its crops.

The fleet stopped in the Canary Islands for fresh water. While anchored there, Newport ordered the detention of two men for mutinous behavior—John Smith and Stephen Galthorpe. Smith remained under guard until the fleet reached Virginia thirteen weeks later. Presumably, he failed to report seditious activity by Galthorpe. The charges against both would later be dropped by Newport without so much as council approval, from which we can infer a tempest in a teacup. But the incident implicates Wingfield in an effort to discredit Smith, whom he may have viewed as a rival.[42] As a founding member of the company that employed Newport, Wingfield may have leaned on the admiral to act, though as yet Wingfield had no official power.[43]

This would indicate that Smith's past had become known. History has produced few men so adventurous, fearless, romantic, and controversial as the swashbuckling Captain John Smith. Son of a prospering farmer, he was twenty-seven when the *Susan Constant* set sail for Virginia, and prior to that time, he had fought more battles, overcome more hardships, and seen more of the known world than any man in the fleet, the hook-handed Newport included. Smith was short and strong, bearded, clear-eyed, reminiscent of Francis Drake in appearance and manner. A throwback to the age of chivalry, at sixteen he had turned his back on a modest inheritance and gone looking for adventure.[44]

His tale began in the Low Countries as a foot soldier fighting for Dutch independence. He then spent time in Rome before crossing the Adriatic to enlist in the army of the Holy Roman Empire fighting in Transylvania to oust the Ottoman Turks from Europe. Three times Smith volunteered for single combat, and each time he emerged victorious and presented the head of his victim to his general. As a reward for these and other exploits, he was made an officer just before being captured by the Turks. With his head and beard shaved, he was taken in chains to Constantinople to be sold into slavery. There he was purchased as a gift for Charatza Trabigzanda, the mistress of the pasha, who took pity on him and after a time sent him to her brother for safe keeping. In Smith's account, there is no mention of a love affair, but it throbs between the lines. Her brother, disapproving of his sister's affection for the "English devil," sent him in chains to Crimea to labor in his wheat fields. There Smith murdered his captor, stole clothing and a horse, and rode for three weeks across the Russian steppes to Astrakhan on the Caspian Sea, searching for civilization and relief from the iron collar around his neck. This accomplished, he returned to Transylvania where he was rewarded by its overlord with money and a coat of arms that included three Turks' heads.[45]

Returning to Europe, Smith toured Germany, France, and Spain, then at Gibraltar he boarded a French ship bound for the Canaries. He became embroiled in piracy off the coast of Africa and, after hand-to-hand combat against boarding parties from two Spanish warships, made landfall in Tunisia from where he returned home, arriving in late 1604. Soon after, he was recruited for the Virginia enterprise by Gosnold, who was by marriage related to Smith's benefactor, a baron familiar with Smith's history and admiring of his accomplishments.[46]

The sole source for Smith's preternatural exploits prior to his going to Virginia is Smith himself. And if you have decided his life to this point smacks of a tall tale, you would not be the first to mark him down as a fabulist. One historian labeled him an "impostor," another, a "liar," and another, "an inordinate braggart, troublemaker and distorter of the true facts of history."[47] On the other hand, his twentieth-century biographers researched his youthful heroics in minute detail and found him remarkably credible.[48]

Smith's reports on happenings in Jamestown were published in England in 1608 and 1612, but it was not until his *Generall Historie of Virginia, New England, and the Summer Isles* was published in 1624 that he revealed for the first time that in the final days of December 1607, a ten- or eleven-year-old Algonquin girl named Pocahontas saved him from being bludgeoned to death.[49] One would imagine such a consequential event would have made the earlier publications, and Smith's detractors point to this as proof that he invented a romantic fiction for his own glorification and monetary gain. On the other hand, one of his Jamestown followers said of Smith that he "hated falsehood and cozenage worse than death."[50] How does one reconcile such extremes?

With regard to his incarceration aboard the *Susan Constant*, the charge against Smith appears borne of jealousy or hostility on the part of his rivals. In March, the fleet anchored for six days off Nevis, an island in the Lesser Antilles, and according to Smith, gallows were erected ashore for executing the mutineers, himself included.[51] Were this true, one can imagine that Smith had stuck his nose into something Newport decided was none of his business, in which case the old salt may have resolved to teach the feisty upstart a lesson by giving him the fright of his life. Such would have been in character for Newport. In light of later events, however, the charges appear baseless. In all likelihood, Smith had overheard crew vilifying their officers or their orders and shrugged it off as the idle grumblings of the rank-and-file that attend every campaign, military or maritime. Little did he expect his silence would be construed as mutiny.[52]

From Nevis the fleet sailed north toward their destination. Nearing the coast of Virginia, they encountered a violent storm and bore off to avoid a lee shore. Reduced to bare poles, the battered fleet navigated mountainous seas with no sun or stars on which to take a measurement for determining their position.[53] Newport was soon hopelessly lost. Four days into the storm, John Ratcliffe, captain of *Discovery*, sent a desperate signal to his admiral to abort and return to England. Before Newport had time to react, however, the storm abated and his crow's nest lookout sighted land, a dune that would later become known as Cape Henry, gateway to the Chesapeake Bay. Newport had seven times sailed across the Atlantic and back, but this particular feat of navigational precision was pure luck.[54]

A first landing was made on the south shore of the bay on April 27. It provoked an attack by five Algonquins of unknown origin. Musket fire forced their retreat, but two Englishmen were injured.[55] It was a disappointing first encounter and in stark contrast to the welcome Raleigh's first reconnaissance mission received twenty-three years earlier.

In 1607 Tidewater Virginia was known by its inhabitants as Tsenacommacah (*TSAY-nah-co-mo-cah*).[56] They spoke a dialect of Algonquin similar to that spoken in Ossomocomuck, and many of their place names ended in "-comoco" or "-commacah," meaning settlement. The English applied the name Powhatan to the alliance of tribes occupying the region and to the supreme chief of Tsenacommacah, known to his own people as Wahunsenacawh ("*wah-hun-SAY-na-cah*").[57]

Tsenacommacah was home to over thirty tribes, most members of the Powhatan chiefdom.[58] Exceptions included the Chickahominy of the Lower Peninsula and the Accowmack and Accohanock who lived on the Eastern Shore.[59] The Chickahominy, a tribe ruled by eight elders, numbered fewer than one thousand people.[60] They maintained a certain autonomy from the Powhatan chiefdom despite being situated in its midst and at its mercy. The Accowmack and Accohanock may have paid tribute to Powhatan, but they were too far distant to be considered allies.[61] Powhatan Nation tribes varied in size, from the small Kecoughtan, who could muster only twenty-five warriors, to the Pamunkey, who could field an army of three hundred.[62] As noted, warriors made up one-third of total tribal population, and Powhatan tribes averaged three to four hundred individuals. Tsenacommacah stretched from the south bank of the Potomac River

south to the Dismal Swamp—roughly today's North Carolina-Virginia line—and inland to the fall line of its mainland rivers, beyond which was Siouan territory.

Like the people of Ossomocomuck, the people of Tsenacommacah lived a Late Woodland period existence that required a habitat of considerable size. Population was constrained by the edible yield a particular territory provided. In 1607 population density was little more than two humans per square mile, whereas in England population density was over seventy per square mile. Total Tsenacommacah population was ten to twelve thousand living in about two hundred villages scattered throughout the six thousand square mile area.[63] As in Ossomocomuck, the people-to-land ratio of Tsenacommacah was at or near full capacity when the English arrived. Tidewater Virginia was suffering a multiyear drought that would continue until 1612.[64] As happened during such times, wildlife suffered, and the white-tailed deer—top of the Algonquin food chain—had been over-hunted during this period.[65] As one would expect, individual tribes were covetous of territory, and loss of habitat had existential repercussions.[66]

Despite having no written language, Powhatan culture was rich in ceremony, mythology, and tradition. A devout people, their religion was polytheistic, and their most prominent gods were the Great Hare, creator of all things, Okee, their equivalent of Satan, and Ahone, their beneficent god.[67] Okee and Ahone took human form. According to Algonquin cosmogony, they were twin sons of Sky Woman, who fell to Earth from the sky.[68] Okee meted out punishment in the form of hurricanes, droughts, defeat in wars, poor harvests, illnesses, death of a child, or infidelity.[69] The English construed the frequent presence of Okee idols as devil-worship, an assertion that denigrated Powhatan culture, relegating its people to a lower order of humanity and in the minds of some, a culture unworthy of dominion over the land they occupied.[70] But devil-fearing Powhatan children learned good behavior in the same way as God-fearing Christian children.[71] The Powhatans bathed every morning in nearby rivers or streams, and their daily ablutions were followed by prayer.[72]

Like their relatives to the south, the people of Tsenacommacah had light skin darkened by sun exposure and often painted. They prepared a scarlet red dye made of walnut oil and a powder from the roots of the puccoon or bloodroot plant.[73] Valued for its appeal and as an insect repellant, puccoon was so prized that Powhatan accepted it as tribute from alliance tribes. He maintained a stockpile in his storehouses along with bows, arrows, and shields for issuing in time of war. The warriors' red faces and shoulders provided a dramatic contrast to their raven hair, smooth hairless and tattooed bodies, dark eyes, and prominent cheek bones—an

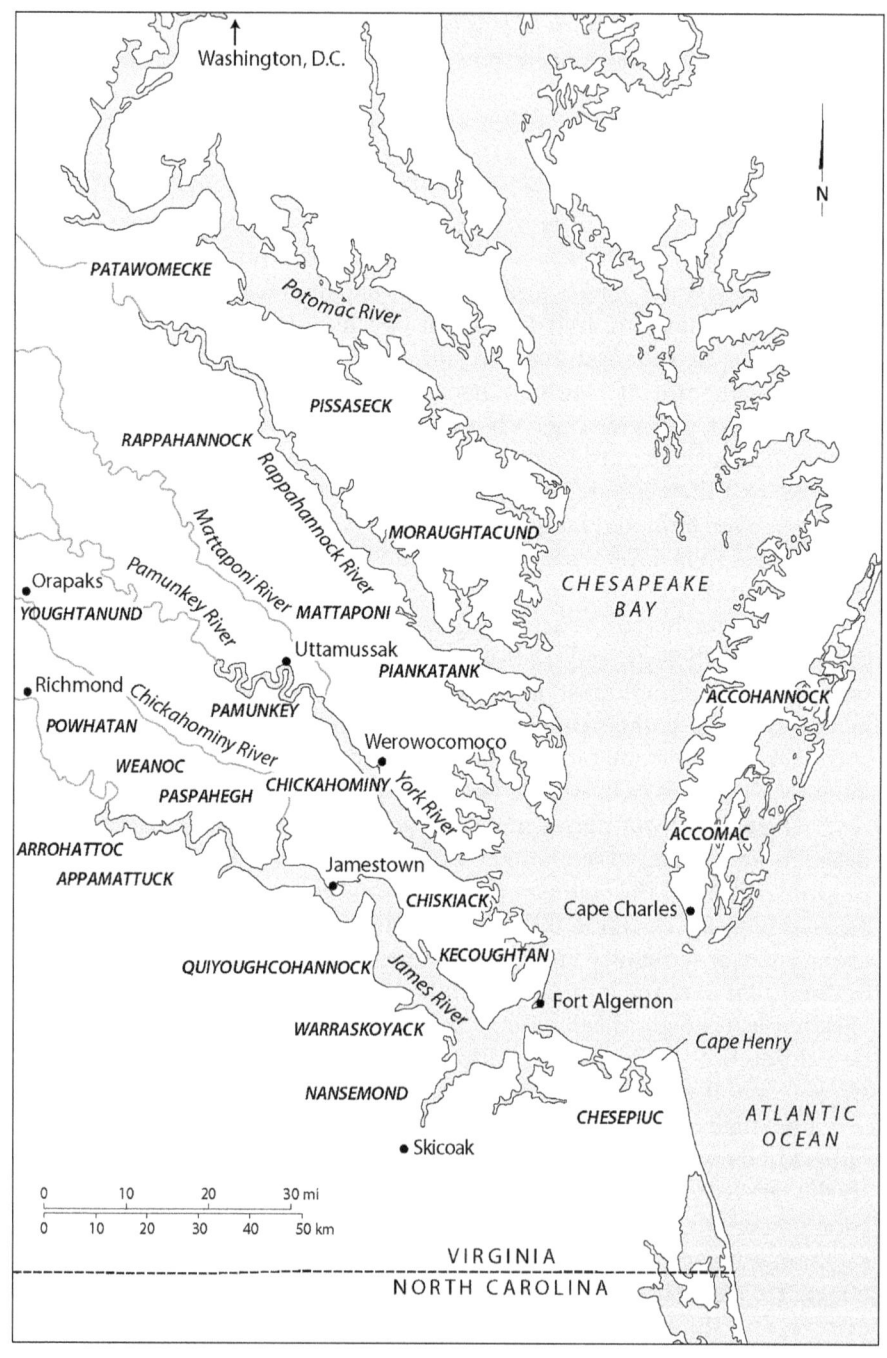

Tsenacommacah.

appearance to inspire fear in their enemies and lust in their women. Using mussel shells, the men shaved the right side of their head—or the left if left-handed—to keep their hair out of the pulled bowstring. The hair on the other side of their head was allowed to grow long and was often done up in a topknot.[74]

The Powhatans practiced polygamy. Multiple wives were a sign of wealth and status, but such was out of reach for all but the most powerful. Powhatan himself had many wives, more than one hundred during his lifetime.[75] When an alliance was made with a new tribe, Powhatan took as a bride a daughter or granddaughter in the line of succession and returned her when she became pregnant, often in exchange for a new bride.[76] In this way, alliance tribes' lines of succession included his own progeny.[77]

Considered the equivalent of deities, weroances could look forward to an afterlife, as could their siblings, wives, children, and the tribes' shamans.[78] A chief had life and death power over his subjects who, being mortal, had no afterlife to look forward to.[79] Punishment for their misdeeds, therefore, was meted out during their lifetime by their weroances and shamans.

In most cases, girls married outside their birth tribe to avoid inbreeding. In this way, Algonquin society was patrilocal.[80] Within her new spouse's tribe, however, were other women of her birth tribe who provided an exogamous bond to ease the transition. These distaff groups were powerful and multigenerational, and they gave a tribe's organizational structure a multidimensional array. Another important aspect of Powhatan polity was matrilineal: the ruling line of succession. The headship passed from Powhatan to his brothers first and then to his sisters, but next in line was his oldest sister's first son.[81] For this reason, Powhatan's own children—Pocahontas included—were outside the sovereign line of succession.[82] In three instances, however, he conquered or forced alliances with new tribes and replaced their chiefs with his own sons.[83]

Twice a year—spring and late fall—tribal hunts were undertaken.[84] People left their villages and trekked into backwoods where deer had not been overhunted.[85] The women were responsible for preparing new accommodations in a distant forest encampment that they occupied for weeks.[86] In this way, the people of Tsenacommacah were still somewhat nomadic. Hunts occurred when food stocks were low, these being periods of hardship that the stoic Powhatans endured as their season of fasting.

When an Algonquin youth decided to mate, he took presents to his intended's parents. Known as bride price, the gifts were recompense for the sacrifice her parents would be making by giving up the benefit of their daughter's labor.[87] The English misconstrued this as trafficking in girls, but the compensation was analogous to an English dowry.[88] It was customary, and the Algonquin people cherished their customs. Divorce was permissible, infidelity was frowned upon. Under certain unnamed circumstances, however, their culture tolerated consensual sex outside of marriage. This too was misrepresented by the English and fostered yet another calumny against Native Americans. These and other such misrepresentations led to a misguided justification for the outright seizure of Algonquin lands.[89]

Powhatan shamans were responsible for preserving and teaching Algonquin founding myths and oral history. As spiritual leaders they exerted significant influence over tribal chiefs and their governing councils, and no important decisions were made without their concurrence.[90] Powhatan's power was impressive but not dictatorial.[91] Called Kwiokos (*qui-O-kos*), a priest or shaman served as tribal counselor, healer, conjuror, and even rainmaker in addition to performing his priestly duties.[92] He had the status of a minor god and officiated on important occasions such as the green corn festival in late July, other wildlife migration and crop-related annual rites, and feasts of the dead for reburial of ancestors' bones after decomposition.

The Powhatans celebrated the coming-of-age of their children. The Huskanaw (*HUSK-a-naw*) for boys and the Huskanasquaw (*HUSK-a-na-squaw*) for girls occurred at puberty and were considered rebirths into adulthood. Training for the milestone was overseen by shamans. In the case of boys, they were taken deep into the forest for a period of months, trained to endure extreme hardship, and often deprived of food and sleep.[93] On at least one occasion the brutality of their treatment was misconstrued by the English to be human sacrifice.[94] Initiates were given drugs to test their wits and ability to withstand the deprivations and torments of mortal combat.[95] The Algonquin pharmacopeia included mind-altering narcotics and psychostimulants like yaupon, jimsonweed, and tobacco.[96] The *Nicotiana rustica* leaf they smoked contained nine times more nicotine than modern cigarette tobacco.[97] The training was punishing but deemed essential, as conflict with other tribes was all but incessant.

Shamans possessed the gift of prophecy. Sometime before the English arrived, Powhatan was warned by his shamans that a hostile force would invade from the east with the intention of destroying the Powhatan nation.[98] It was foretold that they would make three attempts. Twice they would be repelled, but on the third try, they would prevail, and the Powhatan nation would cease to be.[99] Harriot told of a similar prophecy current among the Algonquins of Ossomocomuck.[100]

Powhatan had reason to heed the prophecy. European ships had visited Tsenacommacah before. In 1559 or 1560, an Algonquin youth was lured aboard a Spanish ship and taken to Spain, where he was christened Don Luis de Velasco and given an education. He returned in 1570 with Jesuit missionaries intent on establishing a mission on the Pamunkey River in Kiskiack territory for the purpose of converting the Algonquins to Catholicism. Don Luis betrayed the Jesuits, however, and all but one were killed. A few years later, another Spanish ship discovered their fate and, in retaliation, abducted ten Algonquin men and executed them in full view of their families and compatriots.[101] Don Luis may have been known to Powhatan, perhaps even a relative.[102] Were this the case, Powhatan would have learned a great deal about Europe and Europeans.

Then in 1584, the Roanoke colonists arrived. Though they did not invade Tsenacommacah directly, word of the events that occurred would have reached Powhatan. Recall that Thomas Harriot and others of the Roanoke colony traveled north in the winter of 1585–86 to reconnoiter Chesapeake Bay, believing it better suited for settlement. They wintered with the Chesepioc Tribe who lived east of the Elizabeth River in the area of present-day Norfolk and Virginia Beach. The Chesepioc Tribe was not a member of the Powhatan alliance, and sometime prior to April 1607, Powhatan claimed to have attacked and annihilated the tribe.[103] Was this brutal action somehow related to the prophecy?

Warfare Powhatan-style was cruel and merciless. In the attack on the Chesepioc Tribe, the men would have been killed, and the women and children dispersed as spoils of war to those Powhatan wished to obligate.[104] As was true of the Incas in Peru, when Powhatan conquered a territory and emptied it out in this manner, a community of trusted allies was moved in to occupy and defend it.[105] In effect, a new alliance tribe was created. The Chesepioc territory, however, was likely appropriated by the neighboring Nansemond Tribe that may have been the force that attacked the *Susan Constant* colonists on their first landing at Cape Henry in April 1607.[106]

Wanchese and Manteo spent six months in London in the winter of 1584–85, guests of Walter Raleigh. Something of what they experienced and learned would have been known to Powhatan. Communication and trade with distant tribes was not unusual. Eastern North America from the Arctic tundra to the Everglades was crisscrossed by ancient, well-worn paths, many now modern highways. Despite danger and distance, anything portable moved along these arteries, from prestigious trade goods to news to disease.

European visits to the mid–Atlantic coast of North America were infrequent, but each would have raised alarms. Those who made contact would have been sought out and questioned. It is even possible Wanchese or Manteo traveled to Tsenacommacah to brief Powhatan. We do not know what he knew, only that he must have known much. Could he tell the difference between an English and a Spanish ship? Perhaps not, but it would be a grave mistake to underestimate his knowledge and understanding.

European incursions added credibility to what was foretold. Powhatan probably understood that Spain and England were different tribes. He would have learned that they were enemies or had been recently and that they possessed weapons superior to his. He knew in a second or third-hand sort of way about the carnage wrought by Spanish conquistadors in the West Indies, Mexico, and Peru and of Hernando de Soto's brutal foray into Florida, the Carolinas, and Mississippi Valley that caused so much destruction two generations earlier.[107] He also knew that Europeans were hairy, foul-smelling, avaricious, potentially brutal, and undeniably mortal. But Powhatan had lived many years beyond the average lifespan of his people. He had built a nation and had never been as powerful as he was now. But he was also old and tired of the struggles and responsibilities that attend command. In a remarkable exchange with Smith in December 1608, he claimed a preference "to eat good food, lie well, and sleep quietly with my women and children, laugh and be merry with you," in short, enjoy the trappings of royalty, Algonquin-style. Smith did not trust him, having by this time been warned by Pocahontas that Powhatan intended to kill him. Nevertheless, Smith's reports of Powhatan's words always ring true.[108]

Future encounters with European ships were inevitable. Powhatan and his counselors and priests understood the threat they faced, and subsequent events give evidence of a strategy to foil the prophecy. The April 27 attack on the landing party might have been part of that plan: greet the invader with token resistance, retreat before they have a chance to use their firesticks, and hope they sail away as they had in the past.[109] More likely, it was unpremeditated self-defense on the part of a startled Algonquin hunting party. At any rate, the English had no intention of sailing away, and for the next two weeks, the fleet cruised the lower reaches of the James River, searching for a place to settle.[110] During this time, a shore party led by Newport enjoyed a friendly encounter with Kecougtan chief Pochins, a son of Powhatan, so within hours the supreme weroance himself must have learned the dreaded news.

While the English searched for a suitable tract of land, the sealed instructions were opened and the names of the governing council revealed.[111] Wingfield, Gosnold, Newport, and Smith were among the seven. The others were John Martin, forty-seven, who had sailed with Drake and Gosnold and whose father was once lord mayor of London; John Ratcliffe, fifty-eight, captain of *Discovery* and a veteran of war in the Low Countries; and George Kendall, another soldier in his mid-thirties with connections in high places. As their first act, they elected Edward Maria Wingfield to preside, and on May 14 the new president chose a site for the colony, and there the fleet landed and began unloading. Wingfield named it Jamestown. It was sixty miles upriver from Cape Henry, far enough to escape easy detection by the Spanish who were still intent on extirpating any foreign incursion into what they considered Florida territory.[112] The council then voted to deny John Smith his appointed seat. He remained Newport's prisoner aboard the *Susan Constant*, which was tied to a tree and floating in the James a few yards offshore, its cannon providing protection for the new settlement from attacks by land or sea.[113]

Wingfield's fellow councilors found his patronizing and imperious manner off-putting.[114] Determined to obey orders, he initially refused to fortify Jamestown for fear of offending the Algonquins. Four days after landing, Wowinchopunck, weroance of the Paspahegh tribe—in whose territory Jamestown was to be built—appeared with a welcoming party, gifts of food, and an offer of friendship.[115] The significance of this gesture has been understated. It suggests the existence of a premeditated strategy for dealing with a European intruder. Invasion by another Amerindian tribe would have been met with deadly force, for loss of hunting and foraging territory was an existential threat.

Amid the exuberance of a first friendly encounter, however, a Paspahegh warrior could not resist the temptation of pilfering a hatchet. He was caught, roughly censured, and the bonhomie evaporated. Offended, Wowinchopunck and his delegation stormed off back into the woods.[116] His indignation is understandable. The English, who were squatting uninvited on his land, had the impertinence to berate him on the theft of a hatchet.[117] Wingfield had bungled his first test and succeeded in doing what his instructions ordered him not to do, "offend the naturals."

But the real power was Newport, not Wingfield. One wonders why Newport was made a councilor when he would be absent most of the time. This arrangement was certain to cause problems. London officials sought to micromanage a situation from which they were too far removed in time and distance, and Newport always came with his own separate orders, which always took precedence.[118] Twice he came with instructions to seek the headwaters of the James River in hopes of finding either a route to the Pacific or precious minerals. On his first mission, he chose Smith to accompany him, and on returning to Jamestown, browbeat council members into releasing Smith from custody and permitting him to take his seat on the council.[119] Wingfield may have been inept, but Newport pulled the carpet out from under him. This and Wingfield's inability to earn the respect and support of his fellow councilors undermined his authority. His hubris even turned his cousin Gosnold against him.[120]

What precisely was Jamestown? Though there were many soldiers among the gentlemen adventurers, it was not viewed as a military base. Such would have been seen as too confrontational. Even so, a palisade fortification was built after Algonquins attacked the colony in late May.[121]

Jamestown more resembled a mining camp with men living in tents and one of the ships serving as an alehouse. Descriptions aside, the setting was marked by division, with commoners segregated from gentlemen. There were a few professionals, two or three carpenters, a blacksmith, gunsmith, baker, brewer, basketmaker, thatcher, and shoemaker, but no women were present to fulfill their traditional roles. In effect, Jamestown was a commune with a common garden, a common livestock herd, a common store, and a common stew pot, all maintained by a common effort for the common weal, yet it was overseen by a committee of men with little power and less inclination to work together. There was no pay and—but for an empty stomach—no incentive to work. Private enterprise was forbidden, as were gambling on Sunday, engaging in sodomy, and having a private garden.[122] Men did as little as they could get away with or worked at cross-purposes.[123] They became disenchanted, demoralized, and homesick. Wingfield got the blame.

The fleet had arrived two months behind schedule, too late for planting a large crop, because months would be needed to fell enough trees for cropland.[124] Jamestown was a forested island connected to the mainland by a swampy land bridge.[125] Presumably Wingfield chose the site for the security an island naturally provides and because deep water near the riverbank allowed ships to anchor just offshore for the extra measure of protection their cannon provided.[126] But the island was low, mosquitoes were bad, and there was no fresh water. The colonists drank river water, salty at high tide, slimy at low.[127] It made them sick, and Wingfield got the blame for this too.

The weather was abnormally hot and humid for an Englishman. A colonist was ambushed by Algonquins and died of wounds from six arrows. Another colonist was killed while relieving himself in the woods.[128] Others deserted, deciding to take their chances with the Algonquins. Men started dying, presumably of typhoid, malaria, or dysentery.[129] Gosnold was buried in August, one of nineteen that month.[130] By mid-September forty-six of the original one hundred and five were dead from disease or hostile action.[131] That same month, Wingfield was deposed and replaced by Ratcliffe, who was no better, perhaps worse.[132] Then Kendall was accused of plotting with Wingfield to abscond with one of the ships and return to England.[133] He was condemned by a drumhead tribunal and shot, presumably by firing squad.[134] Newport had returned to England in late June, so by the end of September, the council was down to three—Ratcliffe, Martin, and Smith—and the colony faced starvation. Martin became sick and feared venturing outside the fort, so in desperation Ratcliffe turned to Smith.

The small Paspahegh tribe that occupied the northern shore of the

James was a Powhatan ally, but a somewhat intractable one as we later learn. When he inherited the headship in the 1570s, Powhatan inherited six tribes.[135] The others—like the Paspahegh—were taken by conquest, and Powhatan's control over them varied. Any tribe would have defended its territory against invasion, so the fact that the Paspahegh initially came in peace and bearing gifts could be construed as following the orders of a higher authority. And it is not surprising, therefore, that in response to the hatchet incident, a proud and defiant Wowinchopunck ignored Powhatan's orders and launched a retaliatory attack that killed two English and injured sixteen others.[136] But Jamestown Island was Paspahegh hunting ground, and at over fifteen hundred acres, the island was a large and vital part of the tribe's habitat. Deer are plentiful to this day in the forests that cover the eastern end of the island.

Events give clear evidence of Powhatan's strategy. On hearing of Paspahegh defiance, he seized the initiative. On June 25, he sent greetings to the colony with an offer of peace and friendship.[137] In addition, he offered to join the English in punishing the Paspahegh for their attack, and had the English agreed, Powhatan would have been brutal. He could not control every vengeful Algonquin warrior with a stone in his moccasin, but he could teach them a lesson. Circumventing the prophecy and English trade goods were more important to him than relations with a small alliance tribe. A few days later, his brother Opechancanough, one of the chiefs of the powerful Pamunkey tribe, sent a deer for the Jamestown firepit, and this was soon followed by another from Powhatan himself.[138] The visitation pattern is proof that Powhatan was following a prescribed plan. Wingfield failed to respond to his overture. Perhaps he misread Powhatan's intent. Instead, he forbade Algonquins from entering the English compound, yet another unfriendly gesture.

Powhatan waited patiently. Perhaps he knew by then that the colonists were English, and though uncertain of their motive, he was determined to make allies of them. Threatened on multiple fronts, he wished to procure the iron and steel armaments the English possessed before they fell into the hands of a would-be enemy. The Susquehannocks raided Tsenacommacah from the north with weapons obtained from the French. The Monacans and Massawomekes threatened from the west. With the arrival of the English, Powhatan felt besieged on three fronts and from within by insubordinate allies like Wowinchopunk. He may have concluded that the English could be defeated, that overwhelming numbers could carry the day despite the losses that might result from English cannon. The wayward Paspahegh had defied his orders, and if Wowinchopunk attacked and overcame the nascent colony, securing English weapons for himself, Powhatan could end up with an internecine rebellion on his hands.[139]

Through his spies, he kept close watch. Though the English tried to conceal the many graves being dug, Powhatan knew the colony, weakened by disease, could not feed itself. In early September, he sent a gift of many bushels of corn and a bountiful supply of game birds. The annual return of migrating ducks, geese, and other wildfowl had begun. But amid this plenty, the surviving English were prisoners in their own fort, too ill to take advantage of the bounty. On September 6, the Paspahegh returned a runaway English boy, and more deserters were returned a week later.[140] Powhatan was pulling the strings, biding his time, keeping the English alive and the Paspahegh in check.[141]

Ratcliffe appointed Smith cape merchant, giving him, in effect, responsibility for trading with the Algonquins for food.[142] Rowing the newly constructed barge downriver with a few volunteers, Smith first tried his luck with the Kecoughtans.[143] Thus began a pattern of negotiation that, despite his success, would anger officials in London. He approached in peace and friendship. When this failed, as it often did, he threatened their canoes or houses with destruction. If that failed, he resorted to a volley of harmless musket fire, and with this trading inevitably began.[144] Glass beads, copper pots, and iron tools were eagerly sought by the Algonquins in exchange for food except during their season of want. Pearls of high quality were also acceptable, but the Algonquins possessed nothing else of value to the English. The historical record is silent on the subject of sexual commerce, but it must have occurred, especially the clandestine, one-on-one sorts of transactions that could be sealed privately when Algonquin visits to Jamestown became more prevalent the following spring.

Smith's approach worked well with the Kecoughtans, so next he sailed across the James to try his luck with Chief Tachonekintaco of the Warraskoyacks.[145] This venture was so successful, he tried his luck upriver with the Chickahominy Tribe, where the same stratagem of firmness and fairness proved profitable once again.[146] Doubtless these trading forays were reported to Powhatan as was a description of the colonists' pugnacious leader, recognizable by his short stature. With his spy network, Powhatan had no need to venture forth from Werowocomoco (*WAYR-uh-wah-KOH-muh-koh*)—"settlement of the chief"—his capital on the Pamunkey River, sixteen miles from Jamestown as the crow flies.[147] He preferred to wait for the English to come to him as—sooner or later—they would have to.

John Smith's success in securing food won the respect of many colonists, both of the laboring class and the gentlemen, but his rancorous fellow councilors took offense at the apparent ease with which he triumphed. He was outshining them, so they went looking for fault. The James River had been explored to the fall line by Newport before he returned to England, so Ratcliffe criticized Smith for failing to explore the Chickahominy River while on his errand for food.[148] Ratcliffe claimed it was a missed opportunity to find the desired route to the Pacific, as had been ordered by company directors. Always up for a challenge, Smith accepted and in early December with nine men rowed the barge six miles up the James to the mouth of the Chickahominy, there to go searching for the river's fountainhead. Little did he know that he was heading for a rendezvous with his own resurrection.

◆ 6 ◆

Pocahontas and John Smith

The mouth of the Chickahominy is deceptively wide, but the river soon narrows and snakes its way northwest. It is navigable by shallow-draft boat for forty miles, though the distance as the crow flies is half that. At its mouth, the water is greenish-brown and tidal. It is difficult to judge the extent of a river viewing it from its mouth, but having been on Newport's exploration of the James, Smith must have suspected the river would branch off into spring-fed streams before revealing anything about a route to the Pacific. The color of the water alone discouraged any notion of an inland sea as its source.

It was early December and bitter cold. The seven-month-old colony was desperate for Newport's return, expecting him to come laden with provisions—English victuals and spirits plus draft animals for helping grub stumps and pulling a plow.[1] Passing Chickahominy villages with which he had recently traded and pursued by canoes of Algonquins wishing to trade again, Smith and his crew of nine paddled thirty miles upriver, arriving in the evening at Apokant, a wilderness Chickahominy village beyond which was Pamunkey territory. Birth tribe of Powhatan himself, the Pamunkey were led by a triumvirate of his three brothers, Opitchapam, Opechancanough, and Kekataugh.[2] Beyond Apokant the river narrows, so the expedition spent the night on the barge anchored offshore.

As was Smith's habit, morning began with prayer and song. Anglican hymns brought curious and bemused Algonquin men, women, and children to the waterfront. Following the matins, Smith hired two Chickahominy guides and their canoe to take him to the river's primary source and back. By now, he knew the journey would fail to find the coveted prize, but he wanted proof.[3] With a guide he avoided wrong turns into dead-end creeks that would waste time.

Smith stepped into the canoe with fellow colonists Jehu Robinson and Thomas Emry, leaving the other seven on the barge. Robinson, a gentleman, had become a Smith partisan. Smith's success in feeding a starving colony and the strong morals he evinced were winning the allegiance of Jamestown's more conscientious citizens, the colony's minister Robert Hunt included. Unlike Wingfield, Smith led by example, never asking something of someone that he did not first demonstrate a willingness to do himself. By now no one doubted his courage to lead in the face of danger. Leading by example comes naturally to those who rise from humble beginnings.

With Smith gone, one of the bargemen, George Cassen, enticed by flirtatious women, disobeyed orders and swam ashore.[4] He was captured, but by whom is unclear. Confederates of his captors then ran north through the woods in pursuit of Smith's canoe. Cassen was tortured and died a gruesome death—his fingers cut off and burned and his skin flayed—but the other English escaped and rowed the barge back to Jamestown, convinced Smith, Robinson, and Emry would suffer the same fate as Cassen.

Smith and the canoe party traveled about fifteen miles deeper into wilderness, stopping in the early afternoon to rest. Smith instructed Robinson and Emry to build a fire and prepare something to eat while he and one of the Chickahominy guides hiked into the woods to go "fowling."[5] Smith ordered his English comrades to keep their fuses lit so as to fire a warning shot should hostile Algonquins appear. He carried no musket, only his wheel-lock pistol with an effective range of about fifty yards—not an ideal weapon for bird hunting—so his excuse for leaving his companions at the river poses questions. Whatever his purpose, he had not gone far when he heard a scream accompanied by the whooping of Algonquins and coming from the direction of the canoe. No warning shot had been fired.[6]

Suddenly Smith was surrounded by Algonquin warriors.[7] He seized his Chickahominy guide and bound the two of them together. Sticking the muzzle of his pistol in his captive's ribs, Smith began frog-marching him back toward the river. His guide pleaded with Smith to run for his life, but before he could, Smith was shot in the thigh with an arrow. The wound was superficial, and Smith fired his pistol at two assailants, missed, and reloaded as they fled. More Algonquins attacked, arrows coming at him from many directions, all falling short. Smith fired again and reloaded again using his guide as a human shield. After firing more shots at movements in the brush, he found himself surrounded by Pamunkey warriors, all with arrows nocked and ready.

Again, Smith began retreating toward the river. In desperation, his Chickahominy captive shouted to the attackers that Smith was the leader of the English, this done in hopes the information would save their lives. Still shielded by his guide, Smith backed them both into an unseen icy bog, and there his boots filled with water and became stuck.[8] Having the high ground now, his attackers eased their aggression. Smith's situation hopeless, he surrendered and threw his pistol onto dry ground. Pamunkey warriors then pulled the two out of the morass and walked them back to the river. There, Smith saw that Robinson had been killed, his body riddled with arrows. There was no sign of Emry. Smith's attackers then added fuel to the smoldering fire to warm Smith while others rubbed circulation back into his legs and feet.[9]

At this point either Opechancanough appeared, or Smith was taken to him somewhere in the forest. The chief's presence and the ambush indicate that Smith had wandered into the midst of a large Pamunkey hunting party. He and Opechancanough had met at the falls of the James six months earlier when Smith accompanied Newport on his exploration. No doubt Smith remembered. A man in his fifties and a head taller than Smith, Opechancanough was an impressive presence and, though he may have deferred to his brother Powhatan and obeyed his orders, he seems to not have fully embraced his brother's strategy regarding the English. He was certainly not going to permit an uncontested invasion of his territory. He would have remembered Newport, but perhaps not Smith, so he may have questioned Smith's authority. It was common knowledge that Newport had left Jamestown in the *Susan Constant* back in July, posing yet more questions as to what the English were up to.

Smith's life was now in Opechancanough's hands. Though his mastery of Algonquin could not have been far advanced, he knew enough to try bluffing his way out of the same fate as Robinson. He carried a pocket compass encased in glass. Pulling it from his satchel, he showed the dial to Opechancanough, demonstrating how the needle always pointed in the same direction and no doubt cataloging its potential to a people who spent so much of their lives in the forest. When Opechancanough tried to touch the needle, he was mystified by the glass.[10]

With words and signs, Smith explained how the compass worked and elaborated on this with a description of the Earth as a round object suspended in space. But he did not stop there, perhaps thinking he could delay the inevitable so long as he kept talking. He expounded on the known world, its immense size, the many nations and their people, England and Spain. Enthralled or amused by Smith's logorrhea, Opechancanough ordered him released from the tree to which he had been tied, and he led him through woods to the village of Rasawrack.[11]

Upon their arrival, curious women and children emerged from the thirty-some houses of the village to see an Englishman about whom they had heard so much. There followed a ceremony in which warriors danced and chanted, their faces and shoulders painted red, some wearing feathers, some in headdresses made of the tail hair of the white-tail deer dyed red, a so-called roach headdress.[12] Their winter buckskins were adorned with the fur of fox, otter, and racoon, and they brandished their weapons as they whooped and danced to the rhythm of their rattles and drums.

Led to a longhouse, Smith was served a bounteous meal of bread and venison while officials and warriors watched.[13] He was then left overnight under guard, and he remained in detention either there or at Menapacant, Opechancanough's principal town, for several days. The record is unclear.[14] Though not free to leave, he was otherwise treated as an honored guest, therefore—as was customary—he may have been offered a bedmate for the night.[15] Smith was something of a prude, so he may have refused, but later he confessed that "nymphs more tormented than ever," a clear indication that he was on occasion discomfited by this tempting offer of sexual intimacy with one of their "voluptuous" young women.[16] There is no report of Opechancanough's whereabouts during this time. Most likely he traveled forty miles down the Pamunkey River to Werowocomoco to consult with Powhatan.

John Smith's narratives are the only source of information about his Algonquin captivity. It is natural and prudent, therefore, to question his veracity. Later events corroborate certain elements of his story, though not all, and there is good reason to believe he was *non compos mentis* for a part of his captivity yet to be described. The historical record is, consequently, incomplete and possibly even specious, but to the extent it exists, nothing that follows is inconsistent.

Powhatan's strategic thinking is manifest in his known actions. Attended by his counselors and shamans, he would have questioned his younger brother or whoever reported Smith's capture. Was this the same short-of-stature Englishman he had been told was forcing the Kecoughtans, Warraskoyacks, and Chickahominies to part with their corn? Yes. Furthermore, it was reported that the Chickahominy guide had called this Smith the English weroance. And what of Newport and the ship that sailed away? Having no answer to this question, Powhatan may have reconsidered his plan in the light of putting it into action—a plan he had probably rehearsed in his mind for years. The leader of the English had fallen into his hands. The timing would never be more auspicious.

Powhatan laid it out again for his advisers—his plan to resolve the threat posed by the English colony. From what we know of the man, he was shrewd and pragmatic, not the sort to be duped like Moctezuma in Mexico, but we cannot know to what degree Powhatan believed the prophecy. The Spanish had come in 1570 and had been killed. And though they came again and murdered ten Algonquins, in the end they fled. Was that not a failed invasion? Then came the Roanoke Colony in 1585—granted an invasion of Ossomocomuck, not Tsenacommacah—but Powhatan claimed to have killed the surviving—"lost"—colonists once they moved to the

Chesapeake Bay, so that could be counted as a second failed invasion.[17] This, then, would be the third and fatal one, unless, of course, Powhatan could confound the prophecy by some clever diplomatic finesse.

Though the English possessed powerful weapons, their colony was now weak and vulnerable. Newport had gone back to England, possibly for more soldiers and weapons. Rather than destroy the Jamestown colony and invite deadly retaliation as happened in the past, Powhatan had decided to assimilate the English colony into his nation. In its weakened state, it would have little choice but to comply. This is why he had ordered food sent in late summer when the colonists were starving. This is why he ordered the Paspahegh to return the English deserters. This is why he had not destroyed the colony already. They were to become his ally, and this Smith—this short but brave young weroance—would become his adopted son, perhaps mate with one of his daughters to establish a kinship bond, and move his colony from the James to the Pamunkey River so as to be under Powhatan's watchful eyes. With this accomplished, Newport's return would pose no threat, indeed, the weapons he brought would add to the arsenal of the Powhatan nation. This or something near to this was his plan.

It is possible Opechancanough favored killing Smith and attacking Jamestown. When his time came to rule, he would be ruthless. But Powhatan must have won his brother over. Protocol would have dictated that he then consult the weroances of the other five core tribes, their shamans and principal counselors. The combined strength of the six core tribes was nearly seven hundred warriors, a force too formidable to be overruled by any of the non-core alliance tribes or by the autonomous Chickahominy.

Powhatan's plan required that Smith undergo the equivalent of a Huskanaw—a ritual rebirth. Provided he passed certain tests designed by the shamans, Smith would be transformed into an Algonquin and given a territory of his own. If he failed the test, he would be killed, and his colony and companions would be destroyed, but in either case, the land they occupied would be returned to the Paspahegh to satisfy Wowinchopunk, who had become a thorn in Powhatan's side over his tribe's loss of hunting ground.[18] While Smith was undergoing his tests, Powhatan's envoys would travel to all alliance tribes to inform their weroances of the plan and to order their attendance at the initiation ceremony.

A few days after his captivity began, Smith was attacked by an Algonquin seeking revenge for his son who had been shot by Smith at the quagmire where he was captured. Such revenge was permissible in Algonquin tradition, but Smith's guards thwarted the assassination attempt.[19] Smith was taken to the youth, whose condition appeared hopeless, and he implored his captors to allow him to go to Jamestown for a remedy. They refused and the young warrior died.[20]

During Smith's confinement at Menapacant, Opechancanough reappeared from time to time, apparently with instructions for his aides and more questions for Smith about Newport and his ship. Then he vanished again from Smith's record of these events. Smith's mastery of Algonquin must have improved during this time as did his esteem for his captors and their regard for him.[21] His clothes were returned to him, a welcome development considering the bitter cold.

At this point Wowinchopunk appeared with a delegation of Paspahegh warriors for the purpose of entreating Opechancanough to join him in an attack on Jamestown.[22] He offered Smith every inducement to join them—his life, liberty, land, and women. Smith assured them they would fail, that the English were too strong, but this gave him an idea. He requested permission to send a written message to Jamestown to inform the colony that he was alive and well treated, this to obviate any retaliatory action on the colony's part to avenge his capture and the deaths of Cassen, Robinson, and, presumably, Emry.[23] It so happened that Smith had his "table book" to provide paper for such a note. He does not say what he used for pen and ink, and we are left to imagine a quill dipped in bloodroot oil.

Permission was granted, though it is doubtful Opechancanough comprehended the concept of a written message. Smith wrote to the colonists at Jamestown to send certain unnamed items in return and, as a demonstration of English power, to fire off a cannon to impress the messengers. In snow and freezing cold, three Pamunkey runners delivered the note. As instructed, cannon were fired, the frightened messengers' fears were calmed, and the requested items were returned to Menapacant within a day or so. Witnessing written communication for the first time, the Algonquins were astonished, further enhancing their respect for Smith.

There followed an odyssey the purpose of which was to learn more about Smith and to educate him in the ways of the Algonquin people. Opechancanough ordered him taken upcountry to see and be seen by alliance tribes that included the Youghtamond, Piankatank, Nandtanghtacund, Mattaponi, and others not named.[24] After two weeks of such travel, he was led back to the Pamunkey River to Cinquoteck—today's West Point, Virginia—the town ruled by Kekataugh, Powhatan's youngest brother. Since Smith and Kekataugh had enjoyed a friendly encounter at Jamestown earlier in the year, Smith was well received. From there he was led thirty miles cross-country in still freezing weather to a village on the Rappahannock River—today's Tappahannock—for his most crucial test yet.

Sometime in the past, the Toppohanock tribe had witnessed the murder of their chief by a European ship's captain, and they insisted on knowing if this Smith was the same man.[25] Had he been that person, their revenge would have been swift, but the mystery captain had been taller.[26]

This is the only evidence we have that Smith was less than normal height for an Englishman, and it may explain much about the man that might have been makeweight for a perceived shortcoming. As Smith told it, a ship had sailed up the Rappahannock River "the year before," and its captain killed the tribe's weroance and kidnapped some of his people.[27] The Toppohanocks' desire for justice was understandable. As it was, however, Smith's encounter with them must have been a positive one, for the following summer as he and his crew explored Chesapeake Bay, he attempted to return to Toppohanock to "see his imprisonment-acquaintances upon the River of Rappahannock."[28]

He realized, of course, that escape was futile. His experience must have brought to mind his Turkish enslavement odyssey, though he was not mistreated and later declared that he never feared for his life. He was so well fed that he quipped about being fattened for the spit, but there is no evidence that the Algonquins ever practiced cannibalism.[29] After his test on the Rappahannock, he was returned to Menapacant and from there most likely to Uttamussak, the Powhatans' most sacred religious citadel.[30] This secluded and forbidden sanctuary on the Pamunkey River very near Menapacant was the site of Tsenacommacah's largest temple, overseen by its most revered shamans. It also housed an ossuary for the bones of dead weroances and high priests and was the location of Powhatan's principal storehouses for weapons and treasure. The site was guarded and unauthorized entry was prohibited. Smith was brought here for three days of reeducation in preparation for some future ordeal, a Huskanaw or something akin to it. The lessons took place in the temple and began early each morning, continuing for twelve hours, and ending with a feast. Smith described only one of the sessions.

As he sat facing the fire, a shaman appeared, his face blackened. He wore a frightening headdress of stuffed snakes and weasels. His incantations and rhythmic dance were punctuated by the rattle he shook with each footfall. In his other hand was a gourd containing cornmeal, which, from time to time, he sprinkled out onto the ground until it formed a circle of meal around the fire. Then three more shamans appeared similarly dressed, their faces painted red and black, with white circles around their eyes. They performed a similar dance, chanting and making abrupt and fitful gestures. Then three more appeared with red circles around their eyes. These six danced until breathless and exhausted, they stopped and sat cross-legged on either side of Smith, still chanting their songs and shaking their rattles.

In ceremonial fashion, the first shaman began his dance anew and at intervals laid down five corn kernels followed by another incantation after which he laid down five more. This was repeated until two circles of corn kernels surrounded the circle of meal, and the frenetic shaman was wet with perspiration from his exertions despite the freezing cold outside.[31] Then the ritual was repeated, this time with short sticks being laid down, each pointing to the fire and forming yet another circle outside the others. Each stick was placed with the chanting of an Algonquin prayer.[32]

Smith could not have understood all that was said or the words of the chants and prayers. A word here and there adds up to no more than a gist of what the shamans wished him to know. He reported that the circle of meal represented Tsenacommacah and the fire at the heart of it, Uttamussak. The circles of corn kernels depicted the near and far bounds of the sea, and the circle of sticks denoted England.[33] Rooted in an English bias of superiority, Smith inferred an Algonquin worldview of charming simplicity—the unschooled perspective of a people confined to a remote and isolated region of the world—a people unable to conceive a round Earth suspended in space. Was this a geography lesson or did the soldier in Smith fail to grasp significant and nuanced symbolism often present in the cosmology of an exotic culture? If the shamans of Uttamussak revealed mysteries of such significance that they had transformative power, Smith failed to grasp them or, at least, to express them. But the intention was clearly to prepare him for his reincarnation as an Algonquin.

He remained in Uttamussak for three long days, but all we know of what transpired is this geography lesson which can only have been a small part. From Uttamussak he was taken to the home of Powhatan's oldest brother and heir apparent, Opitchapam, where he was welcomed and feasted while his host and others sat and watched.[34] From there he was returned to Opechancanough, presumably in Menapacant. Christmas would have come and gone with Smith having no opportunity to observe it in a manner he considered fitting. Having been inspected by the royal families and trotted out to be seen by most of the alliance tribes, the time had come to travel to Werowocomoco to appear at last before Powhatan. As he sat in the canoe that frosty morning, gliding swiftly down the Pamunkey River, John Smith must have understood that something of great import was about to happen for which he was to be the centerpiece.

He arrived in Werowocomoco on or about December 29, 1607, probably midday. As his canoe approached the "King's Village," the shoreline would have been filled with spectators, eager to glimpse the man for whom they had been summoned. Delegations from all thirty tribes had come with their bodyguards and servants. Most had traveled far. They could have been there for several days, attending councils for debating Smith's fate and that of his companions in Jamestown. The debates would have been charged with emotion. But Smith had undergone the requisite indoctrination into the ways of the Algonquin, and the shamans had given their approval. Nevertheless, there would have been fierce opposition to Powhatan's proposals by some of the two hundred weroances, weroansquas, counselors, and shamans who had gathered.[35] But by the day of Smith's arrival, the debating was over. Powhatan had prevailed.

Imagine John Smith—hatless and shivering—as he was detained under guard at the river's edge. We know only that it was cold, so perhaps overcast, threatening snow. He would have eyed those staring at him, seeking to read in their faces some hint of what lay in store. He knew their assembly was occasioned by his capture, and he must have feared they had gathered to witness his execution. Here is his narrative, written in the third person:

> At last they brought him to Meronocomoco [Werowocomoco], where was Powhatan their emperor. Here more than two hundred of those grim courtiers stood wondering at him as he had been a monster, till Powhatan and his train had put themselves in their greatest braveries. Before a fire upon a seat like a bedstead [Powhatan] sat covered with a great robe made of rarowcun [raccoon] skins, and all the tails hanging by. On either hand did sit a young wench of 16 or 18 years, and along on each side the house two rows of men, and behind them as many women, with all their heads and shoulders painted red, many of their heads bedecked with white down of birds, but everyone with something, and a great chain of white pearls about their necks.
>
> At [Smith's] entrance before the king, all the people gave a great shout. The Queen of the Appamatuck was appointed to bring him water to wash his hands, and another brought him a bunch of feathers instead of a towel to dry them. Having feasted him after their best barbarous manner they could, a long consultation was held. But the conclusion was two great stones were brought before Powhatan. Then as many as could laid hands on him [Smith], dragged him to them, and thereon laid his head; and being ready with their clubs to beat out his brains, Pocahontas, the king's dearest daughter, when no entreaty could prevail, got his head in her arms and laid her own upon his to save him from death; whereat the emperor was contented he should live to make him hatchets, and her bells, beads, and copper, for they thought him as well of all occupation as themselves. For the king himself will make his own robes, shoes, bows, arrows, pots—plant, hunt, or do anything so well as the rest.[36]

English America's founding myth is based solely on these two paragraphs. Much was omitted from Smith's *Generall Historie* of 1624 for any number of reasons—his limited knowledge of Algonquin, the ceremonial arcana, or simply because he could not remember sixteen years later. The Powhatans cherished tobacco, so pipes would have been lit and passed around.[37] Prayers would have been offered, perhaps hymns chanted, dances performed, offerings thrown into the fire as was their custom.[38] And orations would have been delivered, the long-winded sort customary for Algonquin weroances. Perhaps they debated Smith's fate again. He would have comprehended little of what was said, but he says nothing of these things. We know he was interrogated by Powhatan. In his earlier publication, he related the egregious falsehood he contrived to explain the English coming, blaming it on a Spanish attack and a leaking ship and implying their stay would be temporary. He claimed Newport—referring to him as his "father"—would soon come to "conduct us away."[39] Doubtless, Powhatan realized Smith was lying.

The crux of the ceremony was akin to a Huskanaw in that it was intended to be transformative for the lone initiate—John Smith. Two clues attest to its significance. Smith's statement regarding "two hundred of those grim courtiers" appears to contradict his later statement that Werowocomoco contained only forty "able" men.[40] It was an important village but not a populous one, so on this day, there must have been many visitors, and by calling them "courtiers," Smith implied they were persons of importance.[41] Pair this with the presence at the ceremony of a weroansqua of the Appamatuck tribe, Opussoquonuske.[42] These morsels of information tell much. Opussoquonuske had traveled far—this "fatt, lustie, manly woman" as one Englishman described her.[43] The village she ruled was sixty miles overland and three major river-crossings from Werowocomoco, and she ruled one single village only and answered to Coquonassum, paramount weroance of her tribe. We can conclude from her presence and that of two hundred "courtiers" that officials from all alliance tribes were in attendance.[44] Logistical and security issues alone would dictate that events of this sort were rare. Such an august gathering would not have been protocol for witnessing the execution of a captive, even an English captive.

Many years later, when the United States was still in its infancy, it became a matter of importance for the foremost scholars of the fledgling nation to compile a history of its formative years from the first landing of the English. In so doing, these men studied the writings of the earliest Jamestown colonists and discovered the aforementioned discrepancy: Smith's failure to mention in his publications of 1608 and 1612 the episode that ultimately made him famous. This fact coupled with the improbable accounts of his experiences as soldier, slave, pilgrim, and pirate persuaded these scholars to dismiss Smith's claims as the conceit and self-promotion of a braggart and a fraud. They claimed the incident involving Pocahontas never happened and that Smith was, at best, unreliable.

Other factors further impeach Smith's narrative. The most persuasive is that Pocahontas was a child, and as such, she would not have been permitted to attend the ceremony.[45] Her age has been questioned, but her year of birth is generally accepted as 1595 or 1596.[46] Smith tells us in one version that she was "a child of ten years old" when they met, and in another, "a child of twelve or thirteen" and in another "not past 13 or 14 years of age."[47]

Ten or eleven is more likely when we consider that the following summer, she was seen playing with English boys at Jamestown, turning cartwheels naked as the day she was born.[48] It was normal for Powhatan children to wear little or nothing in hot weather, and this report indicates she was prepubescent at the time. By the by, the report of her nakedness was censored from publication for two hundred and fifty years, judged too indecent for proper English sensibilities.

If we take Smith at his word, he was brought for execution into the presence of the tribe's two hundred most powerful officials. Pocahontas was not one of them. Though called a princess by the English—and she was, indeed, the daughter of the chief—she was not in the line of succession, so her status may not have been as exalted as history has led us to believe. Powhatan had many children. It is easy to believe she was his favorite, for all firsthand accounts agree Pocahontas was an enchanting and gifted young girl. But it is unlikely she was present on this occasion.

Another important consideration that calls Smith's account into question is that Powhatan—though the most powerful chief in Tsenacommacah—lacked the authority to pardon Smith without the consent of others.[49] Powhatan understood the limits of his power. Tribal polity rested on dual sovereignty of both secular and spiritual authorities, and Powhatan lacked the power to make an impulsive and unilateral decision that could endanger his entire nation.[50] Smith's reprieve was preordained, it was not a spur-of-the-moment decision.[51] It was a part all along of Powhatan's strategy to sidestep the prophecy. Smith was not saved by the passionate entreaties and willing self-sacrifice of an eleven-year-old girl, though she be the brightest star in the Powhatan constellation.[52]

Regarding Smith's character, however, scholars of the more recent past have done impressive spadework into his exploits prior to 1604 and declared his claims to be genuine.[53] As a result, the restoration of Captain John Smith's reputation became a cause célèbre in the twentieth century.[54] His biographers argued, furthermore, that his accomplishments at Jamestown—attested to by others—serve to reinforce the credibility of his earlier accomplishments. And Smith's character as reported by others is yet another testament to his probity. As noted, he led by example and disapproved of falsehood. It was said of him that he always shouldered "the greatest task for his own share," and, in dire straits the following year, frustrated with the sloth of so-called gentlemen, he decreed that "he that will not work shall not eat."[55] This statement—so like Drake's declaration in Puerto San Julián that gentlemen were no longer exempt from hard labor—would have been popular with those who were cooperative and diligent in performing their duties.[56] Smith wanted a strong, industrious, and orderly colony.[57]

Once he became president of the council in September 1608, Smith was diligent in following orders. He sent two expeditions with Algonquin guides into the North Carolina interior in search of Lost Colony survivors. Both missions learned only that all were dead, though without physical proof, questions lingered regarding Raleigh's tragic enterprise, as they do to this day. When London sent tools, materials, and craftsmen to manufacture glass, soap, pitch, tar, and lumber, Smith got these projects up and running and returned samples for London's inspection. Not afraid to speak truth to power, he offered opinions and advice to company directors and did so with humor. When troublesome President Ratcliffe returned to England, Smith reported to London, "I have sent you [Ratcliffe], lest the company should cut his throat."[58] He suggested Newport was not worth £100 a year for merely "carrying news."[59] (Neither Smith nor anyone else in Jamestown was paid a salary.) And when he could not prevail upon his men to stop cursing, he took names and at the end of each day—for each curse word uttered—poured cold water down the sleeves of the guilty to the uproarious laughter of the pure in speech.[60] He professed to be perfectly willing to cut timber for naval stores but observed that England could source such material in Scandinavia or Russia at a lower cost.[61] When more colonists arrived—needing to be fed, housed, and protected—he suggested that the original colonists would have been better off "abandoned and, as it were, left to our fortunes."[62]

He was assiduous in the breeding of livestock, reporting on the increase in number of chickens, hogs, and horses. When food became scarce, he billeted colonists with friendly Algonquins or divided the colony to better enable it to survive. His treatment of the Algonquins was rough, but stopped short of inhumane, though one suspects he would have used deadly force if necessary to feed those in his charge. Like most Europeans, he saw the Algonquins as civil or savage depending upon the particular cultural trait under consideration.[63] He tricked them, taking advantage of their naïveté, viewing them as children with whom if you spare the rod, you spoil the child. But the Algonquins were neither children nor primitive creatures longing for an English version of civilization.[64] Smith's attitude may have calcified over time as Algonquin resistance hardened, but he always began an encounter in the spirit of friendship, and he never committed the atrocities perpetrated by the presidents who followed him.[65]

Smith began each day leading his men in prayer, a Psalm, and hymns. He went to fetch them when they deserted, and his congenial nature did not go unappreciated. Most of the colonists became willing followers. In battle, he led the way, urging others to "fight like men and not die like sheep."[66] He did not curse, he did not lie, he did not shrink from his duty, and he was devout. He had all the attributes of a good leader and a good manager, and he was smart enough to comprehend the difference.

Another significant achievement was his exploration and mapping of the Chesapeake Bay. England would continue to search for an expedient passage across North America to the Pacific, but Smith's expeditions in the summer of 1608 dimmed hopes that such a route existed by way of the Chesapeake Bay. He ventured as far north as the mouth of the Susquehanna River, invited the Susquehanna to meet with him, and correctly inferred from the French weapons and birchbark canoes they possessed, that the river ran north toward Canada, not west toward the Pacific.[67] He explored and mapped the Piankatank, Rappahannock, Potomac, and Patuxent Rivers to their fall lines in addition to exploring rivers on the Eastern Shore and learned much about the Native Americans who lived along their banks. Not once did he fail to befriend them and entice them to trade. In all, he devoted three months to two separate expeditions with small crews, rowing most of the way, often with little to eat, and not knowing what hazards lay in store.[68] When done, he knew more about the people and geography of the region than any European alive.

By the end of his term as president of the council in September 1609, John Smith had achieved or resolved four of the five original objectives of the London Company. When one considers the man's character and accomplishments, one wonders if he would concoct a story so preposterous that it would stain his reputation and that he would do it for mere profit or acclaim. So, which version of Captain John Smith are we to believe?

From a distance of over four hundred years, it would appear the two views are irreconcilable. So much has been written and the historical record has been so thoroughly parsed that students of history are left at odds regarding this man. There is, however, a plausible explanation as to what happened that December afternoon in Werowocomoco that would explain everything without impugning John Smith. By reason of the fact that the entire ruling class of the Powhatan nation had assembled, we can only conclude Smith underwent a ritual adoption, initiation, or rebirth—a Huskanaw or something like it.[69] There is, therefore, a plausible explanation for why he may have misremembered what happened.

By Algonquin tradition, jimsonweed would have been administered to the inductee during such a ritual.[70] Also called the devil's snare, "jimsonweed"—the word—is a corruption of Jamestown Weed. Being a hallucinogen, its use became common among English colonists wishing to numb their despair. Jimsonweed is a wild-growing, temperate-climate shrub with white flowers and green thistle-like seedpods. It is poisonous and potentially deadly. Any part of the plant can be used to induce a psychedelic experience but smoking the leaves or eating the seeds yield maximum potency. Its entheogenic properties were such that considerable skill was required to prevent serious harm and even death, and Powhatan shamans were experienced in its dosage. It was used to produce a mystical or spiritual experience. The drug takes effect within an hour, and delirium and hallucinations can last for hours or even days usually leaving the victim with only a vague recollection of his or her experience. Users report heightened perception and enlightenment, blurred vision, difficulty hearing, insecurity, guilt, and an intense fear of dying. Recovery necessitates constant observation and emotional support, aid in breathing and circulation, and vomiting. The Powhatan's emetic of choice was bloodroot, the same plant they used to paint their faces red.

If Smith's food or drink served at the ceremony had been laced with jimsonweed, he would have gradually succumbed to its hallucinogenic effects. As the drug took hold, the ritual killing was enacted so that the profound vision of his own death would elicit the desired illusions to be experienced in the delirium that would follow—the power of suggestion if you will.[71] Just such a technique has been used in our own time in psychedelic drug therapy. Patients under the influence were found to be keenly susceptible to suggestion aimed at producing desired changes in behavior. Most likely, the objective of the ceremony was the reincarnation of John Smith as an Algonquin.

Events that took place in Jamestown later in January and throughout the spring and summer of 1608 give evidence of a bond existing between Smith and Pocahontas that could only have been forged in Werowocomoco. If she was not present at the ceremony, how did this come about? And how did Smith misconstrue her role in his salvation? It may be that in his delirium Smith conflated two semiconscious visions. The first was his assassins' red faces just before he closed his eyes and tensed his body to steel himself for the death blows. Though he had been reassured of his safety during his odyssey around Tsenacommacah, when carried to the stones, he expected to be put to death.[72] The second vision was that of Pocahontas looking down at him, cradling his head in her hands as he went in and out of consciousness during his long recovery. Later, when fully recovered, his mind merged these two visions into one continuous phantasmagoria, and his conscious brain reasoned that they had happened consecutively, not hours apart. He would naturally have credited Powhatan with sparing his life. From his perspective, what else could it have been? And, because she was there, he would have assumed Pocahontas intervened to save him. Nothing else made sense.

It is plausible that Pocahontas would have been among those nursing Smith back to consciousness. Future events suggest that her father wished to forge a union between the two, as this would help him obtain what he desired, a circumvention of the prophecy and dominion over the English. He would have planted the idea in Pocahontas's mind before the ceremony, as her future actions bear the traces of just such a predisposition. For this reason, she would have been there with others to nurse him in the hours it took for him to regain full cognition. She would have wanted to be the one to greet him as he emerged from his drug-induced coma—the first face he saw. As a prodigy, Pocahontas was accustomed to being a center of attention, and she obviously relished and sought celebrity within her nation as would be natural for someone with her gifts. She was also starstruck, for Smith had stolen the limelight. He would later refer to her as the "only nonpareil of his [Powhatan's] country."[73] We are not created equal despite the noble declarations of founding parchments. Pocahontas was special.

The above scenario, of course, is not what happened. But this or something close to it is well within the realm of possibility, and it would explain a lot of things, not the least, the enigma of Captain John Smith and many—otherwise curious—later events. We must, therefore, consider the possibility that Smith did not fabricate the story of his rescue, he confabulated it—which is to say, he filled the gaps in his memory by extrapolating from bits he could remember. Farfetched as this scenario may seem, it is human nature to piece together solutions to conundrums our conscious memory leaves unresolved. In Smith's mind, the only thing that made sense was that Pocahontas saved his life. Early historians were correct, the life-saving event never happened. But Smith's biographers were also correct—Captain John Smith was the genuine article.

Powhatan used poisons and psychoactive drugs on the English on other occasions. In the summer of 1611, a party of English soldiers left Jamestown for the falls. Camping one night near a cornfield, they were awakened by strange noises. Suddenly a yowling Algonquin ran from the cornfield, jumped the soldiers' campfire, then disappeared. In the darkness—confused and alarmed—the English thought they were being attacked and began fighting one another, thinking they were fighting Algonquins. They grabbed their muskets but could not remember how to use them. Gradually, they returned to their senses and order was restored. There had been no attack. Later, this incident was dismissed as a collective dream or anomalous fantasy.[74] Some claimed they had been bewitched by the Algonquins, but the answer was more likely that they had been drugged.[75] Powhatan had warned them not to go, vowing he would make them drunk and then kill them. Tidewater Algonquins also resorted to a poison called "spotted cowbane," a plant that thrived on the Eastern Shore, using it on the English on several occasions.[76] It would be inaccurate to suggest that the Algonquins used poisonous and/or hallucinogenic plants on the English on a regular basis, but fair to say that they put their knowledge of local plants to good purpose in their defense.[77]

On New Year's Day 1608—two days after his ritual execution—Smith was led to "a great house in the woods" and left alone inside, sitting on a mat before a campfire. After a quiet interval, he heard a dreadful noise, then a man painted black and looking "more like a devil" came out from behind a partition followed by two hundred more just as black and fearsome. Smith does not tell us more about this second ceremony except that the first "devil" to appear was Powhatan himself and that in conclusion, Powhatan assured Smith that they were now friends and that he would be returned to Jamestown. And if Smith sent two cannon and a grindstone to Werowocomoco, Powhatan would give him in return, the "country of Capahowosick and forever esteem him as his son Nantaquoud."[78]

Some historians have misconstrued this to mean Powhatan was adopting Smith and giving him an Algonquin name—Nantaquoud. This is incorrect. Powhatan had a natural son of this name whom Smith admired as "the most manliest, comeliest, boldest spirit, I ever saw in a Salvage [sic]."[79] On the contrary, Powhatan was saying he would esteem Smith as much as he esteemed his own son. Nevertheless, John Smith's three-week-long Algonquin trial-by-ordeal resulted in his being adopted or something akin to it.

It is logical that Powhatan would have sought a union between Pocahontas and Smith. In royal European circles at this time, it was common practice to forge alliances through arranged marriages involving minors. Algonquin royalty was no different. Why else would Powhatan thereafter put Pocahontas in the forefront of his dealings with Smith? Smith's own English associates drew the same conclusion. Powhatan was offering Smith an existing tribal territory carved out of Virginia's Middle Peninsula a few miles downriver from Werowocomoco—move Jamestown there, mate with Pocahontas, and thereafter be the weroance of the equivalent of a Powhatan alliance tribe. Had Capahowosick been occupied by Algonquins, Powhatan would have forced their removal to clear the ground for the English. Having control of English prestige goods was that vital. Though different from the English in many ways, Powhatan was just as human, as covetous of security, comfort, and prosperity as the next chap. Considering the precarious situation in Jamestown, his offer merited consideration: Algonquin land, food, and protection in return for English weapons, technology, and fealty.[80]

In Smith's letter of 1608, published as *A True Relation* that same year in London, he stated that he agreed to Powhatan's offer.[81] It was surely not within his authority to do so, but Smith's letter effectively notified London Company officials that the offer was on the table. By its response to Smith's letter, the company acknowledged receipt of the offer, but company records for this period are lost, so we must assume the offer was rejected and that a response was not deemed necessary.[82] Historians have ignored the implications of this rejection but contemplating them is edifying. Powhatan's offer may well have been disingenuous, but it was no more so than Smith's acceptance. One wonders if the offer was not—at the very least—a basis for further talks?[83] The question is purely academic because Powhatan's offer came with strings that hidebound English aristocracy would have considered abhorrent and unnatural: Algonquin dominion over the English.[84] Such an arrangement would have been dismissed out of hand.

But in pursuit of a more profound understanding, consider from an English perspective the positives and negatives of such an arrangement in the light of Virginia Company objectives. At this point in time, the English needed only enough land to raise sufficient crops and livestock to sustain a few hundred people. The territory of Capahowosick was many times the size of Jamestown Island. Its many streams provided an endless supply of clean fresh water that would have saved numerous English lives. Its cleared land, ready for planting or pasturing livestock, would have better enabled the colonists to achieve "an early self-sufficiency," something London Company officials considered vital.[85] And it goes without saying that implicit in Powhatan's offer was "amity with the naturals," at least for the present. Land was not required to achieve many of the company's other objectives: the discovery of a route to the Pacific, a bulwark against further Spanish incursions into North America, the discovery of precious metals and minerals, finding the lost colonists of Roanoke, and converting the Algonquins to Christianity.[86] None of these activities required large swaths of land, indeed, Capahowosick would have been a convenient base for them all. On the other hand, if selling phantom land as Raleigh had envisioned or ridding England of its indigents and criminals were important measures of success, more land would have been needed in the long run than was on offer from Powhatan. This frivolous exercise does nothing more than provide a glimpse into London Company priorities, but the true reason for rejecting Powhatan's offer was the rigid Eurocentric mindset that saw the indigenous inhabitants of the New World as inferior and uncivilized.

A delegation of Powhatans returned Smith to Jamestown on the icy morning of January 2. Welcomed by many, he invited his Powhatan guards into the fort and led them to two demi-culverins, each weighing a ton and a half. Smith invited them to deliver the cannon to Powhatan, and when they could not lift them or a millstone they were offered, Smith ordered a demonstration for his guests instead. A cannon was filled with ballast stones from *Discovery*, and the gunners fired at trees producing a shower of icicles and branches. The explosions and their effects caused the Algonquins to flee in fear, but they were coaxed into returning and presented with consolation presents for themselves and for Powhatan and his family.[87] Here we see Smith's humor on display again, but it was tinged with condescension. He could not have been oblivious to the fact that his prank would prove an affront to Powhatan. But Smith was fortunate in having as an adversary a wise and patient man.

During the three weeks Smith was away, President Ratcliffe disobeyed London's orders and appointed a close ally, Gabriel Archer, to fill the vacancy left by Wingfield's ouster.[88] A few years older than Smith, Archer had graduated from St. John's College, Cambridge, and attended Gray's Inn, and he fancied himself the colony's legal authority. He had been recruited by Gosnold, with whom he had sailed in 1602 when Gosnold discovered and named Cape Cod and Martha's Vineyard.[89] By being left off the original council, Archer had been snubbed by London, and he may have viewed Smith as the personification of that indignity.

The colony would have learned of the execution of George Cassen from the bargemen returning from Chickahominy territory. In the note Smith sent during his captivity, he must have reported the deaths of Jehu Robinson and Thomas Emry. Alarmed by this, Ratcliffe and Archer plotted to take *Discovery*—the small ship left by Newport for the colonists' use—back to England with a handpicked crew, abandoning those for whom there would be no space. Smith's return confounded this plan, so in anger Archer charged Smith with the murder of Cassen, Robinson, and Emry. Ratcliffe concurred and sentenced Smith to hang the following day, so for the third time in under a year and the second time in a week, John Smith faced execution.[90]

That very evening Newport returned with the first resupply plus eighty new male colonists. His first act was to release Smith, thus undermining the authority of yet another council president. Newport viewed Ratcliffe as a divisive and unpopular leader and marginalized him without a second thought. Of the one hundred and five colonists he had brought from England eight months earlier, only thirty-eight survived, and one of them—Edward Maria Wingfield—was imprisoned on *Discovery*. The death toll must have appalled Newport, but he had his orders from London and refused to let Ratcliffe and Archer stand in his way. As Smith was the only councilor to have engaged with the Algonquins and knew something of their language and region, Newport rightly considered him indispensable.[91]

A few days later, Jamestown went up in flames. There is no record of what sparked the conflagration, but fire destroyed all but three buildings, including most of the new colonists' possessions and the provisions

Newport brought from England.[92] Also among the losses were the books and papers of the colony's minister, the Rev. Robert Hunt.[93] The work of months was thereby reduced to ashes, and once again the colony faced starvation.

Powhatan came to the rescue. From Werowocomoco to Jamestown is a mile and a half by canoe across the Pamunkey River and then fifteen miles overland. Despite the distance, a delegation led by Pocahontas on her first visit to Jamestown arrived on or about January 5, bringing enough food to feed the colony for a week.[94] For a child of eleven or twelve to lead the delegation was disarming.[95] Here is further evidence of Powhatan's strategy and patience. Despite not getting his cannon and millstone and despite the arrival of new colonists—a development that proved Smith had lied to him in Werowocomoco—Powhatan had not given up. And by sending his own child as his guarantor, he demonstrated good faith.[96]

From this point on, Pocahontas appeared at the fort with a delegation bearing food every few days.[97] She would continue to come until Smith left on his first exploration of the Chesapeake Bay in early June—five months later. Without Powhatan's help, the colony's survival would have been tested during the annual spring season of want. On each occasion, Pocahontas and Smith spent time together, and one pastime they must have shared was learning each other's language. Evidence of a budding infatuation—a crush on Smith if you will—is suggested in the reports of other Jamestown colonists. Smith returned the affection, but as time passed and neither cannon nor grindstone arrived at Werowocomoco, Powhatan began to doubt that Smith was in earnest.

Newport had arrived with two goldsmiths and an assayer of precious metals. Impatient for a return on their investment, London Company shareholders demanded progress in the hunt for gold.[98] Newport also brought specialists for beginning other projects—the manufacture of tar and pitch for one—but gold was what kept investors salivating. Newport pulled men away from tasks assigned by Ratcliffe and Smith and put them to work panning for gold in the James River.[99] They may as well have been skipping stones.

When Newport learned of Smith's encounter with Powhatan, he organized a trading mission, possibly hoping to find gold in the temples of Werowocomoco despite Smith's claim that none existed. When Newport proved a poor negotiator in trading English manufactured goods for Algonquin corn, Smith compensated by tempting Powhatan with blue glass beads, which he knew the Algonquin chief would find irresistible.[100] The result humiliated Newport and made him appear inept in Smith's eyes, and the two men locked horns.[101] This notwithstanding, Powhatan renewed his pledge—declaring within earshot of Newport and others—that Smith was now a weroance and that the English were free to enjoy "the corn, women and country" as did the Powhatans themselves.¹⁰²

During Newport's stay in Jamestown, a brisk trade developed between his sailors and the Powhatans that doubtless included sexual favors.¹⁰³ Firsthand accounts are silent on this subject, but the oral history of the Algonquins is not. It accuses early Jamestown colonists and sailors of preying on young girls whose mothers offered up themselves instead so as to protect their daughters.¹⁰⁴ That sexual liaisons took place is incontrovertible, as is the likelihood of rape.¹⁰⁵ A few years later, Jamestown officials enacted a law prohibiting sexual abuse of Native American women under penalty of death, an indication such crimes had occurred. Smith complained that the sailors' commerce with the Algonquins was also causing inflation. Newport ignored his complaint, but after he left again for England, Smith cracked down and individual trade ceased. The backwash of this was an increase in thefts.¹⁰⁶

Newport departed for England in early April, his ship freighted with "gilded dirt"—tons of Virginia soil flaked with particles of pyrite—fool's gold. It was worthless. Ten days later the *Phoenix* arrived in Jamestown with forty more colonists—again, all male. The *Phoenix* had sailed with Newport in January but encountered dangerous weather and sheltered in the Caribbean for weeks.¹⁰⁷ It came freighted with provisions that augmented victuals brought by Pocahontas.¹⁰⁸

During her visits to the fort, she and Smith forged a close personal relationship. From him we get the impression it was not love in the romantic sense but that of a parent for a child.¹⁰⁹ Powhatan had called him "son," and Smith returned the favor by calling Pocahontas "daughter," and by all reports, their relationship became an affectionate one.¹¹⁰ But by Smith's inaction, Powhatan began losing patience. With the arrival of new colonists with Newport and then more aboard the *Phoenix*, Powhatan had confirmation that Smith had lied to him in Werowocomoco. But Powhatan was not ready to abandon his strategy despite the Englishman's mendacity.

Following Smith's crackdown on trade, those accompanying Pocahontas began stealing the items they wanted, weapons mostly. In May, an ax was stolen, and Smith took prisoners. Soon after Pocahontas appeared bearing gifts and promises in exchange for the release of the prisoners into her custody.¹¹¹ Until then, she had been a pawn in Powhatan's plans to gain effective control over the English by guile and gifts of food. Now she came as his official emissary. This marked a subtle shift in the relationship, a turning point in the romance, if such it was.¹¹² Pocahontas must have come to realize that fraternization carried a cost. Did she now see that if Smith refused to supply her father with weapons and move his colony to Capahowosick, her affection for him would turn her own people against her?

The realization must have had the same disheartening effect that Queen Elizabeth experienced in the wake of Amy Dudley's death when she realized she could never marry the man she loved. In Pocahontas's case, it may have been fugitive puppy love, but the pain would have been no less acute.

Smith was accused by his fellow councilors of—among several other things—having grandiose ambitions at odds with company goals.[113] His actions belie this assertion. In his last fifteen months in Jamestown, his plate was full to overflowing with assisting Newport with his futile projects, exploring of the Chesapeake Bay, beginning production of glass and naval stores, building dwellings for new arrivals, expanding the colony's livestock resources, and keeping those in his charge fed, productive, and safe. And had he wanted to build a personal empire, he would have leveraged his relationship with Powhatan much like Cortez did in Mexico with Moctezuma. Instead, Smith turned his back on this source of power.

In early June, he began his exploration of the Chesapeake Bay and, except for three days in late July, stayed gone all summer. In all this time, he had no contact with Powhatan or Pocahontas, but on his journey, he was warned that Powhatan had forbidden trade with the English. The supreme weroance wanted a monopoly on such trade, and his newly adopted son was not cooperating. By the time Smith returned to Jamestown in early September, Ratcliffe was imprisoned—having been deposed for mismanagement—and Smith became president.[114]

Soon after—on September 30—Newport arrived with the second resupply—seventy new colonists, including the colony's first women. Two new London Company initiatives—equally farcical—were in the offing. The first was a coronation. To acknowledge England's respect for Powhatan's pre-eminence and to confer upon him the status of a noble subject of King James, Newport came prepared for a crowning ceremony, complete with said crown—copper, not gold—plus other royal paraphernalia, including a bedstead and bedding. Though dismayed by such pointless folly, Smith and four volunteers dutifully sailed to Werowocomoco to make preparations.[115]

They arrived to find Powhatan away, not to return until the following day. In his absence, Pocahontas—delighted to be reunited with Smith after four months apart—arranged entertainment and a feast. Smith and his men were led to a campfire, joined there by other Algonquins—men, women, and presumably children. Hair-raising shouts were then heard from nearby woods, frightening the English, but Pocahontas assured them they had nothing to fear. Then thirty young women—naked but for leaves covering their vulvae—ran out of the woods whooping and dancing. With faces streaked with red paint, they circled the campfire, chanting and brandishing weapons as if they were warriors. They carried bows, arrows, clubs, and animal skins, and some wore antlers on their heads. After an hour of frenetic and seductive cavorting, they disappeared again into the woods, then returned and invited Smith—and presumably the others—into a lodging. There they tormented the men, pressing their bodies against them and crying, "Love you not me? Love you not me?" After this the English were honored with a feast and then led to their sleeping quarters.[116] We are not told if they were offered bedmates, but such was the custom.[117]

Smith expended more ink on this bacchanalia than he did on the ceremony in which Pocahontas saved his life. Was it because this time he was *compos mentis*? Here we witness the Algonquins' frank and open attitude toward sex and reproduction.[118] We can infer that Pocahontas understood full well that the performance was replete with seduction and that it would arouse men long denied the comfort of women. Under certain conditions, sex outside of marriage was not considered sinful in Powhatan culture, but the English conclusion was negative as always—that they were immoral, indecent, and licentious creatures.

As for the coronation, Newport followed orders. Powhatan, wary of treachery, was neither amused nor honored. He refused to kneel as is required in crowning ceremonies, so he was forced to stoop as someone or some men placed the crown on his head. Smith reported that it took three to do the deed, presumably because of Newport's missing appendage. The charade left Smith incandescent with anger. He suspected the senseless pageant would make Powhatan more demanding than ever.[119]

This fiasco was followed by London's second farcical initiative—another expedition up the James River. Newport brought with him from England a pinnace in five pieces to be portaged across the continental divide for reassembling below the fall line of a west-flowing river. It was a Sisyphean task. The boat was so heavy, Smith estimated it would take five hundred men to carry it all the way. The explorers got as far as present-day Goochland, about thirty miles west of Richmond—two thousand, five hundred miles short of the Pacific Ocean.[120] Smith suggested to London that it would have been equally beneficial and considerably less burdensome to burn the boat and portage the ashes.[121]

By the end of 1608, Powhatan had given up on Smith. Pocahontas had ceased her visits to Jamestown back in the summer, and Smith had resumed his trading forays, compelled more often than not to employ greater force and offer more for less in return. While trading with the Warraskoyacks, Chief Tachonekintaco informed Smith that Powhatan planned to cut his throat.[122] Undaunted, Smith returned to Werowocomoco again in January 1609, and Pocahontas risked her life to inform him that Powhatan intended to kill him.[123] Soon after, Powhatan moved his headquarters to Orapaks, deep in the Virginia wilderness. It was a tactical move in response to a more contentious situation. But it was a retreat nonetheless and all that retreat implied: fear of attack and diminished command and control due to Orapaks' remoteness.[124]

Meanwhile, new colonists were dying, many poisoned by the drinking water. Acclimation to Jamestown always included illness. Even Smith had been laid low by an infectious malaise when he first arrived. There is no mention of Algonquins dying of European diseases as was reported by the Roanoke Colony two decades earlier. The Jamestown illnesses and deaths had a range of causes: change of diet, salt poisoning from brackish drinking water, malaria, malnutrition, scurvy, typhoid, and something that came to be called the "bloody flux," amoebic dysentery that could lead to death by dehydration, exhaustion, and cardiac arrest.

Newport returned to England again in December 1608 with a letter from Smith to London Company directors. The ham-handed London board had earlier accused Smith of being too harsh in his dealings with the Algonquins, so he responded with strong criticism.[125] His term as president would be up the following September, so he had little to lose. At this point, it was all he could do to hold things together. In the late spring and early summer of 1609, feeding the colony became a ceaseless and ever more dangerous job. In desperation, Smith adopted a divide-to-survive strategy, sending some colonists downriver to the bay to live on oysters and others upriver where wild game was more plentiful. Exasperated by Newport's bleak report and Smith's strident missive, London company directors at last conceded that, since the colony could neither feed itself nor coerce the Algonquins to provide food, it would have to be sustained from England. To accomplish this, they drafted and approved a new charter and planned a massive reorganization and resupply.[126]

Smith was to have a role in the new government, but he was forced to return to England in October 1609 after an injury sustained a month earlier caused by the igniting of his own gunpowder as he returned by boat to Jamestown from the falls of the James River. Literally hoisted by his own petard, he nearly lost his life. It seems unlikely it was an accident, but the record is vague, perhaps intentionally vague.[127] Writing in the third person fourteen years later, he said only this: "Sleeping in his boat accidentally one fired his powder bag, which tore the flesh from his body and thighs, nine or ten inches square in a most pitiful manner."[128] The ambiguous "one" leaves us uncertain, but other firsthand accounts reported that a few days later another attempt was made on his life about which Smith only stated that Martin, Ratcliffe, and Archer had plotted to execute him.[129] He had enemies both within and beyond the pales of Jamestown.

With Smith gone, Pocahontas vanished. And the tattered remnants of the Jamestown Colony began a precipitous decline toward a pitiful and tragic denouement.

Upon arriving in London, Smith learned that he had been accused of plotting to marry a Powhatan princess and set himself up in Virginia as a king.[130] This was unfair. In fact, he had done the opposite. By his failure to fulfill the conditions of Powhatan's offer, he had in effect declined the very thing he was accused of. Nevertheless, the accusation served to render Smith persona non grata insofar as the London Company was concerned.

For several years Smith said nothing about the two Powhatan ceremonies he had endured. Perhaps he feared that revealing the details of his adoption ceremony would further aggravate the spurious claims regarding Pocahontas that had turned Thomas Smythe and other London Company officials against him. But seven years later, in 1616, he decided the time had come. The London Company was bringing Pocahontas to England to promote its fund-raising and recruitment efforts, and she was to have an audience with Queen Anne. Here was an opportunity for Smith to disprove the rumors, restore his reputation, and renew a relationship with someone he esteemed, perhaps even loved.[131]

He wrote it as he remembered it. Now middle-aged, he was without fortune, unmarried, and so disfigured from the gunpowder explosion that he may have been unable to father children of his own.[132] Making matters worse, his prospects were meeting with frustration at every turn. One thing that must have brought a frisson of pleasure was his memory of Pocahontas. So to prepare Queen Anne for her visit, he wrote that some years earlier, having been taken prisoner by the chief potentate of the Virginia Algonquins and condemned to death by the beating out of his brains, the chief's dearest daughter hazarded her own life to save his and that later she brought food to a colony that without her assistance would have starved. What he did not say in his letter to the queen but that he would publish a few years later was that Pocahontas had intervened in the ceremony, placing her head upon his as he was being pressed against the sacrificial stone, and rather than kill him, her father stayed the execution and spared Smith's life for the sake of his favorite daughter. Such was Smith's recollection, and it is thus our founding legend was born.

♦ 7 ♦

The Wreck of the *Sea Venture*

In July 1609—three months before John Smith returned to England—the *Mary & John*, a ship captained by Samuel Argall, dropped anchor off Jamestown after a passage from England of just nine weeks. Recall that Christopher Newport's first crossing to Jamestown in the *Susan Constant* took four and a half months. Granted, Newport was delayed by adverse winds, but once underway, his fleet still took more than three months to reach Virginia. Argall achieved this feat by hugging the western and northern edges of the trades, thereby keeping to the west of the Canaries and north of the West Indies, proving it was possible to shave hundreds of miles and significant time off the voyage to Jamestown.[1]

For more than a century—beginning with Columbus—European ships were propelled to and from the Americas by a wide, slow-moving, wind-driven series of connecting currents. They were discovered by trial and error over hundreds of years. The first—the Canary Current—led to the discovery of the Canary Islands at about the time of Christ. It flows southwest along the west coast of Africa until it turns due west, becoming the North Equatorial Current and crosses the Atlantic, emptying into the Caribbean Sea. The speed of the current is one to two nautical miles per hour, powered by trade winds that blow between ten and thirty knots. With wind in their sails, Elizabethan ships could average sixty to ninety nautical miles per day.

The Caribbean sits atop the Equator like a teapot on a hot stove. The teapot's spout is the narrow strait between Florida and the Bahamas, through which the heated waters of the tropics rise until—turned by the cold Labrador Current—they stream across the Atlantic to warm the beaches of Brighton and water the flowers of Kensington Gardens despite the fact that lush, green southern England sits on the same parallel as frigid, rocky Newfoundland.

The whole of this oval, clockwise, wind-driven current system is called the North Atlantic Gyre.[2] European ships could not sail faster than the wind, nor could they sail close to the direction of the wind. They were at its mercy, and when opposed by it—as Newport was on his first voyage to Jamestown—they either anchored or, if beyond anchoring depth, "hove to," a maneuver intended to arrest motion until winds become favorable. Trade winds were considered as dependable as gravity, so sailing directions conformed to their known patterns.

Since Spanish possessions in the New World were in the path of the Canary/North Equatorial wind-driven current system, it became the thoroughfare for outward-bound Spanish treasure fleets and the privateers who preyed on them. Newport knew the route like the back of his one hand. But Jamestown was far to the north, and the Spanish were to be avoided since an attack on Jamestown-bound English shipping was tantamount to an attack on Jamestown itself.

Samuel Argall or someone at the London Company hit on an elegant solution: since the currents that make up the North Atlantic Gyre are hundreds of miles wide, why not hug the inside of the gyre? By so doing, a ship could avoid Spanish territorial possessions altogether. And since the course heading was more direct, time and distance could be saved as could supplies and the health and comfort of outbound colonists and crew. The risk was steering too close to the inner edge of the gyre and ending up becalmed in the windless Sargasso Sea.[3]

Argall was in his early thirties. The fourth son of his father's third marriage, he fit the Jamestown profile well: younger son of gentry, few prospects, meager inheritance. But being a distant cousin of Thomas Smythe gave him a leg up. A bold and capable man, Argall brought with him to Jamestown the letter reprimanding Smith for his treatment of the Algonquins and informing him that a large fleet was on its way bearing a new governor and hundreds of new colonists.[4] Smith was now on notice that his replacement was at hand. Argall did not remain long in Virginia, but he would return later for a brush with history.

On June 2, 1609, eight ships and a pinnace departed Plymouth with four hundred and fifty new colonists and enough food to feed the colony for a year. The pinnace was towed behind the flagship, *Sea Venture*.[5] Headwinds forced the fleet to shelter in Falmouth, from whence it departed on June 8. On board the flagship was its captain, Christopher Newport, the fleet admiral, George Somers, and the new Jamestown governor, Thomas Gates. In desperation and in light of Wingfield's abysmal failure, the London Company had elected to send in the big guns, as it were. Apparently, company investors had challenged key founders to personally fulfill their promises.

Why the three most senior officers in the fleet sailed on the same ship is a mystery. Protocol required the admiral to sail on the flagship, and Newport was the flagship's captain. But for reasons of security, Gates should have sailed on the vice admiral, *Diamond*, captained by Smith's nemesis, John Ratcliffe, returning to Jamestown to continue demonstrating his incompetence. Gates carried a sealed box containing the names of those appointed to the new governor's council, the *only* copy in the entire fleet. Everything, therefore, was riding on *Sea Venture* reaching Jamestown safely.

The fleet kept together in fair weather for seven and a half weeks. Newport could not yet have known of Argall's successful crossing, but it appears he too followed the new shorter route to Virginia. Spain had spies everywhere—even in Jamestown—and the London Company was determined to avoid Spanish colonies and shipping.

On the twenty-third, Newport ordered a course change from due west to northwest. By virtue of his experience, Newport also served as the fleet's principal navigator. Taking advantage of favorable winds, he was able to put the fleet on a direct heading for Virginia, and he reckoned they were seven or eight days from Cape Henry. At the time of the course change, the fleet was between twenty-six and twenty-seven-degrees north latitude—approximately the same parallel as today's Palm Beach, Florida. This information comes from a remarkable document penned by William Strachey, a gentleman sailing aboard *Sea Venture*.[6]

Strachey was born into a prominent family in the town of Saffron-Walden in Essex, forty miles northeast of London. His grandfather had been active in local politics and became a large landowner.[7] William's father bought a house in London to which young William gravitated, seduced by the heady exuberance of the 1590s—high tide of the English Renaissance. After studying at Cambridge, young Strachey entered Gray's Inn.[8] He was drawn thereafter to the buzz and excitement of London's obstreperous avant-garde, most in evidence in its theaters that attracted fifteen thousand patrons every week. Something of a dilettante, he fancied himself a poet and became friends with denizens of the Mermaid Tavern in Bread Street—actors and playwrights—George Chapman, Ben Jonson, Christopher Marlowe, Richard Burbage, William Shakespeare, and, on rare occasions, Walter Raleigh.[9]

Like Shakespeare, Strachey married but left his wife and children in the country while he took bachelor's lodgings in London. Over a period of a dozen years, he squandered his inheritance on a dissolute lifestyle and unwise investments. He owned shares in Blackfriars Theatre and a troop of boy actors, the Children of the Chapel, whose rendition of the play *Eastward Ho!* landed the playwrights—Chapman, Jonson, and John Marston—in jail and the theater owners in hot water due to the play's satire of Jacobean knighthoods. Desperate for a more reliable and respectable source of income, Strachey found employment as secretary to the new ambassador to the Levant, but the two quarreled after arriving in Constantinople, and Strachey returned to London in debt and disfavor. Now middle-aged and financially embarrassed, he borrowed money to buy two shares in the London Company at £12 10s each and volunteered to emigrate, hoping his education would lead to gainful employment in the New World.[10]

It is possible to approximate *Sea Venture*'s position at the time Newport ordered the course change. If his arrival estimate was correct, he was anticipating a sixty-day crossing, besting Argall's record of nine weeks by a few days. A fleet of ships of varying sizes is slowed by the effort to stay within sight of one another, so assuming an average speed of eighty knots per day, the fleet must have been about seven hundred statute miles southeast of Cape Henry. At twenty-seven degrees north latitude, therefore, its current position would have been five hundred and fifty statute miles north of Hispaniola and about five hundred miles south-southwest of Bermuda.[11]

As dark clouds gathered on Monday morning, July 24, high winds began blowing from the northeast. Somers and Newport would have hoped it was a nor'easter and not a hurricane, but it was common knowledge that the season for hurricanes had begun. The wind direction may have prevented *Sea Venture* from achieving the precise heading Newport desired, but the north-flowing Gulf Stream would compensate. Nevertheless, towing the pinnace in heavy seas risked collision, so Newport or Somers ordered the towline cut, hoping the small ship could make it to Virginia on its own. The pinnace was captained by Michael Philes. He and his crew were never seen again.[12]

As the day progressed, the storm intensified. At some point Newport and Somers must have concluded that the fleet was being overtaken by a hurricane. They would not have known that the storm's diameter was about three hundred miles or that its forward speed was between fifteen and twenty miles per hour. Shouting above the din, they would have divvied up responsibility. According to Strachey, Somers took command on the poop deck, directing the helmsmen in the steering room below who operated the whipstaff, the steering lever connected to the tiller that guided the ship. This left Newport free to direct crew in securing sails and doubling the lines fastening items on deck, anything that might break loose and wash overboard or kill someone—cannon, penned up livestock, and the two ship's boats. The passengers were petrified, especially the women. The darkness of the lower decks only added to the terror. Strachey had sailed to Constantinople and endured at least one violent storm, but nothing like this. Everyone feared for their life, certain the ship could not withstand the beating it was taking.[13]

The storm worsened during the night. By Tuesday morning, the wind was so fierce steering was difficult despite carrying only a single storm trysail. Six men were needed to hold the whipstaff steady. Somers ordered the helmsmen to keep the bow pointing into the waves in order to plow through them. A broadside could cause the vessel to roll, fill with water, and sink, and *Sea Venture* was said to wallow in high seas. But the risk of plowing headlong into a wave risked being pitchpoled, flipping end over end. Once reduced to bare poles, however, she was propelled by wind pushing against her stern superstructure. She could only run dead downwind. With the wind coming from the northeast, this meant scudding southwest.[14] But winds within a hurricane circle the eye counterclockwise, therefore, as the storm moved on toward the northwest, winds pushing the ship became more northerly then gradually turned westerly, and eventually south, east, and north again. Knowing the direction of the hurricane and the wind directions within it, however, would have mattered little. Somers had no choice but to run with it and hope to stay afloat.[15]

There was no sign of another ship. The storm had dispersed the fleet during the night. Now scattered, all eight ships were on their own to survive if possible and make for Jamestown as best they could.[16]

Dawn on Wednesday revealed five feet of water above the ballast stones. *Sea Venture* was leaking. As news spread so did a sense of dread. Panic on the faces of crew searching with candles for the source of leaks served to infect passengers with despair. The ship was being wrenched apart by the seas, and in the process, hull timbers disgorged the tarred rope fibers called oakum that sealed her joints and made the ship watertight. Gates took command below decks. He divided the male passengers into three sections—one beneath the fo'c'sle, one amidships, and one in the stern—to operate the three bilge pumps and an untold number of bucket brigades. These he divided into watches to keep work going around the clock.[17]

Meanwhile, crew searched for leaks. Clothes were ripped apart and used to plug crevices. Then casks of salted beef were staved, and chunks of meat stuffed into chinks in the hull. Everyone took turns at the pumps, including gentlemen and officers. There were no slackers, no shirkers, no growlers. Men—sweating, their clothing soaked—stripped naked. Little did they know they had only just begun.[18]

A huge wave swamped the ship, filling it to the brim. It wrenched the helmsmen from the whipstaff so that it lurched side to side and battered those trying to wrestle it under control. Below decks, passengers were tossed like tenpins and left submerged, no doubt certain the ship had already slipped beneath the waves and was sinking to the bottom. Even so—full of water and not so much as a handkerchief for a sail—the ship was plowing ahead at six to eight knots per hour.[19]

The storm raged all day Wednesday and into Thursday. Atlantic Ocean hurricanes begin as thunderstorms that form off Equatorial West Africa and are blown west by the prevailing trades. Warm tropical ocean water evaporates and rises to superheat the air within these storms, causing condensation that forms larger and higher clouds. These then cluster with other, similar storms and begin circling an eye. As the system forms, it is blown westward at first, then it tends northward. In the case of the *Sea Venture* hurricane, when it overtook the ship, it was already being pushed northwest by an opposing weather system. From that point, the storm continued its turn to due north, then northeast, and finally east as it encountered the prevailing westerlies of the North Atlantic Gyre. It would end up dissipating over the colder water of the North Atlantic, but that was days later.

Celestial navigation was out of the question. It was impossible even to detect a horizon, much less a star. Nor was it possible to approximate position by dead reckoning in these conditions. It would have served no purpose. Had they known where they were, they could not alter course. No one slept. No one ate. When eyes met, only fear and misery were exchanged. Still the storm raged and still the water level rose.[20]

Tuesday night or early Wednesday bits of ship's biscuit began clogging the bilge pumps. *Sea Venture* carried five tons of biscuit,[21] Made of water, flour, and salt, they were also called hardtack—inedible unless softened by dipping in liquid. Until then, the pumps had been going round the clock, four thousand strokes per four-hour watch. As some worked to clear the pumps of this debris, others went to the half-submerged bread room, hoping to find a major leak. Carpenters ripped the space apart to no avail. If there was one single worst source of the inundation, it escaped detection.[22]

Strachey estimated that during each watch, one hundred tons of water were pumped overboard. Despite this ceaseless effort, by Wednesday morning there was ten feet of water above the ballast stones. No one doubted the ship was sinking. Water was rushing in faster than they could bail. It was a race against the inevitable.[23]

As the leading edge of the storm moved beyond the ship, *Sea Venture*—like a leaf caught in a whirlpool—was drawn deeper into its vortex. Somers directed the helm without sleep or relief, standing on the poop with a rope around his waist tied to the mizzen mast.[24] His concern was twofold: keeping *Sea Venture* from being swamped by following seas or being caught in a trough, turned, and broadsided. Every crest presented a deadly new challenge. Compass and hourglass were useless. As wind direction changed, the seas and the ship's heading changed with it.

There is no indication *Sea Venture* encountered the storm's eye, which would have been a twenty-to-forty-mile-wide respite of sunlight and relative calm. But winds increased to such an extent that the ship must have skirted the eyewall. On the back side of the eye, winds would have moved around, pushing *Sea Venture* east then northeast and finally due north. By then, the hurricane had turned to the northeast and was moving in the same direction and at roughly the same speed as the ship it carried trapped within its rainbands. *Sea Venture* had become enmeshed as if in a vast, wet, moving spider's web.

In desperation, the officers ordered the ship lightened. Trunks and chests were thrown overboard. No one's possessions were spared. Butts of beer and barrels of oil, cider, wine, and vinegar were staved, and this foul soup was pumped up and out along with the inrushing ocean. The officers debated chopping down the main mast to further lighten the ship but considering the monstrous seas, dismissed the idea as too dangerous. Instead, they jettisoned cannon and livestock penned on the open deck.[25]

Thursday night, Somers noticed ephemeral lights shimmering along the yards and up and down the masts. Calling to others to come see, he declared it to be St. Elmo's fire—a favorable omen, so he claimed. Caused by the exchange of electrically charged ions present during thunderstorms, it was well known to sailors. It continued flashing for four hours—coruscating here then there—perhaps raising hopes for a miracle. But as Friday dawned the fugitive lights disappeared, and still the storm raged.[26]

Now came the first hints of resignation and defeat. Deprived of food and rest, wet and exhausted, hands blistered and bleeding, muscles aching, all hope gone, some few broke open the brandy and urged their fellows to cease their efforts, close hatches, and "commending their sinful souls to God," surrender *Sea Venture* to the deep. Here they were—one hundred and fifty spent souls—on a sinking ship trapped in an endless maelstrom, lost in an endless sea.[27]

Then a miracle. Late Friday morning, clouds began to brighten. Somers espied land to the northeast—trees swaying in the wind as the weakening hurricane moved on. Suddenly, those at the point of surrender became reenergized, manning pumps and bailing with anything that would hold water from chamber pots to tea kettles. Newport ordered a trysail set as Somers ordered the helmsman to "bear up" in order to turn *Sea Venture* toward the wind and the shore. As the winds abated, the seas subsided. The boatswain threw out the plumb line and found bottom at seventy-eight feet. Then forty-two. Then twenty-four.[28]

Somers guided *Sea Venture* toward the center of a strip of pink beach.

7. *The Wreck of the* Sea Venture   141

Unseen between ship and shore was a submerged ridge of coral. *Sea Venture* was a one-hundred-foot-long, big-bellied ship built for cargo. She had a draft of fifteen feet when not half full of seawater. Just at midday—July 28, 1609—she struck a coral head three-quarters of a mile offshore and stuck there—still and upright—as if she had come to rest in the very cradle of her birth.[29]

In the sixteenth century, the Isle of Devils—"Los Diablos"—was reputed to be a craggy, desolate, inhospitable rookery—a sanctuary for seabirds, turtles, and a putative but as yet unseen devilish creature that howled in the night in the most terrifying manner.[30] It was to be avoided at all costs, but as misfortune would have it, it lay in the midst of the Gulf Stream, so like Scylla and Charybdis in Homer's *Odyssey*, it preyed on shipping, its rocks and reefs littered with the sargasso-covered ribs of barquentines, carracks, and galleons fraught with the bones of their sailors. On homeward voyages, pilots who guided their ships safely past the coral encrusted hazard were rewarded by their captains with a keg of spirits. The island had another name—for the Spaniard who discovered it—Bermuda.[31]

Consisting of nearly two hundred islands—many, nothing more than limestone skerries—Bermuda is a volcanic-formed archipelago. In 1609 its larger islands contained forests of cedar, palmetto, and Bermuda olivewood, intertidal areas thick with red and black mangrove, and a lush understory that included fifteen endemic plant species. Discovered in 1505 by Juan de Bermúdez, it was thereafter visited only briefly by shipwreck survivors or thirsty crews desperate to replenish fresh water supplies.[32] At some point years earlier, hogs had been released to multiply and provide fresh meat for future castaways. But ringed by destructive coral, the islands were viewed as godforsaken.[33]

Despite its strategic location, no European power had ever attempted to plant a colony on Bermuda. The first Englishman to set foot there was seaman, Henry May, sailing on a Dutch ship under French command. In December 1593, May's ship struck outlying reefs off the northwest coast. He made it to shore—probably Somerset Island—along with the captain and twenty-four others out of a crew of fifty-five. There they built a ship out of native cedar and rigging salvaged from their ship, and they sailed away five months later. May lived to tell the story.[34]

Somers and Newport would have guessed where they were—just off Bermuda's northeast coast. Perhaps they had sensed that *Sea Venture* had been heading northeast for the better part of three days and that they had been caught up in a storm that, had they been stationary, would have blown over in twenty-four hours. And it must have struck them as miraculous, finding the one needle in the proverbial haystack, five hundred miles distant from their last known position. Ten miles either way and they would have missed it. And had the storm not abated when it did, they could not have steered toward it. No wonder the survivors imagined God's hand on the tiller.

First priority was saving lives. The ship's longboat—turned turtle and lashed down on the main deck—was launched, and by late afternoon, all one hundred and fifty passengers and crew were safely ashore.[35] The setting sun appeared, and the reflection of evening clouds would have given an amethyst ambience to wet sand and the placid lagoon between the beach and offshore coral heads. It must have seemed a paradise the instant they stepped ashore. Once all were safe, the longboat went for whatever food could be quickly salvaged, and salted meat and ship's biscuit were passed out to exhausted and starving castaways still dumbstruck by their salvation. With darkness, they surrendered to sleep.

They had come ashore on today's St. Catherine's Beach at the northernmost tip of St. George's Island, most northerly of Bermuda's islands.[36] Had they missed it—and they almost did—the ship would have wrecked on coral reefs that ring the northern edge of the seamount ten miles beyond the island. In such an event, it is doubtful all would have survived. Indeed, they had not only chanced upon Bermuda, they had also chanced upon its best approach. As they awakened Saturday morning from where they slept on beds of scurvy grass, sea rocket, and morning glory, they must have marveled at their good fortune as they gazed up at blue sky, white clouds, green trees, pink sands, and turquoise waters. But as they basked in salubrious sunshine, they could not have guessed the full extent of their serendipity—from death's door to the one single spot on Earth that was lush, pristine, and devoid of human life.[37]

It may be that the affable and loquacious William Strachey was already scribbling in his journal. We can imagine him writing on an upturned barrel, his bare feet toeing the sand, his mind contemplating the beauty of the place despite its loathsome reputation. This put him in mind of watchwords of the late Queen Mary—a woman he disliked but a catchphrase he admired: "Truth is the daughter of time." Time now revealed that Bermuda was a paradise, and it needed describing in words. He must have thought also of his wife and children, wondering how long it would take for them to learn he was missing and presumed lost. Would he ever see them again? Would he ever get off this island? Were there really devils in the interior?[38]

Strachey does not say, but that first morning as people emerged from the woods or the sea, having attended to their necessaries, an assembly would have been called, all hands. The minister, Richard Buck, would have led everyone in prayer. Then one of the leaders stepped forward. Who

7. The Wreck of the Sea Venture 143

would it have been? Newport was outranked, it would not have been him. It would have been Somers or Gates, both of whom performed admirably during the hurricane, Somers most especially. The heroic efforts of Gates, Newport, and others notwithstanding, more than anyone, George Somers was responsible for their salvation. His was an act of courage, endurance, and seamanship that commands admiration. But who was in charge? This would become a critical question and a source of conflict. As admiral, Somers had command at sea, and Gates was governor of Jamestown. So, who was in charge in Bermuda?

The two men sorted things out at least for the near term. Gates took charge of the one hundred colonists, but it is clear he considered himself governor of colonists and mariners alike, Somers and Newport included. With members of the ship's crew and his personal retainers, Somers took responsibility for providing food, a task that included exploring the archipelago to learn if they were alone. He used *Sea Venture*'s tender for this work and for fishing the sheltered harbors and sounds. With the longboat, Newport directed others of the crew to begin salvaging the skeletal remains of *Sea Venture* and its cargo.

Somers found the fishing bountiful. In an hour he and his crew could catch enough fish to feed the entire company for a day. Merely wading into the crystal-clear waters of the inner harbors attracted so many fish, men feared for their toes. At night, fish were attracted by torchlight and could be netted by the bucketful. But this was only a first taste of Bermuda's cornucopia. *Sea Venture* carried a number of hogs, and some were salvaged by Newport's crew. Penned up on shore, they soon attracted Bermuda's feral hogs, which were easily trapped. On one hunt, Somers's men captured thirty-two.[39]

Large birds—herons, egrets, Bermuda longtails—had no fear of humans and could be captured by hand. Strachey tells of an incident during which thousands were killed in two to three hours, and Gates reported taking a thousand eggs the size of hen's eggs in the space of a morning.[40] Two varieties of sea turtle—green and hawksbill—came ashore to lay eggs after mating offshore.[41] They averaged three hundred pounds, and two supplied enough meat to serve the entire company.[42] The season was yet to come for the cahow or Bermuda petrel, a bird native to the archipelago that will be described in greater detail. Also plentiful were prickly pear cactus that produced edible fruit, palmetto fruit and berries, and cedar berries that yielded provender for humans and hogs alike. All sources of food were superabundant, yet there were no venomous creatures, no snakes, rats, scorpions.[43] Bermuda was a primeval paradise.[44]

Gates oversaw construction of a village on St. George's Island. Called Gates' Bay, it consisted of lean-tos roofed with palmetto fronds. People tended to congregate with those they had befriended on the voyage out. There were at least five women and an unknown number of children. Minister Richard Buck was traveling with his wife, Elizabeth, and two daughters. Another couple, John and Sarah Rolfe, were expecting a child.[45] A native of Heacham in Norfolk, East Anglia, Rolfe was twenty-five and aspired to owning farmland in Virginia. There was a Mistress Horton and her maid, Elizabeth Persons. Elizabeth married while marooned on Bermuda, but of Mistress Horton we learn no more than that she arrived safely.[46] There was an Edward Eason and his wife (name unknown) who conceived a child upon reaching the islands. Mrs. Eason gave birth to a boy the following March. Since food was prepared and served communally, the governor divided the company into messes of six or seven individuals.[47]

Apparently, Gates took charge with Somers's tacit consent. From the outset, Somers was captivated by Bermuda. Apparently, he was willing to relinquish the headaches of command and take advantage of freedom from responsibility to hunt, fish, and explore. In early August, he planted a vegetable garden with seeds salvaged from *Sea Venture*—melons, onions, lettuce, herbs. They quickly germinated, but the sprouts were eaten by birds. Gates tried planting sugar cane, but hogs destroyed that crop. Before long—no surprise to anyone—some enterprising tippler found a way to brew an alcoholic beverage by fermenting water mixed with palmetto sap. Dubbed "bibby," it doubtless drew a crowd.[48] There was little Bermuda could not provide, and Somers resolved to take possession of the islands on behalf of the London Company.[49]

Gates, on the other hand, was eager to get to Jamestown. Among the colonists were skilled carpenters and a shipwright, so Gates ordered the longboat decked over with timber salvaged from *Sea Venture*. This work was completed by the end of August, and a call went out for volunteers to sail it to Virginia. Henry Ravens, master's mate aboard *Sea Venture*, agreed to captain the vessel. As master's mate, Ravens had assisted Newport with navigation, so he was well qualified. He was to carry letters from Gates to John Smith, informing Smith of *Sea Venture*'s fate, appointing an interim governor to replace Smith whose term as president was about to expire, and ordering a ship to be sent at once to rescue those marooned on Bermuda.[50]

Why Ravens and not Newport himself? Newport was not needed in Bermuda. His authority was redundant, and his handicap limited his usefulness. He knew the North American coastline better than anyone, and within the Chesapeake Bay, he knew the landmarks, channels, shoals and other hazards plus the all-important entrance to the James River. He knew something of the Algonquins and where they resided. He could have captained a return vessel for rescuing the Bermuda castaways or he could

7. The Wreck of the Sea Venture

have stayed in Jamestown to provide leadership at a critical time. Powhatan was on the warpath, and Smith was about to have the gunpowder accident that forced his return to England, leaving Jamestown in the hands of the incompetent George Percy.[51] At forty-nine, Newport was not too old. The challenge was surely less arduous than the hurricane he had just endured. Strachey mentions Newport's name only three times in his narrative describing the Bermuda captivity: once pleading for Gates to pardon a malefactor and twice as witness at the christenings of the two infants born on the island. One is left to wonder what he did with his time.

Henry Ravens and his crew of seven never reached Jamestown. Later, Powhatan claimed to have captured and killed them all.[52] If this were true—and one must be suspicious—Ravens could have gotten lost after entering the Chesapeake Bay. Perhaps he mistook the Pamunkey River for the James and ended up at Werowocomoco instead of Jamestown. Such a tragic mistake is conceivable, but it would not have happened had Newport been in command. One Algonquin method of execution began with stripping the victim naked and tying him to a tree, then their women flayed his skin with mussel shells, beginning with his scalp and working down his body.[53] They then sliced off his fingers and toes and ripped open his stomach. The body parts were thrown into a fire before the victim's eyes, then the tree itself was set on fire, and he became a human torch as his executioners danced and chanted in celebration.[54] This may have been the fate of the luckless Henry Ravens and his crew.

On the same day Ravens set sail, Gates oversaw the laying of a keel for a ship that would carry colonists to Jamestown in the event the rescue mission failed. Christened *Deliverance*, the ship's keel, ribs, masts, and much of its hull were constructed of timbers salvaged from *Sea Venture*. The remaining boards were hewn from native Bermudan cedar overseen by shipwright Richard Frobisher.[55] It was obvious *Deliverance* would be too small to transport the entire company and that some would be left behind.[56] This gave rise to speculation as to who would be chosen.[57] Experienced crew would be needed, but most of the sailors now wished stay in Bermuda. This, in turn, gave rise to speculation regarding Gates's authority to make this decision or, for that matter, any decision.[58]

For some time now, new colonists had been in close company with those of the crew who had sailed with Newport before and seen Jamestown firsthand. The newcomers were eager to learn something of what they faced in the New World, and what they heard was disconcerting. Many would have experienced buyer's remorse upon hearing about the sickness, hunger, and violence that plagued Jamestown. It was then they realized the disheartening truth: Jamestown was a dystopian hellhole of noxious conditions, meager food, forced labor, constant threat of attack by hostile

Algonquins, and no escape.[59] Indeed, only officers and gentlemen were permitted to return to England.[60] Faced with this grim prospect, many came to view Bermuda as the better option.[61]

By this time, discipline had already been tested. *Sea Venture* carried two Algonquins returning home to Tsenacommacah. Namontack was one of Powhatan's protégés, and Machumps was the brother of one of the chief's favorite wives. Powhatan sent both youths to England with Newport the previous January to learn what they could. Upon landing in Bermuda, the two had disappeared into the bush. They were not pursued. The general presumption was that they preferred to fend for themselves, setting a precedent soon to be exploited.

And just two weeks after the shipwreck, Robert Waters killed Edward Samuel with a shovel. Both were sailors, and the fracas probably stemmed from an old quarrel. Gates sentenced Waters to be executed the following morning, but during the night he escaped and fled into the woods. His escape was aided by shipmates who resented having to answer to Gates, viewing him as outside their chain of command. Thanks to the intercession of Newport and Strachey, Gates pardoned Waters, allowing him to return to camp.[62]

The upshot of all this was the first of several mutinies that tested Gates's authority. In early September—having been in Bermuda little more than a month—several of the men helping construct *Deliverance* realized they were hastening the day of their departure, so they decided to shirk their tasks and thereby impede progress on the ship. When this failed to produce the desired outcome, six of the shirkers conspired to decamp from Gates' Bay and establish their own settlement on another island. When Gates got wind of the conspiracy, he had the wisdom to let them go and ordered them removed to a remote island. In short time a petition arrived, begging the governor's pardon, expressing sincere remorse, and entreating him to permit their return. Gates did so with a show of magnanimity, hoping the lesson learned would not be lost on the entire community.[63]

But an element of hubris in the governor's attitude undermined his intent. Power often comes with an arrogance that stains the appearance of a big-hearted gesture. Cargo salvaged from *Sea Venture* included arms and ammunition that were secured and closely guarded. That Gates commanded the guard was lost on no one. He had the whip hand and could afford to be magnanimous. The pardon was a subtle power play, and the discontented were in no way mollified.

For the next three months, Gates maintained an uneasy peace with assurances of rescue one way or another. By the end of November, however, hopes for a rescue ship from Jamestown had evaporated. To compensate, Gates granted Somers's request for two carpenters and twenty men to begin constructing a second ship. With this group, Somers established a new camp on Bermuda's Main Island, four miles west of Gates' Bay, accessible only by boat across Castle Harbor. Presumably, this was done for easier access to timber. Most of Somers's crew were sailors whose desire to remain in Bermuda was growing by the day. Once again, the grapevine became active with rebellious gossip. It began with the sailors and soon infected the colonists.[64]

As this stew simmered on its way to a boil, the islands were invaded by a species of large, pelagic seabirds that resembled petrels.[65] The name given to this heretofore unknown *rara avis*—"cahow"—was an imitation of its caterwauling howl that inspired the name, Isle of Devils. Most of the cahow's habitat had been destroyed by the feral hogs released long before *Sea Venture* arrived, but the birds had survived by constructing their aeries on the inaccessible, craggy, outlying islets that dot the entrance to Castle Harbor.[66]

In November and December, this remarkable seabird returned to Bermuda to mate and procreate. Mating pairs excavated a burrow and laid a single egg, which they incubated until hatching after which they nursed and fed the chick until it was ready to fledge. To feed their chick, the parents ranged as far as four hundred miles if necessary, using the energy of storms to hasten their journey. After exercising its wings for days, the fledgling climbed out of its burrow, gazed at the stars to memorize its position on the Earth's surface, scaled a nearby tree using its hooked beak and the tiny nails on its webbed feet, then launched itself from the treetop. It remained at sea for four or five years feeding on shrimp, squid, and small fish before returning to Bermuda—guided by celestial navigation—to within inches of its place of birth, there to mate. Since cahows fed only at night, their spine-chilling cries were all the more terrifying.[67]

Having no innate fear of humans, cahows were hunted to near extinction within a dozen years of *Sea Venture*'s crashing into Bermuda's reefs. After 1620 there is no mention of them.[68] Three hundred years later, a nesting pair was discovered on an outer island. Conservation efforts ensued, and by the year 2000 there were fifty-nine nesting pairs, mostly on uninhabited Nonsuch Island, where conservationists created a safe and suitable habitat. By 2019 there were over one hundred and thirty nesting pairs.

In late January 1610—five months into their exile—three men led by Stephen Hopkins went on strike. As lay reader for Minister Buck, the sanctimonious Hopkins could quote scripture with ease, a strength he drew upon to posit the claim that he was under no obligation to obey the governor or anyone else. He professed that English authority ended with the wreck of *Sea Venture* and that the castaways had a legal right to do as they pleased, and that included remaining in Bermuda. Strachey reported that Hopkins postulated arguments "civil and divine" to support his fallacious contention that he had a legal right to essentially live without laws. Here was the very thing that caused men like Gates to go to bed scared and wake up terrified—the same peril that robbed sleep from the likes of Magellan, Drake, and ship's captains everywhere. In a word—anarchy. It lurked just beneath the surface. Here we see the fragility of the armor that shields order from utter disorder, the ease with which a society can slip into the darkness of every-man-for-himself. Stephen Hopkins's defiance had the potential to foment just such a cataclysm.[69]

Confronted by Gates, Hopkins lacked the fortitude to defend his declaration of independence. The governor assembled the entire company and brought him forth—manacled and under guard. Having agreed to testify in return for amnesty, his co-conspirators confessed all. Weeping, Hopkins denied the charge of inciting mutiny. His guilt apparent, however, Gates sentenced him to die as was stipulated under martial law. Hopkins pleaded for his life, citing the indigence of his family back in England, which produced a groundswell of sympathy and support for his pardon. Gates relented again.[70]

The governor's reprieve was commendable, but Gates's compassion stemmed in large part from satisfaction with the progress of construction of the two ships. They were nearing completion. On February 11, Sarah Rolfe gave birth to a daughter, who was named Bermuda. Strachey and Newport stood witness at her christening ceremony. By the end of February, *Deliverance* was being caulked in preparation for launching and rigging. Another six weeks and she would be ready to sail. But as the prospect of departure drew near, grumblings intensified.

Amid this undercurrent of discontent, a plot was laid to attack the storehouse where weapons, tools, rigging, sails, and other items salvaged from *Sea Venture* were kept under guard. The plot was so widespread, however, that the officers soon got wind of it. Conspirators resided in both camps, Gates Bay and on Main Island in Somers's shipyard. Indeed, all of Somers's men were involved, a fact that must have given Gates pause. He doubled the watch, ordered his guards to carry weapons at all times, and kept a close eye on comings and goings between the two settlements.[71]

On March 13, Henry Paine, one of the Gates' Bay conspirators, was called for guard duty. Paine refused, then cursed and struck the captain of the guard. When threatened with punishment, he claimed Gates had no authority to punish anyone, adding that the governor could kiss his arse. In relating this, Strachey left no doubt that these were Paine's exact sentiments. Again, Gates assembled the company to hear testimony from the captain and others who had witnessed the kerfuffle, and he condemned

Paine to be hanged at once. Claiming the privileges of a gentleman, Paine was executed by firing squad just as the sun was setting.[72]

Following Paine's execution, several of Gates's men fled across the harbor to Somers's shipyard. And when Somers's crew learned of the execution, several of them headed for the woods, fearing for their lives. There they drew up a petition demanding to be left in Bermuda with two new suits of clothes and sufficient grain for a year. Taken out of salvage from *Sea Venture*, these items had been promised to anyone left behind when it was thought only one ship would be built, so there was precedent for the demand.[73]

Gates appealed to Somers for help. It is clear Somers wished to establish a permanent English presence in Bermuda so as to lay claim to the islands for the London Company. This necessitated leaving two or more men behind. Gates, on the other hand, was focused on getting to Jamestown, but by asking Somers to mediate, he was giving the admiral license to accomplish his aim without declaring it. In other words, Gates was tacitly signaling his consent for allowing a holding party to remain so long as it was not too large. He asked Somers to remind those in hiding that their passage to Jamestown and the cost of their maintenance had been paid for by investors of the London Company and that they had an obligation to fulfill their part of the bargain.[74] After so many near-mutinies, Gates must have concluded that a colony surrounded by hostile Algonquins might be more manageable than the malcontents he commanded here in Bermuda.[75]

Somers persuaded all but two to return to their duties, and Gates pardoned them. As for the two—Christopher Carter and Robert Waters—recall that Waters had been pardoned of killing Edward Samuel in August of the previous year, just after the shipwreck. Waters believed that, were he to surrender, he would be executed like Henry Paine. Carter had been among those Gates banished to a small island back in September, so he too had a black mark in the governor's ledger. These two stayed in hiding, and since this served Somers's purpose, he let them be.[76]

Deliverance was floated the last day of March and brought around to St. George's Harbor to have her masts stepped and rigging attached. By the time this work was completed, the second ship, *Patience*, was caulked and floated and ready for tackle, and she was towed from Somers's shipyard to lie alongside *Deliverance*.[77] By necessity, *Patience* had been constructed with trunnels, the word, a corruption of "treenails" for wooden pegs. Metal nails salvaged from *Sea Venture* had gone into construction of *Deliverance*. Somers took pride in the fact that *Patience* contained but one metal fastener in her entire hull.[78]

The two ships set sail on Monday, May 10, colonists and crews having been marooned on Bermuda for ten months.[79] During this time, six were buried, including the infant daughter of John and Sarah Rolfe, three dead of natural causes, the executed Henry Paine, and the man Robert Waters killed with a shovel.[80] One disappeared—the Algonquin Namontack. The other Algonquin, Machumps, emerged from the forest just in time to board *Deliverance*. Namontack's fate was never learned.[81] Eight had vanished—Henry Ravens and his crew. One child was born and survived—a son, Bermudas, born to the Eason couple. And two were left behind. This meant *Deliverance* and *Patience* carried one hundred and thirty-four of the original one hundred and fifty.

The survivors owed their lives to George Somers and Thomas Gates. Somers kept *Sea Venture* afloat through the deadly hurricane that pummeled the ship for four long days. Gates kept them safe and civilized in Bermuda for the better part of a year. Gates, in particular, deserves praise. He did his duty and his job, acted forcefully but with compassion, and he relied—as do all good managers—on the advice and consent of others. To Somers and Gates, English America owes much.

Left behind were Christopher Carter and Robert Waters hiding in the brush, watching as the two small ships were towed through a narrow channel and beyond the offshore reefs into open sea. Setting sail—the wind coming from the south—they rounded St. George's Island, heading northwest to keep clear of treacherous reefs that extend ten miles north of Bermuda. As the construction of *Patience* had relied on innovative substitute materials for tackle, caulking, and sails, Somers and Newport kept in close company in the event one or both had problems. This served to slow their progress, but on the tenth day, they sighted land. On May 21, at about noon, *Deliverance* and *Patience* crossed the bar and, taking the lead as captain of *Deliverance*, Newport made for Point Comfort, twenty miles west of Cape Henry.[82]

A cannon shot sounded as the two ships approached Fort Algernon. It was a warning, demanding the ships identify themselves. Due to shoals that extended far out into the bay, *Deliverance* and *Patience* dropped anchor, and the tender was launched carrying an unidentified petty officer to explain to those at Point Comfort that the two ships carried the survivors of *Sea Venture*, all safe including the new governor. The tender came within shouting distance of shore and in a verbal exchange with soldiers on the beach, it was learned that the other ships of the *Sea Venture* fleet had arrived safely, all but the pinnace captained by Michael Philes. The soldiers further reported that, by happenstance, council president Percy was at the fort and that he implored the governor to come ashore. The tender returned to *Deliverance* for Gates, then to *Patience* for Somers, and they went ashore, hopes high, proud of their accomplishments, confident that their return from the dead would be cause for celebration.[83]

◆ 8 ◆

The Starving Time

An astonished George Percy greeted Gates and Somers on the beach. *Sea Venture*'s crew and passengers had, of course, long since been given up for lost. But Percy's amazement at finding Gates and Somers alive and well must have been countered by their alarm at his appearance. Always fastidious in his dress, Percy probably looked emaciated and disheveled. In fact, he had only just arrived at Point Comfort the day before aboard *Discovery*, eager to learn if there was anything there to eat.

Forty men were stationed at Fort Algernon, a crude fortification at the tip of Point Comfort under the command of Captain James Davies. These men appeared in fine fettle, so well nourished they fed their table scraps to their pigs.[1] But Percy and those who came with him from Jamestown told a different story of conditions there. Of the four hundred alive in Jamestown when John Smith departed the previous October, only sixty survived. The rest had either deserted or were dead. For months, Percy and the others at Jamestown had been prisoners in their own fort, harried and besieged by Powhatan's warriors until the chief pulled his men away for spring planting.[2] It was only then Percy could safely escape to inspect conditions at Fort Algernon, or so he claimed.[3]

George Percy was a younger brother of Henry Percy, the Earl of Northumberland. He had accompanied Newport, Wingfield, and Smith with the first group of colonists, so he had now been in Jamestown three years. Passed over for a seat on the original council, Percy's aristocratic status had earned him the post of colony secretary. He considered himself superior to the anti–Smith cabal—Ratcliffe, Martin, Archer—but he also bristled at taking orders from a common soldier. Smith's gunpowder injury occurred just as his term as president expired, and as he awaited return to England, Percy was elected to replace him. As befitting his new status, and "to keep a continual and daily table for gentlemen of fashion about me," Percy had ordered new clothes by way of his noble brother: five suits lined with taffeta, a cloak, a jerkin, a doublet, several pairs of britches, a dozen pairs of shoes plus ribbons for shoestrings, a dozen pairs of worsted stockings, six pairs of garters, six of boots, one of slippers, nine of gloves, twelve shirts, plus handkerchiefs, hats, nightcaps, three knives, and a sword inlaid with gold.[4] Now, eight months later—having been a virtual prisoner for the last six—he could not disguise the fact that under his leadership Jamestown had starved to death.

On Tuesday morning, May 22, the officers gathered aboard *Deliverance*. They may have enjoyed a meal in the small cabin beneath the poop deck, joined there by Newport and perhaps Strachey and others. Strachey would soon become the colony's new secretary, so we can assume he had earned Gates's trust during their ten-month sojourn in Bermuda. During the meal, they would have heard noises indicating the anchor being raised, as the master's mate gave orders to begin their journey upriver with the incoming tide. Percy would have had questions about their shipwreck and survival on the Isle of Devils before beginning his own lamentable tale.

After the meal, they would have adjourned to the poop deck as the three ships—*Deliverance*, *Patience*, and *Discovery*—turned north into the James River. The four-mile-wide mouth of the river reflected bright midday sun. Beyond a fringe of saltmarsh cordgrass, the near shore was thick with pines, the land, flat. The far shore was a thin horizontal line of dark green forest stretching as far upriver as the eye could see. The whole of it appeared virgin—untouched and unpeopled—but Newport or Percy would have cautioned the others that the forest had eyes. Powhatan would soon know of their coming if he did not already.

Carried upriver on the flood and anchored on the ebb, the ships took two days to cover the forty miles from Point Comfort to Jamestown. Several sources indicated there was little wind.[5] We are also told that before arriving in Jamestown, Percy briefed the newcomers on what had transpired in the year since their last being informed. We have his own account published in 1624 from which to glean his version of events, presumably the same version he reported to Gates, Somers, and the others as they drifted upriver on the rising tide.[6]

To begin, Percy would have pointed to the near shore and explained that it was the territory of the Kecoughtans and their chief, Pochins, one of Powhatan's many sons. They had been friendly until recently. Then he would have pointed to the opposite bank—the land of the Warraskoyack, and their chief Tachonekintaco. He too had ceased to be a friend.

Percy began his account with the arrival of the other ships in the *Sea Venture* fleet. They had limped into the bay the previous summer having been battered by the same hurricane that wrecked the flagship on the reefs of Bermuda. At that time—August 1609—John Smith was still president of the council and had not yet suffered his gunpowder injury.

Four of the ships had arrived on August 11—*Blessing* captained by

8. The Starving Time

Gabriel Archer, *Falcon*, John Martin commanding, *Unity*, and *Lion*. A week later the dismasted *Diamond* arrived under the command of John Ratcliffe, and with it *Swallow*, also without a mainmast. Both ships had carried plague and reported thirty-two buried at sea on the voyage out.[7] The captain of *Swallow* had been taken ill before the hurricane struck, and the ship was brought in by first mate, Matthew Somers, George Somers's nephew, who had performed admirably in his first command. Weeks later the dismasted ketch *Virginia* arrived under Captain Davies with sixteen aboard. It was then that *Sea Venture* and the pinnace it had been towing were given up for lost.

Most of the ships were leaking, and all had damage to rigging and sails. They had to be careened and recaulked. Passengers arrived sick and in shock, many of these women and children. Supplies had been damaged or spoiled, especially stocks of food judged sufficient to feed the colony for a year. Most of these were rotten, having marinated for weeks in seawater.

Rather than providing relief for the eighty colonists under Smith's command, the influx of nearly four hundred new mouths to feed put an unmanageable strain on Jamestown. The colony had not planted crops sufficient to feed so many, and within a few days, new colonists picked clean the corn and wheat planted, leaving no crop at all.[8] There were too many mouths to feed, too little housing, and—with the return of Ratcliffe, Martin, and Archer—too much dissension.[9] It was no wonder Smith complained to London that the colony would have been better left to fend for itself.

With the arrival of the bedraggled remains of the *Sea Venture* fleet, Smith learned that the lost flagship carried Virginia's new interim governor along with the names of those appointed to advise him—all under seal. Furthermore, he learned that the new charter stipulated that henceforth Jamestown was to be ruled by a "Captain General and Governor for Life" rather than a president and council. With Gates presumed dead and Smith's term about to expire, the question of headship was in limbo. Ratcliffe, Martin, and Archer connived to promote the candidacy of twenty-three-year-old Francis West to replace Smith.[10] West was the younger brother of the new governor, Thomas West, Lord De La Warr, a powerful baron. Otherwise engaged at the time, De La Warr had been unable to sail with the *Sea Venture* fleet, so the London Company had appointed Gates interim governor until such time as it pleased De La Warr to go himself.

Being the baron's younger brother, Francis West was viewed by the anti–Smith party as a candidate London would approve given the unforeseen circumstances and the directors' predilection for appointing members of the aristocracy to leadership positions without regard to their qualifications. Doubtless, the Smith-hating triumvirate considered the younger West a figurehead, a malleable placeholder until his brother arrived. Smith countered West's nomination by appealing to his own base of support, the eighty veterans who had been in Jamestown before the newcomers arrived. For a short time, Smith and West vied for preeminence, but the organizational structure and daily routines earlier established by Smith remained in place.[11] And as Smith's knowledge of the Algonquins was essential for feeding the colony, he emerged the more powerful. Of course, Percy put his own slant on this. He did not like Smith, but neither was he cozy with the Ratcliffe-Martin-Archer coalition.

In early September 1609—just as *Sea Venture* survivors marooned on Bermuda were discovering the island's remarkable abundance—Smith divided the Jamestown colony to better their chances of avoiding starvation. There was insufficient food for the more than five hundred people to survive the winter. He sent Francis West upriver to the falls of the James River with one hundred and forty colonists and provisions for six months. Then he ordered Percy and John Martin downriver with sixty more into Nansemond tribal territory.[12]

On or about September 6, Smith traveled upriver to the falls to inspect West's progress. West was absent at the time, his whereabouts unknown. Smith saw that the site selected by West for his fortification was in the James River floodplain, so he arranged with Parahunt—weroance of the Powhatan tribe in whose territory West's settlement was to be located—for the purchase of a Powhatan village and its cropland.[13] Smith concluded the arrangements, moved West's encampment, and left before West got back. It was on Smith's return downriver to Jamestown that he suffered his gunpowder accident-cum-assassination attempt.

He convalesced at Jamestown for a month, incapacitated and in agony much of the time. Before returning to England, however, the ship that was to carry him was delayed long enough for Ratcliffe and Archer to draw up charges against him.[14] This took time, as there were many witnesses to depose. Among the charges were several petty grievances made by disgruntled malcontents—some reportedly bribed with travel passes—a third-hand accusation of double-dealing with Powhatan, and the aforementioned allegation that Smith was plotting to marry Pocahontas and set himself up as king.[15]

During this time Martin sent messengers to Weyhohomo, weroance of the Nansemond tribe, offering to buy a small village on an island near the mouth of the Nansemond River. In exchange, he offered iron hatchets and the usual trinkets, including copper utensils, glass and amber beads, bracelets, copper hawks' bells, sewing needles, combs, and mirrors. The messengers never returned, and treachery was suspected, so Martin sent in soldiers who chased the island's residents from their village, destroyed their canoes, looted and burned their dwellings, ravaged a temple, and vandalized the remains of their dead chiefs. Martin took two prisoners, one reputed to be the chief's own son. One was killed, the other escaped, we know not which.[16]

Elected president to replace Smith, George Percy's first act was to order Ratcliffe to construct a fortification at Point Comfort to be called Fort Algernon in honor of Percy's nephew, heir to the earldom of his brother. He envisioned this fort guarding the north entrance to the James River and Martin's Nansemond garrison guarding the south.[17] When Martin unexpectedly resurfaced in Jamestown, claiming urgent business, Percy suspected Martin's dereliction of duty stemmed from his fear of Nansemond retaliation.[18] In Martin's absence, several of his men deserted, fled across the bay, and were captured and killed by the Kecoughtans. When their bodies were later found, their mouths had been stuffed with bread, a grisly message to the English that they would starve to death before getting any more Algonquin corn.[19] The rest of Martin's men then returned to Jamestown, and the Nansemond garrison ceased to exist. Then West and his detachment sent to the falls returned as well. The divide-to-survive strategy had failed. After this Percy put the colony on short rations, but it was clear there was insufficient food to last the winter. Powhatan had forbidden trade with the English, leaving Percy no option but to bargain with the supreme weroance himself.[20]

A detailed inventory of provisions and livestock was sent to England on the ship carrying the injured Smith that sailed on October 1. It noted seven horses, five to six hundred pigs and as many chickens, plus numerous sheep and goats. In addition, there was food in the storehouse to last five hundred people ten weeks. The inventory further stipulated twenty-four cannon, three hundred muskets, ample shot and powder, a large supply of swords, pikes, hatchets, knives, and tools.[21] But what London was not told was that relations with the Algonquins had deteriorated. They were still trading but only in secret—one-on-one—and that mostly with the mariners who refused to be ruled by the president. They stole arms or tools from the ship or the storehouse, waited for cover of darkness, then traded for food, pearls, and, most likely, sex. Day by day, the Powhatans became better armed while the English stockpile of weapons diminished in like proportion. Percy could not stop it, and it was rampant. After all, people were starving.

A short time later and quite out of the blue, an offer came from Powhatan himself inviting the English to bring trade goods to Orapaks. In return, the English ships would be freighted with corn. It may be no coincidence that the invitation came as rumors spread among the Algonquins that John Smith was dead. Orapaks was a wilderness village far up the Pamunkey River, almost inaccessible by boat. No one had attached great significance to Powhatan's move from Werowocomoco to Orapaks earlier in the year, but it should have been seen as a warning of possible trouble.

Powhatan's offer reached Percy in late November or early December 1609, just when things were starting to look especially bleak. Livestock were being slaughtered at an unsustainable rate. In stark contrast, *Sea Venture* survivors marooned on Bermuda at this precise time were feasting on spit-roasted cahows that were flocking to the island to nest. Percy ordered Ratcliffe to lead the trading party to Orapaks, so Captain Davies was sent to replace him as commander of Fort Algernon. Percy had little faith in Martin, and Archer was best suited to administrative tasks. Ratcliffe had been a soldier, serving in the Low Countries as had Percy. He was the obvious choice.

Jamestown had three ships, thirty-eight-foot *Discovery* being the largest. She had helped bring the first colonists to Virginia in 1607. In addition, there were two pinnaces, *Virginia* and *Swallow*. They had come out with the *Sea Venture* fleet. There was also the barge and one or two longboats, all with shallow drafts and oarlocks for rowing and used primarily for fishing. The barge had been constructed at Jamestown early on using materials brought out from England and had been used by Smith to explore Chesapeake Bay. Ratcliffe probably sailed to Orapaks in *Discovery* towing one of the longboats and followed by the barge. The vessels carried twenty-five to fifty men—accounts differ—with hopes of filling all boats with corn.[22]

The trading party descended the James, rounded Point Comfort and Virginia's Lower Peninsula, then headed up the Pamunkey River, sailing when winds were favorable or anchored when opposed by the tide. It was nearly one hundred miles by water from Jamestown to the point where the Pamunkey forks at today's West Point, Virginia. There they left *Discovery* at anchor due to its draft being too deep to proceed. Except for a skeleton crew, *Discovery's* men were transferred to the barge and the longboat. In these two vessels, Ratcliffe's task force paddled another thirty miles of meandering river into deep wilderness, though the distance as the crow flies was less than twenty miles. Rowing through terrains of wetland and scrub pine, around repeated switchbacks, they finally approached the path to Orapaks, which was located half a mile inland from the river.[23] There they dropped anchor, the barge being unable to reach shore due to shallows. Using the longboat, Ratcliffe sent emissaries carrying gifts for Powhatan, and in return, Powhatan sent bread and venison delivered by a delegation led by two of his children. Pocahontas was not one of them, but the gesture was viewed as disarming and friendly. Ratcliffe entertained the two then returned them to shore.[24]

8. The Starving Time

Powhatan invited Ratcliffe and his trading party ashore for the night with plans for conducting their business the following day. Often implicit in such invitations was a sumptuous feast and a comely bed companion to warm the night, so those appointed to attend Ratcliffe would have been eager to accept. He and some of his men went ashore, leaving sufficient crew to guard the boats.

The next morning, they were all led to Powhatan's storehouse, and the trading commenced. It soon became apparent, however, that Powhatan was trying to inveigle the English with clever tactics to reduce the amount of corn proffered in exchange. The English expressed irritation at these devious machinations, and friction intensified. With little notice, Powhatan, with his wives and others, vanished in unceremonious fashion. Alarmed by this, the English hurriedly began carrying their baskets of corn through the woods back to the longboat, but warriors attacked them, killing all save Ratcliffe and two who escaped.[25]

As the Bermuda officers listened in horror, Percy described how Ratcliffe had been stripped naked and tied to a tree. A fire was lit, and using muscle shells, Algonquin women began scraping his flesh from his bones and throwing the detritus into the fire. He died of this mutilation or, failing that, of being burned alive.[26] The longboat and barge escaped, and sixteen men made it back to Jamestown alive—those left onboard, plus one of the two who had escaped by swimming the river and finding his way back through the woods. The attack demonstrated the degree to which relations had deteriorated, and the loss left the colony disheartened.

A desperate Percy then ordered Francis West to take *Swallow* north to the Potomac River to attempt trade with the Patawomeck Tribe.[27] Smith had enjoyed friendly relations with the Patawomecks in the summer of 1608 on his exploration of the bay. It was a large tribe, with 160 to 250 warriors, viewed by the English as being just beyond the ambit of Powhatan's domination.[28] They had been eager traders in Smith's day, and it was hoped they might be bold enough to defy Powhatan's prohibition on trade with the English. West took thirty-six men in a last-ditch effort to secure enough food to last until resupply ships arrived.[29]

What Percy knew about West's venture he had learned from Captain Davies when first arriving at Point Comfort just before the Bermuda ships appeared. West had succeeded in loading *Swallow* with corn, and on his return to Jamestown, Davies spotted the ship approaching Fort Algernon and went out to urge West to hurry, advising him that the colonists were starving. West confessed to Davies that he had been forced to resort to strong measures, that in addition to other extremes, he had put two Patawomeck captives to death by cutting off their heads.

Davies then returned to Fort Algernon, but rather than watch *Swallow* round Point Comfort and turn up into the James River, he watched the ship sail east toward Cape Henry, the Atlantic, and, presumably, England. Percy's outrage at Francis West's betrayal must have been apparent as he related the story to Gates, Somers, and Newport aboard *Discovery*. Percy wanted to believe it had been mutiny, that a brother of Lord De La Warr—a member of the peerage and Jamestown's newly appointed governor—would never forsake his fellow countrymen at a time of dire need.[30]

Percy's telling of events to Gates, Somers, and the others would have been interrupted at dusk when the tide turned. By then *Deliverance* was abreast a marshy spit of land called Mulberry Island. Reaching Jamestown would take another twenty-four hours. Trailing in her wake were *Patience* and *Discovery*, the ketch Percy had taken to Point Comfort two days earlier. Here, though the river widens, the channel narrows, and Newport would have been concerned about running aground. The ships dropped anchor in the middle of the river in twenty feet of water, and the master's mate would have ordered the watch to keep a close eye out for Powhatan canoes.

A dark headland would have been visible three miles up ahead at a bend in the river. Percy would have pointed it out—Hog Island, so named because Smith had released three pigs on the island to run free, forage, and breed in the same way hogs had multiplied in Bermuda.[31] The Algonquins hunted there, but the island was large enough for the hogs to thrive, and soon there were shoats aplenty. But the Warraskoyacks had killed them all, no doubt following Powhatan's orders.[32] Like Powhatan's removal to Orapaks, it was another missed signal of an unspoken declaration of war.

On a moonless night, even with the Milky Way visible, each shore would have been pitch-black. One can imagine some spectacle—perhaps a bonfire—a distant, menacing orange glow, shooting off sparks and silhouetting flickers of kinetic nakedness. The Algonquins often taunted their enemies, and their howling and whooping would have carried across the water. Was it a war dance intended to intimidate the newcomers, a portent of things to come? To the uninitiate, such a specter would have been spine-chilling.

What were the *Sea Venture* officers thinking that sleepless night? Gates would have felt guilt and betrayal, believing his new command a travesty, made even worse by its being of his own making. He should have sailed on *Diamond*, not *Sea Venture*. What fools they had all been—he, Somers, Wingfield, Gosnold, Hakluyt—supposing an undertaking such as this could be easily accomplished. Had they learned nothing from Raleigh's Lost Colony? As for Newport, he might have recalled all the riffraff he had transported to Jamestown in his years with the company—London's unwanted human refuse—and wondered how they could have thought the treachery Percy described would not happen. Of course, it would. It was bound to happen.

Perhaps Somers's thought of Bermuda—how the plenty there could feed the many here. He could get there and back in under a month with a ship full of protein-rich food, a feat that could win Bermuda for England and advance his aspirations. Or perhaps he was thinking the entire colony should be transported to Bermuda, though Gates would have opposed him in this. As for Strachey, he was probably recalling the hurly-burly of London streets, the cozy inglenook of the Mermaid Tavern, and the laughter and wit of his thespian friends. He was surely homesick.

The tide would have turned again in the wee hours of Wednesday morning, May 23. In anticipation, crew would have been rousted to raise the anchor. To lead the way in the darkness, a tender was launched and attached by towline to the bow of *Deliverance*. In the tender were two oarsmen, the boatswain with a lantern, and the bosun's mate tossing the plumbline to sound the depths ahead and keep the ships centered in the channel. As others slept, the ship glided silently upriver pushed by the rising tide. Just at sunrise, she made a ninety-degree turn to port at Hog Island Point, and the tender was brought around to be towed aft as its occupants climbed back aboard. Now two miles ahead, the whole of the forested eastern end of Jamestown Island was in plain sight, though the settlement itself remained hidden around yet another ninety-degree bend in the river.

Sunrise would have brought everyone on deck. No doubt Percy pointed to the right bank and explained to the officers gathered on the poop that it was a frontier separating the Kiskiacks from the Paspaheghs, and the left bank was another frontier dividing the Warraskoyack tribe from the Quiyoughcohannocks.[33] The newcomers were doubtless mystified by so many unpronounceable names. Strachey must have wondered how he could possibly reconstruct them using common English orthography. And each tribe had a chief with a name equally inscrutable. Strachey ended up creating a glossary of Algonquin names and words, useful to this day.

As they covered the final leg to Jamestown under sail, Percy told the rest of his pitiable story. Powhatan, of course, had been incensed over the decapitation of two Patawomecks by Francis West. With *Swallow* gone and the *Virginia* moored at Point Comfort, the colonists' only means of escape was *Discovery*, which was too small to accommodate everyone and too vulnerable to enemy attack. Until Gates and Somers arrived, Jamestown colonists had been as marooned in their fort as the *Sea Venture* survivors had been on Bermuda. But at Jamestown there was no food, and hunting, foraging the forest, and fishing the waters were too dangerous. The

Algonquins could have attacked, but there was no need. Powhatan realized this. He sent his spies to trade and heap scorn on the doomed colonists. Any Englishman who strayed beyond the fort was to be killed, but risking Algonquin lives in a full-scale attack was unnecessary. Time would finish off the English.

Percy was forced to resort to tyrannical measures. After West's shameful desertion, he enacted a new law declaring desertion and stealing to be punishable by death. When, a few days later, someone was caught pilfering from the storehouse, Percy had him hanged forthwith. He insisted that discipline was crucial, that the president must be obeyed, and that their very lives depended on it. Other offenses were punished with equal ruthlessness. Perhaps Percy felt he had no choice, but one expects his quotidian banquets for "gentlemen of fashion" continued, perhaps catered by way of his own private larder.

One morning, a deranged and starving colonist emerged from his dwelling and ran into the marketplace blaspheming God for allowing such misery. In his rage, he ran out of the fort and into the woods, where Algonquin arrows made short work of him. He was found days later, his body consumed by animals.[34] After the livestock had all been slaughtered, hungry colonists killed their dogs and cats, and after that, mice, rats, and snakes.[35] By the first of March there was nothing left to trade, and by the first of April there was nothing left to eat. Then the unspeakable happened. The corpse of an Algonquin buried in Jamestown was exhumed and devoured.[36] Word of this abomination spread, tempting others to acts of similar degradation. To some, the dead became the stay and staff of life.[37]

A man named Collins murdered his pregnant wife then butchered her. He threw the fetus in the river, fed on his wife's body, then salted and hid the remains to be eaten later.[38] The crime was discovered. It was Percy's responsibility to prevent this practice. Collins denied the deed, claiming his wife had died of natural causes and that he had been driven by hunger to eat her. Percy had him hung up by his thumbs until he confessed. He was then burned to death.[39]

Many gave up and waited for death as if life was no more precious than a worn-out pair of boots. Archer died. No one noticed. Bodies were dragged into the marketplace every morning to be buried—two or three each day, though perhaps not for long. Some who seemed sturdy enough at dusk were found dead the next morning. No one had the strength to work. It was all Percy could do to muster enough able bodies for a night watch. Being winter, there was less work to do, but keeping warm was a dangerous challenge. Neglect and freezing weather took its toll. The palisades crumbled from disrepair and were carried off for firewood. More thieves were caught and executed by ever more barbaric means—mutilation, burning at the stake. Deserters were caught and executed too, though many got away, taking their chances with the Algonquins. None were ever seen again.⁴⁰

With this, George Percy concluded his tale of woe as *Deliverance, Patience,* and *Discovery* rounded Jamestown Island's southern cape. The Bermuda survivors would have strained to see the fort in the distance, no doubt dreading what they were about to witness.

Deliverance carried a new colonist—William Pierce—who had come out on *Sea Venture* while his wife and daughter had sailed on *Blessing*. How they came to be separated is not known, but rumors of deaths in Jamestown would have spread throughout the ship, and Pierce would have been eager to learn if his wife and daughter were still alive. Would Percy have known? Perhaps. Either way, the *Sea Venture* officers would have pondered a chilling suspicion that despite his claims, George Percy had sailed to Fort Algernon with no intention of returning to Jamestown.⁴¹

Once *Deliverance* rounded Lower Point—the marshy southern cape of Jamestown Island—the blockhouse at the far corner of the triangular fort would have come into view. Here the channel widens and deepens, hugging the south bank of the island so that with any breeze at all, the ships could have sailed the last two miles almost within spitting distance of shore. The silence was unnatural, and no smoke was seen rising above the treetops from forge or cookfire. One can imagine buzzards circling overhead. As the ships neared the palisade, all appeared peaceful. No one stirred. No sentries guarded the fortification, in fact, the gates of the fort were open, one of them hanging askew as if off one hinge. This we know from Strachey's firsthand account. Weeds were thick and vines creeped up the pales. It appeared a ruin—a derelict, asleep in warm noonday sun.⁴²

After anchors were set, the tender was brought around for the officers, oarsmen, and a squad of soldiers. They crowded into the small boat and rowed to the wharf. No one came out to greet them. It was possible, of course, that since Percy and his party sailed away a few days earlier, Algonquins had overrun the fort and killed those who remained. There was never a mention of Percy having left someone in charge to organize and lead a defense. Natives could have been lying in wait at that very moment, so the shore party advanced with caution, fuses lit, muskets at the ready. They entered the fort, made their way to the church—it too suffering neglect—and Gates ordered a guard to ring the bell.

As the final toll died away, a long figure emerged in the dark doorway of a nearby building. "We are starved," he cried. "We are starved!"⁴³

Soon others emerged. The most able among them made their way to the church, heartened by the sight of ships. Weakened stragglers gathered in the churchyard as more officials and passengers came ashore. William Pierce was among them, searching the gaunt faces for his wife and daughter. They were both alive. This and other reunions—including that of George Somers and his nephew Matthew—were reasons for thanksgiving. Someone must have begun preparations for a meal for the starving, but Gates insisted the minister, Mister Buck, first lead them in prayer. What he said was not recorded. They could be thankful for their lives but little else.

Gates and Somers would have already explained to Percy that *Deliverance* and *Patience* carried little food. Not only had they limited space for provisions, they had also assumed Jamestown would have food to spare. After hearing Percy's shocking account, however, Gates, Somers, and Newport would have discussed options, and they must have viewed the situation as all but hopeless. The Algonquins would be no help, not just because of prevailing hostilities, but also because this was the time of year when they had little or nothing to spare. And even if they had the inclination to trade, the English had nothing to offer in exchange.[44]

Once the starving and critically ill were attended to, Gates assembled the entire company. Those who had suffered through the starving time must have had mixed feelings. This man about to address them—whose coming was saving their lives—was an official of the now hated London Company that had been the cause of all their suffering. The others—the Bermuda survivors—would have likewise been angry and hostile. Gates had forced them to leave Bermuda, many against their will, only to be transported to an alien, hostile wilderness with nothing to eat. They saw their future in the emaciated faces and bodies of the forlorn and helpless creatures before them, so near death that had *Deliverance* and *Patience* arrived a week later, none would have been found alive. In short, the entire company would have been furious—at Gates, at Thomas Smythe, at the London Company for luring them with golden promises into a hellscape of misery, starvation, and death.[45] To them, it all seemed a fraud and a scam, and Gates must have sensed that were he to propose anything other than a return to England, he would unleash a mutinous mob.[46]

In solemn ceremony, Gates presented the official document that authorized the transfer of authority. Percy played his part, reading the document aloud, handing over the seal and official records, and pledging allegiance to the new interim governor. Gates then promised that the victuals carried by the two ships from Bermuda would be shared equally by all. He then vowed to use the resources brought from Bermuda and available at Point Comfort to fish the waters and hunt the forests in order to feed all two hundred surviving colonists. In addition, he vowed to use force if necessary to coerce the Powhatans into sharing what they had while acknowledging that this was their seed time and that their stores from the previous harvest would have been depleted.

These assurances would have appeased no one. Perhaps Gates was reading their faces as he spoke, testing the limits of his ability to maintain authority. If so, he realized he would have to capitulate, that there would be no soldiering on until the next supply arrived. These people were at the end of their tether. He would have to give them what they wanted or risk losing control. This he did, adding that if these measures failed, he would see to their transport and repatriation to England.[47]

Strachey's narrative—the only eyewitness account—maintained that Gates's assurance elicited shouts of joy. This rings of hyperbole. More likely, they were sighs of relief. The same cannot be said for the Powhatans who were doubtless nearby—spying from the tall grass or behind trees at the edge of the forest. Their response would come soon enough. Gates then read the names of those appointed to the council, now limited to an advisory capacity. The council no longer had a vote, only a voice. Named were Somers, John Smith, John Ratcliffe, Matthew Scrivener, Richard Waldo, Peter Winne, Gabriel Archer, John Martin, and two new adventurers, Messrs. Wood and Fleetwood. Smith had returned to England, Ratcliffe had been killed, Scrivener and Waldo drowned in a boating accident the year prior, Winne was dead of unknown causes, and Archer died during the starving time.[48] Of the nine, only Somers, Martin, and the two new adventurers were present for their swearing in, but doubtless Gates intended to also rely on Newport, Percy, Strachey, and others with experience. Why Newport—a past member of the council—was now excluded is not known but must be noted.

There followed a period of assessment. Rules were established and posted in the church. The details are not known but were laid out in twenty-one articles. Gates had no sympathy for the state of things and made no secret of his displeasure, so we can assume his twenty-one articles demanded strict compliance to a rigid daily schedule and to strictures of behavior and that transgressions would meet with harsh punishment. Discipline was his stick, return to England, his carrot. The original form of president-and-council government came in for sharp rebuke, it being considered too weak to govern "so headie a multitude," as Strachey characterized it. By all accounts, with the exception of gentlemen, most of those recruited for Virginia came not from sturdy yeoman stock like John Rolfe—he was the exception—but from London's lowlife and criminal netherworld.[49] We can assume that by "headie" Strachey meant willful and defiant. Some of the gentlemen proved intractable and many among the common folk were depraved, irreligious, and perverse. All required a strong disciplinarian, and Gates was such a man. In the face of what he perceived as "sloth, riot, and vanity," he would not be so forgiving as he had been in Bermuda.[50]

Five days after their arrival, two colonists who had survived the hurricane and ten months in Bermuda were killed by Algonquins. With their deaths came a message from Powhatan demanding that the English keep to the fort and cease all trade with the Algonquins. He threatened to kill any Englishman leaving the fort and to attack any boat attempting to fish the river. Despite this, Powhatan's warriors continued coming to the fort on the pretense of trading but with demands so unreasonable, it was clear they were spies. Gates saw through this duplicity and tried to stop it, but he could not control the sailors. Under cover of darkness, they would have made a pact with the devil for a haunch of venison, a few beaver skins, or a nubile Algonquin maiden.[51]

For a week, the officers debated the colony's future, weighing every conceivable option. Gates certainly considered attacking the Kecoughtans, the small tribe that occupied the Lower Peninsula between Jamestown and Point Comfort. He must have wanted revenge for the outrage they had committed by stuffing the mouths of their English victims with bread. The barbarity of the deed was still fresh in everyone's minds. Gates had helped author the company's amiable Algonquin policy, but as a soldier, he would have decried the desecration of dead English soldiers as a *casus belli*.

Examining the pros and cons of such an attack proves the hopelessness of their situation. On learning of such a plan, would colonists agree to it, their hearts already set on returning to England? And how many trustworthy soldiers could Gates hope to muster? How much shot and powder did they have? As noted, the storehouse was empty. And if they did succeed in capturing the Kecoughtans' stores of food, would it feed all two hundred colonists until the next supply arrived? The entire Kecoughtan tribe did not exceed one hundred people. And if an attack were to succeed, could the colony withstand a Powhatan counterattack? Any other time of the year, the benefit might have outweighed the cost.

Fishing the river and the bay was equally fruitless. From April to June, anadromous Atlantic sturgeon migrate from the ocean to spawn in fresh water. These fish weigh as much as one hundred pounds. Despite Powhatan's warning, Gates sent boats as far as Cape Henry, but they caught no sturgeon. Indeed, their catch was insufficient to even feed the fishermen. Rumor had it Powhatan had chased the deer from the forests. It seemed he also banished the sturgeon from the bay.[52]

To abandon the colony was to bankrupt the London Company. Their investments would be worthless, and they would have nothing to show for years of work and hundreds of lives lost. The failure would reflect on England and King James, a national disgrace that would stain the glory of the defeat the Spanish Armada. The return of the entire colony to England on the heels of the defection of Francis West and his crew of thirty-six aboard *Swallow* would finish forever the London Company's ability to

8. The Starving Time

recruit. And even if a resupply fleet was in transit at that very instant, they would find Jamestown reclaimed by the Algonquins and be faced with having to fight their way ashore against a determined foe. Gates knew, of course, that he would bear the brunt of the blame for Jamestown's failure. More than anyone, his would be the name associated with this disaster, and that prospect must have been deeply disturbing.

A week after the arrival of the Bermuda survivors, an inventory reported sixteen days' supply of food remaining.[53] Gates could delay no longer. He announced that the entire company would sail on the four small ships—the three riding anchors off Jamestown plus the pinnace *Virginia*, at anchor off Point Comfort. A long boat had been sent to alert those stationed at Fort Algernon. The plan was to sail to Newfoundland, there to rendezvous with the English fishing fleet. The company could then be dispersed for better feeding, comfort, and transport home. A week was spent stripping the settlement of everything of value that might be sold in England to help defray London Company debts. There was no space for carrying cannon, however, so they were buried.[54]

On June 7, 1610, the drummer beat a retreat, and Jamestown's two hundred occupants began boarding. There was strong sentiment to torch everything standing—palisades, houses, blockhouse, storehouse. It arose from those determined to prevent any possibility of return, but Gates would not have it, and he kept armed guards ashore until all were aboard their assigned ships. Gates was the last to leave. At noon, with a salute of muskets, anchors were raised, and the fleet drifted downstream with the tide. That evening, with the turn of the tide, they anchored off Hog Island for the night. With the falling tide the next morning, they dropped down as far as Mulberry Island, setting an anchor again there late morning to wait out the next flood.[55]

Jamestown had survived just over a thousand days. Almost eight hundred colonists had been transported there, but the living now numbered little more than two hundred. Three in four perished or disappeared. One could say it had been a tragedy of errors, Shakespearean in scope.[56] Untold numbers of Algonquins had also been killed, but with the English vanquished, the land was theirs once again. Powhatan had outfoxed the prophecy. At this very moment, the triumphal news was wending its way to Orapaks. Doubtless, bonfires were lit, and celebratory dancing and chanting erupted as word spread. All would have welcomed the joyous news with one possible exception—Pocahontas. One cannot help but wonder what was in her mind.

◆ 9 ◆

Redemption

Most of the ships of the *Sea Venture* fleet had returned to England the previous fall, arriving late November 1609. They included *Blessing*, *Diamond*, *Falcon*, *Lion* and *Unity*, and they carried the sad news of the hurricane and the loss of *Sea Venture* and its admiral, captain, and Jamestown's interim governor.

With this, investors who had pledged to purchase London Company shares began backing out. The colony appeared to be in decay, much like Raleigh's Roanoke Island colony, and the company's value collapsed. Recruiting dried up even as Lord De La Warr began chartering ships for what would be the pinnacle of his career—governing the colony of Virginia. Adding insult to injury, sometime during that same winter, Francis West and his fellow deserters arrived aboard *Swallow*. The date is not recorded, presumably because neither West, nor his brother, nor London Company officials wished to advertise a situation so dire that some would risk the gallows to escape Jamestown.

Francis West's return to England must have been a supreme humiliation to his family, the baron most especially. And officials of the London Company must have been incensed by his treachery. Did he claim to have been forced by a mutinous crew? Rumor had it he and his crew agreed to a pact, and there is no record of criminal charges being levied or of mutineers being hanged. We are not told, but one suspects that Lord De La Warr castigated his younger brother and demanded he return to Virginia to redeem his reputation and their family's prestige.

Thomas Smythe now faced a dilemma. To bring everyone home would doom the company and cost a fortune. Not only would he lose his investment, his reputation as London's eminent man of business would be ruined. It was apparent, however, that to continue meant raising more money and enticing more people to emigrate, neither of which could be achieved if Algonquins kept killing Englishmen. He must have recognized, therefore, that the company's goal of forging good relations with the indigenous Amerindians must be compromised. Considering this, Smythe

9. Redemption 167

gave in to a more belligerent policy now that financial success depended on solving the Algonquin problem. No proof exists, but he and De La Warr must have agreed to a more forceful policy prior to the baron's departure in the spring. De La Warr's future actions are proof enough.

For damage control, Smythe needed a publicist, and he found one in the pulpit. The Rev. William Crashaw was a Cambridge-educated cleric who fulminated against Catholics and Puritans alike and championed the cause of English imperialism in the New World.[1] With the latest turn of events, he downplayed his earlier support for converting the Algonquins to Christianity in favor of admonishing the English for abandoning their fellow countrymen by failing to honor their pledges. He urged them not only to invest more but to volunteer to go. It was a matter of national honor.[2] Support for the Jamestown Colony was every Englishman's duty, and to abandon a fellow countryman to suffer and die in the New World was to be guilty of his death. Crashaw imputed the problems in Jamestown to the "vulgar and viler sort."[3] To contend with this, a stronger hand was needed, and that hand belonged to Thomas West, Lord De La Warr.

Despite Crashaw's impassioned sermons, recruitment efforts faced strong headwinds. One suspects the truth of conditions in Jamestown had become common knowledge. The company sought five to six hundred new colonists to embark with De La Warr but got commitments from only one hundred and fifty.[4] They sailed with the baron and his bodyguard of fifty liveried halberdiers on April 1, 1610.[5] Among De La Warr's objectives was the capture of an American flying squirrel for King James. As Robert Cecil, the king's principal secretary, reminded the baron, the king was greatly entertained by such exotic toys.[6] If at this time, the English monarch had any other interests or concerns regarding Virginia, they were not reported. Only the squirrel.[7]

On the opposite side of the Atlantic, on the morning of June 8, 1610—the day after Jamestown was abandoned—three ships, *Deliverance*, *Patience*, and *Discovery*, were anchored single file off Mulberry Island waiting for the tide to turn. By nightfall that same day, they expected to be well out to sea, headed north, bound for Newfoundland.[8] At the southernmost point of Mulberry Island, the James River is nearly four miles wide and shallow except in the narrow mid-river channel. Washed upriver by the rising tide, the ships would have been pointed downriver toward its mouth, ten miles distant.

Imagine standing that late spring morning in the bow of *Deliverance*, the lead ship, peering downriver. The day would have been warm and still, the scene, primeval. Suddenly, a bright flash draws your attention. At a point on the horizon—in the midst of that distant indistinct seam where river meets sky—something had reflected sunlight. Something metal.

Something moving. Others would have noticed and gathered in the narrow peak of the bow or climbed the ratlines for a better view. Someone would have gone for one of the officers. It appeared that a small craft was in the offing, moving toward *Deliverance*, but as yet too far distant to identify. It could have been someone from Point Comfort, coming to deliver a message. It could have been Algonquins. By then all tribes in Tsenacommacah possessed metal objects, but the Powhatans attacked by stealth, and not in broad daylight unless the odds were in their favor. It could have been a party of Kecoughtans or Nansemonds wishing to trade, but that seemed unlikely given recent events. It could have been Spanish spies. Upon seeing English ships, however, they would have turned tail and retreated to their mother ship to prepare for battle. But this object kept coming closer.

In time the observers would have discerned a longboat with several aboard, a craft clearly superior to any the English possessed in Jamestown or Point Comfort. It carried a single lugsail and moved swiftly with the tide. If English—and that seemed certain now—it would mean the resupply had arrived. When the longboat was within hailing distance, an officer stood and holding the boom for balance shouted over the water for the captain. Newport moved to the rail, leaned forward, and identified himself and the ship, *Deliverance*, lately of Jamestown, with Governor Sir Thomas Gates aboard.

There must have been a moment's hesitation as the longboat's captain, Edward Brewster, heard proof of the miracle reported at Point Comfort—that Somers, Gates, and Newport were alive. They had not drowned as all believed. The longboat came alongside *Deliverance*, and Brewster climbed aboard. If he did not know Christopher Newport on sight, the old sea dog's hook hand would have given him away. Brewster saluted and reported that he had come with a letter for the president of Jamestown from his eminence, Captain General and Governor for Life Lord De La Warr. Gates would have stepped forward to receive the letter, identifying himself for the awed Captain Brewster.[9]

Gates's orders were to return to Jamestown at once. De La Warr had learned from Captain Davies at Point Comfort of Gates's intentions, and Brewster had been sent in advance to inform him that the resupply fleet carried provisions for a year for those at Jamestown plus the one hundred and fifty newly arriving colonists. For Gates, this news was nothing less than redemption. His reputation was saved, and he must have been elated. The same could not be said, however, for those in his charge.[10] They had suffered enough hardship and privation. They had wanted to burn Jamestown to the ground. One wonders what was in Newport's mind. He must have been growing weary of the mystifying vicissitudes of his job. After all, he was not a young man. At any rate, he ordered the anchor raised and

9. Redemption 169

signaled to *Patience* and *Discovery* to follow his lead back to Jamestown. With a favorable wind, they were there shortly after sunset to get settled and await the arrival of their new governor.

Powhatan had made a terrible blunder. He knew the English were starving and weak. He had months to finish them off. It could have been easily done, and why he did not is a mystery. He must have known more ships would come, but by destroying the English foothold before those ships arrived, he might have prevented them from planting another colony in his midst. From this day forward, his more combative brother, Opechancanough, began a gradual ascent to power.

Lord De La Warr landed in Jamestown two days later. The colonists were assembled for his disembarkation, and with pomp better suited for another continent, the thirty-three-year-old baron came ashore. He was flanked by an honor guard of fifty soldiers in red uniforms and followed by his retinue of richly clad advisers and personal retainers—including his now disgraced brother Francis and his nephew William—all to the sound of bugle and drumroll. Once ashore, the new governor knelt and prayed in silence as everyone watched. Then, as befits all peaceful transfers of power, official parchments were trotted out and read aloud, followed by the requisite religious service conducted by the dutiful Mr. Buck. Following Buck's sermon, De La Warr delivered one of the most heartless, hypocritical, and ill-timed invectives in the history of humankind. Instead of expressing admiration and sympathy for the hardships his listeners had endured in Virginia, Bermuda, and on the high seas and reassuring them that conditions would improve, he berated them for their vanity and idleness and warned that should their iniquities continue, they would feel the cutting edge of his wrath.[11]

There is no report on the reaction of his audience, but the baron's words must have had a chilling effect on an already demoralized company. The presentiment was that things would get no better. They may not starve to death, but neither would their lives improve.

De La Warr named a five-man advisory council consisting of Gates, Somers, Newport, Percy, and a newcomer, Sir Ferdinando Wainman. Strachey was officially named secretary of the colony.[12] The first order of business was fresh meat. Though the fleet carried food to last a year, it included no livestock. London had not expected that every last chicken, hog, horse, goat, and lamb in Virginia would have been slaughtered by the time De La Warr arrived. London Company officials—even after all this time—had still not awakened to the reality that its New World colony had from the very beginning been totally dependent on the Algonquins for food. Now Somers saw his opportunity. He volunteered to take *Patience*—the ship he and his men had built in Bermuda—back to the islands to fetch hogs, claiming he could be back in Jamestown by mid–August with a boat full of fresh meat. On the nineteenth of June, he sailed away, assisted by his nephew Matthew and in company with *Discovery*, captained by Samuel Argall, and crews totaling twenty men.[13]

Fishing expeditions to the bay proved fruitless—due primarily to a lack of skill—so for a time, Jamestown survived on peas and oatmeal. De La Warr was predisposed to live in peace with the Algonquins so long as the English were free to hunt and fish without being attacked. But a war of attrition was sparked when a canoe bearing one of De La Warr's officers was forced ashore in Kecoughtan territory by opposing winds. The officer, Humphrey Blunt, was captured and executed.[14]

Blunt's death provoked the governor into sending Powhatan an ultimatum demanding that the thefts and killings cease, that all Englishmen living with or imprisoned by the Powhatans be repatriated, and that all arms stolen be returned to Jamestown. What De La Warr specified as punishment for noncompliance is not recorded, but he reminded Powhatan of the crowning ceremony and that by virtue of that event, Powhatan was a subject of the English crown.[15] Powhatan answered with the same warning he had sent to Gates a few weeks earlier: Keep to the fort.[16]

Soon after, two Paspahegh warriors were captured, one a suspected spy. De La Warr ordered the man's right hand cut off and sent him to Powhatan with the message that if all Englishmen and stolen arms were not returned at once, the other captive would be executed and all Algonquin villages and crops within the vicinity of Jamestown would be destroyed.[17]

De La Warr then began implementing a plan, the essence of which was doubtless conceived in England. The goal was control of Tsenacommacah, beginning with the James River. London Company officials had resolved to unleash a reign of terror if necessary to force the Algonquins into submission or push them off their lands. Hostilities began in July with an attack led by Gates on a Kecoughtan village four miles inland from Point Comfort. Twelve to fourteen Kecoughtans were killed, others fled, and the town was sacked. The English suffered no casualties. Thereafter, Kecoughtan cropland near Point Comfort became Jamestown's breadbasket, and the tribe itself ceased to exist, its remnants assimilated into other tribes.[18]

Recent events had persuaded the English that God had preordained North America for England. The many serendipitous incidents proved it: *Sea Venture* surviving the deadly hurricane, the ship coming to rest upright so near shore, the bounty of Bermuda for those marooned there, the arrival of *Deliverance* just in time to save the starving Jamestown colonists, and the arrival of Lord De La Warr just as the colony was being abandoned. These auspicious twists of fate fostered the belief that Virginia was predestined to be English.[19] De La Warr may not have believed such drivel himself, but it served his purpose to promote the notion. It was an age-old ploy—long practiced by autocrats—to use the superstitions of those in their charge as shackles.

Following the attack on the Kecoughtans, Gates left for England. De La Warr then turned to George Percy and ordered him upriver to attack the Paspaheghs. It appears the baron had decided to continue his reign of terror by working his way up the north bank of the James River. In early August, Percy led seventy men in an attack on the principal Paspahegh town. Fifteen Algonquins were killed in the early morning raid. The rest fled except for the Paspahegh weroansqua, her children, and a male, all taken prisoner, against Percy's orders to spare no one. Incensed at having prisoners on his hands, he ordered the male beheaded, then his troops burned the town, destroyed the crops, and returned to their boats with the captured weroansqua and her children.

On board the barge returning to Jamestown, Percy's soldiers groused about the prisoners, so he convened a council to decide their fate. He did not report how many Paspahegh children were on board, but the result was that all were thrown overboard then shot as they splashed about trying to survive or escape. When the barge landed in Jamestown with the distraught weroansqua, De La Warr expressed irritation that she had been spared, so Percy ordered Captain Davies with two men to take her into the woods and kill her with their swords.[20] One can imagine the impact of this gruesome brutality on a people who believed in always sparing the lives of women and children.

In September, Samuel Argall returned to Jamestown from fishing with George Somers on the Grand Banks. Winds had initially opposed their return to Bermuda. Argall then led an attack on the Warraskoyacks just across the river. They fled before Argall's troops arrived, leaving only their houses and crops to be destroyed.[21] De La Warr then turned his attention to the falls. He sent fourteen men in the barge, but on their passage upriver, they were lured ashore for a midday repast at an Appamatuck tribal village. It was a trap, and all but a boy drummer were killed. The drummer escaped by running back to the barge, pushing off, and using its rudder as a shield until out of arrow range.[22] The Appamatuck tribe was one of the core six tribes of the Powhatan nation, and the English should have known better than to accept their hospitality.

Implicit in this wholesale violence is that De La Warr did not bother to discriminate among the many tribes of Tsenacommacah to better understand the multifarious nature of his enemy. It is likely he viewed all Algonquins as one homogeneous mass of savage humanity. This boorish attitude may have resulted from a lethargy caused by the baron's declining health. Like many before him, he contracted *morbus virginiana*—the Virginia disease—shortly after his arrival. He came with gout—the plague of upper-class English toffs—and in-country, he contracted a hot and violent ague followed by distemper, the bloody flux, severe cramps, and scurvy. At last, believing himself near death, he and his council agreed that he should sail to the Caribbean for rest and a fresh diet. At the end of March, the Governor for Life departed Virginia, having spent ten months there. Though he intended to return, while on the mend in Nevis, he was further persuaded, so he claimed, that for a full recovery, the natural air of his own country was indispensable. He set sail again, tarried in the Azores for a few weeks, then arrived back in London in June.[23]

De La Warr's unexpected return infuriated London Company directors.[24] As if Thomas Smythe was not having enough trouble recruiting, now he was forced to defend yet another high-level defection. He gave up trying to fill ships with people like John Rolfe—the honest, hardworking, God-fearing sort. Their lot in England was not so awful as to leave home for the hardships and deaths being reported out of Virginia. A few years on, strong-willed Puritans and adherents to other nonconforming sects would flock to North America for the freedom to worship as they wished, but this trend was yet to come.

Though Smythe advertised for carpenters, shipwrights, masons, farmers, fishermen, and the like, the only prospects he could lay hands on were the dregs of society—criminals, indigents, masterless men, and homeless women and children for whom the promise of basic necessities supplied free of charge had appeal. They were not always given a choice. For many, it was Jamestown or the clink, for some, Jamestown or the gallows.[25] One wonders if in private, Smythe might have preferred to pull the plug on the whole affair, but he was trapped. Indeed, in desperate hopes of achieving greater social stability, the London Company would end up sending boatloads of destitute women and children to Virginia in hopes they would tame the "vulgar and viler" English reprobates already there.[26] The black hole of Jamestown was not for the faint of heart.

De La Warr's replacement was Sir Thomas Dale, a soldier, probably in his forties. Another veteran of the Irish and Dutch wars, he had twenty-three years of military service. He arrived Jamestown in May 1611, six weeks after De La Warr's ignominious departure. His actions in the Netherlands had drawn the attention of the king's son, Henry, Prince of Wales, for whom Cape Henry had been named. As it was universally believed that discipline would remedy all that ailed Jamestown, Henry recommended Dale for assignment there as de facto chief law enforcement officer. Dale would not disappoint.

The English, indeed, the entire European invasion of the Americas, was a clash of such incompatible cultures it could only produce winners and losers. This then became London Company strategy, a winning one insofar as the Powhatan problem was concerned: send wave after wave of colonists, never mind their qualifications, and overwhelm the Algonquins by sheer numbers. It was cheaper to replace a colonist than to protect him. They were, therefore, expendable and sent like lambs to the slaughter. But from the point of view of the Powhatans, they were more like the Hydra—when one head was scalped, two grew back in its place.

Dale arrived with three hundred new colonists, including sixty women.[27] With De La Warr gone, Dale became acting governor and codified draconian new laws recorded by Strachey and later published as *Lawes, Divine, Morall and Martiall, &c*.[28] Using this as his jurisprudence, Dale meted out punishment like a prison warden: the rack, the stake, the wheel, the noose, the firing squad—he employed them all.[29] People were whipped for arriving late for work.[30] Dale had the effrontery to pull the beard of the leonine Christopher Newport and threaten to hang him, an exchange that led to Newport's resignation.[31] Furthermore, Dale laughed in the face of Powhatan's demands.

He led an attack against the Nansemonds with one hundred men, many in body armor, the first use of such in Virginia and a marvel to the Algonquins.[32] An unreported number of Nansemonds were killed.[33] He created new settlements up and downriver from Jamestown—Kecoughtan, Point Charles, Henrico, Bermuda Hundred, West Hundred, Shirley Hundred—all on lands purchased or taken by force from the Powhatans. From the falls to its mouth, the James River was being anglicized.[34]

The war was won but far from over. In August, Gates returned with a fleet of six ships, three hundred new colonists, sixty cows, and two hundred pigs.[35] He had been celebrated and feted in London as a man returned from the dead—the hero of the *Sea Venture* saga. The thrilling news of the wreck and salvation elicited a celebratory national response. This and a lottery marketing initiative injected new life into recruitment efforts and renewed resolve for bolstering England's tenuous foothold in America. The use of a lottery was granted by the king under the aegis of yet another charter—the third—that also granted the London Company jurisdiction over the Bermuda Islands. Once again Gates assumed the governorship of Jamestown, and he was to remain in that post for two and a half years with Dale as his military commander.

As reported, George Somers had left Jamestown in June 1610 with Samuel Argall on a mission to fetch hogs in Bermuda. Delayed for weeks by adverse winds, they gave up and sailed instead to the Grand Banks to fish. Separated in a fog off Newfoundland, Argall decided to return to Jamestown, his ship now freighted with salted codfish.[36] Somers, his nephew

Matthew, and his crew sailed on to Bermuda. There is no record of when they arrived there, but they found Christopher Carter and Robert Waters alive and well.[37] During Somers absence, these two deserters had discovered among the rocks a quantity of ambergris weighing over one hundred pounds.[38] Secreted by sperm whales and used as a fixative in the manufacture of perfume, ambergris was extremely valuable, and the two men concealed their discovery from Somers, believing that if found, their trove would be appropriated by the London Company. Valued at three English pounds per ounce, the ambergris was worth a fortune.

For mysterious reasons, Somers remained in Bermuda for months. During this time, he and his crew presumably captured pigs and caught and preserved fish and fowl with the intention of returning to Jamestown. But sometime in November, George Somers died of what was described as an overindulgence of pork, possibly food poisoning.[39] After this, it became apparent that Matthew Somers lacked the strength of character to command his crew to return to Virginia, so the following spring *Patience* set sail for England with George Somers's body preserved in vinegar.[40] Left behind was his heart, buried at the foot of a cross erected on the highest point of St. George's Island. Also left were three men—Carter, Waters, and one other—to protect England's claim to the islands and their secret hoard of ambergris.[41] Sir George Somers's body was interred in the graveyard of the church in Whitechurch, Dorset, seat of one of his estates.[42] Today, he is celebrated as the Father of Bermuda.

Bermuda's first fifty colonists arrived in July 1612.[43] The first shipment of ambergris—weighing between twenty and thirty pounds—arrived in London a year later, property of the London Company.[44] In 1615, the Somers Islands, as Bermuda was briefly called, were split off into a separate corporation. Rats escaped from a later ship carrying more colonists and, having no natural predators on the islands, they multiplied unchecked. It took years to eradicate them.[45] The feral hogs were hunted to extinction within a few years, and it was thought that cahows became extinct by 1630.[46] Happily, as noted earlier, the cahows survived on outlying islets and are there to this day, though their species is considered endangered. Sea turtles also made a modest recovery after being overhunted.

William Strachey returned to England in September 1611 after two years in Jamestown. Doubtless, his pecuniary circumstances remained dire. His long and fascinating narrative of events in Bermuda and Virginia made the rounds in manuscript form but went unpublished in his lifetime. The London Company saw to publication of his *Lawes, Divine, Morall and Martiall, &c.*, as proof to the public that the colony adhered to the rule of law, but Strachey would have profited little from this. He wrote a more ambitious work, *The Historie of Travell Into Virginia Britania*, but

9. Redemption

could find no publisher, possibly because London Company officials found it too discouraging to prospective recruits. Or perhaps it was eclipsed by John Smith's *A Map of Virginia* published in 1612.[47] Strachey's *Historie* remained unpublished until 1857.[48] In its appendix A is the most extensive translation of English/Algonquin words and phrases extant. Strachey died in London in 1621 at the age of forty-nine. Always the poet, he reviewed his dissolute and profligate life in this contrite little ditty: "I have sinned against Earth and heaven / Early by day and late in the even / All manner of sins, all manner of ways / I have committed in my daies."[49]

Upon his return to England, Christopher Newport leveraged his relationship with Thomas Smythe into command of a ship in the employ of the English East India Company. He made the first of three voyages to England's far eastern entrepôts in 1613.[50] On his third voyage in 1617, accompanied by his son, he died aboard his ship anchored in the bay of Bantam off the island of Java. He was fifty-six. At the time of his death, no Englishman alive had greater maritime experience. He is remembered in Christopher Newport University in Newport News, a city on the Lower Peninsula of Virginia that encompasses Mulberry Island. Aristotle said, "There are three sorts of people: those who are alive, those who are dead, and those who are at sea." Christopher Newport belongs with the last.

As noted, after John Smith left Virginia in October 1609, Pocahontas disappeared. Three and a half years later, Samuel Argall sailed to the Potomac River on orders from Gates to trade with the Patawomecks. Ever since De La Warr's arrival saved Jamestown, Powhatan had been losing his grip on his alliance, and the Patawomecks were willing to trade again, their memory having faded of Thomas West's outrages three years earlier. While there, Argall learned that Pocahontas was living among them, perhaps with a mate, Kocoum.[51] She was now sixteen or seventeen. Argall persuaded a minor Patawomeck weroance named Iapazaws and his weroansqua to bring Pocahontas aboard his ship for supper and a tour. In return, Argall promised Iapazaws a copper kettle and other gifts. By this intrigue, Pocahontas was lured aboard, kidnapped, and brought to Jamestown, pensive and despondent according to eyewitnesses.[52] She may have been fearful, having no doubt learned of English atrocities toward the Paspahegh, but she was well treated. She was held for ransom for the release of all English citizens whether imprisoned or living among the Powhatans of their own volition, the return of all English weapons, and a large quantity of corn.[53]

The fate of Kocoum is not known, if, indeed, he ever existed.[54] There has also been speculation of a child of this union, but future events make this unlikely.[55] Pocahontas was taken to Henrico, a settlement fifty miles upriver from Jamestown founded by Thomas Dale two years earlier. Here she was put in the care of an Anglican minister, the Rev. Alexander Whitaker, to better her command of English and to receive Christian religious instruction.[56] Her father gave only token response to English demands, giving rise to speculation that he was using his daughter as a spy. It is more likely that Powhatan was no longer in a position to meet English demands to the degree necessary to satisfy Gates and Dale. His power was eroding.[57] There was even a rumor that he lived in fear of his brother Opechancanough.[58]

Time passed. Pocahontas was persuaded to adopt English ways: modes of dress, eating, religious worship.[59] She was permitted to have her half-sister come live with her as her handmaid; indeed, Algonquins came and went with a degree of freedom as many were being employed by the English. Though not confined, she was closely observed and protected, and she was saddened by her father's apparent disinclination to buy her freedom. In time she accepted her circumstances and took an English name, Rebecca. She became friendly with her captors and with one in particular, John Rolfe, who with his wife had been marooned in Bermuda. Now a widower, he fell in love with Pocahontas and wrote a long, anguished letter to Dale, a remarkable document expressing his desire to marry Pocahontas despite his misgivings about miscegenation, this based on warnings in the Bible against "marrying strange wives." He laments the devil's "diabolical assaults" that filled him with "unbridled desire of carnal affection" and bears his "troubled soul," begging Dale to advise him.[60]

Dale countenanced the union, and on April 5, 1614, one day after her baptism, Pocahontas and John Rolfe were married by Minister Richard Buck in the church in Jamestown. Powhatan gave his consent and sent a maternal uncle of Pocahontas named Opachisco to represent him accompanied by two of "his sons." Was it age or fear of treachery that kept Powhatan away? The following January, Pocahontas gave birth to a son, Thomas, named after Thomas Dale. With the marriage came a rapprochement between the Powhatans and the English that continued until her death—the so-called Peace of Pocahontas.[61] A separate peace was concluded with the Chickahominies.[62] For the Powhatans, however, it was more a temporary capitulation than genuine, sustainable peace. They were experiencing an internal struggle for leadership, so English incursions continued unopposed for a time.

Dale was so inspired by the marriage that he too resolved to marry an Algonquin. He learned that Powhatan had another comely daughter and in May 1614 sent an emissary, Ralph Hamor, to the paramount chief, proposing the match. The fact that Dale had a wife and children in England did not impinge upon his conscience, but Powhatan disappointed Hamor, informing him that the daughter in question who "was not full twelve years old" had recently been sold to a powerful weroance three days distant.[63] One doubts a decision of such a personal nature was motivated by an urge to forge better relations with the Algonquins but rather to provide Dale himself with amatory comfort from the deprivations of soldiering far from home. As chance would have it, Hamor was the last Englishman to see Powhatan alive.

John Rolfe purchased land in Virginia to grow tobacco, believing the crop had a promising future.[64] At the time, the English smoking public preferred the variety grown in the West Indies and imported into England by Spain. In 1612, by mysterious means, Rolfe came into possession of contraband seeds from Trinidad. He grew the leaf in the friable soil of the tidelands—so-called Pamunkey soil, Virginia's official state soil—and cured his tobacco leaves using the traditional Algonquin method, which he may have learned from Pocahontas.[65] The West Indian variety, *Nicotiana tabacum*, was favored over the harsher *Nicotiana rustica*, indigenous to Virginia and smoked by the Algonquins. First shipped to England in 1613, the milder variety grown in Pamunkey soil was an instant success.[66] Rolfe promoted his leaf as "Orinoco," and the brand proved so profitable that a law was later passed in Jamestown prohibiting colonists from planting tobacco unless they also planted two acres of corn—this to ensure the colony had enough to eat.[67] In 1615, exports of Virginia tobacco to England totaled two thousand pounds. This grew to fifty thousand pounds by 1620 and a million and a half by 1630.[68]

Tobacco was the very gold England had been seeking in the New World since Walter Raleigh first planted a colony on Roanoke Island thirty years earlier.[69] Ironically, King James hated "this precious stinke" and considered smoking a noxious habit. He was correct in claiming it was harmful to the lungs. He even published an acerbic monograph entitled "A Counterblaste to Tobacco" in a futile attempt to discourage its use. But he soon came to appreciate the windfall to his treasury of a tax on a substance that was not only addictive, it was also growing in popularity. If anyone could be said to have saved Jamestown and the English foothold in the New World, it was John Rolfe and Pocahontas by reason of the peace that followed their marriage and their innovations that supplied an insatiable English demand for a highly profitable product—flue-cured Virginia tobacco.[70]

Cultivating tobacco requires abundant land and labor, for which the Algonquins were ill-suited. They did not adapt well to a European agricultural lifestyle, but their land was in great demand. The forests in which they hunted gave way to the plow. In 1619 a Dutch ship returning to Europe from the Caribbean, and running short of victuals, stopped in Jamestown to purchase food in exchange for the only cargo the ship carried—twenty

African slaves. This does not mark the beginning of the southern plantation economy, but it is a portent of what would come later in the century. For the next few decades, tobacco farmers relied on indentured workers to fill their labor needs. The Powhatans could choose not to work the tobacco fields, but those in forced servitude could not. Once their term was up, however, they could collect their headright of fifty acres and begin growing their own tobacco crop. Orinoco tobacco gave English America a reason to be.[71]

In March 1614, Thomas Gates resigned as governor of Virginia and returned to England, leaving Thomas Dale in charge. Gates had become disenchanted with the London Company's policy regarding the Algonquins, thinking it too lenient, and he sold his ownership interest. He returned to the Netherlands and died there in 1622.[72] In 1616 Dale resigned leaving George Yeardley in charge as deputy governor. Like Newport in his post–Jamestown career, Dale found employment with the East India Company and died in India in 1619. A soldier also, Yeardley had served in the Netherlands under Gates. He had sailed on *Sea Venture* and was marooned on Bermuda. He ultimately served three terms as governor of Virginia. Like Somers, Dale, and Argall, George Yeardley was knighted by King James. He gained possession of large land holdings in Virginia, including one thousand acres on Mulberry Island, much of it devoted to growing tobacco. He died in 1627 and was buried in the church in Jamestown.[73]

Yeardley was replaced in May 1617 by Samuel Argall, who served two years as governor, and it was during his tenure that African slaves first arrived in Jamestown. Argall was replaced by Yeardley again, who served another two years, to be replaced by Francis Wyatt in 1621, yet another recipient of a knighthood from King James. These soldier knights—Gates, Dale, Argall, and Yeardley—were resolute and experienced field-grade military officers—capable men and good soldiers.

George Percy had failed so utterly as president of the Virginia council that he is omitted from this list, though he too was a soldier. He sold his shares in the London Company when he returned to England, believing that as an investment, Jamestown was a losing proposition. He went back to soldiering in the Netherlands in the 1620s and died in the early 1630s.

An alumnus of Oxford and Gray's Inn, Francis Wyatt was a born aristocrat. His great, great grandfather Sir Henry Wyatt served as privy councilor to Kings Henry VII and VIII, and his great grandfather Sir Thomas Wyatt was a poet. Briefly imprisoned in the Tower of London in 1536, Sir Thomas was one of several men accused of having had an affair with Queen Anne Boleyn. Francis's grandfather was the infamous Sir Thomas Wyatt the Younger, who lost his head for leading the 1554 rebellion against Queen Mary Tudor that put the future Queen Elizabeth in the Tower of

London, as described at the beginning of this book. With Elizabeth's ascension to the throne, the Wyatt family regained its former favor, status, and estates.

Francis Wyatt was chosen governor of Virginia by way of his connections with important London Company directors. Respected for his "parentage, good education, integrity of life, and fair fortune," Wyatt arrived in Virginia in 1621 with a new constitution that again vowed no harm to the Algonquins. The company wished to bury the hatchet and "to forget old quarrels," but to the natives of Tsenacommacah, old quarrels were anything but buried and forgotten.

Epilogue

In Whitehall Palace on the afternoon of November 1, 1611, King James, Queen Anne and their guests attended a matinee performance by the King's Men of a new play by William Shakespeare. Entitled *The Tempest*, it told of a violent storm, a shipwreck, and castaways on a faraway island. It is quite possible Shakespeare ran into William Strachey at the Mermaid Tavern after Strachey's return from Virginia. Both men were habitués of the ancient inn located in Bread Street just south of Cheapside in the heart of London. In this way, perhaps, the forty-seven-year-old playwright received a copy of Strachey's narrative and was inspired thereby to write one more play. As sole author, it would be his last.

§ § §

Four years later, someone—probably Thomas Dale—had the idea of taking Pocahontas to London. By then, many native Amerindians had visited England, but not a princess and not a princess who was also the wife of an Englishman. She was certain to captivate the English public and attract new subscriptions and recruits for the London Company.

Pocahontas arrived in Plymouth in early June 1616 with her husband, son, and an entourage of ten or twelve Powhatans, all guests of the London Company. They included Matachanna, Pocahontas's half-sister, and Uttamatomakkin, Matachanna's mate. As a priest and senior member of the delegation, Uttamatomakkin had been assigned two important tasks by Powhatan: to learn the truth about John Smith—was he dead or alive?—and to keep a count of the number of people in England by notches on a stick. Regarding the stick, it appears Powhatan could not believe reports of Machumps and others who had traveled to London. Powhatan had never visited Jamestown or any English settlement, therefore, he could not comprehend how so many people could survive packed into so small an area. He wanted proof. Uttamatomakkin attempted to comply, but soon gave up. One imagines his stick had been whittled to pieces.[1]

Pocahontas was in England for nine months. During this time, she was the subject of intense curiosity and deference befitting exotic royalty. She attended an event in her honor hosted by the lord bishop of London.[2] On a tour of the Tower of London, she met the Earl of Northumberland, brother of George Percy, and perhaps also Walter Raleigh.[3] Both men were imprisoned there. In early January 1617, she attended the Twelfth Night masque at Whitehall Palace hosted by the king and queen and may have had a private audience with them then or at another time accompanied by Lord and Lady De La Warr.[4] Uttamatomakkin was interviewed by the Rev. Samuel Purchas, who declared the Powhatan priest a blasphemer for insisting on the supremacy of Algonquin deities.[5] Pocahontas posed for an engraving, the only likeness done in her lifetime. The artist failed to capture the charm Smith wrote about so fervently.

There is no record that Pocahontas visited or was visited by Richard Hakluyt. He may have been too unwell for a visit, as he died in November of 1616 and was buried in Westminster Abbey. His literary executor was the Rev. Samuel Purchas who, using the reams of material collected by Hakluyt over his lifetime, published a twenty-volume collection of discovery narratives in 1625, *Hakluytus Posthumus, or, Purchas His Pilgrimes*. Though voluminous, it remains in print to this day and has inspired an untold number of works, including Samuel Taylor Coleridge's classic poem "Kubla Khan."

Pocahontas must have been flattered by the attention, but not feeling well, she and her family moved to the suburb of Brentford in Middlesex, ten miles west of London. There is speculation that they were guests of the Percy family at Syon House, the imprisoned earl's country estate. Were this the case, she would have met another Syon House resident, Thomas Harriot.[6] It may have been there that John Smith met with Pocahontas in the early months of 1617.[7]

The only eyewitness account of what transpired was written by Smith himself, but since in his telling, he was mildly rebuked by Pocahontas, the account rings true. It is void of self-promotion; indeed, Smith must have been somewhat humbled by the exchange. Close scrutiny of the passage reveals much. It follows here, the words in italics spoken by Pocahontas:

> After a modest salutation, without any word she turned about, obscured her face, as not seeming well contented. And in that humor, her husband with diverse others we all left her two or three hours, repenting myself to have writ she could speak English.
>
> But not long after, she began to talk and rememb'red me well what courtesies she had done, saying:
>
> *"You did promise Powhatan what was yours should be his, and he the like to you. You called him father, being in his land a stranger, and by the same reason so must I do you."*

Which though I would have excused, I durst not allow of that title because she was a king's daughter. With a well-set countenance, she said:

"Were you not afraid to come into my father's country, and caused fear in him and all his people (but me) and fear you here I should call you father? I tell you then I will, and you shall call me child, and so I will be for ever and ever your countryman. They did tell us always you were dead, and I knew no other till I came to Plymouth; yet Powhatan did command Uttamatomakkin to seek you and know the truth, because your countrymen will lie much."[8]

Elizabethan prose requires a degree of annotation for today's reader—not unlike a Shakespearean soliloquy—and so it is with this passage. What is obvious, however, is that Pocahontas was emotionally distressed upon seeing John Smith. This speaks volumes. And after hours of silent brooding, it is clear also that she scolded him, hence the "well-set countenance." We do not know when he wrote this. It was published in his *General Historie of Virginia* in 1624, seven years after the event, therefore, he is relying on old notes or recalling from memory the words of someone for whom English was a second language. Smith met with Pocahontas at least twice during her visit, so he related only a small fragment of their several conversations—that part he remembered best or thought most relevant.

What jumps out at once is the phrase, she "rememb'red me well what *courtesies* she had done." (The italics are mine.) By reminding Smith of those "courtesies" or favors, Pocahontas justified her wish that, in return, he permit her to call him father. We can interpret courtesies in this case as bringing food to the people of Jamestown or feeding and entertaining Smith when he came to visit Powhatan. But in his *Historie* of 1624, Smith reported that Pocahontas saved his life in Werowocomoco the day of his resurrection ceremony. It makes no sense that someone would characterize saving someone's life as a mere courtesy. Rather, Pocahontas would have justified her wish by simply reminding Smith that he owed her his life. To call this evidence that she did not, in fact, save his life, may be stretching things too far, but the comment does fly in the face of Smith's claim that on that frigid December day ten years earlier Pocahontas "got his head in her arms and laid her own upon his to save him from death."

To understand the implications of the first paragraph of Smith's passage, it is helpful to know that after Pocahontas arrived in England, Smith wrote to Queen Anne, urging the queen to receive her. He informed the queen that Pocahontas was the first Powhatan Algonquin to learn to speak English.[9] This may be what he is referencing by the phrase, "repenting myself to have writ she [Pocahontas] could speak English," implying that Pocahontas's English language skills or lack thereof accounted for her two to three hours of silent brooding. Had she, in her audience with the queen, committed some faux pas by reason of her lack of mastery of the English language? There is no record of such a thing, indeed, there is no certainty she ever actually conversed with the queen.[10] And if she were guilty of some solecism in the queen's presence, why would it cause her to brood for two or three hours on seeing Smith? The statement does not fit the context. It is as if Smith wrote a first draft of his *Historie* and on rereading, decided to add the clause, wanting to explain Pocahontas's emotional turmoil so as to distract the reader away from trying to guess the true nature of it. The English language comment appears to be purposeful misdirection.

It is more likely that the cause of Pocahontas's distress is revealed by what she said next, for it provides a clue as to what flashed into her mind upon seeing Smith again after all these years. She reminded him of his compact with Powhatan—the what-is-mine-is-thine-and-vice-versa pledge. And the fact that she felt compelled to remind him of this implies that in her mind, Smith had not kept his part of the bargain.

She went on to remind him that in Tsenacommacah, he called Powhatan "father." Therefore, now that she was in England, she wished to call him—John Smith—"father." She argued that he should not refuse just because her real father was a king. Her reproof is clearly a surrogate for a more painful and private wound, one that may have stemmed from Smith's outward display of acceptance of Powhatan's offer of land, friendship, and perhaps also Pocahontas herself, while in truth Smith was dissembling, and, in the end, he abandoned them, letting them believe he was dead. Was she also including Smith when she later lamented that the English "will lie much"? In a manner of speaking, did Pocahontas feel that she had been left at the altar by the man to whom she believed she was betrothed—a man she loved? This would better explain two or three hours of brooding discontent.

One can imagine that Smith did not want his readers to think Pocahontas's feelings for him caused her emotional distress. For one thing, it would have appeared self-serving, rendering his narrative less credible. In addition, it would have added plausibility to the earlier charge that he had wanted to marry Pocahontas and set himself up as a king. He needed an excuse and invented one that was as unsatisfactory as it was transparent, that Pocahontas lacked proficiency in English.

At this point in their conversation, Pocahontas changed the subject, informing Smith that she and her father distrusted the news of his death and that Powhatan commanded Uttamatomakkin to learn the truth. It is fascinating that after a six-and-a-half-year absence, Smith was still so much in the minds of Powhatan and Pocahontas. Uttamatomakkin made his inquiry upon arriving in Plymouth. Apparently, he could not wait until they traveled to London to learn the truth. Why this urgency to learn Smith's fate if not for some sense of loss or still-simmering hope?

These tantalizing and seemingly trivial details betray something that has been overlooked, something personal for Pocahontas but also something that had the potential to alter the history of the founding of English America in a profound way. Pocahontas, Powhatan, and John Smith were bound together by what appears from this vantage point to be an adoption, alliance, and betrothal all rolled into one Algonquin ritual execution and rebirth. Throughout history, peace was often achieved by a treaty cemented in marriage, including marriages involving a child. Was this a lost opportunity that might have saved her people?

In none of his three Jamestown-related publications does John Smith reveal why he never acted on Powhatan's offer of Capahowosick, the territory on Middle Peninsula that Powhatan offered Smith for the English colony in return for two cannon and a grindstone. We can be certain of only this: despite his being our best source for this history, John Smith did not reveal everything. He held something back, something that might solve the mystery of this captivating relationship and provide insight into what may have happened had he and the London Company accepted Powhatan's offer or some negotiated compromise.

Pocahontas felt betrayed. This is clear, but Smith refrained from giving his opinion as to why. This aspect of his telling is remarkable in its restraint. He could have put his own self-serving slant on the encounter, but, to his credit, he did not. Despite resentment and hurt feelings, however—and even after all these years—Pocahontas still wanted to call Smith "father" and to be called by him "child." Did she consider this some small consolation for unrequited love?[11] Herein is our founding myth *and* our founding mystery.

In March, the Rolfes prepared to return to Virginia. Pocahontas had not been feeling well for several weeks. They boarded ship on the Thames and fell with the tide to Gravesend near the river's mouth. Delayed by adverse winds, Pocahontas disembarked to convalesce in a local inn or private residence. Her condition worsened, and she died sometime between the fifteenth and twentieth and was buried in the church in Gravesend.[12] She was twenty, perhaps twenty-one.

After her burial, John Rolfe and young Thomas sailed on to Plymouth, where John decided his son was not strong enough to survive the crossing. He left Thomas in the care of his brother to be brought up in England.[13] They never met again.

While Pocahontas was abroad, Powhatan quietly ceded power to Opechancanough. The venerable old chief died in April of the following year, well into his seventies.[14]

§ § §

Epilogue

On October 29, 1618, Walter Raleigh awoke early, ate a healthy English breakfast, then enjoyed a smoke. By now, pipe smoking had been fashionable in London for years in large part because of him, but this smoke would be his last. When Raleigh failed to find gold in Guyana in 1617, King James revived the old charge of treason against him for having plotted in 1603 to put James's cousin and rival Arabella Stuart on the throne.[15] The charge was baseless, but except for his fruitless foray to the Orinoco River for gold, Raleigh was imprisoned in the Tower of London for the rest of his life. He filled the hours writing letters, poetry, essays, and a history, *The Historie of the World*, consisting of nearly a million words.[16] Though the work was unfinished, it became immensely popular, went through twenty editions, and remained in print for a hundred years.[17]

On the morning of his execution, his mood was cheerful, one might even say, jaunty. Just outside his gatehouse cell, a well-wisher offered a glass of wine, and, after pausing to imbibe, Raleigh emerged into the morning light of the Westminster Palace yard and was at once surrounded by an armed guard. It was a holiday—the Lord Mayor's Day—a day of pageants to be followed in the evening by fireworks.

A crowd had gathered on the grass surrounding the newly erected scaffold. Among the spectators were gentlemen of rank, a sprinkling of veiled ladies, and several of Raleigh's close confidants. One of them, Thomas Harriot, was there for support and to record Raleigh's last words.[18] Raleigh had a cold, and the overcast morning was chilly and wet. His voice cracked at first as he hushed the crowd, then he excused his trembling as due solely to the dampness and cold of his prison cell.

His valediction lasted three quarters of an hour. He touched on the accusations against him and professed his innocence. He spoke of his old adversary, the Earl of Essex, calling him noble and claiming to have wept at his execution. And he ended by admitting his vanity, confessing his sinfulness, and asking God's mercy and forgiveness, all this in the dispassionate voice of a man at peace with the injustice and indignity that had brought him to this hour. When done, he asked to inspect the headman's axe, and satisfied with its keen edge, he bade farewell to those crowding near the scaffold then knelt to the block and prayed. When he extended his arms, the executioner severed his neck with two blows. Raleigh's lips were still moving as his head dropped into the basket.[19]

"Behold, the head of a traitor!" the executioner is reported to have exclaimed as he lifted Raleigh's severed head by the hair for all to see.

In the awed silence that followed, some stalwart spectator had the temerity to respond, "England hath not another such head."[20]

The response—fitting though it may have been—is doubtless apocryphal. Like many men who inspire, they can also overbear. Raleigh was not without enemies; indeed, he could count many. He had—in former times as the crown's favorite—taken solace in knowing that though he was hated, he was likewise feared, but his power perished with his queen.[21] With his imprisonment, Raleigh's abject humiliation was achieved, but in death he had his revenge. As one historian observed, Raleigh's ghost "pursued the House of Stuart to the scaffold."[22] In truth, his remarkable shadow had already been cast. Raleigh forced England to think big, and English America is the product of his vision.[23] With Elizabeth Tudor and William Shakespeare, Walter Raleigh embodied the zeitgeist of his time.

§ § §

Opechancanough watched as more English arrived. The London Company created a headright system, granting fifty acres to anyone agreeing to emigrate. This attracted some, but to fill quotas, more and more masterless men were forced to migrate, and in turn, scores of destitute women were shipped to Jamestown to become servants or wives for those who could afford the bride price—one hundred and fifty pounds of tobacco.[24] Hundreds of young guttersnipes and mud larks were shipped over as indentured servants or apprentices to serve until they were twenty-one or, in the case of girls, until they married.[25] Treated little better than slaves, most died in their first year and were replaced by others.[26] Between 1618 and 1621, fifty ships brought four thousand English men, women, and children to Jamestown.

As tobacco exhausted the land, more forest was cleared for cultivation.[27] Soon Algonquins began coming into English settlements to trade animal pelts for food. Many now depended on trade with the invader simply to feed themselves, and in return for food, they gave up their land.[28] Opechancanough watched as the virgin forests of Tsenacommacah were cut down and his people displaced. On Friday morning, March 22, 1622, he took his revenge.

He had waited long enough for the English to become complacent. He orchestrated a surprise attack involving all tribes, and he maintained remarkable control, coordination, and secrecy. Three hundred and forty-seven English men, women, and children were killed—one-quarter of all colonists alive at the time—many slain with their own tools and weapons.[29] But for Opechancanough the victory was a pyrrhic one, for even as his warriors returned from the slaughter, nearly double the number of English killed were onboard ships en route to Virginia.

Of the six thousand colonists sent to Jamestown since its inception fifteen years earlier, little more than a thousand remained alive. Nearly five of every six had died or were killed.[30] These were dreadful odds. Being shipped to Virginia was tantamount to a death sentence.[31] In effect,

England cleared the ground for her invasion of North America by using her lowliest and poorest citizens—men, women, and children—as cannon fodder. Jamestown is the dark underbelly of our origin story.

In April of 1623, King James seized control of the Jamestown Colony, wresting it away from the London Company and accusing Thomas Smythe of mismanagement. Despite the company's failure, Smythe was a wealthy man when he died in 1625 at the age of sixty-seven. The king died that same year, age fifty-eight, having suffered from a variety of maladies. Thomas Smythe's role in the creation of the British Overseas Empire cannot be overstated, though his neglect of Jamestown colonists was abominable, and he was hated for it.[32] This notwithstanding, the impetus for this world-changing development did not come from the crown. Elizabeth and James were content to be encased in the chrysalis of their Thames River Valley palaces, and James was determined not to offend his Spanish counterpart.[33] Nor did the impetus come from the nobility. It came from the visionaries—Dee, Hakluyt, and Gilbert—and the entrepreneurs—Raleigh, Smythe, and Rolfe—commoners all.

John Rolfe married again after returning to Virginia, and he and his third wife had a daughter, Elizabeth.[34] He became a member of the Jamestown governing council in 1619 and served until his death. A heavy smoker, his health began to decline in 1621, and he made out his will, leaving parcels of land to his son, Thomas, and his daughter, Elizabeth, both minors at the time. His date of death is given only as 1622. He may have been a victim of the Powhatan Uprising of that year, which was deadly for most English living in the vicinity of Varina, his plantation on the north shore of the James River, but there is no proof of this. He was thirty-seven or thereabouts. He did much that helped save Jamestown: marrying Pocahontas, discovering a strain of tobacco that gave the colony a cash crop, and serving in government.

Thomas Rolfe inherited hundreds of acres of land in Tsenacommacah, some from his father and some from Powhatan himself. Thomas emigrated to Virginia in about 1640. There, he married Jane Poythress or Poyers, and their daughter—also Jane—married Robert Bolling. The Bollings' son John married Mary Kennon, and they had six children and thirty-seven grandchildren. Today, descent from Pocahontas is proudly claimed by countless Americans, and for good reason: in our pantheon of founding luminaries, we have but one female—Pocahontas.

John Smith's last years were frustrating ones. He returned to North America on a reconnaissance mission in 1614 and explored the coast of New England, the naming of which is credited to him. He attempted two additional voyages to New England, but both were thwarted by mishap—a broken mainmast on one, capture by the French on the other. After these failures, venture capital dried up. He went on to write and publish the accounts of his Virginia experiences already mentioned, plus tracts on colonization in general, offering advice that was ignored. After the Powhatan Uprising of 1622, he volunteered to return to Jamestown, but his offer was declined.[35] Unappreciated and alone, Smith spent his last years in obscurity. He never married and died in 1631, his fifty-second year. He was buried in the church of Saint Sepulchre-without-Newgate, destroyed in the Great Fire of London in 1666.

Of this large cast of characters, Opechancanough outlived them all. He survived to make one last desperate attempt to rid Tsenacommacah of the English and take back his land.[36] On April 18, 1644, his warriors killed four hundred colonists before the rebellion was put down. Opechancanough was captured and imprisoned in Jamestown. Now in his late nineties and so weak he could neither walk nor raise his eyelids without help, he was a curiosity for colonists who came to gawk until one of his guards—disobeying orders not to mistreat the intrepid old warrior—shot him in the back.[37]

If tasked to pinpoint the birthdate of English America, one might start with July 13, 1584, the day Walter Raleigh's colony first landed on Roanoke Island. Or one might choose May 14, 1607, the day the *Susan Constant* dropped anchor off Jamestown Island. Or the day in late December 1607 that Captain John Smith claimed Pocahontas saved his life. Or one might choose the day Lord De La Warr stepped ashore at Jamestown to save the colony from abandonment. Some have even suggested the infamous day in August 1619 when African slaves were first landed and sold in Jamestown. Or one might choose July 30, 1619, the day Governor George Yeardley opened the first session of an assembly of democratically elected representatives, two white males from each from the colony's eleven townships.

The original charter of the Virginia Company of London approved by King James in 1606 guaranteed to all citizens of England who agreed to emigrate to Virginia the same "liberties, franchises and immunities" as if they had remained in England. Needless to say, this pledge was ignored for the first thirteen years of the colony's existence, but it had become evident by 1619 that the colony would never thrive were it managed as it had been. When Yeardley arrived in April of that year for his second term as governor, he brought news that the company had decided to abandon martial law in favor of English common law and, furthermore, that the company had approved a legislative assembly in Virginia, but with limited powers.[38] The company was only agreeing to do what its original charter had ordered it to do in the first place.

The assembly included the governor and his council, which included

John Rolfe and Francis West, Lord De La Warr's brother who had deserted Jamestown during the starving time. Both men had been in Virginia for years now. The issues important to them were the same ones that concerned the twenty-two elected assemblymen: relations with the Algonquins, allocation of land, agricultural concerns, trade with England, church attendance, and public disorder which was rife—theft, drunkenness, gambling, and the like. These men—a plutocracy of tobacco plantation owners—seized upon their new powers and enacted legislation deemed appropriate to deal with these issues and more.[39] As men newly empowered tend to do, they went beyond the limits of their authority. They authorized free enterprise and created a taxing authority. For redress of grievances, they created a judiciary. The assembly would continue to grasp for a greater share of power right up to and beyond the American Revolution, one hundred and fifty-six years later. They were motivated, at bottom, by the same urges and desires that have motivated humankind since we became aware that we are aware—the pursuit of happiness. But as has also been the case for millennia, one man's pursuit of happiness often comes at the expense of the happiness of others. In coming years, the Algonquins of Tsenacommacah and Ossomocomuck would suffer extermination and removal to reduce the threat of attack on farmers and to clear more land for growing tobacco. To do the work, thousands upon thousands of indentured servants and, later, African slaves would be brought to Virginia as forced labor in a plantation system and treated as chattel to be bought and sold.[40] From such harsh and degrading servitude, there was no escape in such an alien land. It was inhumane and ugly, but it worked. English America was a fait accompli.

§ § §

Over four hundred years have passed since the colonists of Roanoke Island were given up for lost. John Smith had sent two expeditions into the Carolina interior seeking survivors. He had information, perhaps from Opechancanough, that at least some had settled with the Chesepioc Tribe and, when the first Jamestown fleet arrived in April 1607, that Powhatan had ordered the destruction of the entire tribe plus its English inhabitants. But this source added that four English escaped and survived in an Algonquin village on the Chowan River where it forks into three branches.[41] Smith sent Michael Sicklemore in search of them with two Warraskoyack guides in late December 1608, but this effort "found little hope and less certainty of them."[42] Perhaps unsatisfied with this inconclusive result, Smith later sent Anas Todkill, one of his most trusted acolytes, with Quiyoughcohannock guides again into Chowanoc Territory, "but nothing could they learn but they were all dead."[43]

Powhatan may well have wiped out the Chesepioc Tribe. The Jamestown Colony found no trace of them. It would not have been the last time he resorted to such brutality. In October 1608, for reasons that remain a mystery, Powhatan ordered the destruction of the Piankatank Tribe, killing twenty-four warriors and forcing the tribe's chiefs, women, and children into the Algonquin equivalent of slavery.[44] But recall that the Spanish searched the Chesapeake Bay for Roanoke Colony survivors in 1588 and found none. Of course, the Spanish could have missed them, or the colonists could have arrived later. Perhaps Powhatan destroyed the Chesepioc because he linked them to the prophecy which foretold that his overthrow would come from the direction of the Chesapeake Bay, where the Chesepioc lived.

The London Company was appraised of the rumor regarding survivors and gave orders to Thomas Gates to investigate further. Strachey then reported another rumor, learned from Machumps, with whom he sailed on *Sea Venture*: that there were seven survivors—"four men, two boys, and one young maid"—living at a place called Ochanahoen, having "escaped and fled up the River of Choanoke."[45] Needless to say, Gates had no opportunity to send out a search party after De La Warr declared war on the Powhatans. In contemporary accounts, therefore, there is no further mention of Roanoke colony survivors or of efforts to find them.

In the four hundred years since, several theories have been proposed to explain where they might have gone and dozens of attempts to find evidence of their fate have been undertaken. Powhatan's claim that he killed them all along with the Chesepioc Tribe would indicate that at least some went to live on the Chesapeake Bay. But Powhatan also claimed to have killed Henry Ravens and the others who sailed the *Sea Venture's* long boat from Bermuda to Virginia. The old chief liked to take responsibility for all things, therefore his claim is suspect. He had no reason to kill the Roanoke colony survivors, indeed, for a whole host of reasons, keeping them alive would have been the wiser option. But the fact that the Roanoke colonists knew that the Spanish were looking for them on the Chesapeake Bay is persuasive that they chose not to take that risk.[46]

John White's statement that they intended "to remove fifty miles further up into the main" would also seem to rule out Chesapeake Bay as their destination. His statement implies that the Roanoke colonists intended to go farther inland. In 1937 a tourist from California driving through North Carolina on the Coastal Highway found a stone near the east bank of the Chowan River—which would have been roughly "fifty miles further up into the main" from Roanoke Island—while searching for hickory nuts in the woods. Carved in the stone was a message signed EWD—presumably Eleanor White Dare—stating that the colonists "Cam Hither" after

John White sailed to England where they lived for two years in "Misarie & Warre," that all but seven were ultimately killed including her daughter and husband, and that their bodies were buried four miles east of the Chowan River on a small hill marked by a rock inscribed with their names. The message ended with the pleading offer of a generous reward to any "savage" who showed the stone to White or any other Englishman. Two aspects of the message appeared genuine, the Elizabethan orthography and the apparent age of the carving. And the number seven agreed with Strachey's report from Machumps as to the number of survivors and their general location. This was compelling, but the stone's finder was unable to retrace his steps to the place where he found it, and then he disappeared in mysterious fashion. After more carved stones of dubious authenticity began surfacing elsewhere, doubt was cast on all such artifacts.

Based on the analysis of a map created by John White in 1585 and findings from recent archaeological excavations, there is evidence of a possible English settlement located near the confluence of the Chowan and Roanoke Rivers.[47] If this were true, then White would have known the intended destination before he returned to England for supplies which seems unlikely. But as a refuge for the lost colonists, the Chowan River area was problematic for two reasons. First, the Chowanoc had agreed to Pemisapan's conspiracy to attack Ralph Lane's colony, and its weroance, Menatonon, was not well-disposed toward the English after Lane kidnapped his son, Skiko, and threatened to kill him. And second, the colonists were inordinately dependent on Manteo who, by reason of his siding with the English when Lane attacked the Secotan and killed Pemisapan, would have been considered a traitor by all the northern tribes of Ossomocomuck.[48] The colonists needed Manteo for important reasons: as their interpreter, their advisor and guide, and their primary negotiator. It is likely, therefore, that where he was unwelcome, they were unwelcome also. This augured for establishing the colony within the territory of one or more of the southern tribes, the Croatoan, Pomoiok, Neusiok, or Coree.[49] The message left by the colonists on the pale at Roanoke Island confirmed this, though the fact that the Croatoan territory was too small to absorb all one hundred and eighteen colonists meant that Croatoan Island could not have been their *only* destination.[50]

It was not until 1700—ninety years later—that an Englishman was reported to have returned to the North Carolina Outer Banks. In that year, a young man named John Lawson was employed to survey the Carolina interior. Lawson had arrived in Charleston, South Carolina, a town founded thirty years earlier by the Lords Proprietors of Carolina, eight English aristocrats who were awarded ownership of the vast area by Charles II in 1663 by virtue of their support for the restoration of the

English crown and overthrow of the Commonwealth of England led by Oliver Cromwell.[51] The grant included all of North America between Virginia and Florida, the boundaries of which were ill-defined and, needless to say, disputed by Spain.[52]

Lawson left Charleston on December 28, 1700, and traveled through wilderness northwest as far as present-day Charlotte, North Carolina, where he encountered the Occaneechi or Great Trading Path that ran from today's Petersburg, Virginia, to Augusta, Georgia.[53] He followed the path northeast as far as present-day Hillsborough, North Carolina, then turned east, led by an Amerindian guide named Enoe Will, and he arrived at an English plantation on the Pamlico River in the vicinity of present-day Washington, North Carolina, on February 23, 1701. He had traveled five hundred and fifty miles by himself during winter and maintained a detailed journal of his experiences and observations.

Lawson continued on to Roanoke Island, where he found the ruins of a fort and artifacts—English coins, a powder horn, and "one small Quarter deck–Gun"—in the possession of the "Hatteras Indians" whom he encountered. These people told Lawson that their ancestors were "white People," and that they "could talk in a Book." He reported that some of them had gray eyes unlike any other Native Americans he had ever encountered. They also claimed to have had a frequent vision of a ship under sail which they called "Sir Walter Raleigh's Ship." Lawson claimed this story "has been affirm'd to me, by Men of the best Credit in the Country."[54]

Lawson's report rings true. It is entirely plausible that those colonists who initially went to Croatoan Island returned to the island after the hurricane of 1589 to continue to wait for John White's return and that a legend of English ships had been passed down to children and grandchildren by the original colonists, who would have spent the rest of their days scanning the ocean for a tall ship that would never come.

What became of them is a mystery. Perhaps their descendants intermarried with English whites or African American slaves and remain in the vicinity to this day. Such a claim is made by members of the Lumbee Tribe of southeastern North Carolina. It is conceivable that DNA tests could prove descent from the original colonists if existing relatives were to be found in England from whom DNA samples could be obtained. Farfetched though this may seem, it is not impossible.

As to the fate of those who could not be accommodated on Croatoan Island, and in the interest of leaving no stone unturned, consider the discovery of a fort symbol hidden under a patch on a map drawn in 1585 by John White. Hailed as an important find and the possible landing place for the Lost Colony, the site is at the confluence of the Chowan and Roanoke Rivers in what is today Bertie County, North Carolina. But this theory is problematic for reasons stated earlier, principally, that the site was in the midst of hostile territory, that it would have been difficult to defend and resupply, and that the colonists were entirely dependent on Manteo—their interpreter, guide, and negotiator—who was viewed as a traitor by all the tribes in the vicinity. And as for the aforementioned Eleanor White Dare stone found on the banks of the Chowan River, it has been thoroughly debunked. For one thing, there are few hills in Chowan County, North Carolina and virtually no large stones, plus there are other persuasive reasons to dismiss this artifact as a hoax.[55] We are left to conclude, therefore, that in all probability the Lost Colony will never be found.

§ § §

Along the ancient, sheltered harbor of Plymouth, on the channel coast of Devon in England, stands an impressive Greek Revival portico flanked by flagpoles flying the Union Jack and Stars and Stripes. A carved stone announces the entrance to the Mayflower Steps where they descend to the water. A popular spot with American tourists, it is a memorial to the ship, the *Mayflower*, which sailed from this spot in September 1620 to establish a colony in Massachusetts. Further along on the dock are two unassuming bronze plaques gone green with the verdigris of age. Though now hard to read, with patience one can make them out. The first commemorates the sailing in April 1584 of the reconnaissance voyage sent by Walter Raleigh to Roanoke Island, North Carolina, site of what would become known as the Lost Colony. The second commemorates the sailing of the ill-fated *Sea Venture* in 1609, destination Jamestown. No flags fly here.

Chapter Notes

Introduction

1. George Bruner Parks, *Richard Hakluyt and the English Voyages*, 10–11. Flemish geographer Gerardus Mercator (1512–1594) created the Mercator Projection of cartography which enables a sailing course (rhumb line) to be represented by a straight line. It revolutionized navigation.
2. J.E. Neale, *Queen Elizabeth I*, 48; Benjamin Woolley, *The Queen's Conjuror*, 38.
3. Woolley, 91.
4. Woolley, 131–133.
5. Raleigh Trevelyan, *Sir Walter Raleigh*, 20.
6. One could cite earlier beginnings: Richard Eden's preface to his 1555 translation of Peter Martyr d'Anghiera's *The Decades of the New World*, for example, in which he suggests New World colonies for England. Humphrey Gilbert's *A Discourse of a Discoverie for a New Passage to Catay* of 1576 does the same. Dee's vision of a British Empire, however, and his influence with the queen brought such ideas to a whole new level of national consciousness.
7. Anthony Payne, "Richard Hakluyt: An Essay in Bibliography 1580–88," vii; Beeching, introduction to *Voyages and Discoveries*, by Richard Hakluyt, 13. Payne gives 1552 as Hakluyt's date of birth; Beeching gives 1551 as the date, and Clements Markham gives 1553 as the date. (Markham, "Richard Hakluyt: His Life and Work," 1896, 4.); George Bruner Parks, *Hakluyt and the English Voyages*, 57–58.
8. Markham, "Richard Hakluyt: His Life and Work," 5–6.
9. A.L. Rowse, *Ralegh and the Throckmortons*, 132; Trevelyan, *Sir Walter Raleigh*, 9; David Beers Quinn, *Set Fair for Roanoke*, 4; Karen Kupperman, *Roanoke: The Abandoned Colony*, 9. Kupperman states that Raleigh "was registered at Oriel College, Oxford, in 1568 when he was fourteen and stayed on the rolls until 1572; but for much of that time he was actually in France fighting on the side of the Protestant Huguenots."
10. Beeching, introduction to *Voyages and Discoveries*, by Richard Hakluyt, 14.
11. John Winter Jones, introduction to *Divers Voyages Touching the Discovery of America and the Islands Adjacent*, by Richard Hakluyt, xviii; D.B. Quinn, *Raleigh and the British Empire*, 31.
12. Parks, *Hakluyt and the English Voyages*, 59, 65.
13. Margaret Holmes Williamson, *Powhatan Lords of Life and Death*, 195. Williamson: "The head of an English Protestant congregation in the early 17th century was a minister, a parson, a vicar—not a priest, except to those inimical to his brand of Protestantism."
14. Parks, *Hakluyt and the English Voyages*, 62–63.
15. D.B. Quinn, *Raleigh and the British Empire*, 47; Jones, introduction to *Divers Voyages*, lxxxvii.
16. Payne, "Richard Hakluyt," 168; Markham, "Richard Hakluyt, 5–6; Parks, *Hakluyt and the English Voyages*, 102–103.
17. Parks, *Hakluyt and the English Voyages*, 87, 248; Anthony Payne, "Richard Hakluyt: An Essay in Bibliography 1580–88," PhD diss., National University of Ireland, Galway, 2019. https://aran.library.nuigalway.ie/bitstream/handle/10379/15851/PaynePhD2019.pdf?sequence=1&isAllowed=y, 149. The shortened title

has been variously referred to as *Discourse of Western Planting*, *Discourse Concerning Western Planting*, and *Discourse on Western Planting*, the latter being the one used in the work before you. Only two or three copies were originally made. It was not published until 1831.

18. Williamson, *Powhatan Lords*, 17. Apparently Francis Walsingham requested a copy and was given one. Williamson: "That Raleigh, and not the state, sponsored the effort was contrary to Hakluyt's recommendations. 'Hakluyt envisaged large-scale planting from Newfoundland to the borders of Florida, only possible with State support.'"

19. D.B. Quinn, *Raleigh and the British Empire*, 56–57; Robert Lacey, *Sir Walter Ralegh*, 64; Parks, 96–97; Edmund S. Morgan, *American Slavery, American Freedom*, 31; Giles Milton, *Big Chief Elizabeth*, 76. Parks suggests that Raleigh and Hakluyt may have been seeking "not a government subsidy but merely the Queen's private investment."

20. D.B. Quinn, *Raleigh and the British Empire*, 62; Lacey, 66, 87; Parks, *Hakluyt and the English Voyages*, 85–86. Quinn reports that on its return to England the *Tyger* captured a Spanish ship off Bermuda, the *Santa Maria de San Vicente*, and robbed it of a cargo worth "120,000 ducats." Lacey adds, "To take Spanish prizes was the most rapid way Walter Ralegh's heavy investment in the Virginia enterprise could be recouped." Referring to the same 1585 Virginia (Roanoke Colony) enterprise, Parks maintains that "there is no record of the financing of Virginia." Doubtless, Raleigh invested heavily in it himself. Hakluyt may have invested also, but apparently capturing Spanish prizes was necessary to cover the costs.

21. Kupperman, *Roanoke*, 29, 101. The author points out that Hakluyt believed—since Roanoke Island was on the same parallel as Spain—that the colony could produce "wine, olive oil, sugar, oranges and lemons, rice, and silk." England's manufacturers of woolen cloth depended on olive oil to finish their fabrics. Since it was imported from Spain and Portugal, the Iberian kingdom had, to some degree, a chokehold on England, and Hakluyt sought to provide his nation with its own source.

22. Hakluyt's *A Discourse on Western Planting* was not published until 1831; at least three copies of the manuscript were made, one likely for Francis Walsingham.

23. Kupperman, *Roanoke*, 105.

24. Lacey, 100–101, 153.

25. Lacey, 59, 153; Mark Nichols and Penry Williams, *Sir Walter Raleigh: In Life and Legend*, 41–42.

26. Parks, *Hakluyt and the English Voyages*, 90–93.

27. Kieran Doherty, *Sea Venture: Shipwreck, Survival, and the Salvation of Jamestown*, 12. Doherty: "More than 650 individuals became shareholders along with fifty-six city companies and guilds...."

28. Kupperman, *Roanoke*, 141; Milton, *Big Chief Elizabeth*, 257. Indeed, King James was not interested in America. Milton quotes him, "Shall we ... abase ourselves so far as to imitate these beastly Indians, slaves to the Spaniards, refuse to the world, and as yet aliens from the holy covenant of God." Kupperman: "The entire expedition had been a disaster and a textbook illustration of the difficulties of conducting national policy through private enterprise."

29. Helen C. Rountree, *Manteo's World*, 136; Lawler, *The Secret Token*, 132; Williamson, *Powhatan Lords*, 17; James Horn, *A Land As God Made It*, 103. Williamson states, "The motivation for establishing the Jamestown colony were, for the most part, those that motivated the attempt some 25 years before to settle at Roanoke." Rountree credits King James I with demanding that the Jamestown colonists seek to find the lost Roanoke colonists. Lawler claims the London Company's reason for wanting to find the lost colonists was a selfish one. It stemmed from their need to reassure prospective colonists that Virginia was a safe place and that the Roanoke colonists were alive and well. Horn: "Finding the lost colonists would be a tremendous propaganda coup for the Company ... they would have invaluable information about the region ... might know about sources of gold and copper...."

30. Parks, *Hakluyt and the English Voyages*, 110.

31. Parks, 88; Kupperman, *Roanoke*, 12.

32. Dorothy and Thomas Hoobler, *Captain John Smith: Jamestown and the Birth of the American Dream*, 4. The Hooblers imply that the word "Chesupioc" means "great water" in Algonquin.

Notes—Chapter 1

33. Trevelyan, *Sir Walter Raleigh*, 160; Kupperman, 135.
34. Rountree, *Manteo's World*, 18, 131, 136. Rountree asserts that the Chowanoc and Weapemeoc were in "regular communication with Nansemond people in Virginia."
35. William M. Kelso, *Jamestown, the Truth Revealed*, 218–219.
36. Trevelyan, *Sir Walter Raleigh*, 418–419; Kupperman, *Roanoke*, 159; Williamson, *Powhatan Lords*, 25. But Kupperman states that "No one from the Virginia Company called on him [Raleigh] for advice. Nor was Thomas Harriot consulted." She provides no source for this information, and I cannot find support for her claim. Trevelyan refutes this, providing evidence that both Raleigh and Harriot provided advice, Raleigh in writing according to Don Pedro de Zúñiga, the Spanish ambassador to England at the time.
37. Victor Wolfgang von Hagen, ed., Introduction to *The Incas of Pedro de Cieza de León*, xl. Von Hagen provides the Spanish equivalent for the English gentleman or junior cadet: "*hidalgo* (i.e., a *hijo de algo*, a son of somebody)."
38. Horn, *A Land As God Made It*, 25.
39. D.B. Quinn, *Raleigh and the British Empire*, 19.

Chapter 1

1. Laurence Bergreen, *In Search of Kingdom*, 220. Bergreen: "cloves, the most valuable commodity in the world, itself a form of currency."
2. Ronald Watkins, *Unknown Seas: How Vasco da Gama Opened the East*, 298.
3. Watkins, 21, 30, 38; Ernle Bradford, *A Wind from the North*, 100.
4. Timothy R. Walton, *The Spanish Treasure Fleets*, 8.
5. Peter Russell, *Prince Henry "the Navigator,"* 118. Russel states that "the term 'Guinea' [was used] to describe the lands to the south of the desert [Sahara]."
6. Russell, 112, 215. Watkins, *Unknown Seas*, 24, 67–68, 72; Bradford, *Wind from the North*, 49. Russell states that the Canary Current blown by the northeast trade winds "sometimes flows south-west at a speed of six knots."
7. Bradford, 81.

8. Russell, *Prince Henry*, 228; Watkins, *Unknown Seas*, 154.
9. Russell, 201; Watkins, *Unknown Seas*, 84.
10. Russell, 236; Robin Blackburn, *The Making of New World Slavery*, 101, 103.
11. Russell, 271.
12. Russell, 262.
13. Russell, 228.
14. Paine, *Sea & Civilization*, 384. Paine explains that such ships were called "*naves* in Italian, *não* in Portuguese, and *nao* [or *nau*] in Spanish—while the English used the word 'carrack.'"
15. Paine, 432; Hugh Bicheno, *Elizabeth's Sea Dogs*, 53–54. According to Paine, "galleons developed around the middle of the [16th] century ... longer but narrower than *naus* and had lower forecastles, and they carried four masts with square sails on the fore and main and lateens on the mizzen and bonaventure mizzen, all of which made them faster and more maneuverable than *naus*." Bicheno: "Likewise the Royal Navy's move away from the 'high-charged' carrack, with its tall towers at bow and stern, to the slimmer, faster and more maneuverable galleon followed...."
16. Russell, *Prince Henry*, 229.
17. The *caravella redonda* evolved into usually three-masted ships called carracks or galleons depending on the purpose for which they were built, the former being primarily for cargo, the latter, a warship, but the terms are sometimes used interchangeably. They became the standard oceangoing ships of the sixteenth and seventeenth centuries. They had square sails on the fore- and main-masts, a fore-and-aft sail on the aft mast, an often multistoried superstructure at the stern and a single-story forecastle or fo'c's'le at the bow that often served as crews' quarters.
18. Watkins, *Unknown Seas*, 90.
19. Watkins, 100.
20. Russell, *Prince Henry*, 199.
21. Russell, *Prince Henry*, 199. Russell states that such a decree "could have no international validity unless it was underwritten by the authority of the pope." By "international," of course, he meant Christendom.
22. Neville Williams, *The Life and Times of Elizabeth I*, 121. Philip II inherited the Spanish Netherlands from his father,

Charles V, Holy Roman Emperor, in 1555. The northern provinces, which included Holland and the ports of Amsterdam and Rotterdam, spoke Dutch, and the southern provinces, which included Flanders and the port city of Antwerp, spoke Flemish. Calvinism became popular in the northern provinces while the southern provinces remained predominantly Catholic. The northern provinces rebelled against Spanish rule in the 1570s under William, Prince of Orange, and eventually gained independence in 1648 as the Netherlands. The southern provinces form the modern nations of Belgium and Luxembourg.

23. From the French, *routier*, literally "road," instructions for navigating a course at sea; a pilot's guide.

24. Russell, *Prince Henry*, 100; Watkins, *Unknown Seas*, 86.

25. Carlo M. Cipolla, *Guns, Sails, and Empires*, 23–36, 137.

26. Raleigh Trevelyan, *Sir Walter Raleigh*, 70.

27. Cipolla, *Guns, Sails, and Empires*, 143; Walton, *The Spanish Treasure Fleets*, 64. In Cipolla's words, "The oceans belonged to Europe."

28. George Bruner Parks, *Richard Hakluyt and the English Voyages*, 108; Quinn, *Set Fair for Roanoke*, 250; James Horn, *A Land As God Made It*, 4. Quinn speaks of the Verrazzanian Sea (for Giovanni da Verrazzano) which it was believed, "jutted into western America and made some part of eastern North America accessible to the Pacific."

29. Richard Hakluyt, *Voyages and Discoveries*, 233.

30. Richard Hakluyt, *A Discourse on Western Planting In The Year 1584*, in *Documentary History of the State of Maine*, edited by Leonard Woods, 113.

31. John Winter Jones, introduction to *Divers Voyages Touching the Discovery of America and the Islands Adjacent*, by Richard Hakluyt, lxiii.

32. A.L. Rowse, *The England of Elizabeth*, 136. The Italians may have been first to use such an entity.

33. Paine, *The Sea & Civilization*, 428.

34. Edmund S. Morgan, *American Slavery, American Freedom*, 18.

35. Richard Hakluyt, *A Discourse on Western Planting*, 115.

36. Hakluyt, 95–103; Wesley Frank Craven, *The Southern Colonies in the Seventeenth Century 1607–1689*, 76.

37. A.L. Rowse, *Sir Richard Grenville of the Revenge*, 87; John Sugden, *Sir Francis Drake*, 90–91; Neville Williams, *The Sea Dogs*, 127. Tierra del Fuego, a large island in an archipelago of islands of the same name separated from the South American continent by the Straits of Magellan. Today the island, Tierra del Fuego, is part Argentine and part Chilean. According to Rowse, "...speaking of the Malay peninsula ... the Elizabethans identified these lands with the unknown continent [Terra Australis] in the South Sea." Sugden: "The strait was thus seen as merely a channel between the continents of South America and Terra Australis, and was do depicted in 1541 by the influential Flemish geographer, Gerard Mercator." Francis Drake's circumnavigation voyage was blown south after exiting the Straits of Magellan to beyond Cape Horn, thus discovering that below South America was more ocean, not a continent.

38. Peter Martyr, *De Orbe Novo*, vol. 1, 239–240.

39. Martyr, 276. Parks, *Richard Hakluyt and the English Voyages*, 8; William Gilbert Gosling, *The Life of Sir Humphrey Gilbert*, 62. Gosling states that Gilbert "argues ... that Asia and America must be separated because there is such dissimilarity between both the human and animal species of the two continents," thus indicating the prevalence of such a belief.

40. Parks, 99.

41. Ivor Noël Hume, *The Virginia Adventure: Roanoke to James Towne*, 7.

42. Rowse, *England of Elizabeth*, 135.

43. David Beers Quinn, *Set Fair for Roanoke*, 16–17.

44. J.E. Neale, *Queen Elizabeth I*, 93.

45. Starkey, *Elizabeth*, 21. Williams, *Life and Times of Elizabeth I*, 17.

46. Trevelyan, *Sir Walter Raleigh*, 20; Hibbert, *Virgin Queen*, 72; Weir, *Life of Elizabeth I*, 231.

47. Neale, *Queen Elizabeth I*, 14, 128; David Starkey, *Elizabeth: The Struggle for the Throne*, 26–8, 35, 47, 52, 68, 81, 215, 227. Christopher Hibbert, *The Virgin Queen*, 26–27; Alison Weir, *The Life of Elizabeth I*, 14. All biographers agree she was fluent in French, Italian, and Latin and that she was proficient in Greek. Neale

called her German, "bad." Weir claims Elizabeth "read and conversed fluently in Latin, French, Greek, Spanish, Italian and Welsh." Starkey confirms a fluency in Spanish. Hibbert states she learned Flemish and acquired in addition some Welsh.

48. Starkey, 69. Author provides quote stating Seymour "struck her on the back or buttocks familiarly."

49. Starkey, 71–73; Carolly Erickson, *The First Elizabeth*, 69–70.

50. Williams, *The Sea Dogs*, 35. Williams reminds us that "Spain was still England's traditional ally and England's trade with the Peninsula, and even more so with the Spanish Netherlands, was of overriding importance to the economies of each country." Mary Tudor (1516–1558) is often referred to as "Bloody Mary" for her persecutions of Protestants during her five-year reign. She married Philip of Spain in 1554 who became King Philip II of Spain two years later. Mary Tudor should not be confused with Mary, Queen of Scotts (1542–1587).

51. Neale, *Queen Elizabeth I*, 35–39; MacCaffrey, *Elizabeth I*, 15–17. Wyatt's Rebellion, led by Thomas Wyatt, was widespread, but discovered and put down forcefully on February 7, 1554.

52. Hibbert, *Virgin Queen*, 49–50.

53. Neale, *Queen Elizabeth I*, 40.

54. Starkey, *Elizabeth*, 83, 205; Wallace MacCaffrey, *Elizabeth I*, 11; Hibbert, *Virgin Queen*, 36, 42; Erickson, *First Elizabeth*, 87, 92–93. Starkey quotes biographer Mandell Creighton: "her love of simplicity soon passed away. Indeed, it was never real ... Elizabeth was acting a part" and describes her affectation as playing "the Puritan Maid" and the "the rural Cinderella of Hatfield."

55. Hibbert, 31, 34–35, 53, 111.

56. MacCaffrey, *Elizabeth I*, 19; Starkey, 103. Starkey poses the question, "Were the Wars of the Roses about to be followed by the English Wars of Religion?"

57. Rowse, *The England of Elizabeth*, 311. Rowse translates the Latin as "the religion of the people is determined by that of the prince."

58. Neale, *Queen Elizabeth I*, 77; MacCaffrey, 50, 99, 373. "Act of Supremacy," Starkey, *Elizabeth*, 279. Starkey paraphrases the Archbishop of York who objected, asking how could they give supremacy to a woman, who was forbidden by St Paul even to speak in church, much less be its head.

59. Rowse, *England of Elizabeth*, 35–36, 435; Starkey, 117, 175, 277, 319; Rowse, *Sir Richard Grenville*, 130–131. Starkey refers to the settlement as Elizabeth Protestantism. Rowse calls the compromise, "Catholic in order, Protestant in doctrine," "the new State-made Church" that "hardly anyone cared for."

60. Rowse, England of Elizabeth, 300–301; Benjamin Woolley, *The Queen's Conjuror*, 88; Weir, *Life of Elizabeth I*, 223; Liza Picard, *Elizabeth's England*, 102; Benjamin Woolley, *The Queen's Conjuror: The Life and Magic of Dr. Dee*, 88.

61. MacCaffrey, *Elizabeth I*, 327, 332; Starkey, *Elizabeth*, 260; Hibbert, *Virgin Queen*, 25; Weir, 59.

62. Neale, *Queen Elizabeth I*, 180.

63. Hibbert, *Virgin Queen*, 67; Starkey, *Elizabeth*, 63, 86. Elizabeth expressed this belief in a letter to her father written in December 1545 and in another to her brother, King Edward VI, written in 1551 or 1552.

64. Starkey, 76; MacCaffrey, *Elizabeth I*, 307; A.L. Rowse, *The Elizabethan Renaissance*, 260–261; Weir, *Life of Elizabeth*, 224. Starkey adds: "Nowhere was this truer than in her sexuality." Weir quotes Sir Francis Bacon: "Her majesty loveth peace. Next, she loveth not change."

65. MacCaffrey, 40; Williams, *Life and Times of Elizabeth I*, 44; Weir, 256.

66. Hugh Bicheno, *Elizabeth's Sea Dogs*, 26, 55.

67. Parks, *Richard Hakluyt and the English Voyages*, 8; A.L. Rowse, *Sir Richard Grenville*, 198.

68. Rowse, *England of Elizabeth*, 167–168. Rowse points out that the French and Portuguese were the first to exploit the schools of Atlantic cod on Newfoundland's Grand Banks as early as 1550, but they were soon followed by the Spanish, English, and Dutch.

69. Williams, *The Sea Dogs*, 16–19.

70. Weir, *Life of Elizabeth I*, 228–229. Quoting Elizabeth: "I have not sought to advance my territories and enlarge my dominions."

71. Neale, *Queen Elizabeth I*, 108.

72. Neale, 63; Hibbert, *Virgin Queen*, 66. Hibbert quotes a Norfolk clergyman's

prayer: "Ah, Lord! To take away the empire from a man, and give it to a woman, seemeth to be an evident token of thine anger towards us Englishmen."
73. Starkey, *Elizabeth*, 3.
74. Starkey, 162; Hibbert, *Virgin Queen*, 57; Williams, *Life and Times of Elizabeth I*, 36, 44. She attended Mass regularly and even went to confession.
75. Rowse, *England of Elizabeth*, 316.
76. Hibbert, *Virgin Queen*, 61–62. Hibbert quotes the Spanish ambassador.
77. Hibbert, 79. Author states, "Certainly she liked men and women about her who were sexually attractive; and this led to much gossip, particularly in foreign courts."
78. MacCaffrey, *Elizabeth I*, 375; Hibbert, 67, 123; Weir, *Life of Elizabeth I*, 257.
79. MacCaffrey, 172. Author states, "She demanded a lively wit, a ready tongue, and an eloquent pen ... courtiers cast in the mode of Castiglione."
80. Raleigh Trevelyan, *Sir Walter Raleigh*, 46.
81. A.L. Rowse, *Ralegh and the Throckmortons*, 236; Trevelyan, 48, 80, 365. Trevelyan calls it "the Charybdis pool of the English court" and Rowse states that "At the top, almost anyone would betray almost anyone else."
82. Trevelyan, 50. The author states, "Rowse, though he never said it on paper, was sure that some sort of 'touching' went on between [Elizabeth] and her lovers."
83. Hibbert, *Virgin Queen*, 81. Hibbert reports that Amy Dudley had been playing backgammon with other ladies who were staying in the house when the accident happened.
84. Hibbert, 81–82; Erickson, *First Elizabeth*, 194.
85. Neale, *Queen Elizabeth I*, 84.
86. Hibbert, *Virgin Queen*, 115.
87. Neale, 233. MacCaffrey, *Elizabeth I*, 172. Neale calls it "a dawning respect for the Queen's judgment."
88. MacCaffrey, 67; Hibbert, *Virgin Queen*, 115–117; Trevelyan, Sir Walter Raleigh, 271. MacCaffrey states Elizabeth was "desperately anxious to avoid decisions which could not be reversed."
89. Neale, *Queen Elizabeth I*, 83, 96; Rowse, *England of Elizabeth*, 307–310; Starkey, *Elizabeth*, 157; Hibbert, 258; Erickson, *First Elizabeth*, 232; Trevelyan, *Sir Walter Raleigh*, 77.
90. MacCaffrey, *Elizabeth I*, 182, 390; Williams, *Life and Times of Elizabeth I*, 175; Weir, *Life of Elizabeth I*, 228.
91. MacCaffrey, 75, 364. Starkey, *Elizabeth*, 230, 276. MacCaffrey calls her "a natural snob" and claims that "she found the exercise of power exhilarating, and she was loath to yield it to anyone." Starkey quotes Spanish ambassador, Count de Feria as saying, "she is determined to be governed by no one."
92. Picard, *Elizabeth's London*, xxii.
93. Rule of Thumb in English folklore held that a man could beat his wife with a stick no thicker than his thumb.
94. Picard, *Elizabeth's London*, 48. Between 107 and 100 to be more precise, nearly all could be traced back to 1200.
95. Rowse, *England of Elizabeth*, 249–250; Picard, 270.
96. Picard, *Elizabeth's London*, 272–273; M. St. Clare Byrne, *Elizabethan Life in Town and Country*, 271.
97. Picard, 259. The author explains that among the 100 livery companies were the twelve "great companies"—Mercers, Grocers, Drapers, Fishmongers, Goldsmiths, Skinners, Merchant Taylors, Haberdashers, Salters, Ironmongers, Vintners, and Clothworkers. Average annual wage for a clothworker, blacksmith, or butcher was £6 (Picard, 323).
98. Morgan, *American Slavery, American Freedom*, 62–67.
99. Picard, 180.
100. Rowse, *England of Elizabeth*, 240–241; Edmund S. Morgan, *American Slavery, American Freedom*, 66.
101. "Three quarters of London's male citizens," Picard, 262. "Prices and wages were fixed," Picard, 168.
102. Picard, *Elizabeth's London*, 268, 271.
103. Gosling, *Sir Humphrey Gilbert*, 80. Gosling states that by statute of Henry VII (citing chapter and verse) "were decreed the arms, armour, and horses each squire, knight and noble, according to his degree, was to maintain for the service of the Crown."
104. Picard, 259; Byrne, *Elizabethan Life*, 87.
105. Rowse, *England of Elizabeth*, 256; Morgan, *American Slavery, American Free-*

dom, 65; Picard, 290–291; Lee Miller, *Roanoke, Solving the Mystery of the Lost Colony*, 38. Morgan asserts that England's population was "growing faster than the country could find jobs for them" and reports "rising numbers of hungry, masterless men." Miller: "Classes of thriftless men and women spring up everywhere, earning a living as beggars, of which there were reckoned to be no less than 10,000 persons in the realm."

106. Rowse, 392. The year was 1598.

107. Morgan, *American Slavery, American Freedom*, 62–69.

108. David Howarth, *The Voyage of the Armada*, 31. Howarth: Philip "was bigoted, dogmatic, self-righteous, illogical, ruthless and hopelessly confused; but also, he was appallingly sincere."

109. Geoffrey Parker, *The Grand Strategy of Philip II*, 181.

110. Parker, 124, 195.

111. Parker, 93; MacCaffrey, *Elizabeth I*, 328–9; David Harris Sacks, "Discourses of Western Planting: Richard Hakluyt and the Making of the Atlantic World" in *The Atlantic World and Virginia, 1550–1624*, ed. Peter C. Mancall, 419. Parker: "Spanish imperial power in Europe and the Americas [was] the holy mission of Philip's divinely ordained and absolute rule."

112. Neale, *Queen Elizabeth I*, 183. Rowse, *England of Elizabeth*, 139–142; Walton, *The Spanish Treasure Fleets*, 29, Paine, *Sea & Civilization*, 426–427, 439; Hibbert, *Virgin Queen*, 176; Williams, *Life and Times of Elizabeth I*, 122; MacCaffrey, *Elizabeth I*, 155–156. MacCaffrey calls Antwerp the focal point of English overseas trade, where the whole cloth export of London was sold, and the great bulk of the nation's imports procured. Paine states that after its capture by Spain, "the population of Antwerp fell by more than a half." Hibbert states "The Spanish then closed the port of Antwerp to English ships."

113. Antonia Fraser, *King James*, 20, 26.

114. MacCaffrey, *Elizabeth I* 106–113.

115. Parker, *Grand Strategy of Philip II*, 161.

116. Parker, *Grand Strategy of Philip II*, 160. Indeed, Parker: "Ridolfi ... was almost certainly a double-agent who shared all his information with Elizabeth's ministers." This, however, has not been proven.

117. Neale, *Queen Elizbeth I*, 292; Starkey, *Elizabeth*, 312; Hibbert, *Virgin Queen*, 220, 222–223; Byrne, *Elizabethan Life*, 167; Weir, *Life of Elizabeth I*, 272. Neale adds that "when it came to fighting Spaniards ... all men were Englishmen."

118. Parker, *Grand Strategy of Philip II*, 163. Parker: "The Ridolfi plot proved a turning-point in Anglo-Spanish relations."

119. Parker, *Grand Strategy of Philip II*, 167; Peter H. Wilson, *The Thirty Years War*, 90. The Spanish tercio was a "pike and shot" formation of two hundred and fifty well-trained soldiers advancing against an enemy position. The front ranks carried pikes to defend against a cavalry charge, and they were protected on the flanks and in the rear by ranks of musketeers.

120. Parker, *Grand Strategy of Philip II*, 182. Parker: "nine English governments had been overthrown or seriously undermined by seaborne invasion in the five centuries since the Norman Conquest of 1066."

Chapter 2

1. Timothy R. Walton, *The Spanish Treasure Fleets*, 72.

2. Richard Hakluyt, *Voyages and Discoveries*, 51; Neville Williams, *The Sea Dogs*, 19–20. Williams points out that the senior Hawkins sought to trade for brazilwood, which contains a red dye that was in high demand "by English clothiers," presumably for dying wool yarn and undyed woven cloth for the clothing trade.

3. Harry Kelsey, *Sir Francis Drake*, 30. Kelsey speaks of the "nearly unlimited authority of the commander of a fleet."

4. Herbert S. Klein and Ben Vinson III, *African Slavery in Latin America and the Caribbean*, 122. The authors: "The single largest item of European imports that paid for slaves were textiles.... Next in importance as a trade item were iron bars, which were worked into tools by African blacksmiths.... Finally came tobacco and alcohol."

5. Robin Blackburn, *The Making of New World Slavery*, 220.

6. Kelsey, *Sir Francis Drake*, 18.

7. Kelsey, 34–36; Hugh Bicheno, *Elizabeth's Sea Dogs*, 102–104.

8. Walton, *The Spanish Treasure Fleets*, 74.

9. Bicheno, *Elizabeth's Sea Dogs*, 88.
10. A.L. Rowse, *The England of Elizbeth*, 321; Wallace MacCaffrey, *Elizabeth I*, 185. Rowse claims Elizabeth had no choice but to assist the Dutch. Had she not, they would have lost the war and left Spain free to invade England.
11. Rowse, 179, 371. Rowse limits the high tide of Elizabethan prosperity to the years 1574–85 and calls the years 1585 to Elizabeth's death in 1603 the war years. The Armada year of 1588 was certainly the capstone of her reign.
12. J.E. Neale, *Queen Elizabeth I*, 113; Neville Williams, *The Life and Times of Elizabeth I*, 117–118. The St. Bartholomew's Day Massacre occurred on August 23–24, 1572. It began in Paris and spread to other cities and towns. Following the assassination of Huguenot leader Gaspard de Coligny, French Catholics attacked Huguenot men, women, and children, killing an estimated 10,000 to 30,000. The French Calvinist Protestant movement was thereby damaged irreparably.
13. Christopher Hibbert, *The Virgin Queen*, 175; Neville Williams, *The Life and Times of Elizabeth I*, 92; Walton, *The Spanish Treasure Fleets*, 74. Williams states the ships carried £85,000 in specie, not £100,000 as Hibbert claimed. Walton puts the amount at 450,000 pesos.
14. Mark Nicholls and Penry Williams, *Sir Walter Raleigh: In Life and Legend*, 65.
15. Philip P. Boucher, "Revisioning the 'French Atlantic'" in *The Atlantic World and Virginia, 1550–1624*, ed. Peter C. Mancall, 291–292.
16. Bicheno, *Elizabeth's Sea Dogs*, 113–115.
17. Kelsey, *Sir Francis Drake*, 61; Edmund S. Morgan, *American Slavery, American Freedom*, 11–12.
18. Bicheno, *Elizabeth's Sea Dogs*, 124.
19. Rowse, *England of Elizabeth*, 148; Hibbert, 176.
20. David Starkey, *Elizabeth: The Struggle for the Throne*, 320–321.
21. MacCaffrey, *Elizabeth I*, 165–167. MacCaffrey refers to it as "a feminine revulsion towards blood and violence … that … could be avoided only by playing the dangerous game of diplomatic bluff, a sustained exercise in brinkmanship."
22. Hibbert, *Virgin Queen*, 119; Weir, *Life of Elizabeth I*, 297.
23. Geoffrey Parker, *The Grand Strategy of Philip II*, 157–165; Weir, 363. Parker: "In July 1568 Pope Pius V began to pressure Philip to invade England and restore Catholicism."
24. Parker, 276. Parker quotes Philip II: "the cause of religion must take precedence over everything."
25. Williams, *Life and Times of Elizabeth*, 118. Francis, originally the Duke of Alençon, inherited the title of Anjou in 1574 from his brother, Henry, upon the death of his eldest living brother, King Charles IX. Francis was the youngest son of Henry II of France and Catherine de' Medici.
26. Hibbert, *Virgin Queen*, 198.
27. Parker, *Grand Strategy of Philip II*, 165.
28. Walton, *The Spanish Treasure Fleets*, 72–73.
29. John Sugden, *Sir Francis Drake*, 98. Sugden quotes Drake: Elizabeth "contributed 1,000 crowns to the venture."
30. Kelsey, *Sir Francis Drake*, 105.
31. Lincoln Paine, *The Sea & Civilization*, 401–402.
32. Kelsey, *Sir Francis Drake*, 98; Sugden, *Sir Francis Drake*, 95. Sugden asserts that Drake and Thomas Doughty met in Ireland as soldiers after which Doughty served as personal secretary to Christopher Hatton, who learned of the plan the two soldiers had hatched in Ireland.
33. Kelsey, 79; Sugden, 96; Bicheno, *Elizabeth's Sea Dogs*, 135.
34. Sugden, 98.
35. Kelsey, *Sir Francis Drake*, 83, 95.
36. Kelsey, 247–248.
37. Kelsey, 106–109.
38. Kelsey, 106–107.
39. Kelsey, 108.
40. Bicheno, *Elizabeth's Sea Dogs*, 139–141.
41. Kelsey, *Sir Francis Drake*, 110–112; Sugden, *Sir Francis Drake*, 113–114. Quoting Drake, "I must have the gentleman to haul and draw with the mariner, and the mariner with the gentleman."
42. Kelsey, 113; Bicheno, *Elizabeth's Sea Dogs*, 329. Bicheno speaks of the "sheer ferocity of the English," which "disheartened their Spanish opponents."
43. Bicheno, 11. Bicheno claims that "it's safe to say that while the ale remained drinkable everyone aboard was at least mildly inebriated at all times."

Notes—Chapter 2

44. Kelsey, *Sir Francis Drake*, 156–159; Walton, *The Spanish Treasure Fleets*, 80; Williams, *The Sea Dogs*, 129–130. Kelsey states, "The weight of the gold was eighty pounds. There were thirteen chests of reales, and there was so much uncoined silver that it was used as ballast in place of the usual ballast stones." Walton states that in the years after 1580, "About 250 tons of silver, worth nearly 8 million pesos, came from mines at Potosi (in Peru) every year."

45. Rowse, *England of Elizabeth*, 180; Walton, *The Spanish Treasure Fleets*, 75–76. Rouse puts the cost of Drake's circumnavigation at £5,000 and the returns to investors at £600,000; however, estimates differ wildly as to the value. Walton states that "Drake had more than 25 tons of silver worth about 750,000 pesos and equivalent to almost a year of Elizabeth's normal revenue."

46. Kelsey, *Sir Francis Drake*, 219; Bicheno, *Elizabeth's Sea Dogs*, 155; Williams, *The Sea Dogs*, 147. Williams claims Drake paid the princely sum of £3,400 for the estate.

47. Technically, members of a 1525 Spanish expedition led by García Jofre de Loaísa (1490–1526) who survived shipwreck in the East Indies and were returned to Europe as Portuguese prisoners comprised the second circumnavigation.

48. Rowse, *Ralegh and the Throckmortons*, 134; D.D. Quinn, *Raleigh and the British Empire*, 30; William Gilbert Gosling, *The Life of Sir Humphrey Gilbert*, 18, 24, 32.

49. Raleigh Trevelyan, *Sir Walter Raleigh*, 20; Gosling, *Sir Humphrey Gilbert*, 49–50; Anna Beer, *Patriot or Traitor: The Life and Death of Sir Walter Ralegh*, 19.

50. Gosling, *Sir Humphrey Gilbert*, 58; Robert Lacey, *Sir Walter Ralegh*, 27.

51. Gosling, 63; Lacey, 27–28. The patent was dated 14 June 1578.

52. Peter Russel, *Prince Henry 'the Navigator': A Life*, 240. The "royal fifth (*quinto*)," traditional share due the crowns of Europe in such cases.

53. Lacey, *Sir Walter Ralegh*, 29; William Stebbing, *Sir Walter Ralegh*, 15; Karen Kupperman, *Roanoke: The Abandoned Colony*, 10.

54. Trevelyan, *Sir Walter Raleigh*, 23.

55. Williams, *Life and Times of Elizabeth I*, 132.

56. Leonard Woods, introduction to *A Discourse on Western Planting*, by Richard Hakluyt, lvii.

57. Starkey, *Elizabeth*, 316. Weir, *Life of Elizabeth I*, 324, 340–341.

58. MacCaffrey, *Elizabeth I*, 173; Trevelyan, *Sir Walter Raleigh*, 47; Weir, 341, MacCaffrey's characterization: "In 1581, a new star appeared in the court firmament, dim at first but rising meteor-like to a dazzling brilliance."

59. Stebbing, *Sir Walter Ralegh*, 23–24. As his source for this story, Stebbing cites English historian Thomas Fuller (1608–1661) and his *History of the Worthies of England* (1662).

60. Trevelyan, *Sir Walter Raleigh*, 20.

61. Stebbing, *Sir Walter Ralegh*, 28; Lacey, *Sir Walter Ralegh*, 30; Beer, *Patriot or Traitor*, 27.

62. Nicholls and Williams, *Sir Walter Raleigh*, 255.

63. Lacey, *Sir Walter Ralegh*, 45.

64. Trevelyan, *Sir Walter Raleigh*, 167; Williams, *Life and Times of Elizabeth I*, 166.

65. Stebbing, *Sir Walter Ralegh*, 26. But Stebbing cautions that "Of sensual love between her and Ralegh there is not a tittle of evidence which will be accepted by any who do not start by presuming in her the morals of a courtesan."

66. Rowse, *Ralegh and the Throckmortons*, 139.

67. Trevelyan, *Sir Walter Raleigh*, 61.

68. James Horn, *A Kingdom Strange: The Brief and Tragic History of the Lost Colony of Roanoke*, 27.

69. Gosling, *Sir Humphrey Gilbert*, 207. Gosling reports that "the shares of the Company were to be £5 each, either in money or goods. And as land was plenty in the New World, and promises cheap, each holder of one share was entitled to 1000 acres of land" and "The lands were to be 'in free socage tenure,' paying to Sir Humphrey, his heirs or assigns, after the first seven years, ten shillings for every 1000 acres." Socage was the equivalent of a property tax without any obligation of military service.

70. Gosling, *Sir Humphrey Gilbert*, 230.

71. D.B. Quinn, *Raleigh and the British Empire*, 31, 42; Trevelyan, *Sir Walter Raleigh*, 64; Lacey, *Sir Walter Ralegh*, 28; Margaret Holmes Williamson, *Powhatan Lords of Life and Death*, 23.

72. Gosling, *Sir Humphrey Gilbert*, 229.

73. Gosling, *Sir Humphrey Gilbert*, 259; Williams, *The Sea Dogs*, 79.

74. A pinnace is a shallow draft boat of various sizes with a single deck and one or two masts propelled by sails and/or oars. Sizes ranged from twenty to eighty tons or from roughly twenty-five to thirty-five feet long. They were capable of crossing oceans and often served as message boats ship-to-shore or within fleets or for navigating shallow rivers and estuaries where larger galleons could not go. Other small flat-bottomed watercraft used by the English in the New World were shallops, tilt boats, and wherries.

75. Gosling, *Sir Humphrey Gilbert*, 254.

76. Hakluyt, *Voyages and Discoveries*, 241; Trevelyan, *Sir Walter Raleigh*, 64–65; Bicheno, *Elizabeth's Sea Dogs*, 175. Gilbert was quoted as responding, "We are as near to Heaven by sea as by land" as he sat in the stern of the *Squirrel* reading a book. The story is surely apocryphal. As anyone who has sailed on a small craft in heavy seas can attest, reading a book on deck in such conditions is difficult, not to mention perilous for the book. Gilbert's response appears to be out of context with the request; however, Bicheno suggests his statement was inspired by a quote from Thomas More's *Utopia*: "He that hath no grave is covered with the sky: and the way to heaven out of all places is of like length and distance."

77. Gosling, *Sir Humphrey Gilbert*, 271. During the night of Monday, September 9, 1583.

78. Trevelyan, 4, 77; Paine, *Sea & Civilization*, 429. Paine compares Raleigh's action to that of Russia's Ivan the Terrible who seized Siberia as *"terra nullius*, literally 'no one's land,' the conceit being that land not in productive use ... did not belong to its inhabitants."

79. Trevelyan, 55–56; Woolley, *The Queen's Conjuror*, 198.

80. Rowse, *Ralegh and the Throckmortons*, 132.

81. Trevelyan, *Sir Walter Raleigh*, 17; Benjamin Schmidt, "Reading Ralegh's America: Texts, Books, and Readers in the Early Modern Atlantic World" in *The Atlantic World and Virginia, 1550-1624*, ed. Peter C. Mancall, 454–466.

82. Liza Picard, *Elizabeth's London*, 231, 323; Anna Beer, *Patriot or Traitor*, 216–218. Dating from the twelfth century, the Inns of Court were finishing schools for training in English common law. There are four principal inns — Gray's Inn, Lincoln's Inn, Inner Temple, and Middle Temple. Legal training was originally prohibited within the City of London, so the inns were located outside the old Roman walls in Holborn, now Camden. Over time, impressive residence and dining halls were constructed that serve as fraternal clubs and London residences for alumni. Prospective members — men only — applied for admission and, if accepted, paid dues for as long as they used the facilities. Grey's Inn was the largest with 356 members in 1586, and membership cost about £40 per year. Beer calls the Inns of Court "a breeding ground for a new kind of political actor: the parliamentarian."

83. Trevelyan, *Sir Walter Raleigh*, 48; Nicholls and Williams, *Sir Walter Raleigh*, 20, 26.

84. Stebbing, *Sir Walter Ralegh*, 40.

85. Lacey, *Sir Walter Raleigh*, 271; Nicholls and Williams, *Sir Walter Raleigh*, 29.

86. Trevelyan, *Sir Walter Raleigh*, 80; Rowse, *Ralegh and the Throckmortons*, 143; Lacey, 104; Nicholls and Williams, 213. Lacey provides a quote from the time (though not the source) that Raleigh was "the best hated man of the world, in court, city and country." This is not entirely true, for Raleigh was always quite popular in his native West Country. Nicholls and Williams quote a poem about Raleigh by one Thomas Rogers "dating from 1603" that includes the line, "Hated of all, and pittied of none."

87. Rowse, *England of Elizabeth*, 179. Hakluyt emphasized two things: trade and conversion of the Algonquins to Christianity. This attitude was echoed by the London Council of Virginia in a publication, "A True Declaration," in 1610, "[It is honorable profit if we] by way of merchandising and trade do buy of them the pearls of the earth and sell to them the pearls of heaven." Profit was the motive; religion, the justification.

88. George Bruner Parks, *Richard Hakluyt and the English Voyages*, 88.

89. Trevelyan, *Sir Walter Raleigh*, 184–185; Stebbing, *Sir Walter Ralegh*, 97; Lacey, *Sir Walter Ralegh*, 174. Hawkins applied the

moniker "especial man" to Raleigh by the latter's unique ability to bring order to the chaos that reigned in Plymouth after the arrival there of the Spanish treasure ship, *Madre de Deus* in August 1592. Raleigh restored order and made sure the queen received her share of the booty.

90. Woods, introduction to *A Discourse on Western Planting*, by Richard Hakluyt, lix–lxi.
91. Lacey, *Sir Walter Ralegh*, 52.
92. Christopher Hibbert, *The Virgin Queen*, 31; Trevelyan, 57; Beer, *Patriot or Traitor*, 29.
93. Trevelyan, *Sir Walter Raleigh*, 57–59; M. St. Clare Byrne, *Elizabethan Life in Town and Country*, 57.
94. Trevelyan, 65.
95. Trevelyan, 59; Lacey, *Sir Walter Ralegh*, 60–61.
96. Trevelyan, 72.
97. Gosling, *Sir Humphrey Gilbert*, 13–14.
98. Trevelyan, 119–120, 200–201; Lacey, *Sir Walter Ralegh*, 61.
99. Trevelyan, 149. *The Faerie Queene*, epic poem by Edmund Spenser (1552/3-1599) in six books, the first three of which praise Queen Elizabeth and were encouraged by Walter Raleigh. The last three books of the poem are critical of the queen. Trevelyan states that the first three books were completed at Durham House.
100. Trevelyan, 70.
101. Robyn Arianrhod, *Thomas Harriot: A Life in Science*, 41–46. A nautical mile or one knot is a unit of distance slightly longer than a statute mile (1.15:1) or 6,080 feet equal to 1/60 of one degree of longitude at the Equator. Degrees of latitude are 60 nautical miles or 69± statute miles apart.
102. Lacey, *Sir Walter Ralegh*, 111–113, 195–197; Arianrhod, *Thomas Harriot*, 182; Benjamin Woolley, *The Queen's Conjuror*, 310.
103. Trevelyan, *Sir Walter Raleigh*, 192, 200–201, 208–209.
104. Kupperman, *Roanoke*, 37.
105. Arianrhod, *Thomas Harriot*, 97–98, 155–157, 195.
106. Jack Beeching, introduction to *Voyages and Discoveries*, by Richard Hakluyt, 27; Arianrhod, 148–149, 172–179.
107. Arianrhod, 201.
108. Trevelyan, *Sir Walter Raleigh*, 75;

Parks, *Richard Hakluyt ad the English Voyages*, 84.
109. Kupperman, *Roanoke*, 65–68. The author states that Hakluyt professed "that gentleness was simply good policy." Raleigh and Hakluyt may have agreed in principle on a policy of amity toward the Algonquins at all costs, but the actions of Raleigh's commanders and field officers do not attest to his allegiance to such a policy.
110. Parks, *Richard Hakluyt and the English Voyages*, 100–101; Victor Wolfgang von Hagen, ed., Introduction to *The Incas of Pedro de Cieza de León*, lxxv. Peter Martyr d'Anghiera (1457–1526), Italian historian, his *De Orbe Novo* commissioned by Charles V was translated into English in 1555. Gonzalo Fernández de Oviedo (1478–1557), Spanish colonist, historian; his *Historia general de las Indias* was translated into English in 1555. Bartolomé de las Casas (1484–1566), New World priest, Spanish bishop, and historian, known as "Protector of the Indians," his works published in English in 1583. The translation of his work was dedicated to Sir Walter Raleigh.
111. Jack Beeching, introduction to *Voyages and Discoveries*, by Richard Hakluyt, 19; John Winter Jones, introduction to *Divers Voyages Touching the Discovery of America and the Islands Adjacent*, by Richard Hakluyt, xx; Parks, *Richard Hakluyt and the English Voyages*, 115–117; Nicholls and Williams, *Sir Walter Raleigh*, 50; Andrew Hadfield, "Irish Colonies and the Americas" in *Envisioning an English Empire*, ed. Robert Appelbaum and John Sweet, 180.
112. Boucher, "Revisioning the 'French Atlantic'" in *The Atlantic World and Virginia, 1550-1624*, ed. Peter C. Mancall, 292; Von Hagen, ed., Introduction to *The Incas of Pedro de Cieza de León*, lxxii; G.F. Dille, translator, Biographical Notes in *Writings From the Edge of the World: The Memoirs of Darién, 1514-1527* by Gonzalo Fernández de Oviedo, 37.
113. Bartolomé de Las Casas, *A Short Account of the Destruction of the Indies*, 20; Peter Martyr, *De Orbe Novo*, vol. 1, 284, 331. Las Casas: "A fortune in gold sank beneath the waves that day, among the cargo being the Great Nugget, as big as a loaf of bread and weighing three thousand

six hundred *castilians*." Martyr: "a piece of sapphire larger than a goose's egg."
 114. Martyr, vol. 1, 253–254, 256, 260, 288, 294, 305, 316–317, 338–339, vol. 2, 387.
 115. Martyr, vol. 1, 340, vol. 2, 274–275.
 116. Las Casas, 38, 74. Descriptions of atrocities are too grim to quote.
 117. Von Hagen, xlvii.
 118. Herbert S. Klein and Ben Vinson III, *African Slavery in Latin America and the Caribbean*, 45–46. The authors: "the institution of Indian slavery ... was doomed to failure. The most important factor undermining its importance was the endemic diseases the Europeans brought with them...."
 119. Helen C. Rountree, *Manteo's World*, 111, 115. Rountree quotes Ian Mortimer (*The Time Traveler's Guide to Elizabethan England*, New York: Viking, 2012) "The Elizabethan character is an amalgam of rashness, boldness, resolution, and violence — all mixed in a heady brew of destructive intolerance."
 120. Trevelyan, *Sir Walter Raleigh*, 11, 35–40; Parker, *Grand Strategy of Philip II*, 167; Hibbert, *Virgin Queen*, 128; Lacey, *Sir Walter Ralegh*, 35–38. Lacey: "The sharkpool that was the Elizabethan court did not make for tenderness, nor did the West Country tradition of fierce loyalties and fierce hatreds." Note: Smerwick is a corruption of St. Mary Wick.
 121. Trevelyan, 261; Beer, *Patriot or Traitor*, 124.
 122. David Berke, "'The Undiscover'd Country': Sir Walter Ralegh's Literary Approach to English Colonialism," 3. Berke: "...he (Raleigh) writes, 'Charles the fifth [the king of Spain] ... had the Maydenhead [virginity] of Peru,'" adding, "Since colonization is parallel with sexual consummation, it is made as singular as the act of deflowering a virgin."
 123. Hobson Woodward, *A Brave Vessel*, 173.
 124. Arthur Barlowe, "Arthur Barlowe's Narrative of the 1584 Voyage," in *The First Colonists: Documents on the Planting of the First English Settlements in North America 1584–1590*, ed. David B. Quinn and Alison M. Quinn, 8. The term "Golden Age" in this context comes from this quote by Barlowe: "Wee found the people most gentle, loving, and faithfull, void of all guile, and treason, and such as lived after the manner of the golden age."
 125. Quinn, *Raleigh and the British Empire*, 157–159.

Chapter 3

1. Arthur Barlowe, "Arthur Barlowe's Narrative of the 1584 Voyage," in *The First Colonists: Documents on the Planting of the First English Settlements in North America 1584–1590*, ed. David B. Quinn and Alison M. Quinn, 2; D.B. Quinn, *Raleigh and the British Empire*, 60; David Beers Quinn, *The Roanoke Voyages*, Vol. I, 94 (footnote 3). Quinn states that Port Ferdinando was in the vicinity of today's Oregon Inlet.
 2. Arthur Barlowe, "Arthur Barlowe's Narrative of the 1584 Voyage," in *The First Colonists: Documents on the Planting of the First English Settlements in North America 1584–1590*, ed. David B. Quinn and Alison M. Quinn, 2–9; Thomas Harriot, "A briefe and true report of the new found land of Virginia (1588)," 5; Richard Hakluyt, *Voyages and Discoveries*, 270–275.
 3. Raleigh Trevelyan, *Sir Walter Raleigh*, 75.
 4. Robyn Arianrhod, *Thomas Harriot: A Life in Science*, 58–61; Giles Milton, *Big Chief Elizabeth*, 67.
 5. Trevelyan, 21.
 6. Robert Lacey, *Sir Walter Ralegh*, 73–74.
 7. The Treaty of Joinville signed in secret on December 31, 1584.
 8. A letter of reprisal, also known as a letter of marque, was an official license issued by the government authorizing a private entity to attack the shipping of an enemy of that government.
 9. Edmund S. Morgan, *American Slavery, American Freedom*, 32.
 10. Quinn, *Raleigh and the British Empire*, 58; James Horn, *A Kingdom Strange: The Brief and Tragic History of the Lost Colony of Roanoke*, 35.
 11. Richard Hakluyt, *A Discourse on Western Planting in the Year 1584*, in *Documentary History of the State of Maine*, edited by Leonard Woods, 7–12, 36–44, 108–117, 153, 159. Robert Lacey, *Sir Walter Ralegh*, 57–58; James Horn, *A Land as God Made It*, 24.
 12. Laurence Bergreen, *In Search of*

Kingdom, 59. Bergreen: "The Spanish treasure fleet expanded quickly in Drake's day, with seventeen ships in 1550 and more than fifty by the end of the century."

13. Horn, *A Land As God Made It*, 202. Horn pointed out another reason why a privateering base there was impractical: "There was also little risk that English privateers would be able to attack Spanish possessions in the Caribbean because contrary winds and currents effectively blocked their way southerly along the coast."

14. Carlo M. Cipolla, *Guns, Sails, and Empires*, 136.

15. Karen Kupperman, *Roanoke: The Abandoned Colony*, 101.

16. Trevelyan, 109–110; Lacey, 82.

17. David Beers Quinn, *Set Fair for Roanoke*, 56.

18. Kupperman, *Roanoke*, 12. Author states that "Ralegh's first colonists were largely veterans of the Irish or European wars." Soldiering and the ministry were common career choices for the younger sons of nobility and gentry.

19. Scott Dawson, *The Lost Colony and Hatteras Island*, 31. According to Dawson, "The Spanish colonies in Florida and the Caribbean followed the Gulf Stream current northeast to get back to Spain, and at no point is the land closer to this massive ocean current than at Croatoan.... In order to rob a ship, one must be able to spot the ship. Croatoan and Wokokon (now Hatteras and Ocracoke) are the only places this can be accomplished because as soon as the Gulf Stream reaches the north end of Croatoan, it crashes headlong into the cold-water Labrador Current that turns violently east away from land."

20. Helen C. Rountree, *Manteo's World*, 25; Martin D. Gallivan, *The Powhatan Landscape*, 30. Rountree estimates Ossomocomuck population at less than ten thousand. Gallivan: "archaeologists have arrived at an overall estimate of 12,000–15,000 Algonquian speakers for Virginia's Tidewater region (Tsenacomoco)...."

21. Grace Steele Woodward, *Pocahontas*, 17–18; Gallivan, 30. Writing about the Powhatans of Tidewater Virginia, Steele states: "By 1607 the total population of the (Powhatan) confederacy was between 8,500 and 9,000 persons, approximately 3,000 of whom were warriors." While I agree with Woodward's estimate of the ratio of warriors to the whole, I believe her estimate of total population for the Powhatan polity was low. Gallivan computes from Smith's accounts a "ratio of about 3.33 people per warrior" or 30%, not one-third.

22. Harriot, "A briefe and true report," 13–15; Daniel K. Richter, *Facing East from Indian Country*, 55; Rountree, 38; Kupperman, *Roanoke*, 44; Alan Gallay, *The Indian Slave Trade*, 23–24. The symbiotic trio of corn, beans, and squash came to be called the "Three Sisters." Kupperman and Rountree point out that "beans, being legumes, fix nitrogen in the soil, which continually fertilizes the corn," and the trailing squash kept weeds down and prevented moisture from evaporating. Eating maize and beans together boosted the amount of protein in the Algonquin diet. Gallay indicates that maize production increased substantially from about A.D. 1000 and that "With the rise of maize, hunting and gathering did not end, but intensive agricultural production allowed the native peoples to spend less time attaining subsistence and more time in craft production, religious and leisure activities, and warfare."

23. William H. Prescott, *History of the Conquest of Peru*, 83–84. Prescott: "Of the four varieties of Peruvian sheep, the llama ... chiefly employed as a beast of burden ... the employment of domestic animals distinguished the Peruvians from the other races of the New World."

24. Rountree, 20, 118.

25. Morgan, *American Slavery, American Freedom*, 23, 57–58; David Beers Quinn, *Set Fair for Roanoke*, 211; Richter, 57. As Morgan points out, in *Utopia*, Sir Thomas More—anticipating a colony in Ireland or the New World—expressed the opinion that the English had a right to "unoccupied and uncultivated land." He added that his countrymen had "just cause for war when a people which does not use its soil but keeps it idle and waste nevertheless forbids the use and possession of it to others who by the rule of nature ought to be maintained by it." More could not anticipate the hunter-gatherer culture of the coastal Algonquins who depended on their "unoccupied and uncultivated" land for foraging and wild game. This was, nevertheless, the English mindset.

26. Quinn, *Set Fair for Roanoke*, 185; Gallivan, *The Powhatan Landscape*, 73, 100-101. Quinn refers to the Algonquin's culture as "a Woodland culture that had existed in eastern North America for more than 1,500 years before this time." Gallivan: "While not all in agreement, interpretations of this language spread point to the arrival of Alqonquian speech communities in the Chesapeake sometime between 500 BC and AD 900."

27. Arthur Barlowe, "Arthur Barlowe's Narrative of the 1584 Voyage," in *The First Colonists: Documents on the Planting of the First English Settlements in North America 1584-1590*, ed. David B. Quinn and Alison M. Quinn, 9.

28. James Horn, *A Kingdom Strange*, 46; Anna Beer, *Patriot or Traitor: The Life and Death of Sir Walter Ralegh*, 48.

29. Lee Miller, *Roanoke: Solving the Mystery of the Lost Colony*, 241.

30. Ralph Lane, "Narrative of the Settlement of Roanoke Island 1585-1586," in *The First Colonists: Documents on the Planting of the First English Settlements in North America 1584-1590*, ed. David B. Quinn and Alison M. Quinn, 26; Andy Gabriel-Powell, *Richard Grenville and the Lost Colony of Roanoke*, 36; Rountree, *Manteo's World*, 123; Dawson, *Croatoan*, 156. Lane states that the Chawanoc Tribe was headed by weroance Menatonon and that the tribe could muster 700 warriors. The tribe is further reported by Harriot to have contained eighteen villages (Harriot, "A briefe and true report," 25). The Croatoan Tribe's weroance is not named but was probably a relative of Manteo, perhaps his mother according to Daniel Beers Quinn (*Set Fair for Roanoke*, 39). The tribe could muster approximately 325 warriors. This number is derived from Quinn's estimate of 1,000 inhabitants living on Croatoan Island at the time, however; Dawson puts the number at 1,500 in the year 1600. For this work, I have adhered to Quinn's estimates, as do most historians.

31. Miller, *Roanoke*, 267. Miller argues that the Algonquins of Roanoke did not constitute a separate tribe as Quinn asserts.

32. Horn, *A Kingdom Strange*, 47; Brandon Fullam, *The Lost Colony of Roanoke: New Perspectives*, 106. Horn claims they were Iroquoian, disputing the earlier opinion of James Mooney, an American ethnographer, who studied Southeastern tribes in the late nineteenth and earlier twentieth century. Mooney believed that the Pomouik were Algonquin and that by reason of their alliance with the Neusiok, that the Neusiok were also.

33. Arthur Barlowe, "Narrative of the 1584 Voyage," in *The First Colonists: Documents on the Planting of the First English Settlements in North America 1584-1590*, ed. David B. Quinn and Alison M. Quinn, 4.

34. Miller, *Roanoke*, 98-99; Brandon Fullam, *Manteo and the Algonquins of the Roanoke Voyages*, 123. Fullam estimates total Weapemeoc population at 1,300. Miller calls the Weapemeoc a confederacy, consisting of "the Yeopim proper, the Perquiman, Pasquotank, and Poteskeet." The first three of these names survive as the names of rivers that flow into the Albemarle Sound. Perquimans and Pasquotank also survive as the names of North Carolina counties, and the name Poteskeet survives as a community on the Outer Banks in Duck, North Carolina.

35. Dawson, *The Lost Colony*, 45.

36. Rountree, *Manteo's World*, 12-13; Rountree, Clark, and Mountford, *John Smith's Chesapeake Voyages*, 174.

37. Helen C. Rountree, Wayne E. Clark, and Kent Mountford, *John Smith's Chesapeake Voyages 1607-1609*, 30; Camilla Townsend, *Pocahontas and the Powhatan Dilemma*, 18.

38. Harriot, "A briefe and true report," 19-21.

39. Harriot, 7-12, 18, 22-25; William Strachey, *Historie of Travell into Virginia Britania*, 118-133; Helen C. Rountree, *The Powhatan Indians of Virginia*, 42.

40. Quinn, *Set Fair for Roanoke*, 175, 178. Much was made of the "medicinal virtues of sassafras" as a "cure for many diseases from syphilis to sore throats." So much of it was shipped to England and its efficacy proved to be so minimal that its value plummeted.

41. Quinn, *Set Fair for Roanoke*, 194; Rountree, *Manteo's World*, 36. Quinn tells us that "The wood of the white cedar and the tulip tree was especially suited for this purpose as the inner layers are not necessarily as hard as the outer. The art and craft

of making these canoes ... was a task for the winter, when leaves were off and the sap was down."

42. Quinn, *Set Fair for Roanoke*, 197; Rountree, *The Powhatan Indians of Virginia*, 65–70.

43. Margaret Holmes Williamson, *Powhatan Lords of Life and Death*, 214. Williamson: "The women provided the vegetable component of the Powhatan diet and the men the animal."

44. Barlowe, "Narrative of the 1584 Voyage," 10; Strachey, *Historie of Travell*, 108–109; Quinn, *Set Fair for Roanoke*, 266; Rountree, *The Powhatan Indians of Virginia*, 32. Quinn maintains that "stout buff (leather) coats would turn most Indian arrows."

45. Harriot, "A briefe and true report," 24; Henry Spelman, "Relation of Virginia, 1609" in *Jamestown Narratives: Eyewitness Accounts of the Virginia Colony*, ed. Edward Wright Haile, 494; Strachey, *Historie of Travell*, 109.

46. Morgan, 31. The *Tyger* was a royal navy ship on loan from Queen Elizabeth, her contribution to Raleigh's enterprise.

47. Gabriel-Powell, *Richard Grenville and the Lost Colony*, 28, quoting Hakluyt's *The Principall Navigations*. Regarding the charge against Simon Fernandez, the author quotes from Haklyut's *The Principall Navigations*. Over the years hurricanes and other violent storms have opened and closed breaches in the North Carolina Outer Banks. The inlet used by Grenville became known as Wococon Inlet. The islands immediately north and south of it were small and uninhabited. The small island to the north was called Wococon, and north of Wococon Island was Croatoan Island. The name Ocracoke is a corruption of Ocacock or Wococock, as the inlet has been called in the past.

48. Morgan, *American Slavery, American Freedom*, 34; Giles Milton, *Big Chief Elizabeth*, 96–101.

49. Brandon Fullam, *The Lost Colony of Roanoke: New Perspectives*, 25, 29; Miller, *Roanoke*, 162–163. Sir Francis Walsingham was one of the accused saboteurs, but as Fullam later points out, Walsingham invested in the 1587 Roanoke Colony, so the accusation is highly suspect. Miller opines that the Earl of Leicester may have sabotaged Raleigh's 1587 colony.

50. Christopher Hibbert, *Virgin Queen*, 128–129; Alison Weir, *The Life of Elizabeth I*, 343–344.

51. Quinn, *Set Fair for Roanoke*, 54.

52. Quinn, *Raleigh and the British Empire*, 54–55.

53. Anonymous, "Anonymous Journal of the 1585 Virginia Voyage," in *The First Colonists*, ed. David B. Quinn and Alison M. Quinn, 18.

54. Anonymous, 18; Trevelyan, *Sir Walter Raleigh*, 86–87; Quinn, *Set Fair for Roanoke*, 71–72.

55. Quinn, *Set Fair for Roanoke*, 32–33, 71. The Algonquin word "succotash" means beans and corn cooked together.

56. Quinn, *Set Fair for Roanoke*, 193–194; Rountree, *The Powhatan Indians of Virginia*, 137. Rountree: "The celebration of first gathering of corn was the Powhatans' most elaborate festival."

57. Trevelyan, 89.

58. David Beers Quinn, *The Roanoke Voyages*, Vol. I, 212; Mark Nicholls and Penry Williams, *Sir Walter Raleigh*, 52.

59. Rountree, *The Powhatan Indians of Virginia*, 114; Andrew Lawler, *The Secret Token*, 62. Lawler expresses an opinion common among historians that "Native Americans would often accept payment for land, but they typically did so with the assumption that it was a temporary lease rather than a final purchase." More likely, they had no concept of land as something a person could own. Land could only be occupied until lost to an invading force, Native American or foreign.

60. Daniel K. Richter, "Tsenacommacah and the Atlantic World" in *The Atlantic World and Virginia, 1550–1624*, ed. Peter C. Mancall, 35. Richter quotes anthropologist Margaret Holmes Williamson in speaking of Powhatan himself, "Indeed, he really has nothing of 'his own' as a private person. Rather, he is the steward of the group's wealth, deploying it on their behalf for their benefit."

61. Rountree, *The Powhatan Indians of Virginia*, 57; Richter, *Facing East from Indian Country*, 54.

62. Morgan, *American Slavery, American Freedom*, 41.

63. Horn, *A Kingdom Strange*, 54–55; Lawler, *The Secret Token*, 59. Lawler states that Amadas led an exploration of Weapemeoc territory that came upon a Green

Corn Festival with 700 revelers during which an incident occurred in which twenty Algonquins were killed. Lawler cites Richard Butler as the source. According to another source, Butler was deposed by the Spanish twelve years later, but there is no Richard Butler listed among the colonists under Ralph Lane as reported by Richard Hakluyt, and the Quinns do not include Butler's account in *The First Colonists: Documents on the Planting of the First English Settlements in North America 1584–1590*, so I am unable to verify this incident.

64. Rountree, *Manteo's World*, 9–10. Rountree names four breaches that have since silted up.

65. Williamson, *Powhatan Lords*, 205.

66. Williamson, 165–170. Williamson: "...colonists translate the term 'cockarouse' as 'captain,' 'elder,' 'councilor,' 'brave fellow,' and possibly 'chief man.'"

67. Kupperman, *Roanoke*, 50.

68. Helen Rountree, *Pocahontas's People*, 11.

69. Trevelyan, *Sir Walter Raleigh*, 63; Lacey, *Sir Walter Ralegh*, 119.

70. Quinn, *Set Fair for Roanoke*, 76; Milton, *Big Chief Elizabeth*, 113.

71. Quinn, *Set Fair for Roanoke*, 36.

72. Quinn, *Set Fair for Roanoke*, 89, 96. Quinn opines that "Its bias on the military side emphasized the colony's position as an outpost against Spain ... and a possible target for Spanish attack." Most of the soldiers would have been the younger sons of nobles and gentry.

73. Harriot, "A briefe and true report," 28.

74. David Beers Quinn, *Set Fair for Roanoke*, 228; Lawler, *The Secret Token*, 65.

75. Harriot, "A briefe and true report," 29; Milton, 91, 103. Without citing his source, Milton claims that the colonists were under orders "to refrayne from carnall lust," and he quotes from Raleigh's code of conduct "that no souldier do violat any woman" and that the punishment for rape was death.

76. Quinn, *Set Fair for Roanoke*, 72; Quinn, *The Roanoke Voyages*, Vol. I, 138; Arianrhod, *Thomas Harriot*, 70.

77. Quinn, *Set Fair for Roanoke*, 87–88, 121.

78. Ralph Lane, "Narrative of the Settlement of Roanoke Island 1585–1586" in *The First Colonists*, ed. David B. Quinn and Alison M. Quinn, 36.

79. Nicholls and Williams, *Sir Walter Raleigh*, 53. Authors claim the expedition "stayed for two or three months."

80. Trevelyan, *Sir Walter Raleigh*, 108.

81. Lane, "Narrative of the Settlement of Roanoke," 24–25. Ralph Lane's three sentences relating to the Chesapeake Bay: "First therefore touching the particularities of the Countrey, you shall understand our discovery of the same hath bene extended from the Iland of Roanoak (the same having bene the place of our settlement or inhabitation) into the South, into the North, into the Northwest, and into the West.... To the Northwarde our furthest discoverie was to the Chesepians, distant from Roanoak about 130. miles, the passage to it was very shallow and most dangerous, by reason of the breadth of the sound, and the little succour that upon any flawe was there to be had. But the Territorie and soyle of the Chesepians (being distant fifteene miles from the shoare) was for pleasantness of seate, for temperature of Climate, for fertilitie of soyle, and for the comoditie of the Sea, besides multitude of beares (being an excellent good victual, with great woods of Sassafras, and Wall nut trees) is not to be excelled by any other whatsoever."

82. Chesepioc Tribe, also spelled Chesepioc and Chesepiuc from the Algonquin word for "Great Water." Before being destroyed by Powhatan, the tribe could muster approximately 100 warriors.

83. Horn, *A Land As God Made It*, 30.

84. Horn, *A Kingdom Strange*, 87–88.

85. Quinn, *Set Fair for Roanoke*, 106–108; Dawson, *Croatoan*, 22. Dawson explains that Skicóac (he spelled it Skico) was located in today's Portsmouth, Virginia.

86. George Bruner Parks, *Richard Hakluyt and the English Voyages*, 110; D.B. Quinn, *Raleigh and the British Empire*, 50. Quinn relates the following story corroborating the hiding of evidence: "But there is evidence which strongly suggests that Barlow's story was pruned of some awkward incident on Chesapeake Bay ... when the Indians, apparently the Powhatan Indians of Tidewater Virginia, attacked them and killed some of the Englishmen, even eating them, according to one Spanish

report." In Quinn, *Set Fair for Roanoke*, 250, he quotes from a letter from Hakluyt to Raleigh of 30 December 1586, "...your best planting will be about the bay of the Chesepians."
87. Harriot, "A briefe and true report," 32.
88. Quinn, *Set Fair for Roanoke*, 77.
89. Quinn, *Set Fair for Roanoke*, 103–104.
90. Milton, *Big Chief Elizabeth*, 153.
91. Quinn, *Set Fair for Roanoke*, 115.
92. James D. Rice, "Escape from Tsenacommacah" in *The Atlantic World and Virginia, 1550–1624*, ed. Peter C. Mancall, 119. Author states: "An influx of spiritually potent goods from this new source could be used to strengthen a weroance's position, both within his nation and in diplomatic affairs. English copper and beads, as well as more mundane items such as metal tools, also made the newcomers sufficiently useful that they need not be killed or left to starve."
93. Helen C. Rountree, *Pocahontas Powhatan Opechancanough*, 211. Rountree: "perhaps connected with a ceremony intended to imbue them and their followers with a new determination...."
94. Benjamin Woolley, *Savage Kingdom*, 380. In yet another example, Wooley reports that in 1621 Opechancanough "changed his name to Mangopeesomon." This would have been shortly before the massacre 1622 in which 347 English were killed.
95. Fullam, *The Lost Colony*, 17.
96. Lane, "Narrative of the Settlement of Roanoke, 31.
97. Harriot, "A briefe and true report," 10.
98. April Lee Hatfield, *Atlantic Virginia: Intercolonial Relations in the Seventeenth Century*, 29; Fullam, *The Lost Colony*, 138; Miller, *Roanoke*, 247–249. The Great Trading Path also called Occaneechee Path was an ancient Amerindian trading artery running northeast to southwest from Petersburg, VA (formerly Fort Henry) through North and South Carolina to near Augusta, GA. At the point where Occaneechee Island was located in the Roanoke (Moratux) River, the river "was fordable, not above knee deep." Fullam states that the island trading center was at point where the Dan River flows into the Roanoke River. Miller suggests that Occaneechee or Ocaneechi was also a pidgin language used for trading purposes that consisted of fragments of Algonquin, Siouan, and Iroquois.
99. Lane, "Narrative of the Settlement of Roanoke," 33; Morgan, *American Slavery, American Freedom*, 41.
100. Miller, *Roanoke*, 244–245.
101. Lane, "Narrative of the Settlement of Roanoke," 34.
102. Wesley Frank Craven, *The Southern Colonies in the Seventeenth Century 1607–1689*, 67. Craven: As the adventurers pointed out, there was a chance that the river system of the North American continent was similar to that of Russia, where the Volga and Dvina from sources close together flowed in opposite directions to provide water transportation over most of the distance from the White to the Caspian Seas."
103. Gabriel-Powell, *Richard Grenville and the Lost Colony*, 37, quoting Hakluyt's *The Principall Navigations*.
104. Horn, *A Kingdom Strange*, 79.
105. Gabriel-Powell, *Richard Grenville and the Lost Colony*, 40, quoting Hakluyt's *The Principall Navigations*.
106. Lane, "Narrative of the Settlement of Roanoke," 38; Quinn, *Set Fair for Roanoke*, 36; Horn, *A Kingdom Strange*, 93
107. Lane, 35.
108. Lane, 37.
109. Trevelyan, *Sir Walter Raleigh*, 109; Horn, *A Kingdom Strange*, 100. Horn claims Pemisapan was shot by Philip Amadas.
110. Lane, "Narrative of the Settlement of Roanoke, 40–42; Horn, *A Kingdom Strange*, 100. Lane names the executioner as Edward Nugent.
111. Lane, 42; Milton, *Big Chief Elizabeth*, 148. While sailing along the Atlantic coastline, Drake was alerted to the location of the Roanoke Colony by a signal fire set by English Captain Edward Stafford.
112. Timothy R. Walton, *The Spanish Treasure Fleets*, 90–92.
113. Quinn, *Set Fair for Roanoke*, 137. A lee shore is a shore toward which the wind is blowing. A ship anchored off a lee shore, therefore, risks being blown and wrecked on shallows should its anchor cable fail to hold.
114. Robert Lacey, *Sir Walter Ralegh*, 86; Horn, *A Kingdom Strange*, 104–107;

Kupperman, *Roanoke*, 92. Lacey opines that "It was quite possible that national priorities had detained all Ralegh's ships in the English Channel," hence Lane's decision to abandon the colony. Horn calls the storm a hurricane and it could have been, but it was very early in the hurricane season. Kupperman quotes Hakluyt: "the hand of God came upon them for the cruelty, and outrages, committed by some of them against the native inhabitants of that country."

115. Lane, "Narrative of the Settlement of Roanoke," 44; Quinn, *Set Fair for Roanoke*, 138; Lacey, 86.

116. Richard Hakluyt, "Narrative of the 1586 Virginia Voyages" in *The First Colonists*, ed. David B. Quinn and Alison M. Quinn, 86; Quinn, *Set Fair for Roanoke*, 142–143. Quinn cites Hakluyt, saying, "the English Channel was difficult to sail from during the winter months, and, if the ship had not set out by mid–March, she might be held back further by the frequent storms of that period."

117. Quinn, *Set Fair for Roanoke*, 144; Kupperman, *Roanoke*, 92.

118. Quinn, *Raleigh and the British Empire*, 84.

119. Fullam, *The Lost Colony*, 19. A Spaniard, Pedro Dias, captured by Grenville reported that eighteen men were left.

120. Quinn, 116; Hibbert, *Virgin Queen*, 129; Lacey, *Sir Walter Ralegh*, 106–107; Anna Beer, *Patriot or Traitor*, 29.

121. Nicholls and Williams, *Sir Walter Raleigh*, 38, A.L. Rowse, *Ralegh and the Throckmortons*, 141; Quinn, *Set Fair for Roanoke*, 243–245. Quinn states, "Munster and its plantation was the greatest disincentive Ralegh could have had at that moment from entertaining further elaborate plans for American colonization."

122. Quinn, *Raleigh and the British Empire*, 112–113.

123. Anthony Payne, "Richard Hakluyt: An Essay in Bibliography 1580–88," 182.

124. Kupperman, *Roanoke*, 107. Kupperman estimates there were fourteen families, including "one child ... so young that he was still being nursed," and "six were married couples without children." And, of course, there was also a pregnant Eleanor Dare.

125. Trevelyan, 113.

126. Strachey, *Historie of Travell*, 147.

127. Nicholls and Williams, *Sir Walter Raleigh: In Life and Legend*, 65; Kupperman, *Roanoke*, 96.

128. Horn, *A Kingdom Strange*, 126; Kupperman, 107.

129. Quinn, *Set Fair for Roanoke*, 260; Horn, 131; Miller, *Roanoke*, 49–51.

130. Trevelyan, 166–167; Rowse, *Ralegh and the Throckmortons*, 172. Trevelyan quotes Edward Edwards's nineteenth century biography of Raleigh that it is not easy to "ascertain Raleigh's precise views, in regard to theological matters, at any epoch" but opines that his "support for Puritans had its roots in his experiences during the French wars of religion."

131. Quinn, *Raleigh and the British Empire*, 138; Trevelyan, 115; Lacey, *Sir Walter Ralegh*, 97; Weir, *Life of Elizabeth*, 386.

132. John White, "Narrative of the 1587 Virginia Voyage," in *The First Colonists*, ed. David B. Quinn and Alison M. Quinn, 93–94.

133. David Starkey, *Elizabeth: The Struggle for the Throne*, 127; Liza Picard, *Elizabeth's London*, 126–128, 281; Miller, *Roanoke*, 133. Miller: "Fernandez is Protestant, has become an English citizen, and will soon take an English wife."

134. White, "Narrative of the 1587 Virginia Voyage," 97. White (writing in the third person): "The two and twentieth of Julie, we arrived safe at Hatoraske, where our shippe and pinnesse ankered: the Governor [White] went aboord the pinnesse, accompanied with fortie of his best men, intending to passe up to Roanoke forthwith, hoping there to finde those fifteen Englishmen, which Sir Richard Grenvill had left there the yeere before, with whom he meant to have conference, concerning the state of the Countrey, and Savages, meaning after he had so done, to returne againe to the fleete, and pass along the coast, to the Baye of Chesepiok, where we intended to make our seate and forte, according to the charge given us among other directions in writing, under the hande of Sir Walter Raleigh, but assoone as we were put with our pinnesse from the shippe, a Gentleman by the meanes of Fernando, who was appointed to returne for England, called to the sailers in the pinnesse, charging them not to bring any of

the planters back againe, but leave them in the Island, except the Governour, and two or three such as he approved, saying that the Summer was farre spent, wherefore hee would land all the planters in no other place."
135. White, 97.
136. Quinn, *Raleigh and the British Empire*, 87; Lacey, *Sir Walter Ralegh*, 122; Gabriel-Powell, *Richard Grenville and the Lost Colony*, 71, quoting Hakluyt's *The Principall Navigations*.
137. Trevelyan, *Sir Walter Raleigh*, 125.
138. White, "Narrative of the 1587 Virginia Voyage," 97.
139. Fullam, *The Lost Colony*, 28. Fullam observed that Fernandez served as "a deck officer aboard the *Triumph*, the largest ship in the English fleet, commanded by Martin Frobisher."
140. Trevelyan, *Sir Walter Raleigh*, 89; Kupperman, *Roanoke*, 130.
141. Quinn, *Set Fair for Roanoke*, 281; Fullam, *The Lost Colony*, 52.
142. Lawler, *The Secret Token*, 87. Lawler goes so far as to suggest that Mary's execution "doomed White's settlers before they even left home."
143. Gabriel-Powell, *Richard Grenville and the Lost Colony*, 70, quoting Hakluyt's *The Principall Navigations*; Milton, *Big Chief Elizabeth*, 191.
144. Horn, *A Kingdom Strange*, 146, 165–166, 173–174.
145. Parks, *Richard Hakluyt and the English Voyages*, 114.
146. Philip P. Boucher, "Revisioning the 'French Atlantic'" in *The Atlantic World and Virginia, 1550–1624*, ed. Peter C. Mancall, 290; Fullam, *The Lost Colony*, 33–34.
147. Joseph I. Doran, *Sir George Yeardley and His Voyage of 1609–1610 to Virginia in the Sea Adventure and Deliverance*, 5.
148. Kupperman, *Roanoke*, 173; Fullam, *The Lost Colony*, 67–68. Fullam concludes also that "This provides convincing, first-hand evidence that White's colonists did not relocate to the Chesapeake Bay." This may be, but the Chesapeake Bay is very large, and it is also doubtful that the search of the bay by the Spanish captain, Vincente Gonzalez, was exhaustive.
149. Quinn, *Set Fair for Roanoke*, 298.
150. John White, "Narrative of the 1587 Virginia Voyage," 103.

151. Gabriel-Powell, *Richard Grenville and the Lost Colony*, 72, quoting Hakluyt's *The Principall Navigations*.
152. White, 98–99.
153. Kupperman, *Roanoke*, 114; Lawler, *The Secret Token*, 91–92; Dawson, *Croatoan*, 165. Lawler reports that the thirty Secotan attackers were led by Wanchese. Dawson opines that the English survivors initially took refuge five miles away on today's Cedar Island, between Roanoke Island and Nags Head. This is certainly logical if their plan was to sail north to rendezvous with the Grand Banks fishing fleets.
154. Quinn, *Set Fair for Roanoke*, 150–154.
155. Brandon Fullam, *A Lost Colony Hoax*, 102–103.
156. Lacey, *Sir Walter Ralegh*, 124.
157. Quinn, *Set Fair for Roanoke*, 284–285. Quinn identifies her as "the wife of Manatoan, one of the *weroances* of the Croatoan group." Not to be confused with Menatonon, weroance of the Chowanoc tribe.
158. White, "Narrative of the 1587 Virginia Voyage," 101–102; Gabriel-Powell, *Richard Grenville and the Lost Colony*, 74, quoting Hakluyt's *The Principall Navigations*.
159. White, 102.
160. Kupperman, *Roanoke*, 116.
161. John White, "John White's Narrative of the 1590 Virginia Voyage" in *The First Colonists*, ed. David B. Quinn and Alison M. Quinn, 120. White states that "we found many barres of Iron, two pigges of Lead, four yron fowlers, Iron sacker-shotte, and such like heavie things." The iron "fowlers" would have been small cannon, but too heavy to carry easily. A saker was a medium-sized cannon weighing nearly a ton. Its round shot weighed five pounds but would have been useless without the cannon itself which they would not have been able to carry.
162. Miller, *Roanoke*, 100; William M. Kelso, *Jamestown, The Truth Revealed*, 152. Miller: "it will be the worst drought to hit the coast in eight hundred years."
163. Gabriel-Powell, *Richard Grenville and the Lost Colony*, 75, quoting Hakluyt's *The Principall Navigations*.
164. White, "Narrative of the 1587 Virginia Voyage," 102.

165. White, 102–3. Writing in the third person, White states: "The next day, the 22. of August, the whole companie, both of the Assistants, and planters, came to the Governor, and with one voice requested him to return himself into England, for the better and sooner obtaining of supplies, and other necessaries for them: but he refused it, and alleaged many sufficient causes, why he would not: the one was, that he could not so suddenly returne back again, without his great discredite, leaving the action, and so many, whom he partly had procured through his perswasions to leave their native Countrey, and undertake that voyage, and that some enemies to him, and the action at his returne into England, would not spare to slander falsely both him, and the action, by saying he went to Virginia, but politikely, and to no other ende, but to leade so many into a Countrey in which he never meant to stay himself, and there to leave them behind him. Also he alleaged, that seeing they intended to remove 50. miles further up into the maine presently he being then absent, his stuffe and goods, might be both spoiled, and most of it pilfered away in the carriage, so that at his returne, hee should be either forced to provide himself of all such things againe, or els at his coming againe to Virginia, finde himself utterly unfurnished, whereof already he had found some proofe, being but once from them but three daies. Wherefore, he concluded, that he would not goe himselfe."

166. White, 103–104.

167. White, 108.

168. Quinn, *Set Fair for Roanoke*, 266. Quinn speculates that Wright and/or Lacie might have been able to "make themselves understood" by the Algonquins of Ossomocomuck.

169. J.E. Neale, *Queen Elizabeth I*, 305; Trevelyan, *Sir Walter Raleigh*, 127; Lacey, *Sir Walter Ralegh*, 126–127. Neale writes, "Elizabeth prudently kept the greater part of her fleet, immobilized." Lacey adds, "The comfort of distant colonies would have to wait on the salvation of the realm."

Chapter 4

1. Harry Kelsey, *Sir Francis Drake*, 289–290.

2. D.B. Quinn, *Set Fair for Ronaoke: Voyages and Colonies, 1584–1606*, p. 300; Brandon Fullam, *The Lost Colony of Roanoke: New Perspectives*, 63: "on October 9 [1587] Elizabeth issued a general stay, prohibiting ships from leaving English ports."

3. Fullam, 65.

4. John White, "Narrative of the Abortive Virginia Voyage 1588," in *The First Colonists*, ed. David B. Quinn and Alison M. Quinn, 110–114.

5. Geoffrey Parker, *The Grand Strategy of Philip II*, 186.

6. Parker, 202; David Howarth, *The Voyage of the Armada*, 16, 45; Carolly Erickson, *The First Elizabeth*, 367.

7. Howarth, *The Voyage of the Armada*, 119; Alison Weir, *The Life of Elizabeth I*, 389. Plymouth Hoe is the grassy hill that rises to the town of Plymouth.

8. Howarth, 62.

9. Huch Bicheno, *Elizabeth's Sea Dogs*, 253.

10. Howarth, *The Voyage of the Armada*, 62–63. Howarth: "...the Baltic urcas and the Mediterranean naos … only twice as long as they were wide … their sailing performance was laughable … the (Spanish) galleons had to shorten sail to avoid leaving them astern."

11. Howarth, 93–94.

12. Wallace MacCaffrey, *Elizabeth I*, 236–7; Carlo M. Cipolla, *Guns, Sails, and Empires*, 83–89; Parker, *Grand Strategy of Philip II*, 253; Neville Williams, *The Life and Times of Elizabeth I*, 180.

13. Howarth, *The Voyage of the Armada*, 124–125, 135–137; Parker, 251, 259–260. Howarth: The Spanish ships were in such close formation that though "the English wanted to cannonade, but their longest shots could only reach the nearest edges of the Spanish fleet, leaving the mass of it unscathed." Parker explains that the English directed their cannon barrage toward the Spanish hulls, trying to sink the ships. They would have fired at rigging had their strategy been to disable and board the Spanish ships, but that was not their intent. By contrast, the Spanish inflicted "precious little … structural damage to (English) hulls."

14. Howarth, 151–152; Parker, 235. Parker: Parma's army at "Nieuwpoort (for 18,000 Walloons, Germans and Italians) or Dunkirk (for the 9,000 Spaniards, Irish,

Burgundians and cavalry); and he had supervised two 'rehersals.'"

15. Howarth, 156–163; Parker, 238–248, 268 Parker: "Philip's flawed 'management style' frustrated the Armada's success far more than the loss of secrecy, the lack of communication between the two threater commanders and the technical differences between the two fleets."

16. Howarth, 169–173. Howarth: "Nearly three hundred anchors were lying on the sea-bed off Calais, and no doubt they are lying there still; and losing their anchors in the end caused more destruction among the armada ships than anything else."

17. Howarth, 196.

18. Bradford Smith, Captain John Smith, 21.

19. Howarth, The Voyage of the Armada, 216. Howarth: "six thousand Spaniards met the most miserable deaths in Ireland or off its shores."

20. Erickson, First Elizabeth, 377. Quoting the Secretary of Ireland in a letter to William Cecil after walking on the beach near Sligo.

21. Howarth, The Voyage of the Armada, 243.

22. Parker, Grand Strategy of Philip II, 214. Parker explains that the rumor of a reserve fleet preparing to follow the Armada to England "contributed directly towards the ruthless treatment of the Armada survivors forced ashore on the coasts of Ireland" and that "as a panic measure the government decided 'to apprehend and execute all Spanish found, of what quality soever.'"

23. Raleigh Trevelyan, Sir Walter Raleigh, 132.

24. Robert Lacey, Sir Walter Ralegh, 129.

25. Weir, Life of Elizabeth I, 392.

26. J.E. Neale, Queen Elizabeth I, 368–369, 404. Of Essex and his execution for treason, Elizabeth said, "Those who touch the scepters of princes deserve no pity."

27. Neale, 308. The author quotes Robert Dudley, who likened Elizabeth's performance that day to that of an "Amazonian empress."

28. MacCaffrey, Elizabeth I, 66; Margaret Holmes Williamson, Powhatan Lords of Life and Death, 22. MacCaffrey refers to Elizabeth I as the "general patroness of a Protestant internationale." Williamson: "Protestants regarded the queen as their sheet anchor."

29. Christopher Hibbert, The Virgin Queen, 80; Williams, Life and Times of Elizabeth I, 175; Weir, Life of Elizabeth, 399. Pope Sixtus V is quoted as saying: "She is only a woman, only a mistress of half an island, and yet she makes herself feared by Spain, by France, by the Empire...."

30. Thomas Harriot, "A briefe and true report of the new found land of Virginia (1588)," 5–6.

31. Harriot, 31.

32. Ivor Noël Hume, The Virginia Adventure: Roanoke to James Towne, 308. Hume: "The notion that the China Sea might indeed be close at hand persisted as late as the mid–seventeenth century...."

33. Harriot, 29–30.

34. Edmund S. Morgan, American Slavery, American Freedom, 38.

35. Karen Kupperman, Roanoke: The Abandoned Colony, 96–97.

36. Lacey, Sir Walter Ralegh, 87; Mark Nicholls and Penry Williams, Sir Walter Raleigh: In Life and Legend, 59.

37. Lytton Strachey, Elizabeth and Essex, 266.

38. A.L. Rowse, The England of Elizabeth, 172.

39. Lacey, Sir Walter Ralegh, 152–153; John Winter Jones, introduction to Divers Voyages Touching the Discovery of America and the Islands Adjacent, by Richard Hakluyt, xiv; Kupperman, Roanoke, 123.

40. George Bruner Parks, Richard Hakluyt and the English Voyages, 134–135.

41. John White, "John White to Richard Hakluyt, 4 February 1593," in The First Colonists, ed. David B. Quinn and Alison M. Quinn, 115–116.

42. Trevelyan, Sir Walter Raleigh, 153–154; Nicholls and Williams, Sir Walter Raleigh, 62.

43. Kupperman, Roanoke, 7–8, 139; Bicheno, Elizabeth's Sea Dogs, 314. John Watts (ca. 1554–1616), English merchant, "lost heavily in the Spanish confiscation of English ships in 1585 and sued for letters of reprisal." He was "knighted when King James I came to the throne in 1603" and was later active in the Virginia Company. Bicheno observed that the Spanish Ambassador claimed Watts was "the

greatest pirate that has ever been in this kingdom."

44. Lee Miller, *Roanoke: Solving the Mystery of the Lost Colony*, 5; A. Bryant Nichols, Jr., *Captain Christopher Newport*, 23.

45. White, "White to Hakluyt, 4 February 1593," in *The First Colonists: Documents on the Planting of the First English Settlements in North America 1584–1590*, ed. David B. Quinn and Alison M. Quinn, 115–116. White's letter states: "Whereupon he [Walter Raleigh] by his good means obtained license of the Queenes Majestie, and order to be taken, that the owner of the 3 ships should be bound unto Sir Walter Raleigh or his assignes, in 3000 pounds, that those 3 ships in consideration of their releasement should take in, & transport a convenient number of passengers, with their furnitures and necessaries to be landed in Virginia. Neverthelesse that order was not observed, neither was the bond taken according to the intention aforesaid. But rather in contempt of the aforesaid order, I was by the owner and Commanders of the ships denied to have any passengers, or any thing els transported in any of the said ships saving only my selfe & my chest; no not so much as a boy to attend upon me, although I made great sute, & earnest intreatie aswell to the chiefe Commanders, as to the owner of the said ships."

46. John White, "Narrative of the 1590 Voyage," in *The First Colonists*, ed. David B. Quinn and Alison M. Quinn, 117–122.

47. Fullam, *The Lost Colony*, 42. Fullam suggests that "This inconsistency is persuasive evidence of White's intention to fabricate a false narrative about Fernandez."

48. Fullam, 113. Fullam observes that the fact that White directed the two ships to Wococon Inlet gives evidence to support his contention that that the colonists did not intend to go to the Chesapeake Bay. That may not be the case, however. By sounding Chacandepeco Inlet a few days later, it seems clear that White's destination was Croatoan Island where he expected to find some of the colonists who would direct him to the others wherever they might be.

49. White, "Narrative of the 1590 Voyage," 122–123. Wococon or Wokokon or Wococok Inlet is today's Ocracoke Inlet. Over time it has been the most stable inlet into the Pamlico Sound from the Atlantic Ocean, though it has shifted slightly north of its 1585 position. In 1846 a hurricane cut Croatoan Island in half. The southern half became Ocracoke Island, the name a corruption of "Woccocock." The northern half became part of Hatteras Island when the inlet separating Croatoan and Hatoraske Islands silted up in 1672.

50. Fullam, *The Lost Colony*, 39.

51. Quinn, *Set Fair for Roanoke*, 345. My count: one hundred and eighteen original colonists minus White and Howe plus Virginia Dare and the Harvie's child = 118. Quinn maintains there were 114, "85 men, 17 women, and 11 children (10 male and 1 female)."

52. Fullam, *The Lost Colony*, 66.

53. Fullam, *The Lost Colony*, 51, 55–58. There was another reason: the need for a navigable inlet. Wococon Inlet (today's Ocracoke Inlet), south of Croatoan Inlet, was the deepest and most stable of all the inlets the English had discovered. It has continued to be the deepest and most stable to this day. It was not deep enough then to allow tall ships, but pinnaces with a draft of six feet could enter Wococon, but not Port Ferdinando (Oregon Inlet).

54. White, "Narrative of the 1590 Voyage," 122–123.

55. Scott Dawson, *The Lost Colony and Hatteras Island*, 31. Chacandepeco Inlet no longer exists. It "was located just north of the modern-day village of Buxton." For more, see endnote number 58 below.

56. White, 123.

57. The silting up of Chacandepeco Inlet (at today's Chicamacomico Channel) in 1672 joined Hatoraske Island with Croatoan Island to form today's Hatteras Island. The point at which they were joined is just north of today's Cape Hatteras, offshore of which is Diamond Shoals. The inlet called Port Ferdinando closed in 1798, and as the result of the same hurricane that cut Croatoan Island in half, it opened again in 1846 and was then renamed Oregon Inlet.

58. White, "Narrative of the 1590 Voyage," 123.

59. Brandon Fullam, *Manteo and the Algonquins of the Roanoke Voyages*, 76.

60. Fullam, *The Lost Colony*, 91–101.

Evidence of a September 1589 hurricane was found in the Archivo General de Indias in Seville, Spain, published in the *Journal of Geophysical Research*, Volume 110, Issue D3, Feb. 4, 2005, and cited by Fullam as a reason that Croatoan Island may have been uninhabited for some time after 1589.
 61. Fullam, *The Lost Colony*, 104, 119.
 62. Helen C. Rountree, *Manteo's World*, 12; Kupperman, *Roanoke*, 19. Kupperman states, "In the 1580s the Outer Banks were one mile east of their present location." This may be an exaggeration, but these barrier islands have been steadily migrating westward for eons. This said, in 2009 the famous Cora live oak on Hatteras Island was estimated to be five hundred years old.
 63. White, "Narrative of the 1590 Voyage," 123–124.
 64. White, 124–125.
 65. White, 125.
 66. Trevelyan, *Sir Walter Raleigh*, 156.
 67. Fullam, *The Lost Colony*, 45.
 68. Fullam, *The Lost Colony*, 83–85. The pinnace was too small to accommodate the entire colony. Only a third of it by Fullam's account.
 69. White, "Narrative of the 1590 Voyage," 125–126.
 70. White, 126–127.
 71. Fullam, *The Lost Colony*, 114–116.
 72. Lacey, *Sir Walter Ralegh*, 155.
 73. White, "Narrative of the 1590 Voyage," 127–130.
 74. Quinn, *The Roanoke Voyages*, 589 footnote 6, citing Richard Hakluyt, ed., *The Principall Navigations, Voiages, Traffiques and Discoueries of the English Nation*, vol. III, 1600, 288–295.
 75. Fullam, *The Lost Colony*, 117–118. Fullam suggests, however, that White's motive was to keep Raleigh's patent alive. It is certainly a plausible explanation for White's implication that the colonists were alive on Croatoan Island despite the overwhelming circumstantial evidence that indicates he knew they were not there.
 76. Trevelyan, 158. Trevelyan quotes White peroration: "thus committing the relief of my discomfortable company, the planters in Virginia, to the merciful help of the Almighty."
 77. Quinn, *Raleigh and the British Empire*, 119; James Horn, *A Kingdom Strange*, 197; Kupperman, *Roanoke*, 129.

 78. John White, "White to Richard Hakluyt, 4 February 1593," 116. In this letter White laments, "I would to God my wealth were answerable to my will."
 79. Quinn, 104. Quinn makes the point that the colonists "might in the long run be more valuable to [Raleigh] if they stayed lost." So long as they were presumed to be alive, he could claim that his patent was still valid.
 80. Giles Milton, *Big Chief Elizabeth*, 167–168. Hakluyt urged Raleigh that by persevering he would "leave to posterity an imperishable monument of your name and fame, such as age will never obliterate."
 81. Hibbert, *Virgin Queen*, 106; Laurence Bergreen, *In Search of a Kingdom*, 49. Hibbert counted seventeen: "seven married ladies of high rank, four of lesser rank known as the Queen's Women and six Maids-in-Waiting." Bergreen: "...six or seven women in the Privy Chamber and three or four women in the Bedchamber."
 82. A.L. Rowse, *The Elizabethan Renaissance*, 53–54; Alison Weir, *The Life of Elizabeth I*, 258.
 83. David Starkey, *Elizabeth*, 76; Hibbert, *Virgin Queen*, 83. Starkey writes, "she enforced a reluctant celibacy on her favourites and maids." Hibbert adds that "by an act of 1536 it was treason for a person of royal blood to [marry] without the sovereign's permission."
 84. Anna Beer, *My Just Desire: The Life of Bess Ralegh, Wife to Sir Walter*, xxii.
 85. Lacey, *Sir Walter Ralegh*, 150.
 86. Liza Picard, *Elizabeth's London*, 149.
 87. Quinn, *Raleigh and the British Empire*, 162; Lacey, *Sir Walter Ralegh*, 233, 237; Kupperman, *Roanoke*, 146.
 88. Robyn Arianrhod, *Thomas Harriot: A Life in Science*, 126–127, 138.
 89. Lacey, 192–193; Fullam, *The Lost Colony*, 121.
 90. Quinn, *Raleigh and the British Empire*, 136–137; William H. Prescott, *History of the Conquest of Peru*, 354–356.
 91. Sir Walter Raleigh, *The Discoverie of the Large, Rich and Bewtiful Empyre of Guiana*, 141; Lacey, *Sir Walter Ralegh*, 203; Timothy R. Walton, *The Spanish Treasure Fleets*, 23.
 92. Trevelyan, *Sir Walter Raleigh*, 206–207, 216–217, 261.

93. MacCaffrey, *Elizabeth I*, 399.
94. Hibbert, *Virgin Queen*, 255.
95. Starkey, 97. According to Starkey, Elizabeth ran a "tight ship" in her household and her kingdom.
96. MacCaffrey, *Elizabeth I*, 329–330.
97. Trevelyan, *Sir Walter Raleigh*, 290; Hibbert, *Virgin Queen*, 253; Weir, *Life of Elizabeth*, 431; Erickson, *First Elizabeth*, 383–384. Weir claims that the ambassador concluded Elizabeth was "trying to bewitch him with her faded charms." More likely she was oblivious to the exposé.
98. MacCaffrey, 243; Erickson, *First Elizabeth*, 397.
99. MacCaffrey, 437. Author states of James VI of Scotland that "the succession to the English throne ... was the ruling ambition of his life."
100. Benjamin Woolley, *Savage Kingdom*, 290. Indeed, James inherited a crown deeply in debt. Selling aristocratic titles was seen as a remedy. "Rumor spread of baronies being offered at £5,000 apiece, and a new semi-aristocratic order of baronet, aimed at the gentry and costing £1,000."
101. Trevelyan, *Sir Walter Raleigh*, 430; Antonia Fraser, *King James*, 94.
102. Fraser, 67–68, 101–102: Williamson, *Powhatan Lords*, 99–101. Indeed, quoted by Williamson, James claimed that "kings were gods, adorned and furnished with some sparkles of divinity ... the King is above the law."
103. MacCaffrey, 7, 378–390, Erickson, *First Elizabeth*, 400–401.
104. Rowse, *England of Elizabeth*, 193; MacCaffrey, 214. MacCaffrey refers to the transition as the first stages of an early modern nation state. Rowse calls the reign of Elizabeth a transition from medieval to modern.

Chapter 5

1. Raleigh Trevelyan, *Sir Walter Raleigh*, 342, 350–354.
2. A.L. Rowse, *Ralegh and the Throckmortons*, 230.
3. William Stebbing, *Sir Walter Ralegh*, 180.
4. Trevelyan, *Sir Walter Raleigh*, 346–347, 358; Robert Lacey, *Sir Walter Ralegh*, 189–190; Stebbing, 181–182. Trevelyan alludes to Raleigh's enthusiasm for parliament as follows: "It has been said that if nothing else contributed to Raleigh's renown he would have been remembered as one of the most active parliament men of his time ... he had spoken with conviction and in some degree in the manner of parliamentarians of the next century." Lacey refers to his "posthumous reputation as a 'parliament man.'"
5. Trevelyan, 360–361; Lacey, 283–284.
6. Trevelyan, 266; Lacey, 208 (map); Mark Nicholls and Penry Williams, *Sir Walter Raleigh: In Life and Legend*, 118.
7. William Strachey, *Historie of Travell into Virginia Britania*, 151; Trevelyan, 348.
8. Brandon Fullam, *The Lost Colony of Roanoke: New Perspectives*, 124–125; Lawler, *The Secret Token*, 112–113. Lawler asserts that Mace's primary mission was to trade for sassafras, which at the time was selling for £300 per ton. This may well be true, but Raleigh needed some means to pay for the venture; otherwise, it would not have been possible.
9. David Beers Quinn, *Set Fair for Roanoke*, 355–358. For consistency in this narrative, I shall refer to the York River as the Pamunkey River.
10. John Winter Jones, introduction to *Divers Voyages Touching the Discovery of America and the Islands Adjacent*, by Richard Hakluyt, xiv, xxi.
11. Margaret Holmes Williamson, *Powhatan Lords of Life and Death*, 18.
12. The Hudson River was then called the North River by the Dutch, who called the Delaware River the South River. Spain had never established a colony north of the town of Santa Elena on South Carolina's Parris Island, considered the capital of La Florida from 1566 to 1587. This may explain why the Cape Fear River was considered by the English to be safely beyond reasonable Spanish claims.
13. Edward D. Neill, *History of the Virginia Company of London*, 3. Neill: "... prebendary of Westminster...."
14. George Bruner Parks, *Richard Hakluyt and the English Voyages*, 205–206.
15. Philip L. Barbour, *The Three Worlds of Captain John Smith*, 100–101.
16. Jocelyn R. Wingfield, *Virginia's True Founder: Edward Maria Wingfield*, 15, 48–49, 66, 96, 143. 151.
17. John Smith, *The Generall Historie*

of Virginia, New England, and the Summer Isles, Book 3, 222, in *Jamestown Narratives*, ed. Edward Wright Haile; Barbour, 105. Barbour: "He (Gosnold) and Wingfield were apparently responsible for almost 40 per cent of the colonists whose names are known...."

18. A. Bryant Nichols, Jr., *Captain Christopher Newport*, 66. Nichols: "According to legend, the initial meeting to plan the voyage to Virginia was held in the great room of Otley Hall, Gosnold's ancestral home in Suffolk, England." He lists the attendees as Newport, Wingifeld, Gosnold, Sir Thomas Smythe and Captain John Smith.

19. Edmund S. Morgan, *American Slavery, American Freedom*, 45–47; Parks, *Hakluyt and the English Voyages*, 204; Ivor Noël Hume, *The Virginia Adventure: Roanoke to James Towne*, 206.

20. Quinn, *Set Fair for Roanoke*, 49–50. Regarding amity with the Algonquins, Quinn summarizes with this general characterization: "proceed in amity with the inhabitants so long as they were docile, but kill, conquer, and settle, as suited the colonists, if they resisted intervention."

21. Wesley Frank Craven, *The Southern Colonies in the Seventeenth Century 1607–1689*, 78; David Harris Sacks, "Discourses of Western Planting: Richard Hakluyt and the Making of the Atlantic World" in *The Atlantic World and Virginia, 1550–1624*, ed. Peter C. Mancall, 446. Citing as his source Hakluyt's dedication to Sir Walter Ralegh in his publication of Peter Martyr d'Anghera's *De orbe novo*, Sacks concludes that Hakluyt believed "that the Native peoples must be removed from their state of near-savagery to civil order before their conversion to Christianity can be completed."

22. Craven, *The Southern Colonies*, 76. Craven quotes a 1609 sermon in England: "The first objection is by what right or warrant we can enter into the land of these Savages, take away their rightfull inheritance from them, and plant ourselves in their places, being unwronged or unprovoked by them."

23. Quinn, *Set Fair for Roanoke*, 237; Andrew Fitzmaurice, "Moral Uncertainty in the Dispossession of Native Americans" in *The Atlantic World and Virginia, 1550–1624*, ed. Peter C. Mancall, 383–409. Fitzmaurice's essay is an excellent overview of the English philosophical conundrum regarding the acquisition of Algonquin lands. Quinn states unequivocally "that Englishmen, from Ralegh downward, regarded it as their right to intrude on American soil and to occupy such parts of it as they felt necessary, ultimately without regard to the desires of the inhabitants."

24. Everett Emerson, *Captain John Smith Revised Edition*, 27. Emerson: "elaborate instructions from the Virginia Company of London: 'In all your passages, you must have great care not to offend the naturals, if you can eschew it, and employ some few of your company to trade with them for corn and other lasting victuals.'"

25. Neill, *History of the Virginia Company*, 11; J.A. Leo Lemay, *The American Dream of Captain John Smith*, 147.

26. April Lee Hatfield, *Atlantic Virginia: Intercolonial Relations in the Seventeenth Century*, 7. As Hatfield affirms, "Early promoters understood Virginia to be one piece of a larger English project to challenge Spain in the Americas."

27. Morgan, 86. Bridewell and the Clink were prisons, the former located where the Fleet River empties into the Thames and the latter across the Thames in Southwark.

28. Craven, *The Southern Colonies*, 99.

29. Smith, *Generall Historie*, Book 3, 290.

30. Quinn, *Set Fair for Roanoke*, 322; Nichols, *Captain Christopher Newport*, 29, 47, 52.

31. Marcy Norton and Daviken Studnicki-Gizbert, "The Multinational Commodification of Tobacco, 1492–1650" in *The Atlantic World and Virginia, 1550–1624*, ed. Peter C. Mancall, 261. In a portent of things to come, the authors relate that "In 1591, Christopher Newport intercepted a frigate heading for Havana laden with '50 hogs-heads and two-hundred weight of excellent tobacco.'"

32. Nichols, *Captain Christopher Newport*, 71. Nichols: *Susan Constant* "overall length was 110', her beam was 24'3", and her draft was 7'11". The *Godspeed* and *Discovery*, which were 61' and 49'6" long respectively...."

33. Benjamin Woolley, *Savage Kingdom*, 33. Woolley: "Thirty-six of the company were identified as 'gentlemen.'"

34. Lacey, *Sir Walter Ralegh*, 128.
35. Smith, *Generall Historie*, Book 3, 223.
36. Smith, 222.
37. Wingfield, *Virginia's True Founder*, 154.
38. Wingfield, 165.
39. Hume, *Virginia Adventure*, 121–122. Hume: "…what was meant by gentleman … a person entitled to possess heraldic arms but not a member of the nobility … as playwright Ben Jonson noted in 1600, many still had mud on their boots."
40. J.H. Elliott, "The Iberian Atlantic and Virginia" in *The Atlantic World and Virginia, 1550–1624*, ed. Peter C. Mancall, 551–552.
41. Morgan, *American Slavery, American Freedom*, 63.
42. Smith, *Generall Historie*, Book 3, 225–226; Bradford Smith, *Captain John Smith*, 93. Bradford Smith: "Wingfield practically confesses that he was one of the accusers.…"
43. Barbour, *Captain John Smith*, 114; Wingfield, *Virginia's True Founder*, 174.
44. David S. Shields, "The Genius of Ancient Britain" in *The Atlantic World and Virginia, 1550–1624*, ed. Peter C. Mancall, 500. Though he does not necessarily agree with this characterization, Shields writes, "Smith seemed a Beowulf incarnate—an avatar of ancient energy—at times a martial Roman, at others a freedom-loving Saxon, or, in his more refined moments, a latter-day member of Arthur's round table, an embodiment of knightly virtue."
45. Barbour, *Captain John Smith*, 17–73.
46. Barbour, 86–87.
47. Bradford Smith, *Captain John Smith*, 41, 161, 296–299; Frances Mossiker, *Pocahontas: The Life and the Legend*, 85. Bradford Smith: "(Thomas) Fuller in his *Worthies of England* cast the first stone in 1662" and "Charles Deane of Boston first challenged the story in 1859 … Smith is left at last as an adventurer, a braggart and a liar without any serious claim to remembrance." A native of Texas, Mossiker singles out noted Boston historian Henry Adams (1838–1918) as leading the attack on Smith in an article published in 1867 "out of spite, an anti–Southern bias in a post–Civil War period marked by vicious sectionalism." In a review of *The First Republic in America* by Alexander Brown published in 1898, the *New York Times* stated (Saturday, June 18, 1898), "Even if Capt. John Smith had been the verist scamp and the greatest rascal unhung we could not but admire his bravery and his fortitude, and it seems to us that the controversial spirit has led Mr. Brown to forget that these rare and great qualities 'shine afar in a naughty world,' and should cover a multitude of sins."
48. Bradford Smith, 50, 54, 60. Bradford Smith: "(Capt. John) Smith is better informed about Hungarian affairs than his critics … the facts support him in an amazing way … the surprising accuracy of Smith's other statements about Hungary require us to be more cautious about condemning him than past critics have been.… Still, a man who blows his own horn is always suspect."
49. Captain John Smith's *The Generall Historie of Virginia, New-England, and the Summer Isles* is a work in six books published in 1624. Book one contains reprints of narratives related to the Roanoke Island Colony. Book two is a reprint of Smith's own *Map of Virginia* published in 1612 with minor revisions. Books three and four pertain to Virginia and the Jamestown Colony, expanding on Book two with much new material. Smith attributes authorship of some of the chapters of Books three and four to one or more of fifteen associates. Book five pertains to Bermuda or the Summer or Somers Islands and Book six pertains to New England.
50. Smith, *Generall Historie*, Book 3, 334.
51. Woolley, *Savage Kingdom*, 40.
52. Edward Maria Wingfield, "A Discourse of Virginia" in *Jamestown Narratives*, ed. Edward Wright Haile, 192, 200. Wingfield writes that Smith accused him of saying that "he [Smith] did conceal an intended mutiny."
53. Bare poles meant that a ship had furled or taken in all sails, the "poles" referring to the ship's masts and spars. Sails were furled because they could not withstand the force of severe winds without being torn apart. Without sails, the ship would lose steerageway and be blown downwind.
54. Smith, *Generall Historie*, Book 3,

223; Bradford Smith, *Captain John Smith*, 94.

55. Smith, 223–224; George Percy, "Observations gathered out of a discourse of the plantation of the southern colony in Virginia by the English, 1606" in *Jamestown Narratives*, ed. Edward Wright Haile, 90.

56. Helen C. Rountree, *The Powhatan Indians of Virginia*, 13. Rountree credits Strachey with recording the name.

57. Powhatan was the name of one of the tribes of the Algonquin alliance of thirty tribes occupying Tidewater Virginia. In 1600 the name was pronounced "*po-HAT-un*." Today it is commonly pronounced "*POW-a-tun*." The English applied the name also to the alliance collectively and to its principal chief, Wahunsenacawh (ca. 1545–1618) aka Powhatan, principal chief of the Powhatan Nation and father of Pocahontas.

58. Williamson, *Powhatan Lords*, 47. Regarding the organizational structure of the Powhatans and citing Helen Rountree, anthropologist Williamson says, "This polity can reasonably be called a paramount chiefdom."

59. Strachey, *Historie of Travell*, 68–69. The Chickahominy (*Chicahamania* according to Strachey) tribe occupied the lower Chickahominy River, which empties into the James River six miles upriver from Jamestown. Independent of the Powhatan Nation, the tribe could muster 300 warriors.

60. Ralph Hamor, "A True Discourse," in *Jamestown Narratives*, ed. Edward Wright Haile, 811, 845; Williamson, *Powhatan Lords*, 71. Hamor and Dale claimed the Chickahominy had "at the least five hundred" fighting men and "five hundred bowmen" respectively, which would indicate a total population of fifteen hundred or so. This is at odds with Strachey's estimate of 300 Chickahominy warriors. For the sake of consistency, I have used Strachey's estimates for all tribes.

61. William Strachey, *Historie of Travell into Virginia Britania*, 49. The Accohmack and Accohanock tribes occupied the lower Delmarva Peninsula on the eastern shore of the Chesapeake Bay. They could muster approximately eighty warriors and forty warriors respectively.

62. Strachey, 67–68. The Kecoughtan (*key-CAW-tan*) tribe and its chief, Pochins, a son of Powhatan, was a Powhatan alliance tribe that occupied the point of Virginia's Lower Peninsula between the James River and the Chesapeake Bay, site of present-day Newport News and Hampton. The Kecoughtans could muster only 30 warriors. It was ruled by Pochins, a son of Wahunsenacawh (Powhatan) and, therefore, a brother or half-brother of Pocahontas. The Pamunkey tribe was ruled by Powhatan's three brothers—Opitchapam, Opechancanough, and Kekataugh—and it occupied the Pamunkey River Basin, a tributary of today's York River.

63. Rountree, *The Powhatan Indians*, 15; Daniel K. Richter, *Facing East from Indian Country*, 70; Barbour, *Captain John Smith*, 140; Williamson, *Powhatan Lords*, 40; Grace Steele Woodward, *Pocahontas*, 17–18; Keith Egloff and Deborah Woodward, *First People: The Early Indians of Virginia*, 52–53; James Horn, *A Land As God Made It*, 16. Rountree: "13,000 or a minimum of 14,300 people in the very first years after the English arrived ... about 6,350 square miles." Barbour: "...numbering perhaps 8500 souls scattered over an area of about as many square miles." Steele: "By 1607 the total population of the (Powhatan) confederacy was between 8,500 and 9,000 persons, approximately 3,000 of whom were warriors." Williams estimates total Algonquin population at 14,000 and land area, 8,000 square miles. Egloff and Woodward: "...a population of approximately 14,000 to 21,000 ... in over 150 villages...." Horn: "Perhaps 15,000 people ... lived in territories belonging to the Powhatan chiefdom."

64. Helen C. Rountree, *Pocahontas Powhatan Opechancanough*, 13; William M. Kelso, Jamestown, *The Truth Revealed*, 152, 200; Hobson Woodward, *A Brave Vessel*, 102–103. Woodward: "Virginia began its driest seven-year span in seven hundred and seventy years."

65. Rountree, *The Powhatan Indians*, 40; Woolley, *Savage Kingdom*, 97.

66. Rice, "Escape from Tsenacommacah," 97–108. The author explains in excellent detail the survival stress imposed on the Algonquins of the Middle Atlantic region by the Little Ice Age of 1300 to 1850 by the shortening of the growing season.

67. Williamson, *Powhatan Lords*, 173–174. Williamson: Ahone was "the good

and peaceable god," Okee "in whom they recognized the Devil," and the Great Hare, "creator of the land, water, the first people, deer, and fish."

68. Quinn, *Set Fair for Roanoke*, 223.

69. John Smith, *Captain John Smith's History of Virginia*, 14; Strachey, *Historie of Travell*, 88–89; Uttamatomakkin (Tomocomo), "An Interview in London," 1617, conducted by Samuel Purchas in *Jamestown Narratives*, ed. Edward Wright Haile, 881–882.

70. Henry Spelman, "Relation of Virginia, 1609" in *Jamestown Narratives*, ed. Edward Wright Haile, 486; Williamson, *Powhatan Lords*, 179, 199; Fitzmaurice, "Moral Uncertainty in the Dispossession of Native Americans," 383–409. Williamson: "they (English colonists) took Virginian religion as a perverted version of their own religion, one that made much of the worst aspects of Christianity and paid insufficient attention to the good and valuable aspects." Fitzmaurice cites the work of Spanish theologian José de Acosta (ca. 1539–1600) who reasoned that human societies could be divided into three categories, the lowest being nomadic "savages similar to wild animals" who had no right to possession of the land they occupied. This fallacious understanding of Algonquin culture became a high-minded and immoral justification for appropriation of land in the New World.

71. Richter, *Facing East from Indian Country*, 84. Richter explains, "other-than-human persons bent on harm required much more ritual attention than those more kindly disposed."

72. William White, "Excerpt published by *Purchas His Pilgrimage*: The Black Boys Ceremony," in *Jamestown Narratives*, ed. Edward Wright Haile, 141; Rountree, *The Powhatan Indians of Virginia*, 78.

73. Strachey, *Historie of Travell*, 71; Helen C. Rountree, *Manteo's World*, 74. Bloodroot, *Sanguinaria canadensis*, also known as Canada puccoon, bloodwort, or redroot and is native to eastern North America. Rountree explains that the plant grows only in the sand hills of southern South Carolina, far remote from Algonquin territory.

74. Spelman, "Relation of Virginia, 1609," 494; Strachey, 73; Percy, "Observations," 92.

75. Strachey, 61.

76. Spelman, "Relation of Virginia, 1609," 488–489; Rountree, *The Powhatan Indians of Virginia*, 112; Williamson, *Powhatan Lords*, 64, 68. Williamson points out that in this way "after only two or three generations all the werowances of the polity would have been kin to one another."

77. Linwood Custalow, *The True Story of Pocahontas*, 6; Camilla Townsend, *Pocahontas and the Powhatan Dilemma*, 15. Custalow: "It was a temporary marriage in order to infuse royal blood into the alliance tribe and establish kinship ties."

78. Rountree, *The Powhatan Indians of Virginia*, 139; Williamson, *Powhatan Lords*, 204.

79. Strachey, *Historie of Travell*, 100; White, "Excerpt published by *Purchas His Pilgrimage*," in *Jamestown Narratives*, ed. Edward Wright Haile, 141; Rountree, *Manteo's World*, 62.

80. Williamson, *Powhatan Lords*, 212, 221. Williamson: "Strachey confirms the virilocal (patrilocal) rule of postmarital residence, adding that the groom married only after he had built a house for the couple to live in." Algonquin dwellings were not single-family, however, but shared with extended family and, perhaps, nonfamily, so a groom's preparations for marriage were probably not an all-new structure.

81. Smith, *Captain John Smith's History of Virginia*, 19; Strachey, 77.

82. Custalow, *The True Story of Pocahontas*, 6; Richter, *Facing East from Indian Country*, 71. Custalow: "…her mother was Mattaponi; her father was Pamunkey (Wahunsenacawh).

83. Williamson, *Powhatan Lords*, 65.

84. Rountree, *The Powhatan Indians of Virginia*, 45.

85. Helen C. Rountree, Wayne E. Clark, and Kent Mountford, *John Smith's Chesapeake Voyages 1607–1609*, 299.

86. Spelman, "Relation of Virginia, 1609," 487–488; Strachey, 82–84.

87. Rountree, *The Powhatan Indians of Virginia*, 90; Williamson, *Powhatan Lords*, 212.

88. Spelman, "Relation of Virginia, 1609," 488.

89. Andrew Fitzmaurice, "Moral Uncertainty in the Dispossession of Native Americans" in *The Atlantic World and*

Virginia, 1550-1624, ed. Peter C. Mancall, 402-403, 407, citing José de Acosta's "pro-gressive theory of barbarism" and John Locke's "famous dismissal ... of the natural-law rights of Native Americans."
90. Strachey, *Historie of Travell*, 89; Rice, "Escape from Tsenacommacah," 115. Strachey: "...they (priests) doe at all tymes so absolutely governe and direct the Weroances or Lords of Countryes in all their accions and this Custome he hath politquely maynteyned and doth yet vniversally...."
91. Rice, 118. Author explains that "people who were ideologically committed to their own weroance's sacred lineage but who merely acquiesced in Powhatan's rule were perfectly willing to consider working with the English to rid themselves of Powhatan. For, notwithstanding the accumulation of power in Powhatan's hands, each weroance, including Powhatan's thirty-plus tributary chiefs, remained the head of a distinct nation."
92. Thomas Harriot, "A briefe and true report of the new found land of Virginia (1588)," 26; Rountree, *Manteo's World*, 61; Williamson, *Powhatan Lords*, 195-196. Harriot spelled the word, "Kewasowok." Rountree asserts that the name was also applied to images of Okee. Williamson: "...the quiyoughcosough was a 'priest' because he was imposed on his 'congregation' from above (as in the Catholic Church) ... the Jamestown colonists saw him as the Devil's agent."
93. Williamson, 207-209. Williamson quoting John Smith, the boys "were kept in the wildernesse by the young men till nine months were expired," and she observes, "a period corresponding to the length of human gestation."
94. Strachey, *Historie of Travell*, 92, 94; 98-99; Uttamatomakkin, "An Interview in London," 1617, 882-883; Rountree, *Manteo's World*, 55-56, 65; Williamson, 208. Williamson: "this was an initiation and not a sacrifice."
95. Martin D. Gallivan, *The Powhatan Landscape*, 176-177.
96. Rountree, *Manteo's World*, 66-67. Yaupon holly, *Ilex vomitoria*, is a shrub or small tree having leaves and twigs that contain caffeine. It was a common hospitality drink. Jimsonweed will be discussed later in greater detail.

97. Rountree, 36.
98. D.B. Quinn, *Raleigh and the British Empire*, 105; Bernal Díaz, *The Conquest of New Spain*, 181, 220-223, 264, 322. Interestingly, the Aztec had an almost identical prophecy that told of "the coming of men from distant lands in the direction of the sunrise, who would conquer them and rule them." Could there be a connection?
99. Strachey, *Historie of Travell*, 104-105.
100. Harriot, "A briefe and true report," 29.
101. Townsend, *Pocahontas*, 7-10; Horn, *A Land As God Made It*, 8; Woodward, *Pocahontas*, 43-44.
102. Williamson, *Powhatan Lords*, 144; Daniel K. Richter, "Tsenacommacah and the Atlantic World" in *The Atlantic World and Virginia, 1550-1624*, ed. Peter C. Mancall, 37-43; Custalow, *The True Story of Pocahontas*, 17. Custalow: "According to Mattaponi sacred oral history, Luis and Wahunsenaca were the same person." This seems highly unlikely.
103. Quinn, *Raleigh and the British Empire*, 105; Helen Rountree, *Pocahontas's People*, 22; Fullam, *The Lost Colony*, 158-161.
104. Rountree, *The Powhatan Indians of Virginia*, 121; Williamson, *Powhatan Lords*, 145-147. Williamson: "...adoption, slavery, or sacrifice to be the usual fate of captives" ... the most important reason for the chief engaging in warfare was that a raid or battle provided captives to be sacrificed. "Providing the sacrificial victim and by this means ensuring the life of the community are obligations of kings worldwide...."
105. Pedro de Cieza de León, *The Incas*, trans. Harriet de Onis, 75-76; William H. Prescott, *History of the Conquest of Peru*, 50.
106. Strachey, *Historie of Travell*, 66; Rountree, *Pocahontas's People*, 27. Nansemond (*NANS-mund*) tribal territory was along the Nansemond River south of the James River. A Powhatan alliance tribe, they could muster an estimated 200 warriors. Its chief was Weyhohomo.
107. Richter, "Tsenacommach and the Atlantic World," 39; Francis Maguel, "Report of what Francisco Maguel, an Irishman, learned, etc., July 1, 1610" in *Jamestown Narratives*, ed. Edward Wright Haile,

450. Don Luis de Velasco spent considerable time in Mexico before being repatriated to Tsenacommacah in the summer of 1570, so it is certain that he related to others what he had observed there of Spanish brutality to the indigene of Mexico. Powhatan's year of birth is estimated at 1547, so he was in his twenties when Don Luis returned. Maguel was surely exaggerating when he wrote that Powhatan sent men to the West Indies and Newfoundland to bring him news, but this Spanish spy must have heard something in Jamestown regarding Powhatan's intelligence network that led him to believe what he reported to the Spanish ambassador in London was true.

108. Smith, *Generall Historie*, Book 3, 297–303.

109. Percy, "Observations," 90.

110. John Smith, *A True Relation* in *Jamestown Narratives*, ed. Edward Wright Haile, 145.

111. Smith, *Generall Historie*, Book 3, 224.

112. Morgan, *American Slavery, American Freedom*, 71.

113. Percy, "Observations," 94.

114. Barbour, *Captain John Smith*, 142–143.

115. Strachey, *Historie of Travell*, 66–67; Percy, "Observations," 92, 94. Wowinchopunck (*"wo-WEEN-cha-punk"*), chief of the Paspahegh (*"PAS-pah-hey"*), a Powhatan alliance tribe located on the north bank of the James River, a tribe that could muster 40 warriors. Jamestown was established in Paspahegh tribal territory. Of Wowinchopunck, Strachey says, "he being one of the mightiest and strongest Saluadges that Powhatan had vnder him."

116. Percy, "Observations," 94–95.

117. Bradford Smith, *Captain John Smith*, 98; Craven, *The Southern Colonies*, 79; Hume, *Virginia Adventure*, 272. Craven: "Among his (Powhatan's) 'subjects' were the Indians of Paspahegh, the region in the immediate vicinity of Jamestown, from whom the colonists by a payment in copper purchased the right of settlement." He cites Strachey's *Historie of Travaile* (sic., *Travell*) as a source for this claim: "that the English would pay for every foot of land used." Hume disagrees: "Furthermore, the Jamestown Island site was not purchased from the Indians either legitimately or by ... cheating—at least not directly." I tend to agree with Hume.

118. Barbour, *Captain John Smith*, 233. Barbour: "It appears that the Council in London sent word that Captain Newport's verbal instructions must be obeyed."

119. Gabriel Archer, "A relation of the discovery of our river from James Fort into the main, made by Captain Christofer Newport, and sincerely written and observed by a gentleman of the colony" in *Jamestown Narratives*, ed. Edward Wright Haile, 117; Bradford Smith, *Captain John Smith*, 100–101. Bradford Smith: "On June 10 Smith was at last sworn a member of the council ... through the mediation of Newport and (Richard) Hunt, the chaplain, matters were patched up."

120. Smith, *A True Relation*, 148; Wingfield, "A Discourse of Virginia," 200; Barbour, *Captain John Smith*, 149; Wingfield, *Virginia's True Founder*, 204, 212.

121. Smith, *A True Relation*, 147; Archer, "A relation," 115. The Algonquin attack on either May 26 or 27, 1607—presumably by Paspahegh warriors—left one English boy killed, eleven wounded of which one died later, and twenty Algonquins killed. Wingfield estimated the attack force numbered four hundred, but this is an exaggeration; although Smith reports the same number. Archer estimated two hundred. According to Strachey's estimate, the Paspahegh could muster only about 40 warriors, so other tribes may have been involved.

122. Craven, *The Southern Colonies*, 87–88.

123. Craven 99.

124. Smith, *Generall Historie*, Book 3, 231; Hamor, "A True Discourse," 827; The Ancient Planters of Virginia, "A Brief Declaration" in *Jamestown Narratives*, ed. Edward Wright Haile, 894–895; John Ratcliffe, *alias* Sicklemore, "Letter to Salisbury, 4 October 1609 in *Jamestown Narratives*, ed. Edward Wright Haile, 355; Kelso, *Jamestown The Truth Revealed*, 147. Hamor clearly states that Jamestown was "when we first seated upon it a thick wood." The ancient planters speak of only four acres being cleared for planting crops at the arrival of the first supply in January 1608, and later "not being above seven acres." Jamestown Island is 1,561 acres. It was even larger in 1607. Kelso disagrees:

"And the settlement (Jamestown) was built on an abandoned, open Indian field," but he cites no source for this claim.

125. Hume, *Virginia Adventure*, 139. Hume: "That trees were cut is undisputed ... growth in the chosen area was less than a century old...."

126. Hume, 131. Hume quoting Percy: "...where our shippes doe lie so neere the shoare that they are moored to the Trees in six fathom water."

127. Percy, "Observations," 100.

128. Gabriel Archer, "A relation," 116.

129. Barbour, *Captain John Smith*, 145–146.

130. Smith, *A True Relation*, 149, Percy, "Observations," 99; Kelso, *Jamestown The Truth Revealed*, 119–122. Kelso describes a grave unearthed by archeologists at Jamestown that may contain the remains of Gosnold as it contained with the bones a ceremonial captain's staff or half pike.

131. Smith, *A True Relation*, 149.

132. Wingfield, "A Discourse of Virginia," 188–192; Percy, "Observations," 100.

133. Smith, *Generall Historie*, Book 3, 233; Kelso, *Jamestown The Truth Revealed*, 43. Kelso: "...Captain George Kendall seems to have been ... a suspected agent of the Spanish."

134. Smith, *A True Relation*, 154; Wingfield, "A Discourse of Virginia," 194; Maguel, "Report of what Franscisco Maguel learned," 453; Barbour, *Captain John Smith*, 153–154. Maguel calls Kendall a Catholic who wanted to go to Spain "in order to reveal to His Majesty all about this country (Virginia) and many plans of the English." In other words, Kendall is accused of being a Spanish spy, but Maguel is wrong about so much else in his deposition that one cannot accept this as fact. Nevertheless, here is Barbour on Kendall: "...almost certainly a former Continental spy for Lord Salisbury (Robert Cecil). Kendall planned to supply King Philip with full information on the colony—undoubtedly for a price." Apparently, Barbour accepted Maguel's theory.

135. Smith, *Captain John Smith's History of Virginia*, 18; Strachey, 57. The six core tribes were the Appamatuck (estimated at 100 warriors), Arrohateck (60), Kiskiack (*KISS-kee-ack*) (50), Mattaponi (*mah-tah-PON-ie*) or Mattapanient (140), Pamunkey (300), and Powhatan (45).

136. Smith, *Generall Historie*, Book 3, 224–225.

137. Smith, *Generall Historie*, Book 3, 231. Smith, *A True Relation*, 148; Wingfield, "A Discourse of Virginia," 184. Smith indicates the peace greeting was delivered by "the King of Pamunke" which would indicate Opechancanough.

138. Smith, *A True Relation*, 149, Wingfield, 185. Opechancanough (*o-pe-CAN-ca-no*) (ca. 1554–1646), tribal chief of the Pamunkey, younger brother or half-brother of Powhatan (Wahunsenacawh). He succeeded his brother Opitchapam as chief of all Powhatan tribes sometime before 1622.

139. Richter, *Facing East from Indian Country*, 52. Richter states that "Formerly weak villages that may have owed tribute to larger and more powerful neighbors could be transformed into dominant powers by their geographical proximity or political ties to European trading partners."

140. Wingfield, "A Discourse of Virginia," 186.

141. Williamson, *Powhatan Lords*, 62.

142. Smith, *A True Relation*, 149; Smith, *Generall Historie*, Book 3, 231.

143. Smith, *A True Relation*, 149–150.

144. Smith, *Generall Historie*, Book 3, 232; Lemay, *The American Dream of Captain John Smith*, 143.

145. Smith, *A True Relation*, 150; Strachey, *Historie of Travell*, 65–66; The Warraskoyack (*rar-as-KO-yak*) were a Powhatan alliance tribe whose territory was across the James River from the Kecoughtans. Under their chief, Tachonekintaco (*toc-one-kin-TAC-o*), the tribe could muster approximately 60 warriors.

146. Smith, *A True Relation*, 151–154.

147. Horn, *A Land As God Made It*, 66; Mossiker, *Pocahontas*, 222. Regarding Werowocomoco, Mossiker: "a total population of perhaps two hundred, at the most." The Pamunkey River, so called by the Powhatans in 1607, included what is today the York River plus a tributary of the York still bearing the name, Pamunkey. Early Jamestown colonists originally named it Prince Henry's River. For consistency in this narrative, I shall refer to the York and Pamunkey as the Pamunkey.

148. Smith, *Generall Historie*, Book 3, 234.

Chapter 6

1. Ivor Noël Hume, *The Virginia Adventure: Roanoke to James Towne*, 132. Hume: "...the planters lacked horses or oxen to pull the stumps."
2. James Horn, *A Land As God Made It*, 269–270. Opitchapam (*o-PITCH-a-pam*) (before 1554–ca. 1623), younger brother/half-brother of Powhatan (Wahunsenacawh) whom he succeeded as chief of the Powhatan nation upon Powhatan's death in April 1618. He was succeeded by Opechancanough before 1622. According to Horn, he was poisoned by the English in 1623 and may have died as a result. Kekataugh (*KEY-ka-taw*) (1557–1618), youngest brother/half-brother of Powhatan (Wahunsenacawh).
3. John Smith, *A True Relation* in *Jamestown Narratives*, ed. Edward Wright Haile, 156.
4. John Smith, *Generall Historie of Virginia, New England and the Summer Isles*, Book 3, in *Jamestown Narratives*, ed. Edward Wright Haile, 234; William Strachey, *Historie of Travell into Virginia Britania*, 60. Strachey: "...they executed an Englishman one George Cawson, whom the women enticed vp from the barge vnto their howses at a place called Appocant."
5. Smith, *A True Relation*, 156; Smith, *Generall Historie*, Book 3, 234. In the former (1608) work, Smith claimed that "During the boiling of our victuals, one of the Indians I took with me to see the nature of the soil, and to cross the boughts (bends) of the river," while in the latter work (published in 1624), he claimed that "by fowling [he] sought them victual." Perhaps at this point, it was easier to explore farther upriver on foot than by canoe due to shallows and the many switchbacks.
6. Smith, *A True Relation*, 156. Invented in the late fifteenth century, the matchlock musket had an effective range of two hundred yards. It relied on a lighted taper to ignite priming gunpowder in a flash pan at the base of the barrel, which in turn ignited the main charge. From time to time, the musketeer had to blow on the taper to keep it lit.
7. Smith, *Generall Historie*, Book 3, 234–235. Smith stated that "he was beset with 200 savages, two of them he slew" then later he stated that "they followed him with 300 bowmen, conducted by the King of Pamunkee (Opechancanough).
8. Smith, 234.
9. Smith, *A True Relation*, 157; Smith, *Generall Historie*, Book 3, 235. Smith's two versions of this are inconsistent. In *True Relation* (1608) he wrote "...he (Opechancanough) requited me, conducting me where the canoe lay and John Robinson slain, with 20 or 30 arrows in him. Emry I saw not." In *The Generall Historie* (1624), Smith wrote that Opechancanough "found Robinson and Emry by the fireside. Those they shot full of arrows and slew."
10. Smith, *A True Relation*, 157; Smith, *Generall Historie*, Book 3, 235.
11. Smith, *A True Relation*, 159; Smith, *Generall Historie*, Book 3, 235. Smith's accounts differ. In the former, Smith states he was first taken to Rasawrack and then to Menacapute (Menapacant) "where the king (Opechancanough) inhabited," but in his *Generall Historie*, Smith indicates that he was taken to Orapaks where he was "kindly feasted and well used."
12. Gabriel Archer, "A Brief Description of the People" in *Jamestown Narratives*, ed. Edward Wright Haile, 122.
13. Lee Miller, *Roanoke: Solving the Mystery of the Lost Colony*, 90. Miller points out that corn was "pounded in mortars into lavender-tinted flour. Worked into moist bread called *ponap*, the 'corn pone' of English settlers" this being bread made without milk or eggs and baked or fried.
14. Smith, *A True Relation*, 157–158.
15. John Smith, *Captain John Smith's History of Virginia*, ed. David Freeman Hawke, 13; Helen C. Rountree, *Manteo's World*, 80; Margaret Holmes Williamson, *Powhatan Lords of Life and Death*, 213. Smith states that "at night where his [the honored guest's] lodging is appointed they set a woman fresh painted red with puccoon and oil to be his bedfellow."
16. Philip L. Barbour, *Pocahontas and Her World*, 39; Bradford Smith, *Captain John Smith*, 65, 126. Bradford Smith: "...from his (Capt. John Smith's) reading, he draws the trait of purity as his special characteristic. It is already clearly there in the code of Christian chivalry, this ideal of ascetic purity." Quoting Strachey, Bradford Smith: "...they are a people most voluptuous" by which he meant a people addicted to sensual pleasure.

17. D.B. Quinn, *Raleigh and the British Empire*, 50. Quinn: "But there is evidence which strongly suggests that Barlow's story was pruned of some awkward incident on Chesapeake Bay ... when the Indians, apparently the Powhatan Indians of Tidewater Virginia, attacked them and killed some of the Englishmen, even eating them, according to one Spanish report."

18. Williamson, *Powhatan Lords*, 67.

19. Smith, *A True Relation*, 159.

20. Smith, *Generall Historie*, Book 3, 236–237.

21. Smith, *A True Relation*, 158.

22. Smith, *A True Relation*, 158.

23. Smith, *A True Relation*, 158–159; Smith, *Generall Historie*, 237; Philip L. Barbour, *The Three Worlds of Captain John Smith*, 161. Barbour: "William Strachey noted that the Indians made wars 'principally for revenge.' They may have thought that the English would do the same thing."

24. Smith, *Generall Historie*, Book 3, 237; Strachey, *Historie of Travell*, 45. Youghtamond (*yough-ta-MUND*), a Powhatan alliance tribe that occupied the coastal plain area of the Pamunkey (York) River west of Pamunkey territory and could muster sixty-five warriors. Piankatank (*pee-ANK-a-tank*) a Powhatan alliance tribe that lived along the Piankatank River, its warriors numbering forty to fifty. Nandtaughtacund (*nan-tow-tah-CHUND*) a Powhatan alliance tribe with 150 warriors that lived along the south shore of the lower Rappahannock River. Mattiponi (or Mattapanient) with 140 warriors. The spelling of all tribal names conforms with Strachey; however, he used "y" for our "i" as in Pyankatank for Piankatank and Wyghcomoco for Wighcomoco. I have used the "i" for clarity. Warrior population conforms to Strachey's estimate in all cases, warrior numbers being approximately one-third of total tribal population.

25. Strachey, *Historie of Travell*, 45; Edward Maria Wingfield, "A Discourse of Virginia" in *Jamestown Narratives*, ed. Edward Wright Haile,195. Toppahanock, a Powhatan alliance tribe that occupied the south bank of the coastal plain area of the Rappahannock River and could muster one hundred warriors. Tappahannock is forty miles below the fall line at Fredericksburg.

26. Smith, *A True Relation*, 160; Grace Steele Woodward, *Pocahontas*, 68–69.

27. Smith, *A True Relation*, 160.

28. Smith, *Generall Historie*, 262.

29. Smith, *Generall Historie*, 236.

30. Strachey, *Historie of Travell*, 95. Uttamussak was the site of the Powhatans' holiest temple and was located on a sharp bend in the Pamunkey River ten miles upriver from the confluence of the Pamunkey and Mattaponi Rivers at today's West Point, Virginia.

31. Smith, *A True Relation*, 163–164.

32. Smith, *Generall Historie*, 237–238; Strachey, 96–97.

33. Smith, *Generall Historie*, 238.

34. Smith, *Generall Historie*, 238.

35. Weroansqua (*WEAR-o-an-squa*), a female chief, leader, or queen of a territory or village.

36. Smith, *Generall Historie*, 239.

37. Thomas Harriot, "A briefe and true report of the new found land of Virginia (1588)," 16.

38. Williamson, *Powhatan Lords*, 159. Williamson: "chiefly speech was important." Quoting anthropologist Robert H. Lowie, "a 'typical American chief' must be among other things a 'prolix Polonius.'"

39. Smith, *A True Relation*, 161. Published in 1608.

40. Martin D. Gallivan, *The Powhatan Landscape*, 166.

41. Courtier—"one who attends the court of a sovereign." This is the definition Smith would have known. From Anglo-French, *corteour*, "to be at court," from *cort*, "king's court; princely residence."

42. Smith, *Generall Historie*, 239. Opussoquonuske (*OH-po-so-quo-NUS-keh*) (died 1610), a weroansqua of the Appamatuck tribe who ruled a town near the mouth of the Appomattox River where it flows into the James.

43. Archer, "A relation," 112.

44. Frances Mossiker, *Pocahontas: The Life and the Legend*, 80.

45. Linwood Custalow, *The True Story of Pocahontas*, 19–20. Custalow: "...the quiakros would not have allowed Pocahontas to be there."

46. Helen C. Rountree, *Pocahontas Powhatan Opechancanough*, 36; Woodward, *Pocahontas*, 19. Rountree: "She was probably born sometime during 1596."

47. Smith, *A True Relation*, 181, Smith, *Generall Historie*, Book 3, 336; Book 4, 861.
48. Strachey, *Historie of Travell*, 72.
49. Williamson, *Powhatan Lords*, 166; Martin D. Gallivan, *The Powhatan Landscape*, 40, 50. Williamson quotes Thomas Hamor that Powhatan "could not without long aduise & delibertion with his Councell, resolue vpon any thing." Gallivan: "priests possessed the ultimate authority to ordain strategic actions and to declare war, while weroances held the complementary power to make tactical decisions and to enact plans."
50. Strachey, 91, 104; Williamson, *Powhatan Lords*, 256. Williamson: "...dual sovereignty was present among the Powhatan at the time of contact with the English." Williamson's work discusses the nature of this dual sovereignty throughout. Indeed, the understanding that Powhatan did not have absolute power is borne out by the fact that the English later blamed the Algonquin priesthood for the decision to kill the surviving lost colonists of Roanoke—"he (Powhatan) himself perswaded therevnto by his Priests." Calling for an attack on the Algonquin priesthood, Strachey says that the king "hath given order that Powhatan himself with his Weroances, and all his people shall be spared, and revenge only taken upon his Quiyoughquisocks (shamans)."
51. Helen C. Rountree, *The Powhatan Indians of Virginia*, 121–122.
52. Rountree, *Pocahontas's People*, 39.
53. For detailed information about Smith's early years refer to *Captain John Smith* by Edward Keble Chatterton (1927); *Captain John Smith* by Bradford Smith (1953); and *The Three Worlds of Captain John Smith* by Philip L. Barbour (1964). See bibliography.
54. Gallivan, *The Powhatan Landscape*, 28.
55. Smith, *Generall Historie*, Book 3, 314. He continued, "For the labors of thirty of forty honest and industrious men shall not be consumed to maintain an hundred and fifty idle loiterers."
56. Bradford Smith, *Captain John Smith*, 77. Bradford Smith: "John Smith's admiration for Sir Francis Drake is a matter of record."
57. Barbour, *Captain John Smith*, 231.
58. Smith, *Generall Historie*, Book 3, 290.
59. Smith, *Generall Historie*, Book 3, 290.
60. Smith, *Generall Historie*, Book 3, 284–285.
61. Smith, *Generall Historie*, Book 3, 289; Edmund S. Morgan, *American Slavery, American Freedom*, 87; David Beers Quinn, *Set Fair for Roanoke*, 176.
62. Smith, *Generall Historie*, Book 3, 329.
63. Williamson, *Powhatan Lords*, 94. See Williamson for an excellent discussion of how Europeans viewed the Algonquins on a scale of "civil" to "savage" depending on the cultural aspect under consideration. For instance, they were "civil" in that they had "ordered society hierarchically" and "expressed due deference to superiors." They were "savage" in that "they were pagan and not Christian, and that they could or would not recognize the obvious superiority of the English."
64. Karen Kupperman, *Roanoke: The Abandoned Colony*, 102.
65. Bradford Smith, *Captain John Smith*, 162; April Lee Hatfield, *Atlantic Virginia: Intercolonial Relations in the Seventeenth Century*, 16.
66. Smith, *Generall Historie*, Book 3, 306.
67. Barbour, *Captain John Smith*, 216–219.
68. Smith, *Generall Historie*, Book 3, 254–277. Smith's narrative of his two Chesapeake Bay expeditions is covered in chapters five and six of his *Generall Historie*.
69. Barbour, *Pocahontas and Her World*, 24–25; Rountree, *Pocahontas Powhatan Opechancanough*, 80; Frances Mossiker, *Pocahontas: The Life and the Legend*, 80–82. Rountree: "...the sequence of actions echoes the public phase of the *huskanaw* or initiation of boys into manhood." Mossiker believes that the lifesaving event *did* occur, and that Smith was, in effect, adopted by Pocahontas. Mossiker cites the right of women in many Native American cultures to claim the life of an enemy captive as "compensation for a war casualty" if their mates had been killed in the action and they were, thereby, denied his protection and keeping. This explanation, however, does not fit Pocahontas's circumstances, and in Smith's case, the person doing the adopting was clearly Powhatan, not his daughter.

70. Rountree, *The Powhatan Indians of Virginia*, 82. Jimsonweed—*Datura stramonium*, a toxic plant of the nightshade family also known as thorn apple. The name is a corruption of "Jamestown Weed."

71. Daniel K. Richter, *Facing East from Indian Country*, 81. Richter: "Vision quests through fasts, sweats, self-induced pain, or mind-altering substances similarly can be understood as means of achieving altered states of consciousness in which more direct relationships with other-than-human persons and the *manitou* they could mobilize might be established."

72. Custalow, *The True Story of Pocahontas*, 19. Custalow: "...his life was never in danger.... Why would the Powhatan want to kill a person they were initiating to be a werowance ... either a figment of his own imagination or an embellishment to dramatize his narrative."

73. Smith, *A True Relation*, 181.

74. Horn, *A Land As God Made It*, 199–200; Hobson Woodward, *A Brave Vessel*, 139.

75. George Percy, "A True Relation" in *Jamestown Narratives*, ed. Edward Wright Haile, 515; Alexander Whitaker, "Letter to the Reverend William Crashaw, 9 August 1611" in *Jamestown Narratives*, ed. Edward Wright Haile, 549.

76. Barbour, *Captain John Smith*, 256; Rountree, *Pocahontas Powhatan Opechancanough*, 209.

77. Smith, *Generall Historie*, Book 3, 303, 310–311. In support of the allegation that the Powhatans used poison on occasion, in one incident at Werowocomoco in early January 1609, Smith so suspected poisoning that he insisted his Powhatan servers first taste the cooked food they brought for him and his men to eat. On another occasion later that same month, Francis West and others were poisoned but survived.

78. Smith, *Generall Historie*, Book 3, 240.

79. Smith, *A True Relation*, 166; Smith, *Generall Historie*, Book 4, 861. "Salvage," an obsolete spelling of "savage," commonly used in sixteenth-century England.

80. Rountree, *Pocahontas Powhatan Opechancanough*, 83; Horn, *A Land As God Made It*, 70. Rountree: "Finally Powhatan concluded that the Strangers were worth gathering in as allies against his inland enemies ... his intention ... to assimilate the Strangers...."

81. Smith, *A True Relation*, 162. Smith wrote, referring to Powhatan: "He desired me to forsake Paspaliegh and to live with him upon his river, a country called Capa Howasicke; he promised to give me corn, venison, or what I wanted to feed us; hatchets and copper we should make him, and none should disturb us. This request I promised to perform."

82. The Council of Virginia, "A True Declaration of the estate of the colony in Virginia," 1610 in *Jamestown Narratives*, ed. Edward Wright Haile, 470. That the Council received Powhatan's offer is confirmed by this document which states "Principally when Captain Newport was with Powhatan at Warow a comaco, he desired him to come from James town as a place unwholesome, and to take possession of another whole kingdom which he gave unto him."

83. Richter, *Facing East from Indian Country*, 78. Richter explores this theme, "The story of Pocahontas, then, does represent a road of intercultural cooperation that tragically was not taken—but a road toward cooperation on Indian, rather than English, terms.... But Pocahontas's diplomatic marriage suggests that there was a genuine moment when an alternative history might have been made."

84. James Horn, "Imperfect Understandings: Rumor, Knowledge, and Uncertainty in Early Virginia" in *The Atlantic World and Virginia, 1550–1624*, ed. Peter C. Mancall, 526.

85. John Smith, "A Map of Virginia" in *Jamestown Narratives*, ed. Edward Wright Haile, 207; Rountree, *The Powhatan Indians of Virginia*, 109. According to Smith's map, Capahowosick was a village located on the north bank of the Pamunkey (York) River about eight miles upriver from its mouth at today's Gloucester Point. The territory likely included all land between the Piankatank and Pamunkey (York) Rivers that surrounded Mobjack Bay on Virginia's Middle Peninsula, an area of roughly one hundred square miles; whereas Jamestown Island is 2½ square miles. Rountree calls this Powhatan's "hunting preserve" as it was directly east of Werowocomoco.

86. J.H. Elliott, "The Iberian Atlantic and Virginia" in *The Atlantic World and Virginia, 1550-1624*, ed. Peter C. Mancall, 546. Elliott, the renowned Oxford historian, states English New World objectives very succinctly here.

87. Smith, *Generall Historie*, Book 3, 240.

88. Wingfield, "A Discourse of Virginia," 196.

89. Hume, *Virginia Adventure*, 101-102.

90. Smith, *A True Relation*, 164-165; Smith, *Generall Historie*, Book 3, 240; Wingfield, 196.

91. Smith, *Generall Historie*, Book 3, 242; Horn, *A Land As God Made It*, 74-75.

92. Smith, *A True Relation*, 165; Francis Perkins, "Letter from Jamestown to a Friend, 28 March 1608" in *Jamestown Narratives*, ed. Edward Wright Haile, 134-135. New colonists were left with little more than the clothes on their backs. Perkins letter includes an appeal to his benefactor for "such clothes as he may have that are worn out, whether it be large or small garments, doublets, trousers, stockings, capes, or whatever may appear fit to them, since, the fire having burnt all we possessed, everything is needed and whatever may be sent will be useful."

93. Smith, *Generall Historie*, Book 3, 246.

94. Smith, *Generall Historie*, Book 3, 241; Book 4, 862.

95. Camilla Townsend, *Pocahontas and the Powhatan Dilemma*, 70.

96. Custalow, *The True Story of Pocahontas*, 26-28.

97. Smith, *Generall Historie*, Book 3, 243.

98. Horn, *A Land As God Made It*, 103-104.

99. Smith, *Generall Historie*, Book 3, 247-248.

100. Smith, *A True Relation*, 169; Barbour, *Captain John Smith*, 182. Barbour: "...two to three hundred bushels of corn for a pound or two of cheap Venetian glass beads, of quite negligible value compared with copper pots."

101. Smith, *Generall Historie*, 246; Barbour, *Captain John Smith*, 181; Williamson, *Powhatan Lords*, 155. Williamson takes issue with this interpretation, claiming that Newport recognized that Powhatan, by his status, did not engage in ordinary commerce: "Newport, more sympathetic to Powhatan meanings, understands that this is an exchange of gifts and responds accordingly." But Powhatan's eager acceptance of blue glass beads in exchange for a more considerable quantity of corn augurs otherwise.

102. Smith, *A True Relation*, 167.

103. Hume, *Virginia Adventure*, 222.

104. Custalow, *The True Story of Pocahontas*, 35-36.

105. Rountree, *Pocahontas Powhatan Opechancanough*, 101.

106. Smith, *Generall Historie*, Book 3, 286-287.

107. Smith, *A True Relation*, 175.

108. Smith, *Generall Historie*, Book 3, 249.

109. Bradford Smith, *Captain John Smith*, 234.

110. Bradford Smith, *Captain John Smith*, 146, 173. Bradford Smith: "...there was a warm relationship between John Smith and Pocahontas which was publicly on record as early as 1608, was vouched for by half a dozen Virginia settlers in 1612, and was never challenged by anyone during Smith's lifetime or for over two hundred years after."

111. Smith, *A True Relation*, 181; Smith, *Generall Historie*, 250.

112. Bradford Smith, *Captain John Smith*, 128. Bradford Smith: "Powhatan had sons as well as daughters. Why did he send a young girl, unless there was some strong bond between her and the colony? Smith's critics have never answered this."

113. John Ratcliffe, *alias* Sicklemore, "Letter to Salisbury, 4 October 1609" in *Jamestown Narratives*, ed. Edward Wright Haile, 354; Barbour, *Captain John Smith*, 278-279. Barbour: "One colonist 'calculated' that Smith had the savages in such subjection that he was going to make himself King, by marrying Pocahontas....'"

114. Smith, *Generall Historie*, Book 3, 277-278.

115. Hume, *Virginia Adventure*, 213. Hume: "...one of the most ludicrous decisions ever to come out of a committee."

116. Smith, *Generall Historie*, Book 3, 280-281; Joseph Kelly, *Marooned*, 311. Smith does not say that Pocahontas was one of the dancers or that she ever tried to seduce him. Kelly speculates: "In Werowocomoco she had danced provocatively

for the English captain's delectation and had tried to lure him to bed.... We have no reason to suppose that she was less sexually active than the typical young Indian." No other historian or biographer goes so far out on this very insubstantial limb, but rumors did persist of a mutual attraction and warm relationship, and this is borne out by her comments to him when they visited in England in January 1617.

117. Barbour, *Captain John Smith*, 235. Barbour: "...they invited the Englishmen to their wigwams and their beds." Barbour in inferring what I also inferred, but there was no firsthand account saying sex was offered that night.

118. Frances Mossiker, *Pocahontas: The Life and the Legend*, 112.

119. Smith, *Generall Historie*, Book 3, 282–283.

120. Barbour, *Captain John Smith*, 238.

121. Smith, *Generall Historie*, Book 3, 288; Francis Maguel, "Report of what Franacisco Maguel, an Irishman, learned, etc., July 1, 1610" in *Jamestown Narratives*, ed. Edward Wright Haile, 450. In his deposition, Spanish spy Maguel reported that the natives of Virginia could "easily take them [the English] to the South Sea by three routes," then he names the three riverine routes. Though untrue, this claim demonstrates the wild rumors regarding such a passage and the emphasis placed by the English on this particular objective of the Virginia colony.

122. Smith, *Generall Historie*, Book 3, 296.

123. Smith, *Generall Historie*, Book 3, 303; Book 4, 862. Smith explained that "the dark night could not affright her from coming through the irksome woods, and with watered eyes gave me intelligence with her best advice to escape his fury; which had he known, he had surely slain her."

124. Barbour, *Pocahontas and Her World*, 57. Barbour: "The retreat to Orapaks showed that Powhatan realized he could not defeat the whitemen."

125. Bradford Smith, *Captain John Smith*, 151.

126. Horn, *A Land As God Made It*, 134–136; William M. Kelso, Jamestown, *The Truth Revealed*, 225. Horn: "...the extension of territories from 'sea to sea' reflected the continuing hope of finding a river passage somewhere near the head of the (Chesapeake) Bay that would ultimately lead to the Pacific and beyond to the Far East." Kelso: "he (King James) 'gives, grants, and confirms' corporation status to more than 650 named individuals and companies ... that include eight earls, fourteen lords, more than one hundred knights and fifty-four captains."

127. Percy, *A True Relation*, 502; Bradford Smith, *Captain John Smith*, 156. Bradford Smith: "Someone had touched off his powder bag," implying it was not accidental, but John Smith's own words are ambiguous on this point.

128. Smith, *Generall Historie*, Book 3, 332.

129. Smith, *Generall Historie*, Book 3, 333; Barbour, *Captain John Smith*, 278; Benjamin Woolley, *Savage Kingdom*, 228–229. Woolley: "Ratcliffe, Archer, and Martin ... apparently commissioned Thomas Coe and William Dyer to do the job, though the 'heart did fail him that should have given fire to that merciless pistol,' and Smith survived" the attempted assassination.

130. Smith, *Generall Historie*, Book 3, 335–336; Percy, *A True Relation*, 502; Barbour, *Captain John Smith*, 279.

131. Bradford Smith, *Captain John Smith*, 218. Bradford Smith makes the insightful point: He (Capt. John Smith) would not have dared say he had sent her (Queen Anne) a 'little book' if he had not done so, nor would he in 1616 have been likely to lie to the Queen about an event she might soon discuss with Pocahontas herself."

132. J.A. Leo Lemay, *The American Dream of Captain John Smith*, 225; Karen Kupperman, *Pocahontas and the English Boys*, 180. Lemay opines that the explosion "mutilated his genitals." Kupperman: "If Smith had been circumcised, the telltale evidence was destroyed when his powder bag exploded in his lap." There is, however, no contemporary record of the extent of Smith's injuries.

Chapter 7

1. Gabriel Archer, "Letter from Jamestown, 31 August 1609" in *Jamestown Narratives*, ed. Edward Wright Haile, 352; The

Council of Virginia, "A True and Sincere Declaration of the purposes and ends of the plantation of Virginia..." in *Jamestown Narratives*, ed. Edward Wright Haile, 361; Philip L. Barbour, *Pocahontas and Her World*, 73; Wesley Frank Craven, *The Southern Colonies in the Seventeenth Century 1607–1689*, 92. Craven: "Having followed a course from England southwestward to about the thirtieth degree of north latitude, he then ran directly westward for America."

2. Hugh Bicheno, *Elizabeth's Sea Dogs*, 60.

3. David Beers Quinn, *Set Fair for Roanoke*, 144.

4. Bradford Smith, *Captain John Smith*, 151; Craven, *The Southern Colonies*, 72. Craven: "Though his methods and procedures were for the most part unauthorized, significantly they were in line with policies soon to be enforced by order from London."

5. Hobson Woodward, *A Brave Vessel*, 47; Kieran Doherty, *Sea Venture: Shipwreck, Survival, and the Salvation of Jamestown*, 16. Woodward: "The *Sea Venture* had a draft of fifteen feet when it was not carrying a hold full of seawater." Doherty: "Believed to have been built in East Anglia in about 1603, the *Sea Venture* (or more rarely, *Sea Adventure*) was a three-masted vessel roughly a hundred feet long from the end of her bowsprit to her stern post."

6. William Strachey, "A True Reportory of the wrack and redemption of Sir Thomas Gates, knight," etc., in *Jamestown Narratives*, ed. Edward Wright Haile, 383–384; George Somers, "Letter to Salisbury (Robert Cecil), 15 June 1610" in *Jamestown Narratives*, ed. Edward Wright Haile, 445. Somers claimed they were "some 100 leagues from the Bermooda" when the storm hit which would have been 345 nautical miles. For what it is worth, my estimate of their position is approximately 100 nautical miles farther west than Somers's estimate.

7. S.G. Culliford, *William Strachey 1572–1621*, 29–30.

8. Culliford, 31.

9. Culliford, 49; William Stebbing, *Sir Walter Ralegh*, 157.

10. Culliford, 32–33, 53, 56–57, 66, 82, 96, 101–102; James Horn, *A Land As God Made It*, 136; Doherty, *Sea Venture*, 13. Horn: "'Bills of adventure' (shares) could be purchased for £12 10s. each, or an individual could volunteer to join the expedition for an equivalent according to his or her rank...."

11. Archer, "Letter from Jamestown," 351; David F. Raine, *Sir George Somers*, 120. Archer states, "Upon Saint James' Day, being about one hundred and fifty leagues distant from the West Indies, in crossing the Gulf of Bahoma, there hap'ned a most terrible and vehement storm, which was a tail of the West Indian hurricano." One hundred and fifty leagues is 517 statute miles. By the context, Archer makes it clear they were north of the West Indies. Raine's estimate that "they were about 1,000 miles west of the Azores" cannot be right if Newport is to be believed.

12. Strachey, "A True Reportory," 384.

13. Strachey, 384–387. The poop deck or stern deck is an open deck on the roof of the stern superstructure of a ship, its elevated position being ideal for observation in all directions.

14. Woodward, *A Brave Vessel*, 39. Woodward: "Somers veered from his Virginia-bound path to point the bow toward the Caribbean."

15. Strachey, "A True Reportory," 385. The "half forecourse" mentioned was equivalent to a storm trysail, a small triangular sail hoisted in heavy winds in place of a larger sail for powering the vessel forward so that the ship will continue to respond to the commands of the helm.

16. Silvester Jourdain, *A Discovery of the Bermudas*, 105.

17. Strachey, "A True Reportory," 386–387; Somers, "Letter to Salisbury," 445.

18. Strachey, 387.

19. Strachey, 387–388; Doherty, *Sea Venture*, 42. Doherty: "...the ship ... was being driven nine or ten leagues (roughly thirty miles) in each four-hour watch." This computes to approximately 7.5 knots, the knot being a unit of speed equal to one nautical mile per hour.

20. Strachey, 388.

21. Raine, *Sir George Somers*, 119. Raine: "...an estimated 10,000 lbs. of beef and a stock of biscuits...."

22. Strachey, "A True Reportory," 386.

23. Strachey, 390; Jourdain, *Discovery of the Bermudas*, 105. Jourdain: "...covered two tier of hogshead above the ballast."

24. Jourdain, 106.
25. Strachey, "A True Reportory," 389.
26. Strachey, 388–389; Raleigh Trevelyan, *Sir Walter Raleigh*, 65. Trevelyan states that St Elmo's fire was "always considered a bad omen by sailors," but most sources disagree as, apparently, did Somers.
27. Strachey, 390; Jourdain, *Discovery of the Bermudas*, 106. Yards are the tapered horizontal or angled spars of sailing ships to which the sails are attached and from which they hang.
28. Strachey, 390; Somers, "Letter to Salisbury," 445.
29. Strachey, 390; Jourdain, *Discovery of the Bermudas*, 107; Ivor Noël Hume, *The Virginia Adventure: Roanoke to James Towne*, 243. Hume: "The wreck was discovered in 1958 by the Bermudian diver Edmund Downing...."
30. Raine, *Sir George Somers*, 129.
31. Strachey, "A True Reportory," 390–391.
32. Joseph Kelly, *Marooned*, 261–262. Kelly notes Spanish shipwrecks on Bermuda in 1533, 1538, one in the 1540s and another in the 1550s, one in 1563, two in 1582, and one each in 1588, 1591, 1593, 1596, and 1603 and the French shipwreck in 1594.
33. Strachey, "A True Reportory," 392, 395. Strachey quotes from Oviedo, "the *Summary or Abridgment* of his *General History of the West Indies* that 'In the year 1515 ... I sailed above the Island Bermudas, otherwise called Gorza ... I determined to send some of the ship to land, as well to make search of such things as were there as also to leave in the island certain hogs for increase.'"
34. *Hakluyt's Voyages*, Vol. 10, 184–203; Neville Williams, *The Sea Dogs*, 252; Doherty, *Sea Venture*, 54–55.
35. The *Sea Venture* apparently carried two lifeboats, a larger longboat and a smaller tender. The longboat would have carried a single mast that could be unstepped and with oarlocks also could be rowed or sailed. The tender was an oared vessel used for communication or transportation between ships or from ship to shore.
36. Doherty, *Sea Venture*, 57.
37. Strachey, "A True Reportory," 394.
38. Strachey, 391.
39. Jourdain, *Discovery of the Bermudas*, 110.
40. Jourdain, 110.
41. Woodward, *A Brave Vessel*, 83. Woodward: "The Sea Venture, in fact, had come to rest in one of the most active sea-turtle nurseries of the Atlantic.... The average sea turtle weighted three hundred pounds."
42. Jourdain, *Discovery of the Bermudas*, 111.
43. Jourdain, 112.
44. Strachey, "A True Reportory," 394–401.
45. Brandon Fullam, *The Lost Colony of Roanoke: New Perspectives*, 206. Fullam names John Rolfe's wife, Sarah "Goody" Hacker Rolfe. Her given name does not appear in any other source, but Fullam does not cite his source.
46. Edward D. Neill, *History of the Virginia Company of London*, 34. Miss Persons married George Somers's cook, Thomas Powell.
47. Strachey, "A True Reportory," 413.
48. Woodward, *A Brave Vessel*, 63; Doherty, *Sea Venture*, 77.
49. Strachey, "A True Reportory," 394–395.
50. Strachey, 401–403.
51. John Smith, *The Generall Historie of Virginia, New England and the Summer Isles*, Book 3, in *Jamestown Narratives*, ed. Edward Wright Haile, 332–333; George Percy, "A True Relation" in *Jamestown Narratives*, ed. Edward Wright Haile, 502.
52. Woodward, *A Brave Vessel*, 119.
53. Thomas Dale, "Letter from Henrico, 10 June 1613" in *Jamestown Narratives*, ed. Edward Wright Haile, 777.
54. Strachey, *Historie of Travell into Virginia Britania*, 60.
55. Woodward, *A Brave Vessel*, 64, 66. Woodward: "Bermuda cedar was resistant to shipworms ... largest cedars growing on the island were fifteen feet in circumference." Strachey spelled the name of the shipwright, Frubbusher.
56. A. Bryant Nichols, Jr., *Captain Christopher Newport*, 119. Nichols: *Deliverance* "was forty feet long, had a beam of nineteen feet, and rode in eight feet of water."
57. Woodward, *A Brave Vessel*, 78. Woodward: "The assumption by the laborers was that the elite voyagers would take

the skilled workmen and the best mariners and sail to safety, leaving them behind."
58. Strachey, "A True Reportory," 403.
59. Bradford Smith, *Captain John Smith*, 164, 242.
60. The Ancient Planters of Virginia, "A Brief Declaration" in *Jamestown Narratives*, ed. Edward Wright Haile, 906-907; Nichols, *Captain Christopher Newport*, 171; William M. Kelso, *Jamestown, The Truth Revealed*, 146. Nichols: "Captain Newport helped ensure the success of the Jamestown colony by enforcing the Virginia Company's rule prohibiting settlers sent to Virginia from returning to England without authorization from the company."
61. Strachey, "A True Reportory," 404.
62. Strachey, 413.
63. Strachey, 405-406.
64. Strachey, 403.
65. Jenn Dean, "The Keepers of the Ghost Bird," in *When Birds are Near, Dispatches from Contemporary Writers*, editor Susan Fox Rogers, Cornell University Press, 147. Dean: "Prior to 1600, it is estimated that almost half a million pairs of (cahows) bred on Bermuda, making it, in essence, a gigantic seabird colony."
66. Jourdain, *Discovery of the Bermudas*, 111.
67. Strachey, "A True Reportory," 398-399; Jenn Dean, "The Keepers of the Ghost Bird," in "Working Titles," *Massachusetts Review*, September/October 2017, Vol. 2 No. 4, 27. The cahow or Bermuda petrel (*Pterodroma cahow*), a nocturnal ground-nesting seabird, Bermuda's national bird. It spends most of its life on the open sea, visiting land—Bermuda only—for nesting. Its cry was thought to resemble that of a devil. One writer called it "a bone-chilling, caterwauling, and plaintive bleating."
68. Dean, 148.
69. Strachey, "A True Reportory," 406-407.
70. Strachey, 407; Kelly, *Marooned*, 424. Stephen Hopkins later sailed on the *Mayflower* to Plymouth Bay in 1620.
71. Strachey, 408-409.
72. Strachey, 409-410. Strachey paraphrased Paine's response to Gates which was to "let the governor (said he) kiss, etc. Which words being with the omitted additions brought the next day unto every common and public discourse...."
73. Strachey, 410.
74. Kelly, *Marooned*, 326, 363. Kelly: "One contemporary estimate, rough as it might be, put the value of each settler's transportation to Virginia and their clothes and tools and food at twenty pounds."
75. Strachey, "A True Reportory," 410-412.
76. Strachey, 412; Doherty, *Sea Venture*, 89. Doherty quotes future Bermuda governor Nathaniel Butler, who knew Carter personally, as saying Somers made Carter and Waters "a faithful promise that he would speedily return to their relief."
77. Jourdain, *Discovery of the Bermudas*, 114; Benjamin Woolley, *Savage Kingdom*, 252. Jourdain: "...instead whereof we were forced to make lime there of a hard kind of stone and use it ... with some wax we found cast up by the sea from some shipwreck ... to pay the seams of the pinnace." Woolley: "...a smaller pinnace (*Patience*) 29 foot long and 15 foot wide."
78. Strachey, "A True Reportory," 413-416; Jourdain, *Discovery of the Bermudas*, 116; Smith, *Generall Historie*, Book 3, 342.
79. Jourdain, 115.
80. Woodward, *A Brave Vessel*, 97. Quoting Strachey Woodward: "Left behind was a cemetery of graves. 'We buried five of our company, Jeffery Briars, Richard Lewis, William Hitchman, and my goddaughter Bermuda Rolfe, and one untimely Edward Samuel.' Two others ... Henry Paine ... Namontack," making a total of seven.
81. Woodward, 71-72, 131. Woodward: "Eventually Machumps would be cast as the perpetrator of a grisly murder."
82. Strachey, "A True Reportory," 416-417. Point Comfort is the point of land at the tip of Virginia's Lower Peninsula that ends at Hampton Roads, the large harbor and roadstead just west of which is the mouth of the James River. It is forty miles downriver from Jamestown. Fort Algernon was an earthwork fortification constructed at Point Comfort in 1609; it is now the site of Fort Monroe National Monument.
83. Strachey, 418.

Chapter 8

1. George Percy, "A True Relation" in *Jamestown Narratives*, ed. Edward Wright Haile, 506. Referring to this essay, the

editor says, "I find it a piece of grimness relieved by sheer horror."

2. Ivor Noël Hume, *The Virginia Adventure: Roanoke to James Towne*, 260; James Horn, *A Land As God Made It*, 177.

3. William Strachey, "A True Reportory of the wrack and redemption of Sir Thomas Gates, knight," etc., in *Jamestown Narratives*, ed. Edward Wright Haile, 418-419.

4. George Percy, "Letter to Northumberland (his brother the earl), 17 August 1611" in *Jamestown Narratives*, ed. Edward Wright Haile, 559.

5. Hume, *Virginia Adventure*, 262.

6. Percy, "A True Relation," 506-507.

7. Gabriel Archer, "Letter from Jamestown, 31 August 1609" in *Jamestown Narratives*, ed. Edward Wright Haile, 351.

8. The Ancient Planters of Virginia, "A Brief Declaration" in *Jamestown Narratives*, ed. Edward Wright Haile, 895; Hobson Woodward, *A Brave Vessel*, 105. Woodward: "...they fell upon the small quantity of corn—not being above seven acres ... and in three days at the most wholly devoured it."

9. Bradford Smith, *Captain John Smith*, 152-154; Joseph Kelly, *Marooned*, 339. Citing Philip Barbour, Kelly refers to Archer, Martin and Radcliffe as the "unholy triumvirate."

10. Archer, "Letter from Jamestown, 31 August 1609," 353.

11. Barbour, *Captain John Smith*, 273.

12. John Smith, *The Generall Historie of Virginia, New England and the Summer Isles*, Book 3, in *Jamestown Narratives*, ed. Edward Wright Haile, 329; The Ancient Planters of Virginia, "A Brief Declaration," 895.

13. Smith, *Generall Historie*, Book 3, 330; William Strachey, *Historie of Travell into Virginia Britania*, 63-64. The Powhatan tribe of the Powhatan nation occupied an area near the falls of the James River—today's Richmond. The tribe could muster fifty warriors. Its chief was Parahunt, a son of Wahunsenacawh (Powhatan) and, therefore, a brother or half-brother of Pocahontas.

14. Smith, *Generall Historie*, Book 3, 335; John Ratcliffe, "Letter to Salisbury (Robert Cecil)," in *Jamestown Narratives*, ed. Edward Wright Haile, 354.

15. Smith, *Generall Historie*, Book 3, 336; Barbour, *Captain John Smith*, 278-279.

16. Percy, "A True Relation," 501-502.

17. Percy, 503.

18. Smith, *Generall Historie*, Book 3, 330.

19. Kelly, *Marooned*, 343.

20. Percy, "A True Relation," 503-504.

21. Smith, *Generall Historie*, Book 3, 334-335; Hume, *Virginia Adventure*, 252. Hume: "...inventory showed that the colony could boast more helmets, body armor, swords, and pikes than it could muster men to wear and bear them."

22. William White, "The Black Boys Ceremony" in *Jamestown Narratives*, ed. Edward Wright Haile, 141; Smith, *Generall Historie*, Book 3, 339; William Strachey, "A True Reportory," 441; Henry Spelman, "Relation of Virginia, 1609" in *Jamestown Narratives*, ed. Edward Wright Haile, 483; Percy, "A True Relation,"504. White, Smith, and Strachey put the number at thirty. Spellman, who was there at the time as a ward of Powhatan, claimed Ratcliffe came with twenty-four or twenty-five men, but in another version, he claimed twenty-six or twenty-seven were killed. Percy claimed that Radcliffe carried fifty men. He was present in Jamestown at the time, whereas White, Smith, and Strachey were not.

23. Spelman, "Relation of Virginia, 1609," 484.

24. Percy, "A True Relation," 504. Percy blamed Ratcliffe for releasing Powhatan's children, claiming they could have been used as hostages to insure his men's safety during the entire proceedings.

25. Spelman, "Relation of Virginia, 1609," 482-485; Strachey, "A True Reportory," 441; Percy, "A True Relation," 504.

26. Percy, "A True Relation," 504; Spelman, 482-486. Henry Spelman (1595-1623) was consigned to the Powhatans as surety in exchange for the village at the falls of the James River that Captain John Smith purchased from Parahunt. Spelman claimed that Smith sold him to the Powhatans, but on several occasions, youths were billeted with the Algonquins as hostages to ensure compliance with some agreement but also to learn the language so that, when repatriated, they could serve as guides and interpreters. Spelman regained

his freedom, returned to England, and published an account of his experiences.

27. Strachey, *Historie of Travell*, 46. Patawomeck, a large and powerful Powhatan alliance tribe that lived along the south bank of the coastal plain area of the Potomac River. It was estimated that the tribe could muster between 160 (Strachey's number) and 250 warriors. Henry Spelman gives the name of the tribe's weroance as "King Patomecke" (Spelman, "Relation of Virginia, 1609" in *Jamestown Narratives: Eyewitness Accounts of the Virginia Colony*, ed. Edward Wright Haile, 485). In March 1613 a sub-weroance by the name of Japazaws or Iopassus assisted English Captain Samuel Argall in capturing and kidnapping Pocahontas. Argall also purchased the freedom of Henry Spelman on this voyage.

28. April Lee Hatfield, *Atlantic Virginia: Intercolonial Relations in the Seventeenth Century*, 15. Hatfield attributes Powhatan's tenuous control over the Patawomecks to the tribe's independent access to "western goods," i.e., copper and bloodroot, via alternative, long-established trade routes to the southwest and northeast.

29. Percy, "A True Relation," 504.

30. Strachey, "A True Reportory," 439–440; Percy, 504–505; Edward D. Neill, *History of the Virginia Company of London*, 33. Percy mentioned Francis West by name and, though Strachey did not, he described the shameful event with considerable acrimony. Percy implied that West's desertion of the colony was "by the persuasion, or rather by the enforcement, of his company," implying that West's crew mutinied, but there is no other evidence of this. Neill states that West and his crew "bound themselves (made a pact) to agree in one report and declare that they were driven away by famine."

31. John Smith, *The Generall Historie*, Book 3, 319.

32. Strachey, "A True Reportory," 441.

33. Strachey, *Historie of Travell*, 65. Quiyoughcohannock (*kwe-yo-ko-HAHN-awk*), a Powhatan alliance tribe located on the south bank of the James River across the river from Jamestown Island. The tribe could muster an estimated 60 warriors. The name of its weroance is variously given as Tatahcoope (one of Powhatan's sons), Chaopock, or Pepiscunimah.

34. Percy, "A True Relation," 507.

35. William M. Kelso, *Jamestown: The Truth Revealed*, 88–89.

36. Smith, *Generall Historie*, Book 3, 340; The Ancient Planters of Virginia, "A Brief Declaration," 895–896; The Virginia General Assembly, "The Answer of the General Assembly, 20 February 1624," in *Jamestown Narratives*, ed. Edward Wright Haile, 913.

37. Kelso, *Jamestown: The Truth Revealed*, 196, 200–202.

38. Smith, *Generall Historie*, Book 3, 340.

39. Percy, "A True Relation," 505.

40. The Ancient Planters of Virginia, "A Brief Declaration," 896.

41. Kelly, *Marooned*, 385–386. Kelly: "It's more likely that Percy ... decamped when he and his own favorites started to starve. The captain and officers left a sinking ship in the last lifeboat ... left the wretched to their fate."

42. Strachey, "A True Reportory," 419; Thomas West, et al., "Letter to the Virginia Company of London, 7 July 1610" in *Jamestown Narratives*, ed. Edward Wright Haile, 456.

43. Percy, "A True Relation," 507.

44. Strachey, "A True Reportory," 419.

45. The Ancient Planters of Virginia, "A Brief Declaration," 906, 908.

46. Kelly, *Marooned*, 389–390.

47. Strachey, "A True Reportory," 420.

48. Smith, *Generall Historie*, Book 3, 308.

49. Lincoln Paine, *The Sea & Civilization*, 459.

50. Strachey, "A True Reportory," 420–423.

51. Strachey, 424, 440–441; West, et al., "Letter ... 7 July 1610," 457.

52. Strachey, 425–426, 441.

53. Strachey, 426; George Somers, "Letter to Salisbury, 15 June 1610" in *Jamestown Narratives*, ed. Edward Wright Haile, 446. Strachey claimed sixteen days; Somers, fourteen.

54. Strachey, 426–427; West, et al., "Letter ... 7 July 1610," 457.

55. Strachey, 427; West, 458.

56. Edmund S. Morgan, *American Slavery, American Freedom*, 72.

Chapter 9

1. William Crashaw (1572-1626), English cleric, served as minister of Inner Temple, one of the Inns of Court located just outside London in the suburb of Holborn. On February 21, 1609, he preached a sermon in the presence of Lord De La Warr and other London Company officials promoting England's effort to colonize North America.

2. Benjamin Woolley, *Savage Kingdom*, 263. Woolley: "...no mere commercial enterprise, but an imperial and religious one."

3. Andrew Fitzmaurice, "Moral Uncertainty in the Dispossession of Native Americans" in *The Atlantic World and Virginia, 1550-1624*, ed. Peter C. Mancall, 389-391, 396; Hobson Woodward, *A Brave Vessel*, 113. William Crashaw (1572-1626) cleric, scholar, essayist, and poet. Crashaw wrote, "We will take nothing from the Savages by power nor pillage, by craft nor violence, neither goods, lands nor libertie, much lesse life." Woodward quoting Crashaw regarding the "vulger and violent sort": "...the very excrements of a full and swelling state."

4. Lorri Glover and Daniel Blake Smith, *The Shipwreck that Saved Jamestown*, 122-123.

5. William Strachey, "A True Reportory of the wrack and redemption of Sir Thomas Gates, knight," etc., in *Jamestown Narratives*, ed. Edward Wright Haile, 429; Thomas West, "Letter to Salisbury (Robert Cecil), rec'd September 1610," in *Jamestown Narratives*, ed. Edward Wright Haile, 465. Strachey reports that the livery of De La Warr's fifty halberdiers was red.

6. Glover and Smith, *Shipwreck that Saved Jamestown*, 122.

7. Joseph I. Doran, *Sir George Yeardley and His Voyage of 1609-1610 to Virginia in the Sea Adventure and Deliverance*, 16.

8. West, "Letter to Salisbury, rec'd September 1610," 466. West claimed that Gates had "a determination to stay some ten days at Cape Comfort to expect our coming, and otherwise so to go for England, having but 30 days' victuals left him and his hungry company." In fact, Gates had victuals for only sixteen days according to several sources (including West himself), so he would not have lingered at Point Comfort for fear of running out of food and also because of the discomfort of so many colonists packed on such small boats for so long. For the entire company to disembark at Point Comfort would have been impractical due to the extensive shoals that precluded anchoring close by.

9. Percy, "A True Relation," 508; Strachey, "A True Reportory," 427. Percy spelled his name Bruster, as did Strachey. Thomas West spelled it Brewister. Dale spelled it Breuster. The Ancient Planters spelled it Brewster. At this time spelling was determined by the whim of the composer.

10. The Ancient Planters of Virginia, "A Brief Declaration" in *Jamestown Narratives*, ed. Edward Wright Haile, 897. Gates, "to the great grief of all his company ... returned his whole company with charge to take possession again of those poor ruinated habitations at James Town."

11. Strachey, "A True Reportory," 432; Thomas West, et al., "Letter to the Virginia Company of London, 7 July 1610" in *Jamestown Narratives*, ed. Edward Wright Haile, 458-459.

12. S.G. Culliford, *William Strachey 1572-1621*, 120.

13. George Somers, "Letter to Salisbury (Robert Cecil), 15 June 1610" in *Jamestown Narratives*, ed. Edward Wright Haile, 446; Strachey, 432-434; West et al., "Letter to the Virginia Company," 459-460; West, "Letter to Salisbury," 467. West states with confidence that Somers "will store us with hog's flesh and fish enough to serve the whole colony this winter" so he clearly expected Somers to return within two to three months. Sir Ferdinando Wainman (1576-1610) was a soldier and cousin of Lord De La Warr. He died within months of his arrival in Jamestown.

14. Strachey, 434.

15. James Horn, *A Land As God Made It*, 184.

16. Strachey, "A True Reportory," 435-437.

17. Percy, "A True Relation," 511; Strachey, 437.

18. Percy, 508; Strachey, "A True Reportory," 435; The Ancient Planters of Virginia, "A Brief Declaration." 897-898.

19. The Council of Virginia, "A True Declaration of the estate of the colony in

Virginia," 1610 in *Jamestown Narratives*, ed. Edward Wright Haile, 474.

20. Percy, "A True Relation," 509–511.

21. Percy, 511.

22. Percy, 511–512.

23. Thomas West, "A Short Relation, 25-June-1611" in *Jamestown Narratives*, ed. Edward Wright Haile, 529–530; Percy, 513.

24. Wesley Frank Craven, *The Southern Colonies in the Seventeenth Century 1607–1689*, 102, 109; Ivor Noël Hume, *The Virginia Adventure: Roanoke to James Towne*, 294.

25. John Smith, *The Generall Historie of Virginia, New England and the Summer Isles*, Book 3, in *Jamestown Narratives*, ed. Edward Wright Haile, 335. Speaking of them, Smith remarked "poor gentlemen, tradesmen, serving men, libertines, and suchlike, ten times more fit to spoil a commonwealth than either begin one or but help to maintain one. For when neither the fear of God nor the law, nor shame, nor displeasure of their friends could rule them here, there is small hope ever to bring one in twenty of them ever to be good there."

26. Edmund S. Morgan, *American Slavery, American Freedom*, 98; Philip P. Boucher, "Revisioning the 'French Atlantic'" in *The Atlantic World and Virginia, 1550–1624*, ed. Peter C. Mancall, 275. Boucher lists the factors "essential for colonization: a badly needed staple to export to the metropole; agricultural lands for long-term support; women for reproduction and social stability; and official imprimaturs to legitimate land grants and inheritances."

27. Percy, "A True Relation," 514.

28. The Ancient Planters of Virginia, "A Brief Declaration," 899–900; Woodward, *A Brave Vessel*, 146. Also called Dale's Code, it was probably conceived by Sir Thomas Smythe. It was published in England in 1613 and remained in force in Virginia until 1618.

29. The Virginia General Assembly, "The Answer of the General Assembly, 20 February 1624," in *Jamestown Narratives*, ed. Edward Wright Haile, 913; Bradford Smith, *Captain John Smith*, 185; Hume, *Virginia Adventure*, 320. Bradford Smith; "…death penalty for such crimes as bearing false witness, blasphemy, picking a flower in a public or private garden, gaming on the Sabbath, sodomy—and private enterprise." Note that sodomy would not have been included had there not been occurrences of it. Hume: "Dale may have been cruel, but he was not unusual."

30. Percy, "A True Relation," 517–518; Ralph Hamor, "A True Discourse," in *Jamestown Narratives*, ed. Edward Wright Haile, 822–823; The Ancient Planters of Virginia, 900–901. Ralph Hamor (1589–1626) was a colonist and the author of *A True Discourse of the Present State of Virginia*, 1615.

31. The Ancient Planters of Virginia, "A Brief Declaration," 907; Philip L. Barbour, *Pocahontas and Her World*, 90; Edward D. Neill, *History of the Virginia Company of London*, Neill, *History of the Virginia Company*, 73–74. Neill: "…pulling the beard of Captain Newport he threatened to hang him for some statement relative to Sir Thomas Smith."

32. Horn, *A Land As God Made It*, 198.

33. Percy, "A True Relation," 514.

34. Thomas Dale, "Letter to Salisbury, 17 August 1611" in *Jamestown Narratives*, ed. Edward Wright Haile, 554–556; Percy, 517; Hamor, "A True Discourse," 824–827; John Rolfe, "A True Relation of the State of Virginia" in *Jamestown Narratives*, ed. Edward Wright Haile, 870, 872–874; The Ancient Planters of Virginia, "A Brief Declaration," 907. A hundred is a term derived from an old English administrative subdivision encompassing one hundred families or twelve hundred acres.

35. West, "A Short Relation, 25-June-1611," 531; The Ancient Planters of Virginia, "A Brief Declaration," 899; Craven, *The Southern Colonies*, 103–104; Neill, *History of the Virginia Company*, 51–52. Craven: "one hundred cattle, approximately two hundred swine, and with conies, pigeons, and poultry to boot." Neill: Gates sailed with his wife and daughters, but "The wife of Gates died on the passage."

36. Percy, "A True Relation," 509.

37. Hume, *Virginia Adventure*, 285. Hume: "Where Somers had been and what he had been doing between the time his last message reached Argall on July 26 and his arrival in Bermuda at the beginning of November is one of early American history's enduring mysteries." Hume is assuming the early November arrival.

38. Neill, *History of the Virginia Company*, 59; Kieran Doherty, *Sea Venture*, 194. Doherty: "...a man-sized grayish white chunk of material wedged in the rocks that fronted the beach ... roughly 180-pound chunk of ambergris."

39. John Smith, *The General History*, 343; Percy, *A True Relation*, 509; Woodward, *A Brave Vessel*, 186; David F. Raine, *Sir George Somers*, 136. Raine quotes chronicler John Stowe as attributing Somers's death to "a surfeit of pig."

40. Hume, *Virginia Adventure*; 286; Woodward, 187. Hume: "...George's nephew Mathew, ignoring the dying admiral's instruction to return to Virginia, sailed on to England...." It seems more likely to me that Matthew was forced by a demanding crew.

41. Raine, *Sir George Somers*, 142. According to Raine, the third crewman staying in Bermuda was Edward Charde.

42. Raine, 146.

43. Woolley, *Savage Kingdom*, 300; Doherty, *Sea Venture*, 195–196. Woolley: "...an inner circle of directors paid £2,000 into the Virginia Company coffers in return for the rights to settle Bermuda, which would be done by an 'under-company' or subsidiary."

44. Neill, *History of the Virginia Company*, 54; Doherty, 204–206.

45. Doherty, 209.

46. Woodward, *A Brave Vessel*, 195.

47. Culliford, *William Strachey*, 126, 130.

48. Brandon Fullam, *The Lost Colony of Roanoke: New Perspectives*, 6.

49. Culliford, *William Strachey*, 141.

50. A. Bryant Nichols, Jr., *Captain Christopher Newport*, 145. Nichols: "Newport agreed to sail to India once again (Second East India Voyage) for £180 a year.

51. William Strachey, *Historie of Travell into Virginia Britania*, 62.

52. Samuel Argall, "Letter to Hawes, June 1613" in *Jamestown Narratives*, ed. Edward Wright Haile, 754–755.

53. Hamor, "A True Discourse," 802–84.

54. Linwood Custalow, *The True Story of Pocahontas*, 51. Custalow: "Mattaponi sacred oral history states that before Argall took sail, Several of Argall's men returned to Pocahontas's home and killed her husband Kocoum." This is unconfirmed.

55. Helen C. Rountree, *Pocahontas Powhatan Opechancanough*, 143; Paula Gunn Allen, *Pocahontas*, 218; Custalow, 80. Rountree: "The historical record is also completely silent about whether or not the couple had children." Allen is speculating, but Pocahontas later proved to be fertile, so it is entirely possible given her age and Powhatan cultural norms that she would have taken a mate and given birth. Custalow: "The colonists did not recognize Pocahontas's marriage to Kocoum; they considered it to be pagan. Neither did they acknowledge her son by this marriage." Custalow may have been referring to the legend of Ka Okee "Jane" (1611 or 1612–1642 or 1670), a daughter, not a son, believed by the Patawomecke tribe to be the child of Pocahontas and Kocoum. She married Thomas Pettus, and they had a son, Christian Pettus, in 1636. The truth of this cannot be verified.

56. Hamor, 845.

57. Hamor, 808.

58. Uttamatomakkin (Tomocomo), "An Interview in London," 1617, conducted by Samuel Purchas in *Jamestown Narratives*, ed. Edward Wright Haile, 884. Samuel Purchas (ca. 1577–1626), Anglican cleric, compiler and editor of *Purchas His Pilgrimes*, a 20-volume compendium of voyage of discovery narratives published in 1625, building on the work of Richard Hakluyt.

59. Custalow, *The True Story of Pocahontas*, 58. Custalow: "...the stealing of wives and children was a known practice in Powhatan society ... Pocahontas would have known that the way to survive and to prolong her life would have been to submit to the circumstances."

60. Hamor, 850–853; Bradford Smith, *Captain John Smith*, 221. Bradford Smith: "Yet when the Council for Virginia in London heard about the marriage, they debated very seriously whether Rolfe had committed treason in marrying a royal princess."

61. Hamor, 809.

62. Hamor, 809–813, 845–846.

63. Hamor, 833–834, 843. Hamor offered Powhatan "treble the price" he had received in payment for the child to retrieve her and send her to Dale, but Powhatan refused because he loved the child and wished to keep her nearby where he

could see her from time to time, professing that he would never be able to go to an English settlement to see her for fear of his life.
64. Robin Blackburn, *The Making of New World Slavery*, 149, 223, 234–235. Blackburn: "...the smoking of tobacco spread from the Indians and the (African) slaves to English, Dutch and French sailors."
65. Grace Steele Woodward, *Pocahontas*, 162. Woodward opines: "Pocahontas demonstrated for him (Rolfe) Powhatan methods of growing tobacco." This may be supposition on her part.
66. Hamor, 819–820, 828; Marcy Norton and Daviken Studnicki-Gizbert, "The Multinational Commodification of Tobacco, 1492–1650" in *The Atlantic World and Virginia, 1550–1624*, ed. Peter C. Mancall, 264.
67. Rolfe, "A True Relation" 871.
68. April Lee Hatfield, *Atlantic Virginia: Intercolonial Relations in the Seventeenth Century*, 39; Doherty, *Sea Venture*, 221. Doherty puts the 1620 amount exported at 40,000 pounds.
69. Morgan, *American Slavery, American Freedom*, 110.
70. Rolfe, "A True Relation" 869.
71. A.L. Rowse, *England of Elizabeth*, 183.
72. Hume, *Virginia Adventure*, 390. Hume: "...Sir Thomas Gates followed him (Thomas Dale) to the East Indies and reportedly died there." I am unable to corroborate this.
73. Joseph I. Doran, *Sir George Yeardley and His Voyage of 1609–1610 to Virginia in the Sea Adventure and Deliverance*, 3–34.

Epilogue

1. Uttamatomakkin (Tomocomo), "An Interview in London," 1617, conducted by Samuel Purchas in *Jamestown Narratives*, ed. Edward Wright Haile, 884–885.
2. Uttamatomakkin (Tomocomo), "An Interview in London," 883–884.
3. Grace Steele Woodward, *Pocahontas*, 179. Woodward: "Raleigh also escorted Pocahontas to the Tower of London to introduce her to his good friend, the Earl of Northumberland, the older brother of George Percy." Woodward cites no source for this claim. Raleigh had been released from the Tower by King James to prepare for his voyage to Guyana.
4. John Smith, *The Generall Historie of Virginia, New England and the Summer Isles*, Book 4, in *Jamestown Narratives*, ed. Edward Wright Haile, 864.
5. Uttamatomakkin, "An Interview in London," 883–884.
6. Bradford Smith, *Captain John Smith*, 224.
7. Bradford Smith, 227. Bradford Smith: "John Smith went more than once to the house in Brentford...." Smith cites no source for this information, so it may be supposition.
8. Smith, *The Generall Historie*, Book 4, 864.
9. Smith, *The Generall Historie*, Book 4, 863.
10. Benjamin Woolley, *Savage Kingdom*, 338. Woolley cites "one account" (not named), "She (Pocahontas) was introduced to the Queen by Cecilia, Lord Delaware's wife, and afterwards 'was frequently admitted to wait on her Majesty,' who took her to 'many Plays, Balls, and other public Entertainments.'" I am unable to corroborate this. One would imagine more extensive records were this the case.
11. Helen Rountree, *Pocahontas's People*, 44.
12. Karen Kupperman, *Pocahontas and the English Boys*, 138. Kupperman: "...the name 'Gravesend' originally referred to the medieval office of landgrave, or count, and the edge of his jurisdiction."
13. John Rolfe, "Letter to Sandys, 8 June 1617" in *Jamestown Narratives*, ed. Edward Wright Haile, 888–889.
14. Rountree, *Pocahontas Powhatan Opechancanough*, 189.
15. Raleigh Trevelyan, *Sir Walter Raleigh*, 379; William Stebbing, *Sir Walter Ralegh*, 207; Robert Lacey, *Sir Walter Ralegh*, 286–287; Anna Beer, *Patriot or Traitor: The Life and Death of Sir Walter Ralegh*, 159.
16. Trevelyan, 423–427.
17. A.L. Rowse, *Ralegh and the Throckmortons*, 271–272; Lacey, *Sir Walter Ralegh*, 325–331.
18. Robyn Arianrhod, *Thomas Harriot: A Life in Science*, 251.
19. Trevelyan, *Sir Walter Raleigh*, 547–552.

20. Rowse, *Ralegh and the Throckmortons*, 318; Lacey, *Sir Walter Ralegh*, 382; Mark Nicholls and Penry Williams, *Sir Walter Raleigh: In Life and Legend*, 322.

21. Stebbing, *Sir Walter Ralegh*, 58–59.

22. Nicholls and Williams, 331. The authors were quoting from *History of England* by G.M. Trevelyan (London, 1926), 388.

23. Stebbing, *Sir Walter Ralegh*, 356, 389, 397–398; D.B. Quinn, *Raleigh and the British Empire*, 206. "The flood of enthusiasm for him swept away the interest in his guilt or innocence in respect of particular charges. Public opinion hallowed him as saint and martyr, and put the Court and Government on their defence."

24. Ivor Noël Hume, *The Virginia Adventure: Roanoke to James Towne*, 387.

25. Edward D. Neill, *History of the Virginia Company of London*, 161, 246, 262; Horn, *A Land As God Made It*, 244–245.

26. The Virginia General Assembly, "The Answer of 20 February 1624," 913; Edmund S. Morgan, *American Slavery, American Freedom*, 116–129.

27. Rountree, *Pocahontas's People*, 61. Rountree: "Tobacco farming would soon ruin any hopes of true coexistence between the two peoples."

28. John Rolfe, "A True Relation of the State of Virginia" in *Jamestown Narratives*, ed. Edward Wright Haile, 870; Rountree, *Pocahontas's People*, 61; Daniel K. Richter, *Facing East from Indian Country*, 51. Rolfe: "some of their pettie kings have this last year borrowed four or five hundred bushels of sheate, for payment whereof, this harvest they have mortgaged their whole countries...."

29. Neill, *History of the Virginia Company of London*, 319.

30. Karen Kupperman, *Roanoke: The Abandoned Colony*, 163; Kieran Doherty, *Sea Venture*, 242–243.

31. Morgan, *American Slavery, American Freedom*, 158–159.

32. The Ancient Planters of Virginia, "A Brief Declaration" in *Jamestown Narratives*, ed. Edward Wright Haile, 906, 908; The Virginia General Assembly, "The Answer of the General Assembly, 20 February 1624," in *Jamestown Narratives*, ed. Edward Wright Haile, 912–914; Bradford Smith, *Captain John Smith*, 25. The sentiment of the colonists after the Algonquins killed a horse and cooked it was that "whilst she [the horse] was a-boiling that Sir Thomas Smith were upon her back in the kettle." Bradford Smith: "This is one reason why he (Capt. John Smith) is remembered today while Sir Thomas Smith, who actually had much more to do with starting the Virginia colony, is unknown to most Americans."

33. J.H. Elliott, "The Iberian Atlantic and Virginia" in *The Atlantic World and Virginia, 1550–1624*, ed. Peter C. Mancall, 549.

34. After the death of Pocahontas in 1617, John Rolfe married Jane Pierce in 1619. She was the daughter of William Pierce, who had sailed aboard the *Sea Venture* and was marooned with Rolfe on Bermuda while Pierce's wife and daughter arrived in Jamestown aboard the *Blessing* and survived the Starving Time until reunited with William.

35. Bradford Smith, *Captain John Smith*, 251.

36. Helen C. Rountree, *Pocahontas Powhatan Opechancanough*, 231–232. Rountree: "...he (Powhatan) had heard about the outbreak of civil war in England and had decided to strike while that government was in disarray and unable to help its battered subjects across the Atlantic."

37. Rountree, 233–235.

38. The Ancient Planters of Virginia, "A Brief Declaration," 908–909.

39. Carl Bridenbaugh, *Jamestown 1544–1699*, 78–82. Bridenbaugh: "the tobacco plutocracy."

40. Morgan, *American Slavery, American Freedom*, 123–130; Elliott, "The Iberian Atlantic and Virginia" 557; Robin Blackburn, *The Making of New World Slavery*, 240, 256.

41. James Horn, *A Land As God Made It*, 144–145.

42. John Smith, *The Generall Historie of Virginia, New England and the Summer Isles*, Book 3, in *Jamestown Narratives*, ed. Edward Wright Haile, 296, 323.

43. Smith, *Generall Historie*, Book 3, 323; Quinn, *Raleigh and the British Empire*, 106–107; Lee Miller, *Roanoke: Solving the Mystery of the Lost Colony*, 216–217. Miller makes the point: "the information was suppressed ... it was never in

their interests to disclose the whereabouts of White's colony. The meager information we have is deliberately vague." Later it became politically prudent to admit the lost colonists were dead, killed by Powhatan, in order to justify Lord De La Warr's decision to kill and/or remove all Algonquins from the James River valley.

44. John Smith, *Captain John Smith's History of Virginia*, 20; Helen C. Rountree, *Manteo's World*, 84, 98; Helen C. Rountree, Wayne E. Clark, and Kent Mountford, *John Smith's Chesapeake Voyages 1607–1609*, 131. Rountree asserts that the reason for the attack was that Powhatan had been angered by the Piankatank tribe's willingness to trade with Smith while he was on his exploration of the Chesapeake Bay. In such attacks, women and children were captured and kept as the spoils of war. Men were killed, but killing a chief was considered an unforgivable offense.

45. John Smith, *A True Relation* in *Jamestown Narratives*, ed. Edward Wright Haile, 158, 162, 165; James Horn, *A Kingdom Strange: The Brief and Tragic History of the Lost Colony of Roanoke*, 233–234; Miller, *Roanoke*, 258–259. The name of this village was variously spelled Ocanahonon, Ohanahorn or Ocanahowan. Miller states that the word is Siouan for the Algonquin word, Occaneechi. In other words, the selfsame place. This cannot be confirmed. The Choanoke was doubtless the Chowanoc, now the Chowan River.

46. Brandon Fullam, *The Lost Colony of Roanoke: New Perspectives*, 37, 40.

47. Eric Klingelhofer, ed., *Excavating the Lost Colony Mystery*, 123–124.

48. Horn, *A Kingdom Strange*, 224. Horn: "…leaving a small group on Roanoke Island to wait for White's return was too risky. They … opted to send them to Croatoan Island instead, where they would be safe with Manteo's people." He believes that "approximately two dozen settlers were transported to Croatoan Island." This is a good guess as to how many colonists the Croatoans could reasonably absorb.

49. Fullam, *The Lost Colony*, 60–61, 69.

50. Rountree, *Manteo's World*, 100–101. By Rountree's count, "Ninety men, seventeen women, nine boys, and two newborn babies."

51. The area was named Carolina, adopted from the Latin spelling of the name Charles, to honor King Charles II of England, grandson of James I.

52. The Virginia–North Carolina border was ultimately fixed at 36°30' north latitude, and the Lords Proprietors' grant extended west indefinitely.

53. Fullam, *The Lost Colony*, 138.

54. Horn, *A Kingdom Strange*, 235–238.

55. Brandon Fullam, *A Lost Colony Hoax*, 143–158.

Bibliography

Primary Sources

Barlowe, Arthur. "Arthur Barlowe's Narrative of the 1584 Voyage." In *The First Colonists: Documents on the Planting of the First English Settlements in North America 1584–1590*, edited by David B. Quinn and Alison M. Quinn, 1–12. Raleigh: North Carolina Department of Cultural Resources, 1982.

Cieza de León, Pedro de. *The Incas* (Harriet de Onis, translator). Norman: University of Oklahoma Press, 1959.

de las Casas, Bartolemé. *A Short History of the Destruction of the Indies* (Nigel Griffin, editor and translator). London: Penguin, 1992.

Díaz, Bernal. *The Conquest of New Spain* (J.M. Cohen, translator). London: Penguin Books, 1963.

Haile, Edward Wright, ed. *Jamestown Narratives: Eyewitness Accounts of the Virginia Colony, the First Decade: 1607–1617*. Champlain, VA: Roundhouse, 1998.

Hakluyt, Richard. *A Discourse on Western Planting Written in the Year 1584*. In *Documentary History of the State of Maine*, edited by Leonard Woods. Alpha Editions: www.alphaedis.com, 2021.

Hakluyt, Richard. *Divers Voyages Touching the Discovery of America and the Islands Adjacent*, edited by John Winter Jones. Elibron Classics, www.elibron.com, 2005.

Hamor, Ralph. *A Ture Discourse of the Present Estate of Virginia* (facsimile). India: Pranava Books (Original work published 1615).

Harriot, Thomas. "A briefe and true report of the new found land of Virginia (1588)." New York: Dover Publications, Inc., 1972.

Jourdain, Silvester. *A Discovery of the Bermudas, Otherwise Called the Isle of Devils*. In *A Voyage to Virginia in 1609*, edited by Louis B. Wright, 103–116. Charlottesville: University Press of Virginia, 1973.

Lane, Ralph. "Narrative of the Settlement of Roanoke Island 1585–1586." In *The First Colonists: Documents on the Planting of the First English Settlements in North America 1584–1590*, edited by David B. Quinn and Alison M. Quinn, 24–45. Raleigh: North Carolina Department of Cultural Resources, 1982.

Martyr D'Anghiera, Peter. *De Orbe Novo, The Eight Decades of Peter Martyr D'Anghera, Vol. I*. Leopold Classic Library reproduction, 1530.

Martyr D'Anghiera, Peter. *De Orbe Novo, The Eight Decades of Peter Martyr D'Anghera, Vol. II* (F.A. Macnutt, translator). New York: G.P. Putnam's Sons, reproduction, 1912.

Oviedo, Gonzalo Fernández. *Writing from the Edge of the World: The Memoirs of Darién, 1514–1527* (G.F. Dille, translator). Tuscaloosa: The University of Alabama Press, 2006.

Percy, George. "Observations gathered out of a discourse of the plantation of the southern colony in Virginia by the English, 1606" and "A True Relation of the proceedings and occurrents of moment which have hap'ned in Virginia from the time Sir Thomas Gates was shipwrack'd upon the Bermudes, anno 1609, until my departure out of the country, which was in anno Domini 1612." In *Jamestown Narratives:*

Eyewitness Accounts of the Virginia Colony, edited by Edward Wright Haile, 85–100 and 497–519. Champlain, VA: Roundhouse, 1998.

Quinn, David B., and Alison M. Quinn, eds. *The First Colonists: Documents on the Planting of The First English Settlements in North America 1584-1590*. Raleigh: North Carolina Department of Cultural Resources, 1982.

Ralegh, Sir Walter. *The Discoverie of the Large, Rich and Bewtiful Empyre of Guiana*. Manchester, England: Manchester University Press, 1997.

Raleigh, Sir Walter. *Selected Prose and Poetry*, ed. Agnes M.C. Latham. London: The Athlone Press, 1965.

Smith, John. *A True Relation* (1608), 142–183; *A Map of Virginia* (1612), 205–214; *The Generall Historie of Virginia, New-England, and the Summer Isles* (1624), 215–349. In *Jamestown Narratives: Eyewitness Accounts of the Virginia Colony, The First Decade: 1607-1617*, edited by Edward Wright Haile. Champlain, VA: Roundhouse, 1998.

Smith, John. *The True Travels, Adventures, and Observations of Captain John Smith Into Europe, Asia, Africa, and America*. Project Gutenberg Ebook (Print on demand), 2017.

Spellman, Henry. "Relation of Virginia, 1609." In *Jamestown Narratives: Eyewitness Accounts of the Virginia Colony*, edited by Edward Wright Haile, 481–495. Champlain, VA: Roundhouse, 1998.

Strachey, William. *Historie of Travell into Virginia Britania*. London: The Hakluyt Society, 1951.

Strachey, William. "A true reportory of the wracke, and redemption of Sir Thomas Gates, Knight, etc." Charlottesville: University Press of Virginia, 1978.

White, John. "Narrative of the 1587 Virginia Voyage," "Narrative of the Abortive Virginia Voyage, 1588," and "Narrative of the 1590 Virginia Voyage." In *The First Colonists: Documents on the Planting of The First English Settlements in North America 1584-1590*, edited by David B. Quinn and Alison M. Quinn, 93–130. Raleigh: North Carolina Department of Cultural Resources, 1982.

Wingfield, Edward Maria. "A Discourse of Virginia." In *Jamestown Narratives: Eyewitness Accounts of the Virginia Colony*, edited by Edward Wright Haile, 183–201. Champlain, VA: Roundhouse, 1998.

Secondary Sources

Allen, Paula Gunn. *Pocahontas: Medicine Woman, Spy, Entrepreneur, Diplomat*. New York: HarperCollins, 2003.

Andrews, Kenneth R. "Christopher Newport of Limehouse, Mariner." *The William and Mary Quarterly* 11, no. 1 (1954): 28–41.

Applebaum, Robert, and John Wood Sweet, eds. *Envisioning an English Empire: Jamestown and the Making of the North Atlantic World*. Philadelphia: University of Pennsylvania Press, 2005.

Arianrhod, Robyn. *Thomas Harriot, A Life in Science*. New York: Oxford University Press, 2019.

Aronson, Marc, and Marina Budhos. *Sugar Changed the World*. Boston: Houghton Mifflin Harcourt, 2010.

Bailyn, Bernard. *The Barbarous Years*. New York: Vintage Books, 2013.

Barbour, Philip L. *Pocahontas and Her World*. London: Robert Hale & Company, 1969.

Barbour, Philip L. *The Three Worlds of Captain John Smith*. Boston: Houghton Mifflin Co., 1964.

Beeching, Jack, ed. *Hakluyt Voyages and Discoveries*. Middlesex, England: Penguin Books Ltd., 1972.

Beer, Anna. *My Just Desire: The Life of Bess Ralegh, Wife to Sir Walter*. New York: Ballantine Books, 2003.

Beer, Anna. *Patriot or Traitor: The Life and Death of Sir Walter Ralegh*. London: Oneworld Publications, 2018.

Bemiss, Samuel M., President. *The Three Charters of the Virginia Company of London*. Williamsburg: Virginia 350th Anniversary Celebration, 1957.

Bergreen, Laurence. *In Search of a Kingdom*. New York: HarperCollins, 2021.

Bicheno, Hugh. *Elizabeth's Sea Dogs*. London: Bloomsbury Publishing, 2014.

Blackburn, Robin. *The Making of New World Slavery: From the Baroque to the Modern, 1492-1800*. London: Verso Books, 2010.

Bovill, E.W. "The Madre De Dios." *The*

Mariner's Mirror. Vol. 54, no. 2 (May 1968): 129–152.

Bradford, Ernle. *A Wind from the North: The Life of Henry the Navigator.* New York: Open Road Integrated Media, Inc., 2014.

Bradley, A.G. *Captain John Smith.* London: Macmillan & Co. Ltd., 1905.

Bridenbaugh, Carl. *Jamestown 1544–1699.* New York: Oxford University Press, 1980.

Butman, John, and Simon Targett. *New World, Inc: The Story of the British Empire's Most Successful Start-Up.* Great Britain: Atlantic Books, 2019.

Byrne, M. St. Clare. *Elizabethan Life in Town and Country.* London: Methuen & Co. Ltd., 1934.

Chatterton, E. Keble. *Captain John Smith.* London: John Lane, The Bodley Head Ltd., 1927.

Chatterton, E. Keble. *Fore and Aft: The Story of the Fore & Aft Rig.* London: Seeley Service & Co., 1912.

Cipolla, Carlo M. *Guns, Sails, and Empires: Technological Innovation and the Early Phases of European Expansion 1400–1700.* New York: Minerva Press, Funk & Wagnalls Publishing Company, Inc., 1965.

Craven, Wesley Frank. *The Southern Colonies in the Seventeenth Century 1607–1689.* Baton Rouge: Louisiana State University Press, 1970.

Craven, Wesley Frank. "The Virginia Company of London, 1606–1624." Williamsburg: Virginia 350th Anniversary Celebration Corp., 1957.

Custalow, Linwood, and Angela L. Daniel. *The True Story of Pocahontas: The Other Side of History.* Golden CO: Fulcrum Publishing, 2007.

Dalrymple, William. *The Anarchy: The Relentless Rise of the East India Company.* New York: Bloomsbury Publishing, 2019.

Dawson, Scott. *Croatoan: Birthplace of America.* Conshohocken PA: Infinity Publishing, 2009.

Dawson, Scott. *The Lost Colony and Hatteras Island.* Charleston SC: The History Press, 2020.

Defoe, Daniel. *A Journal of the Plague Year.* London: Penguin Books, 2003.

Doherty, Kieran. *Sea Venture: Shipwreck, Survival, and the Salvation of Jamestown.* New York: St. Martin's Press, 2007.

Doran, Joseph I. *Sir George Yeardley and His Voyage of 1609–1610 to Virginia in the Sea Adventure and Deliverance.* Philadelphia: Council of the Pennsylvania Society of Colonial Governors, April 6, 1914.

Egloff, Keith, and Deborah Woodward. *First People: The Early Indians of Virginia.* Charlottesville: University of Virginia Press, 2006.

Emerson, Everett. *Captain John Smith Revised Edition.* New York: Twayne Publishers, 1993.

Erickson, Carolly. *The First Elizabeth.* New York: Simon & Schuster, 1992.

Fishwick, Marshall W. *Jamestown.* New York: American Heritage Publishing Co., Harper & Row, 1965.

Fraser, Antonia. *King James I of England.* London: Weidenfeld & Nicolson, 1974.

Fullam, Brandon. *A Lost Colony Hoax: The Chowan River Dare Stone.* Jefferson NC: McFarland, 2021.

Fullam, Brandon. *The Lost Colony of Roanoke: New Perspectives.* Jefferson, NC: McFarland, 2017.

Fullam, Brandon. *Manteo and the Algonquins of the Roanoke Voyages.* Jefferson, NC: McFarland, 2020.

Gabriel-Powell, Andy. *Richard Grenville and the Lost Colony of Roanoke.* Jefferson, NC: McFarland, 2016.

Gallay, Alan. *The Indian Slave Trade: The Rise of the English Empire in the American South, 1670–1717.* New Haven: Yale University Press, 2002.

Gallivan, Martin D. *The Powhatan Landscape: An Archaeological History of the Algonquian Chesapeake.* Gainesville: University Press of Florida, 2016.

Gately, Iain. *Tobacco: A Cultural History of How an Exotic Plant Seduced Civilization.* New York: Grove Press, 2001.

Gerson, Noel B. *The Glorious Scoundrel: A Biography of Captain John Smith.* New York: Dodd, Mead & Company, 1978.

Glover, Lorrie, and Daniel Blake Smith. *The Shipwreck That Saved Jamestown.* New York: Henry Holt & Co., 2008.

Gosling, William Gilbert. *The Life of Sir Humphrey Gilbert.* London: Constable & Co. Ld., 1911.

Green, Matthew. *London: A Travel Guide Through Time.* United Kingdom: Penguin Random House, 2016.

Greenblatt, Stephen J. *Sir Walter Ralegh—*

The Renaissance Man and His Roles. New Haven: Yale University Press, 1973.

Hatch, Charles E., Jr. *Virginia 1607–1624: The First Seventeen Years.* Charlottesville: University Press of Virginia, 1957.

Hatfield, April Lee. *Atlantic Virginia: Intercolonial Relations in the Seventeenth Century.* Philadelphia: University of Pennsylvania Press, 2004.

Hawke, David Freeman, editor. *Captain John Smith's History of Virginia.* Indianapolis: Bobbs-Merrill Company, Inc., 1970.

Hibbert, Christopher. *The Virgin Queen: Elizabeth I, Genius of the Golden Age.* Reading, MA: Addison-Wesley Publishing Company, Inc., 1991.

Hoffman, Paul E. *Spain and the Roanoke Voyages.* Raleigh: North Carolina Department of Cultural Resources, 1987.

Hoobler, Dorothy, and Thomas Hoobler. *Captain John Smith: Jamestown and the Birth of the American Dream.* Hoboken: John Wiley & Sons, Inc., 2006.

Horn, James. *A Kingdom Strange: The Brief and Tragic History of the Lost Colony of Roanoke.* New York: Perseus Books Group, 2010.

Horn, James. *A Land As God Made It: Jamestown and the Birth of America.* New York: Perseus Books Group, 2005.

Howarth, David. *1066, The Year of the Conquest.* New York: Penguin Books, 1977.

Howarth, David. *The Voyage of the Armada.* Guilford, CT: The Globe Pequot Press, 1981.

Hume, Ivor Noël. *The Virginia Adventure: Roanoke to James Towne.* Charlottesville: University of Virginia Press, 1994.

Kazimiroff, Theodore. *The Last Algonquin.* New York: Walker and Company, 1982.

Kelly, Joseph. *Marooned: Jamestown, Shipwreck, and a New History of America's Origin.* New York: Bloomsbury Publishing Inc., 2019.

Kelsey, Harry. *Sir Francis Drake, The Queen's Pirate.* New Haven: Yale University Press, 1998.

Kelso, William M. *Jamestown, the Truth Revealed.* Charlottesville: University of Virginia Press, 2017.

Killeen, Richard. *Ireland—Land, People, History.* London: Little, Brown, 2012.

Klein, Herbert S., and Ben Vinson III. *African Slavery in Latin America and the Caribbean.* Oxford: Oxford University Press, 1986.

Klingelhofer, Eric, ed. *Excavating the Lost Colony Mystery: The May, the Search, the Discovery.* Chapel Hill: University of North Carolina Press, 2023.

Kupperman, Karen Ordahl. *Pocahontas and the English Boys.* New York: New York University Press, 2019.

Kupperman, Karen Ordahl. *Roanoke: The Abandoned Colony.* Lanham, MD: Rowman & Littlefield Publishers, Inc., 2007.

Lacy, Robert. *Sir Walter Raleigh.* New York: Atheneum, 1974.

Lawler, Andrew. *The Secret Token: Myth, Obsession, and the Search for the Lost Colony of Roanoke.* New York: Anchor Books, 2018.

Lawson, John. *A New Voyage to Carolina.* Chapel Hill: The University of North Carolina Press, 1967.

Lemay, J.A. Leo. *The American Dream of Captain John Smith.* Charlottesville: University Press of Virginia, 1991.

Lewis, Matthew. *Henry III, The Son of Magna Carta.* Gloucestershire: Amberley Publishing, 2016.

MacCaffrey, Wallace. *Elizabeth I.* London: Edward Arnold, 1993.

Mancall, Peter C., ed. *The Atlantic World and Virginia, 1550–1624.* Chapel Hill: University of North Carolina Press, 2007.

Markham, Clements. "Richard Hakluyt: His Life and Work." Address presented on the occasion of the Fiftieth Anniversary of the Foundation of the Hakluyt Society, London, December 15, 1896.

Mason, F. Van Wyck. *The Sea 'Venture.* New York: Doubleday & Company, 1963.

McIntyre, Ruth A. "William Sanderson: Elizabeth Financier of Discovery." *The William and Mary Quarterly*, Vol. 13, No. 2 (April 1956): 184–201.

Miles, Rosalind. *I, Elizabeth.* New York: Doubleday, 1994.

Miller, Helen Hill. *Passage to America: Ralegh's Colonists Take Ship for Roanoke.* Raleigh: North Carolina Department of Cultural Resources, 1983.

Miller, Lee. *Roanoke: Solving the Mystery of the Lost Colony.* New York: Arcade Publishing, 2000.

Milton, Giles. *Big Chief Elizabeth: The Adventures and Fate of the First English Colonists in America.* New York: Farrar, Straus and Giroux, 2000.

Morgan, Edmund S. *American Slavery, American Freedom*. New York: W.W. Norton & Company, 2003.
Mossiker, Frances. *Pocahontas: The Life and the Legend*. New York: Alfred A. Knopf, 1976.
Neale, J.E. *Queen Elizabeth I*. Chicago: Academy Chicago Publishers, 1992.
Neill, Edward D. *History of the Virginia Company of London*. Albany, NY: Joel Munsell, 1869 (Alpha Editions Reprint, 2019).
Nicholls, Mark, and Penry Williams. *Sir Walter Raleigh, In Life & Legend*. New York: Continuum International Publishing Group, 2011.
Nichols, A. Bryant, Jr., *Captain Christopher Newport: Admiral of Virginia*. Newport News, VA: Sea Venture, 2007.
Núñez Cabeza de Vaca, Alvar. *Chronicle of the Narváez Expedition* (Fanny Bandelier, translator). New York: Penguin Books, 2002.
O'Dell, Scott. *The Serpent Never Sleeps*. New York: Fawcett Juniper, 1987.
Paine, Lincoln. *The Sea & Civilization: A Maritime History of the World*. New York: Vintage Books, 2015.
Parker, Geoffrey. *The Grand Strategy of Philip II*. New Haven: Yale University Press, 1998.
Parks, George Bruner. *Richard Hakluyt and the English Voyages*. New York: Frederick Ungar Publishing Co., 1961.
Patton, Willoughby. *Sea Venture*. Hamilton, Bermuda: Engravers Limited, 1983.
Payne, Anthony. "Richard Hakluyt: An Essay in Bibliography 1580-88." PhD diss., National University of Ireland, Galway, 2019. https://aran.library.nuigalway.ie /bitstream/ handle/ 10379/15851/ PaynePhD2019.pdf?sequence=1&isAllowed=y
Percy, George. *A True Relation*. London, 1624.
Picard, Liza. *Elizabeth's London*. London: Orion Books Ltd., 2003.
Powell, Andrew Thomas. *Grenville & the Lost Colony of Roanoke*. Leicester, England: Matador, 2011.
Prescott, William H. *History of the Conquest of Peru*. Mineola, NY: Dover Publications, Inc., 2005.
Price, David A. *Love and Hate in Jamestown, John Smith, Pocahontas, and the Start of a New Nation*. New York: Vintage Books, 2005.
Pritchard, Evan T. *No Word for Time: The Way of the Algonquin People*. Graham, NC: Millichap Books, 1997.
Quinn, David Beers. *Raleigh & the British Empire*. New York: Collier Books, 1962.
Quinn, David Beers. *The Roanoke Voyages 1584-1590, Volumes I & II*. New York: Dover Publications, Inc., 1991.
Quinn, David Beers. *Set Fair for Roanoke: Voyages and Colonies, 1584-1606*. Chapel Hill: University of North Carolina Press, 1985.
Raine, David F. *Sir George Somers—A Man and His Times*. Bermuda: Pompano Publications, 1984.
Richter, Daniel K. *Facing East from Indian Country: A Native History of Early America*. Cambridge: Harvard University Press, 2001.
Rights, Douglas L. *The American Indian in North Carolina*. Winston-Salem, NC: John F. Blair, 1957.
Rolfe, John. *A True Relation of the State of Virginia Left by Sir Thomas Dale Knight in May Last 1616*. Charlottesville: The University Press of Virginia, 1971.
Rountree, Helen C. *Manteo's World: Native American Life in Carolina's Sound Country Before and After the Lost Colony*. Chapel Hill: University of North Carolina Press, 2021.
Rountree, Helen C. *Pocahontas, Powhatan, Opechancanough*. Charlottesville: University of Virginia Press, 2005.
Rountree, Helen C. *Pocahontas's People: The Powhatan Indians of Virginia through Four Centuries*. Norman: University of Oklahoma Press, 1990.
Rountree, Helen C. *The Powhatan Indians of Virginia, Their Traditional Culture*. Norman: University of Oklahoma Press, 1989.
Rountree, Helen C. *Young Pocahontas in the Indian World*. Yorktown, VA: J & R Graphics, 1995.
Rountree, Helen C., and Thomas E. Davidson. *Eastern Shore Indians of Virginia and Maryland*. Charlottesville: University of Virginia Press, 1997.
Rountree, Helen C., Wayne E. Clark, and Kent Mountford, *John Smith's Chesapeake Voyages: 1607-1609*. Charlottesville: University of Virginia Press, 2007.
Rowse, A.L. *The Case Books of Simon*

Forman, *Sex and Society in Shakespeare's Age*. London: Pan Books Ltd., 1974.
Rowse, A.L. *The Elizabethan Renaissance: The Life of the Society*. Chicago: Ivan R. Dee, 1971.
Rowse, A.L. *The England of Elizabeth*. London: Palgrave Macmillan, 2003.
Rowse, A.L. *Ralegh and the Throckmortons*. London: Macmillan & Co. Ltd, 1962.
Rowse, A.L. *Shakespeare's Southampton*. New York: Harper & Row Publishers, 1965.
Rowse, A.L. *Sir Richard Grenville of the Revenge*. London: Faber & Faber, 2013.
Russell, Peter. *Prince Henry 'the Navigator': A Life*. Yale University Press, 2000.
Shirley, John W. "George Percy at Jamestown, 1607–1612" *Virginia Magazine of History and Biography* 57, no. 3 (July 1949): 227–43.
Smith, Bradford. *Captain John Smith: His Life & Legend*. New York: J.B. Lippincott Co., 1953.
Smith, Lacey Baldwin. *The Elizabethan World*. Boston: Houghton Mifflin Company, 1991.
Somerset, Anne. *Elizabeth I*. New York: St Martin's Press., 1991.
Starkey, David. *Elizabeth: The Struggle for the Throne*. New York, HarperCollins, 2001.
Stebbing, William. *Sir Walter Raleigh: A Biography*. Honolulu: University Press of the Pacific, 2004.
Strachey, Lytton. *Elizabeth and Essex*. New York: Harcourt Brace Jovanovich, 1956.
Sugden, John. *Sir Francis Drake*. New York: Simon & Schuster, 1990.
Teems, David. *Majestie, The King Behind the King James Bible*. Nashville: Thomas Nelson, 2010.
Tillyard, E.M.W. *The Elizabethan World Picture*. New York: Vintage Books, 1959.
Tombs, Robert. *The English and Their History*. New York: Vintage Books, 2014.
Townsend, Camilla. *Pocahontas and the Powhatan Dilemma*. New York: Hill and Wang, 2004.
Trevelyan, Raleigh. *Sir Walter Raleigh*. New York: Henry Holt & Company, 2002.
Tyler, Lyon Gardiner. *The Cradle of the Republic: Jamestown and James River*. Richmond, VA: The Hermitage Press, Inc., 1906.
Walton, Timothy R. *The Spanish Treasure Fleets*. Sarasota: Pineapple Press, Inc., 1994.
Warner, Charles Dudley. *Captain John Smith*. New York: Henry Holt and Company, 1881.
Watkins, Ronald. *Unknown Seas: How Vasco da Gama Opened the East*. London: John Murray, 2003.
Weir, Alison. *The Life of Elizabeth I*. New York: Ballantine Books, 1998.
Williams, Neville. *The Life and Times of Elizabeth I*. London: Weidenfeld and Nicolson, 1992.
Williams, Neville. *The Sea Dogs: Privateers, Plunder & Piracy in the Elizabethan Age*. New York: Macmillan Publishing, 1975.
Williamson, Margaret Holmes. *Powhatan Lords of Life and Death: Command and Consent in Seventeenth-Century Virginia*. Lincoln: University of Nebraska Press, 2003.
Wilson, John Dover. *Life in Shakespeare's England*. Middlesex, England: Penguin Books, 1949.
Wilson, Peter H. *The Thirty Years War: Europe's Tragedy*. Cambridge: Harvard University Press, 2009.
Wingfield, Jocelyn R. *Virginia's True Founder: Edward Maria Wingfield and His Times*. North Charleston, SC: Booksurge LLC, 2007.
Woodward, Grace Steele. *Pocahontas*. Norman: University of Oklahoma Press, 1969.
Woodward, Hobson. *A Brave Vessel: The True Tale of the Castaways Who Rescued Jamestown and Inspired Shakespeare's 'The Tempest.'* New York: Viking, 2009.
Woolley, Benjamin. *The Queen's Conjuror: The Life and Magic of Dr. Dee*. London: Flamingo, 2002.
Woolley, Benjamin. *Savage Kingdom: The True Story of Jamestown, 1607, and the Settlement of America*. New York: Harper Perennial, 2007.

Index

Africa 21, 22, 34; Portugal and 17–19; west coast of 134, 139
African slave trade and slaves 10, 18, 34, 36, 49, 190, 201n4; Jamestown and 172, 177–78, 189
agriculture: English 177, 224–25n124; Native American 58, 207n22
Albemarle Sound 53, 54, 208n34; exploration 5, 59, 62
Alexander VI, Pope 19–20, 21
Algonquin peoples 6, 82, 84, 162, 165, 168, 177, 207n25, 221n66; amity with 52, 57, 58, 64, 126, 205n109, 219n20; attacks against 91, 157; attacks by 98, 106, 146, 160, 164, 166, 224n121; in clash of cultures 172–73; diet 207n22, 209n43, 209n55, 226n13; in England 50–51; English view of 78, 171, 205n109, 228n63; hopeful conversion 93, 126, 167, 204n87; hostility 149, 158, 162; Huskanaw ceremony 102, 114, 116, 119, 122; Jamestown and 14–15, 105, 169, 187; language 159, 175, 208n26, 209n55, 210n82, 211n98; London Company and 5, 126, 155; naming traditions 61–62; painted by White 51, 57; patrilocalism 101, 222n80; pharmacopeia 102, 229n77; removal and extermination 78, 190, 222n70, 242n43; rituals 182, 185, 223n93, 223n94, 228n69, 229n71; sex and sexuality 129, 130–31, 155, 157; Smith and 114, 117, 121, 229n72; Spanish and 102–3; in Tidewater 53–57; tortures by 145, 157; as victims of English land lust 78, 177, 187, 219n23, 241n27; *see also* Native Americans; Powhatan people; Secotan people
Allen, Thomas 46
Amadas, Philip 46, 50, 57–59, 209n63; identified 4
ambergis discovered on Bermuda 174, 239n38

Anglican church 29, 93, 110, 176
Anjou, Duke of *see* Francis, Duke of Alençon and Anjou
Anne of Denmark, Queen Consort of Scotland, England, and Ireland 133, 181, 183, 231n131, 240n10
Antilles 79, 97
Antwerp 31, 33, 34, 201n112
Apokant village 110
apprenticeship, apprentices 3, 29, 30, 187
Aquascogoc village 4, 57, 59
Arabs and spice trade 17, 19
archeology 6, 207n20, 225n130
Archer, Gabriel 8, 156, 224n121, 231n129, 232n11, 235n9; death 160, 163; identified 6; Smith and 127, 132, 151, 153–54
Argall, Samuel 178, 238n37; Bermuda mission 170, 171, 173; identified 6; Pocahontas and 175, 236n27, 239n54; shortens voyage to Jamestown 134, 135
Aristotle 175
Ark Raleigh 95
Ashley, Katherine Champernowne 41
Asia 22, 23, 198n39; *see also* China; Far East; Orient
Atlantic Ocean 20, 23; currents 134–35, 137; hurricanes 82, 139
Augusta, Georgia 193, 211n98
Azores 43, 85, 94, 172, 232n11; Portugal and 4, 18, 46; privateers and 5, 52, 64, 67–68, 72
Aztecs 52, 62, 87, 223n98

Babington, Anthony 65
Baffin Island 21
Bahamas 57, 134
Balboa, Vasco Núñez de 23
Barents Sea 22
Barentsz, William 22
Barlowe, Arthur 46, 50, 53; identified 4
Bay of Biscay 41

249

Bay of Fundy 91
Bedford, John 85
Belgium 1, 198n22
Bermuda (Isle of Devils) 6, 9, 137, 147, 158, 163, 174, 176, 196n20, 233n33; deaths on 234n80; London Company and 159, 173, 239n43; reefs 141, 142, 150, 152; *Sea Venture* wrecked on 10, 141; Somers and 169–70, 171; wrecks along 233n29, 233n32
Bermuda Hundred 173
Bermúdez, Juan de 141
Bertie County, North Carolina 193
Black Legend 48
Blackfriars Theatre, London 9, 136
Blessing 152, 166, 241n34
Bloody Mary *see* Mary, Queen of England
Blunt, Humphrey 170
Bogue Sound 54
Boleyn, Anne 1, 23, 24, 178; identified 1
Bolling, Jane Rolfe 188
Bolling, John 188
Bolling, Mary Kennon 188
Bolling, Robert 188
Borgia, Rodrigo *see* Alexander VI, Pope
Brazil 21, 22, 33, 87
brazilwood 201n2
Brentford, Middlesex 182, 240n7
Brewster, Edward 168
Briars, Jeffery 234n80
A Briefe & True Report of the New Found Land of Virginia (Harriot, 1588) 77–78
British Empire 12, 188; Dee on 11, 23–24, 44
Buck, Elizabeth 144
Buck, Richard 142, 144, 147, 162, 169, 176; identified 6
Burbage, Richard 136
Burghley, 1st Baron *see* Cecil, William, 1st Baron Burghley

Cabot, John (Giovanni Caboto) 20, 21, 26, 45; identified 3
Cabot, Sebastian 21, 22, 26; identified 3
Cadiz 7, 73
cahows 143, 147, 174, 234n65, 234n67
Calais 73, 74
California coast: Drake explores 41
Cambridge University 3, 6, 9, 23, 24, 27, 126–27, 136; St. John's College 2, 127; Trinity College 2, 11
Canary Current 134, 135, 197n6
Canary Islands 34, 96, 97, 134
cannibalism 116, 160, 227n17
canoes 50, 56, 110–11, 117, 128, 170, 208–9n41, 226n5, 226n9

Capahowosick 126, 185, 229n81, 229n85
Cape Bojador 17, 18
Cape Cod 6, 7, 127
Cape Comfort 237n8
Cape Fear River 90, 91
Cape Henry 60, 61, 98, 103–4, 136, 150, 158, 164, 172
Cape of Good Hope 19, 21
Cape Verde Islands 18, 20
caravels, lateen-rigged 18, 197n17
Caribbean Sea 33, 79, 85, 97, 129, 172, 207n13; currents and 134, 207n19; Drake's raids in 36, 39
carracks 19, 197n14, 197n15
Carter, Christopher 150, 174
Cartier, Jacques 21
Cassen, George 110, 115, 127
Catherine of Aragon, Queen Consort of England 23, 24
Catholicism 19, 43, 48; Elizabeth and 25, 27; in England 31–32, 74, 91; England vs. 23, 24, 51, 52, 65; Mary and 24, 25; Philip and 31, 202n23
Cavendish, Thomas 46, 53; identified 3
Cawson, George 226n4
Cecil, Robert, Earl of Salisbury 87, 88, 167, 225n134; identified 2
Cecil, William, 1st Baron Burghley 2, 3, 7, 87, 88, 90, 215n20; Elizabeth and 13, 26–27, 33, 45; identified 2
Chacandepco Inlet 81, 82, 216n48, 216n55, 216n57
Chapman, George 46, 136
Charde, Edward 239n41
Charles, archduke of Austria 26, 27
Charles II, King of England 192
Charles IX, King of France 202n25
Charles V, Holy Roman Emperor 25, 197–98n22, 205n110, 206n122; identified 1
Charleston, South Carolina 192, 193
Charlotte, North Carolina 193
Chaunis Temoatan 62
Chesapeake Bay 14, 98, 114, 145, 196n32, 210–11n86, 212n134, 221n61, 227n17; explored by Harriot and White 60–61; Lost Colonists and 90, 191, 213n148, 216n48; Native Americans along 14–15; Smith and 116, 122, 128, 130, 156, 228n68, 242n44; Spain and 191, 213n148; White's vison 65, 66–67, 72
Chickahominy River 109, 221n59; Smith explores 110, 127
children: Algonquin 53, 56, 102, 120; Jamestown and 144, 153, 172, 187
China (Cathay) 19, 20; *see also* Asia; Far East; Orient

Index

Choanoke River 191
Chowan River 190, 193, 242n45; artifacts found along 191–92, 194; exploration 5, 62
Christianity 17, 222n70; conversion to 9, 14, 18, 45, 52, 58, 93, 126, 167, 204n87, 219n21; *see also* Anglican church; Catholicism; Protestants, Protestantism; religion
Cieza de León, Pedro de 48
Cimarrons 36
Cinquoteck (West Point, Virginia) 115, 156, 227n30
circumnavigation of globe 3, 20, 38–41, 45, 46, 198n37, 203n45, 203n47
Cocke, Abraham 79, 83, 85
codfish 21, 26, 91, 173, 199n68; *see also* fishing, fisheries; Grand Banks; Newfoundland
Coe, Thomas 231n129
Columbus, Christopher 19, 20, 134
Constantinople 17, 96, 137
copper 62
Coquonassum 119
Cornwall 5, 13, 46; Raleigh and 45, 51, 65, 86
cottons 20, 21
Crashaw, William 167, 237n1, 237n3
Croatoan Island 63, 80, 82, 86, 207n19, 208n30, 209n47, 216n57, 217n60, 217n75; Lost Colonists and 85, 192, 193, 216n48, 242n48
Cromwell, Oliver 192
Cuba 79, 94
Currituck Sound 60, 69

da Gama, Vasco 19
Dale, Thomas 177, 178, 221n60, 237n9, 238n29, 240n72; founds Henrico 173, 175; identified 6–7; Pocahontas and 7, 8, 176, 181, 239n63; replaces De La Warr 172, 173
Dale's Code 238n28, 238n29
Dare, Ananias 66
Dare, Eleanor White 66, 191–92, 194, 212n124
Dare, Virginia 51, 71, 91, 192, 194, 216n51
Dasemunkepeuc village 63, 70
Davies, James 151, 153, 156, 157, 168, 171
Dee, John 12, 13, 46, 88, 188; envisions British Empire 11, 23–24, 44, 195n6; *General and Rare Memorials Pertaining to the Perfect Art of Navigation* (1576) 11; identified 2
deer, white-tailed 56, 69, 99, 101, 107, 113, 164; venison 113, 156, 164, 229n81

Delaware Bay 91
Delaware River 218n12
De La Warr, Baron *see* West, Thomas, Baron De La Warr
Deliverance 145–46, 149–52, 158–59, 161, 167–68, 170, 233n56
democracy 189–90
Descartes, René 47
de Soto, Hernando 104
Devereaux, Robert, Earl of Essex 8, 28, 66, 76, 86, 186, 215n26; identified 2
Devonshire 9, 12, 13, 30, 91, 194; Drake and Hawkins and 3, 33, 43, 45; Raleigh and 43, 44, 45, 51, 65, 86; seamen from 4, 5, 41
Diamond 136, 153, 158, 166
Díaz, Bernal 48
Diggs, Thomas 46
Discourse of a Discoverie for a New Passage to Catay (Gilbert, 1576) 41, 195n6
A Discourse on Western Planting (Hakluyt, 1584) 13, 14, 51, 195–96n17, 196n22
Discovery 94, 98, 127, 151, 156, 158–59, 161, 167, 170, 219n32
diseases 25, 42, 153; dysentery 40, 106, 132; European 60, 206n118; at Jamestown 106, 108, 172; malaria 106, 132; scurvy 40, 132; tuberculosis 1, 24; typhus 1, 40, 106, 132
Divers Voyages Touching the Discoverie of America... (Hakluyt, 1582) 12, 45
dogs 48, 62, 160
Doughty, Thomas 39–40, 202n32
Drake, Francis 87, 88, 96, 104, 120, 148, 202n32, 203n46, 228n56; arrives in North Carolina 63, 211n111; circumnavigates globe 38–41, 45, 198n37, 203n45; as fleet commander 66, 74, 75; Hawkins and 35, 39; identified 3; as privateer 7, 13, 36, 38, 45, 63, 73, 91
drought 70, 99, 213n162, 221n64
drugs 122–23, 124–25
Dudley, Amy 27, 28, 130, 200n83
Dudley, Robert, Earl of Leicester 2, 3, 44, 87, 88, 209n49; Elizabeth and 13, 27–28, 45, 51, 75–77, 215n27; identified 2
Durham House 3, 4, 48–49, 51, 61, 77, 78, 87, 205n99; as Raleigh's headquarters 5, 46, 47, 90
Dyer, William 231n129
dyes for Native American skins 99, 101

Eason, Bermudas 150
Eason, Edward 144

East India Company 8, 175, 178
East Indies 19, 240*n*72
Eastern Shore 98, 122
Eastward Ho! (play) 136–37
Edward VI, King of England 24, 199*n*63; identified 1
Effingham, 2nd Baron Howard *see* Howard, Charles, 1st earl of Nottingham and 2nd Baron Howard of Effingham
El Dorado 13, 49, 52, 87
Elizabeth I, Queen of England 3, 5, 8, 41, 42, 51, 89, 187, 188, 195*n*6, 215*n*27; attempted assassinations 65, 76; birth and death 2, 14, 23, 88, 90, 91; court 44, 86, 200*n*77, 200*n*79, 200*n*81, 206*n*120, 217*n*81, 217*n*83; as defender of Protestantism 77, 215*n*28, 215*n*29; Drake and 36, 38, 39; excommunication 31, 32; favorites 2, 3, 27–28, 42–43, 66, 86, 130; Gilbert and 41; Hakluyt and 13, 196*n*19; Hawkins and 34–35; identified 1; Mary and 24, 31, 32, 178–79; personality 24–25, 87–88, 199*n*54, 200*n*91, 218*n*95; Philip vs. 13, 27, 30–37, 51, 64; as polyglot 24, 198–99*n*47; pomp and ceremony 75–76; prohibits ships from leaving England 72, 78, 79, 214*n*3, 214*n*169; Raleigh and 13, 28, 42–43, 44, 49, 50, 51, 66, 68, 73, 86, 87, 187, 203*n*58, 205*n*99; reign 25–27, 87–88, 202*n*11, 218*n*104; Virginia named after 12, 25, 44
Elizabeth River 61, 103
Emry, Thomas 110, 112, 115, 127, 226*n*9
England 20, 21, 91, 134, 201*n*105; army 75–76; Catholicism in 31–32, 202*n*23; common law 189, 204*n*82; fishing vessels from 43, 91, 199*n*68; foreign relations 37, 42, 65, 68, 91, 199*n*50, 201*n*118; Ireland and 26, 41, 49, 52–53, 65; Native Americans in 50–51, 103, 133, 181–82; social order 30, 44, 46; Spain vs. 6, 11, 13, 14, 31–32, 45, 51, 87; tobacco in 177, 186; woolens and wool trade in 22, 23, 31, 33, 93, 196*n*21, 201*n*2, 201*n*112
English America 11, 42, 187, 189
English Channel 26, 44, 212*n*116
English Renaissance 25, 88–89, 136
Enoe Will 193
Ensenor 58, 61, 63
Essex, Earl of *see* Devereaux, Robert, Earl of Essex
Eurocentrism 22, 121, 126, 228*n*63
Europe, Europeans: diseases 132, 206*n*118; religion in 31, 48, 51, 77, 201*n*111; rivalry 20, 21, 32; spice trade and 17, 19

The Faerie Queen (Spenser, 1590) 76, 205*n*99
Falcon 153, 166
Far East 17, 19, 22, 231*n*126; *see also* Asia; China; Orient
Farnese, Ranuccio I, Duke of Parma 74–77, 214–15*n*14
Ferdinand II, King of Aragon, Castille, and León 48
Fernandez, Simon 41, 46, 69–70, 73, 79, 82, 209*n*47, 212–13*n*134, 212*n*133, 213*n*139, 216*n*47; as English navigator 50, 52, 57, 60, 66–68, 72; identified 4–5
fireships 74–75
fishing, fisheries 21, 26, 43, 56, 91, 143, 165, 237*n*13; of Grand Banks 171, 173, 199*n*68, 213*n*153; in Virginia 162, 164, 170
FitzGerald, James, 1st Earl of Desmond 65
Florida 13, 21, 23, 57, 59, 63, 68, 104–5, 136, 193, 196*n*18, 207*n*19
Florida Straits 83, 134
Fort Algernon 150, 151, 155–57, 165, 234*n*82
Fort Caroline 68
France 1, 13, 19, 20, 23, 26, 34, 42, 49, 88, 97, 188, 215*n*29; Huguenots 35–37, 44, 51, 68, 195*n*9, 202*n*12; in North America 6, 21, 22, 43; Raleigh in 44, 78, 195*n*9; Susquehannocks armed by 107, 122
Francis, Duke of Alençon and Anjou 38, 42, 202*n*25; identified 1
Fredericksburg, Virginia 227*n*25
Frobisher, Martin 51, 75, 213*n*139; identified 4
Frobisher, Richard 145

galleons 19, 47, 82, 197*n*15; Spanish 72, 74, 83, 94
Galthorpe, Stephen 96
Gates, Thomas 6, 10, 153, 158, 169, 171, 173, 178, 191, 238*n*35, 240*n*72; during Bermuda interlude 143–46, 148–50; identified 9; as Jamestown governor 135, 136, 143, 161–65, 168; as principal of London Company 91, 92
Gates' Bay village 143, 146–48
Generall Historie of Virginia, New England, and the Summer Isles (Smith, 1624) 97, 118–20, 183, 220*n*49
Genoa 3, 17, 20, 36
gentry 12, 44, 149, 200*n*103, 220*n*39; as Jamestown colonists 95–96, 219*n*33; landed 30, 65
Germany 23, 25, 97
Gilbert, Humphrey 5, 12, 41–44, 51, 198*n*39, 203*n*69, 204*n*76; *A Discourse*

Index 253

of a Discoverie for a New Passage to Catay 41, 195n6; Elizabeth and 41, 42; identified 4; Newfoundland and 12, 51, 202n69
glass production at Jamestown 130
Glaven, Darbie 68, 69
Gloucester Point, Virginia 229n85
Godspeed 94, 219n32
gold 4, 13, 51, 62, 96, 129; in Africa 17, 18, 19, 34; London Company and 92, 105, 126, 128, 196n29; in New Spain 21, 36, 41, 48, 90, 203n44, 205n113; Raleigh and 52, 186; royal fifth 41, 48, 203n52; see also El Dorado
Goochland, Virginia 131
Gosnold, Batholomew 6, 97, 104, 158, 219n18; death and burial 106, 225n130; discovers Cape Cod and Martha's Vineyard 7, 127; identified 7; Wingfield and 92, 95, 105, 219n17
Grand Banks 21, 26, 43, 91, 171, 199n68, 213n153
Granganimeo 50, 58, 61
Gravesend, Pocahontas's burial at 185
"Graveyard of the Atlantic" 53
Gray's Inn 2, 3, 9, 127, 136, 178, 204n82
Great Dismal Swamp 54, 99
Great Trading Path 62, 211n98
Greenwich Palace 42, 44
Grenville, Richard 46, 50, 52, 60, 64, 65, 67, 69, 70, 209n47, 212n119; commands fleet to Roanoke 52, 57–58, 80; identified 3
Grey, Lady Katherine 25
Guinea 18, 34, 197n5
Guinea Track 18
Gulf of Mexico 62
Gulf of St. Lawrence 21
Gulf Stream 53, 63, 137, 141, 207n19
Guyana 49, 87, 186, 240n3

Hakluyt, Richard 11–15, 37, 52, 61, 78, 85, 182, 195n7, 209n47; *A Discourse on Western Planting* (1584) 13, 14, 51, 195–96n17, 196n22; *Divers Voyages Touching the Discoverie of America ...* (1582) 12, 45; identified 5; Native Americans and 49, 93, 204n87, 205n109, 219n21; Raleigh and 44, 46, 47, 49, 196n19, 217n80, 219n21; Virginia Company and 91, 92, 196n20, 196n21; writings 12–13, 158, 196n18
Hakluyt, Richard, the Elder 12
Hakluytus Posthumus, or, Purchas His Pilgrimes (Purchas, 1625) 182
Hamor, Ralph 176–77, 238n30

Hampton, Virginia 221n62
Hampton Court 75
Hampton Roads 234n82
Harriot, Thomas 47, 64, 71, 182, 197n36; *A Briefe & True Report* (1588) 61, 77–78; Chesapeake Bay reconnoitered by 60–61, 66, 70, 103; compiles Algonquin dictionary 14–15, 51; identified 5; Raleigh and 46, 186
Hatoraske Island 50, 81, 82, 83, 216n49, 216n57
Hatteras Island 63, 66–67, 216n57
Hatton, Christopher 28, 43, 88, 202n32; identified 3
Hawkins, John 13, 43, 45, 75, 87, 88, 204n89; identified 4; Royal Navy and 39, 74; trade voyages 34, 35
Henrico 8, 173, 175–76
Henry II, King of France 1, 202n25
Henry VII, King of England 21, 178, 200n103
Henry VIII, King of England 1, 2, 12, 26, 46, 92, 178; Elizabeth and 23, 24; identified 1
Henry Frederick, Prince of Wales 172; identified 1
Henry the Navigator (Dom Henrique, Duke of Viseu) 17–19
Hillsborough, North Carolina 193
Hispaniola 7, 34, 79, 94, 137
The Historie of the World (Raleigh) 186
Hitchman, Richard 234n80
Hog Island 158, 159, 165
Holland 20, 21, 22, 218n12; see also Netherlands
Holy Land 19
Holy Roman Empire 1, 8, 23, 25, 96
Hood, Thomas 46
Hopewell 79, 82, 85, 94
Hopkins, Stephen 147–48
hostages 62, 63, 64
Howard, Charles, 1st Earl of Nottingham and 2nd Baron Howard of Effingham 4, 74; identified 3
Howard, Thomas, Fourth Duke of Norfolk 31–32
Howe, George 69, 70, 81
Hudson Bay 21
Hudson River (North River) 91, 218n12
Hues, Robert 46, 47
Huguenots 44, 51, 68, 195n9, 202n12; as privateers 35–37
Hunt, Robert 95, 111, 128, 224n119; identified 7
hunting 101, 107
hurricanes 63, 82, 166, 193, 209n47,

216n49, 217n60; *Sea Venture* wrecked by 137–41, 150, 152, 232n6, 232n11

imperialism 20, 78; English 12, 14, 167; *see also* British Empire
Incas 52, 62, 87
indentured workers 177, 187
India 17, 19, 20, 23, 178, 239n50
Indian Ocean 41
Inner Temple 237n1
Inns of Court 204n82, 237n1
Ireland 5, 8, 9, 23, 202n32, 207n25; England vs. 26, 41, 49, 52–53, 65, 92, 172; Raleigh in 4, 44, 46, 49, 78, 86; Raleigh's land grants 65, 86, 212n121; Spanish Armada and 75, 215n19, 215n22
Italy: explorers from 3, 20; Philip and 30, 31; spice trade and 17
Ivan the Terrible, Czar 22

James I, King of England (James VI of Scotland) 1, 7, 8, 88, 91, 130, 167, 172, 177, 178, 181, 188, 196n28, 215n43, 218n99, 218n100; identified 2; Jamestown and 14, 104, 188, 189; Raleigh and 2, 90, 186, 240n3
James VI, King of Scotland *see* James I, King of England
James River 9, 128, 156, 158, 170, 221n59, 225n145, 227n42, 236n33; entrance to 144, 155; exploration 104, 108, 110, 131; falls and headwaters 105, 154, 235n13, 235n26; north shore 106, 188, 223n115; plantations on 7, 173
Jamestown colonists 14–15, 94; diversity 106, 108, 135, 173, 219n33, 238n25; social origins 15, 30, 163, 172
Jamestown colony 107, 115, 121, 132, 189, 221n59; abandonment 165, 167; African slaves at 172, 177–78, 189; cannibalism and starvation 154, 160; church in 7, 178; drinking water 106, 132; as dystopian hellhole 145–46, 162; executive officers 8, 9, 91, 95, 104, 135, 168, 189; fire and 7, 127–28; James I and 14, 104, 188, 189; livestock 173, 226n1; mortality 106, 127, 132, 165, 187; palisade 105, 161; in Paspahegh terriory 224n115, 224n117; recruitment for 166, 172, 173; resupply fleet for 135–38, 150, 152–53, 156, 168, 172; secretaries 9, 151, 152; shortened voyages 134, 135; Smith returns to 126–27; supplies for 95, 127, 140
Jamestown council 104, 106, 153; becomes democratic assembly 189–90; members 7–8, 9, 163, 169, 188; sealed instructions for 95, 136; Smith and 105, 121, 122, 130, 224n119
Jamestown Island 126, 159, 161, 189, 224–25n124
Japan 19
Jesuits 103
jimsonweed 122–23, 223n96, 229n70
John Evangelist 79
joint-stock companies 22, 91
Jonson, Ben 46, 136, 220n39

Kecoughtan 98, 173
Kekatough 110, 115, 221n62, 226n2
Kendall, George 104, 106, 225n133, 225n134; identified 7
Kendrick's Mounts 83, 85
Kennebec River colony 91
Kiskiacks 103, 159, 225n135
Kocoum, as mate of Pocahontas 175, 239n54, 239n55

Labrador Current 53, 134, 207n19
Lacie, James 71
Lake Mattamuskeet 54
land: English acquisition of Native American 58, 224n117; Native American concept 209n59; as resource 93, 94
Lane, Ralph 58, 62, 92, 210n81; explores up Chowan River 63, 192; as governor of Roanoke colony 52, 60, 67, 80, 91; identified 5
Las Casas, Bartolomé de 48, 49, 96, 205n110
latitude, determining 47
Laws, Divine, Morall and Martiall, &c. (Strachey) 173, 174
Lawson, John 192–93
Leicester, Earl of *see* Dudley, Robert, Earl of Leicester
Levant *see* Holy Land
Lewis, Richard 234n80
Limeys 40
Lincoln's Inn 92, 204n82
Lion 153, 166
Little Ice Age 221n66
Little John 79, 94
livery companies 29, 30
livestock: hogs, 143, 144, 147, 155, 158, 169–70, 173, 174; horses 1, 18, 46, 121, 155, 200n103, 226n1; at Jamestown 121, 130, 155, 156, 160, 169, 173; sheep 23, 32, 155
London 11, 75, 88, 136, 189, 200n97; Algonquins in 51, 182; foreigners in 31, 39; governance 29, 104; London Company and 91, 92, 172, 173, 181;

merchants 13–14, 78; population 28–29, 163; theaters in 9, 136
London Company subsidiary of The Virginia Company 121–22, 128, 130, 153, 169, 174, 185, 187, 237n1; Algonquin policy 126, 170, 173, 178, 179, 181; Bermuda and 144, 149, 239n43; investors in 91, 93, 135, 149, 166, 178; Jamestown's failure and 132, 162, 164–65; Lost Colonists and 92, 126, 191, 196n29; objectives 91–92, 231n121; recruitment by 92, 93, 95, 167, 172, 173, 181; Smith and 125–26, 132, 133
Lost Colonists 6, 14, 15, 50–72, 158, 193, 194, 196n29, 216n51; artifacts 191–92; left by Grenville 64, 65; London Company and 92, 126, 191, 216n51; mystery 190–94, 242n43; Powhatan and 113–14; Raleigh and 86, 90–91; Smith and 121, 190; White and 73, 78, 79–86; *see also* Roanoke Island Colony
lotteries 173
Low Countries 9, 11, 104, 156
Luxembourg 1, 198n22
Lyme Regis 9, 91
Lynnhaven Bay 61

Mace, Samuel 90–91, 218n8
Machumps 146, 150, 181, 191, 192, 234n81
Madeira Islands 18, 73
Madre de Deus 205n89
Magellan, Ferdinand 3, 20, 38–39, 41, 148
Manatoan 213n157
Mandoags 54, 62, 63
Manteo 69, 70, 80, 103, 242n48; in England 50, 53, 58; as interpreter 62–63, 72, 192, 194
A Map of Virginia (Smith, 1612) 175, 220n49
mapmaking, maps 22–23, 122
Marlowe, Christopher 46, 88, 136; identified 5
Marston, John 136
Martha's Vineyard 6, 7, 127
Martin, John 154–56, 231n129, 235n9; identified 7; on Jamestown council 104, 106, 163; Smith vs. 8, 132, 151, 153
Martin's Brandon Plantation 7
Martyr d'Anghera, Peter: *De Orbe Novo* 48, 96, 205n110, 219n21; *The Decades of the New World* 195n6
Mary & John 134
Mary of Guise 2
Mary, Queen of England 2, 9, 11, 25, 36, 41, 92, 142, 199n50; Elizabeth and 24, 31, 32, 178–79; identified 2

Mary, Queen of Scots 2, 3, 25, 31, 32, 68, 199n50; execution 65–66, 68, 213n142
Massawomekes 107
"masterless men" 15, 30, 45, 51, 93, 96, 172, 187, 201n105
Matachanna 181
Mattaponi River 227n30
Mattaponis (Mattapanients) 115, 222n82, 223n102, 225n135, 227n24, 239n54
May, Henry 141
Mayflower 194
Medici, Catherine de' 1, 202n25
Medina Sidonia, Alonso Pérez de Guzmán y Sotomayor, 7th Duke of 73–74
Mediterranean 17, 39, 214n10
Menapacant 115, 116, 117
Menatonon 62, 80–81, 192, 208n30, 213n157
Mercator, Geradus 11, 195n1, 198n37
Mermaid Tavern 136, 181
Mexico 22, 52, 62, 104, 113, 223n106
Middle East 17
Middle Temple 44, 204n82
Mississippi River Valley 104
Mobjack Bay 229n85
Molyneux, Emery 46
Monacans 107
Montaigne, Michel de 49
Moonlight 78, 82, 85, 94
Moratucs 54, 62
More, Thomas 207n25
Moscow 22
Mozambique 21
Mulberry Island 158, 165, 167, 175, 178
Muscovy Company (Company of Merchant Adventurers to New Lands) 22
Muslims 17, 18
mutinies 158, 162, 166, 220n52; on Bermuda 146, 147–49

Namontack 146, 150, 234n80
Nansemond River 154, 223n106
nationalism 23, 24
Native Americans 62, 193; Accohanocks 98, 221n61; Accohmacks (Accowmacks) 98, 221n61; amity with 52, 64; anticipated Christianization 9, 14, 45, 52, 58, 93, 126, 167, 204n87, 219n21; Appamatucks 119, 171, 225n135, 227n42; Arrohatecks, 225n135; attacks against 4, 90–91, 155; Chawanocs 54, 208n30; Chesepiocs 60, 61, 66, 69, 103, 190–91, 210n82; Chickahominies 98, 108, 110–12, 113, 176, 221n59, 221n60; Chowanocs 54, 62, 63, 64,

80, 190, 192, 242*n*45; Corees 54, 192; Croatoans 50, 54, 63, 70, 192, 208*n*30; English treatment 57, 166, 212*n*114; English view 45, 49, 52, 77–78, 93, 101–2, 126, 209*n*59, 237*n*3; English viewed by 60; in Europe 49, 50–51, 103; Hakluyt and 49, 93, 204*n*87, 205*n*109, 219*n*21; Iroquois-speaking people 54, 208*n*32; Kecoughtans 104, 108, 113, 152, 155, 164, 168, 170, 221*n*62, 225*n*145; Kiskiacks 103, 159, 225*n*135; Lumbees 193; Mandoags 54, 62, 63; Mattaponis (Mattapanients) 115, 222*n*82, 223*n*102, 225*n*135, 227*n*24, 239*n*54; Nandtanghtacunds 115, 227*n*24; Nansemonds 103, 154, 168, 173, 223*n*106; natural-law rights 223*n*89; Neusioks 54, 192, 208*n*32; Pamunkeys 98, 110, 115, 221*n*62, 222*n*82, 225*n*135, 225*n*137, 225*n*138; Paspaheghs 105, 106–7, 108, 114–15, 159, 170–71, 175, 223*n*115, 223*n*117, 224*n*121; Patawomecks 157, 159, 175, 236*n*27; Piankatanks 115, 191, 227*n*24, 242*n*44; Pomoioks 54, 192, 208*n*32; Quiyoughcohannocks 159, 190, 236*n*33; shamans 59, 72, 102, 113–14, 116–18; Siouan peoples 99; as slaves 48, 206*n*118; Spanish and 48–49, 104; Susquehannocks 107, 122; Toppohanocks 115, 116, 227*n*25; Tuscaroras 54; as victims of English land lust 78, 177, 187, 190, 219*n*22; Warraskoyacks 108, 113, 131, 152, 158, 159, 171, 190, 225*n*145; Weapemeocs 54, 59, 208*n*34, 209–10*n*63; weroances 54, 58–59, 62–63, 72, 101, 105, 116, 118–19, 129, 154; weroansquas 118, 119, 171, 175, 227*n*35, 227*n*42; Youghtamonds 115, 227*n*24; *see also* Algonquin peoples; Powhatan people; Secotan people
naval stores 130
naval technology and architecture 18, 19, 20, 33, 74
navigation 47
Netherlands 1, 6, 30, 34, 37, 66, 92, 96–97, 172, 178, 199*n*50, 199*n*68; African slaves on ships from 177–78; Duke of Parma as Spanish commander in 74, 214–15*n*14; Spain vs. 31–36, 38, 51, 96, 197–98*n*22, 202*n*10
Neuse River 54
Nevis 97, 98
New England 188
New Spain (Nueva España) 13, 21, 35, 45, 48, 52, 63, 135

New World 19, 41, 43, 48, 126; European invasion 172–73; gold and silver in 21, 35, 45
Newfoundland 22, 23, 69, 134, 173, 198*n*68, 224*n*107; discovery 3, 21, 45; Gilbert and 12, 51; Virginia colonists leave for 69, 165, 167, 213*n*153
Newport, Christopher 79, 94, 114, 119, 144–45, 146, 151, 158, 162, 168, 173, 234*n*60, 238*n*31, 239*n*50; as captain of *Sea Venture* 135–37; during Bermuda interlude 144–45, 146, 148; during wreck of *Sea Venture* 137, 140, 141, 143; explores James River 104, 108, 110; identified 7; on Jamestown council 104, 169; Jamestown voyages and 134, 135; Powhatan and 130–31, 229*n*82, 230*n*101; returns to England 106, 108, 112, 113, 129, 132, 175; Smith and 96, 98, 121, 127, 128–29, 130, 224*n*119
Newport News, Virginia 175, 221*n*62
Newtown 86
Nicotiana rustica 177
Nicotiana tabacum 177
nobility 30, 31, 46, 200*n*103
Nonsuch Island 147
Norfolk, Duke of *see* Howard, Thomas, Fourth Duke of Norfolk
Norfolk, Virginia 69, 103
North Africa 17
North America 21, 23, 41, 170; Virginia in 12–13, 45–46
North Atlantic Gyre 135, 139
North Carolina 53, 99, 104, 121, 242*n*51, 242*n*52
North Equatorial Current 134, 135
North Sea 75
Northeast Passage 21, 22
Northumberland, eighth earl of 7
Northwest Passage 4, 21, 22, 51, 92; Gilbert and 12, 41, 42, 43
Nottingham, 1st Earl of *see* Howard, Charles, 1st Earl of Nottingham and 2nd Baron Howard of Ef
Nova Scotia 43
Nugent, Edward 211*n*110

Occaneechee River 62–63
Occaneechi (Great Trading Path) 193, 211*n*98, 242*n*45
Ochanahoen 191
Ocracoke Island *see* Wococon (Wokokon) Island and Inlet
olive oil 196*n*21
Opachisco 176
Opechancanough (Mangopeesomon)

107, 110, 189, 221*n*62, 225*n*137, 225*n*138, 226*n*2; Powhatan and 113–14, 169, 176, 185; 1622 Massacre 187, 189, 211*n*94; 1644 rebellion 189; Smith and 112–15, 117, 190, 226*n*7, 226*n*9, 226*n*11
Opitchapam 110, 117, 221*n*62, 225*n*138, 226*n*2
Opussoquonuske 119, 227*n*42
Orapaks 132, 165, 231*n*124; trade expedition to 155–57
Orient 12, 19, 21, 22, 41; *see also* Asia; China; Far East
Orinoco River 90
Orinoco tobacco 177, 178
Ossomocomuck 54–56, 98, 99, 102, 190, 192, 207*n*20; invasion 113; map 55
Ottoman Empire 31, 96
Outer Banks of North Carolina 5, 53, 54, 192, 209*n*47, 217*n*62
Oviedo, Gonzalo Fernández de 48, 96, 205*n*110
Oxford University 3, 5, 8, 44, 46, 49, 178; Christ Church College 12; Eton College 8; Oriel College 12, 195*n*9
oysters 132

Pacific Ocean 21, 22, 23, 41, 198*n*28; inland route to 51, 62, 93, 105, 109, 110, 126, 131, 231*n*121, 231*n*126
Paine, Henry 148–49, 150, 234*n*72, 234*n*80
Pamlico River 54, 193
Pamlico Sound 50, 53, 57, 59, 69, 80, 216*n*49
Pamunkey River 91, 103, 108, 113–15, 128, 143, 156, 218*n*9, 221*n*62, 225*n*147, 227*n*24, 227*n*30, 229*n*85
Panama 23, 36, 41
Parahunt 154, 235*n*26
Paris 28; Hakluyt in 13, 45, 47
Parliament 25, 90; Members 4, 8, 9, 34, 51, 91, 218*n*4
Parma, Duke of *see* Farnese, Ranuccio I, Duke of Parma
Patience 149, 150, 158, 161, 167, 169–70, 174
Patuxent River 122
Peace of Pocahontas 176
Pemisapan (formerly Wingina) 192; beheading 63, 64; English and 61–62; *see also* Wingina
Percy, Algernon, 10th Earl of Northumberland, 4th Baron Percy 155, 182, 240*n*3
Percy, George 150–52, 157, 161, 169, 182, 240*n*3; election 151, 155; identified 7–8; Paspaheghs murdered by 171, 175; Powhatan trade mission and 150, 154, 157, 159; tyranny and incompetence 145, 160, 178
Percy, Henry, Earl of Northumberland 151
Persons, Elizabeth 144, 233*n*46
Peru 22, 36, 41, 48, 52, 62, 104, 203*n*44, 207*n*23
Petersburg, Virginia 193, 211*n*98
Pettus, Christian 239*n*55
Pettus, Thomas 239*n*55
Philes, Michael 137, 150
Philip II, King of Spain 1, 21, 39, 201*n*108, 201*n*111, 215*n*15, 225*n*134; Elizabeth vs. 13, 27, 30–32, 35–37; The Enterprise of England and 37, 66, 73, 202*n*23; Hawkins and 33, 34, 35; identified 2; Mary and 2, 11, 24, 199*n*50; Netherlands and 197–98*n*22
Philippines 21
Phoenix 129
Piankatank River 122, 229*n*85
Pierce, William 161–62, 241*n*34
Pigafetta, Antonio, *Report of the First Voyage Around the World* 38–39
Pius V, Pope 31, 32, 202*n*23
plantation system 190
Plymouth, England 4, 33, 34, 37, 52, 66, 85, 184, 194, 205*n*89, 214*n*7; Pocahontas at 181, 183
Plymouth Company (subsidiary of The Virginia Company) 91
Pocahontas 165, 177, 227*n*45, 227*n*46, 229*n*83, Argall and 175, 236*n*27, 239*n*54; in England 133, 181–83; English life 61, 188; ill health and death 182, 185, 241*n*34; at Jamestown, 128, 129; kidnapping 6, 8–9, 175, 236*n*27; marriage 6, 7, 9, 61, 176, 188, 239*n*60; in Powhatan context 221*n*62, 230–31*n*116; Smith and 15, 97, 104, 119–24, 128–33, 154, 182–85, 189, 228*n*69, 230*n*110, 230*n*113, 231*n*123; Smith's last meeting with 182–85, 231*n*116
Pochins 104, 152, 221*n*62
Pocosins 55, 86
Point Charles 173
Point Comfort 150, 151–52, 155–59, 162, 164–65, 168, 170, 234*n*82
polygamy 101
porcelain 20–21
Port Ferdinando 50, 82, 83, 206*n*1, 216*n*53, 216*n*57
Portsmouth, Virginia 210*n*85
Portsmouth Island 57
Portugal 5, 20–23, 26, 30, 78; Africa and 17–19; Azores and 4, 18, 46; fishing

vessels from 43, 199*n*68; slave trade and 18, 34
Potomac River 6, 98, 122, 157, 175
Powell, Thomas 233*n*46
Powhatan (Wahunsenacawh) 8, 102, 146, 151, 241*n*36; alliances 103, 107, 114, 115, 117, 175, 221*n*57, 221*n*62, 223*n*91, 225*n*145, 227*n*24, 229*n*80, 236*n*27, 236*n*33; Chesepioc and Roanoke refugees killed by 70, 113–14, 190–91, 210*n*82; children 152, 230*n*112, 235*n*24, 236*n*33; death 185, 226*n*2; English and 130–31, 155–57, 160, 170, 173, 176–77; Jamestown and 102, 103, 108, 113–14, 128, 151, 152, 158, 164, 229*n*82; Opechancanough and 113, 169, 176, 185, 225*n*138; Pocahontas and 176, 239–40*n*63; *see also* Wahunsenacawh
Powhatan Massacre of 1622 187, 189, 211*n*94
Powhatan people 98, 107, 168, 173, 207*n*21, 221*n*57, 225*n*135, 235*n*13; culture 99, 101, 209*n*56; in England 181–82; English and 128–29, 130, 155–57, 163, 176, 227*n*17, 229*n*80; politics 176, 221*n*58, 228*n*49, 228*n*50; religion 221–22*n*67, 222*n*70, 223*n*92, 227*n*30, 228*n*49, 228*n*50; Smith and 104, 123, 125–29, 131, 154, 181, 182–85, 229*n*72; success and failure 165, 169; warfare 103, 145, 227*n*23; women 129, 130–31, 209*n*43, 226*n*15, 239*n*59
Prince Henry's River *see* Pamunkey River
privateering, privateers 14, 40, 66, 206*n*8; base for 51, 52, 65, 207*n*13; English 3, 4, 5, 7, 9, 13, 33–34, 38, 52, 73, 79, 85, 91, 216*n*43; Gilbert and 41–42; Huguenot 35, 36, 37; Newport and 94, 135, 219*n*31; Raleigh and 41, 45, 51, 52, 196*n*20, 202*n*13, 205*n*89; *see also* sea dogs
privy council of Elizabeth 2, 13, 26, 45, 75
Protestantism, Protestants 25, 31, 45, 48, 91, 195*n*13, 198*n*22, 199*n*50, 202*n*12; American colonization and 36, 52; Elizabeth and 24, 51, 77; Reformation and 34–35, 46; *see also* Anglican church; Huguenots; Puritans
puccoon 99, 222*n*73
Puerto Rico 68, 69
Puerto San Julián, Argentina 38, 39, 40
Purchas, Samuel 182
Puritans 6, 8, 66, 172, 212*n*130
pursuit of happiness 190

Ralegh, Walter *see* Raleigh (Ralegh), Walter
Raleigh, Catherine Champernowne 44

Raleigh (Ralegh), Elizabeth Throckmorton 86, 87; identified 6
Raleigh (Ralegh), Walter 88, 136, 155, 182, 188, 197*n*36, 204*n*86, 218*n*4, 240*n*3; character 45, 57; Elizabeth and 13, 28, 42–44, 51, 53, 66, 68, 73, 78, 87, 196*n*19, 205*n*99; execution 186–87; Fernandez and 67, 212*n*134; financier 13–14; in France 195*n*9, 212*n*130; Gilbert and 4, 12, 41; *The Historie of the World* 186; identified 6; imprisonment 1, 2, 15, 87, 90, 91, 182; Lost Colonists and 86, 91–92; Native Americans and 49, 95, 103, 205*n*109; Virginia colony and 12–13, 50, 52, 61, 62, 64–65, 80, 85, 177, 189, 194, 196*n*20, 216*n*45, 217*n*75, 217*n*79
Raleigh, Walter, Senior 44
Raleigh, Wat 90
Rappahannock River 91, 115, 116, 122, 227*n*24, 227*n*25
Rasawrack village 112
Ratcliffe, John 121, 153, 155, 156, 235*n*22, 235*n*24; as captain of *Discovery* 98, 104; death 157, 163; identified 8; Smith vs. 106–9, 121, 127–30, 132, 136, 151, 154, 231*n*129
rats 40, 160, 174
Ravens, Henry 144–45, 150, 191
religion 29, 46, 172; of Algonquins 53, 99, 102, 116–17, 182, 221–22*n*67; Bermuda castaways and 142–43; Elizabethan Religious Settlement and 25, 30, 199*n*56, 199*n*59; at Jamestown 162, 169; Smith and 121–22; struggles over 36, 199*n*56, 212*n*130; *see also and names of sects*; Catholicism; Protestantism, Protestants
Ribault, Jean 68
Richmond, Virginia 131, 235*n*13
Richmond Palace 44, 88
Ridolfi, Roberto 31–32, 201*n*116
Roanoke colonists 212*n*124; fleet 3, 52–53; origins 15, 207*n*18; recruitment 51, 219*n*17; soldiers among 60, 207*n*18; *see also* Lost Colonists
Roanoke colony 61, 64, 73, 166, 194, 209*n*49, 211*n*111; Algonquins and 14–15, 50, 93; Raleigh and 6, 177; *see also* Virginia colony
Roanoke Island 65, 80, 82, 193, 210*n*81; clues on 84, 193; fortified 50–60, 193; as site of England's first New World colony 51, 189
Roanoke (Moratuc) River 5, 62, 192, 193, 211*n*98
Robinson, Jehu 110, 112, 115, 127, 226*n*9
Rodanthe, North Carolina 83

Index

Rolfe, Bermuda 148, 149, 234*n*80
Rolfe, Elizabeth 188
Rolfe, Jane Pierce 241*n*34
Rolfe, Jane Poythress (Poyers) 188
Rolfe, John 144, 149, 188, 190, 233*n*45, 241*n*28, 241*n*34; identification 9; Pocahontas married to 7, 9, 61, 176, 177, 185, 239*n*60; tobacco and 177, 240*n*65; of yeoman stock 163, 172
Rolfe, Rebecca *see* Pocahontas
Rolfe, Sarah Hacker 9, 144, 148, 149, 176, 233*n*45
Rolfe, Thomas 7, 176, 185, 188
Royal Navy 26, 30, 34, 65, 74–75, 197*n*15
Russia 22
rutters 20

Sahara Desert 17, 197*n*5
Sahel 18
St. Bartholomew's Day Massacre (1572) 36, 37, 202*n*12
St. Elmo's fire 140, 233*n*26
St. George's Harbor 149
St. George's Island, Bermuda 142–50, 174
St. James Palace 75
St. Lawrence River 21
Salisbury, Earl of *see* Cecil, Robert, Earl of Salisbury
Samuel, Edward 146, 150, 234*n*80
Sanderson, William 13, 78; identified 6
Sargasso Sea 135
sassafras 56, 208*n*40, 210*n*81, 218*n*8
Scandinavia 22
Scotland 23, 75
Scrivener, Matthew 163
sea dogs 37, 40, 41, 45, 74, 75, 79, 88; *see also* privateering, privateers
Sea Venture 6, 9–10, 153, 158, 170, 191, 194, 232*n*5, 233*n*35; Bermuda adventure 134–50, 178; as flagship of Jamestown resupply fleet 135, 166; wreck 9, 10, 15, 137–41
Secotan people 4, 50, 54, 63, 64, 65, 192; attack by 69, 83, 213*n*153; Roanoke colonists' relations with 57–59, 68, 80
Senegal River 18
sex and sexuality 60, 129, 155, 199*n*64, 206*n*122; miscegenation and 176–77; of Powhatans 130–31, 226*n*15, 226*n*16, 231*n*116, 231*n*117
Seymour, Jane 1
Shakespeare, William 75, 88, 136, 187; *The Tempest* 15, 181
Shirley, Cecilia, Lady De La Warr 9, 153, 182, 240*n*10
Shirley Hundred 173

Sicklemore, John *see* Ratcliffe, John
Sicklemore, Michael 190
silk 21
silver 21, 51, 52; London Company and 92, 105, 126; in New Spain 41, 48, 203*n*44; royal fifth 41, 48, 203*n*52
Skicóac village 61, 210*n*85
Skiko 62, 63, 64, 192
Smith, John 7, 108, 111, 144, 151, 228*n*56, 231*n*129; accomplishments 121–23; Algonquin reeducation 115–17, 154; capture 112, 226*n*7; character 120, 220*n*44, 220*n*47, 220*n*48; Chesapeake Bay explored by 128, 130, 156, 157, 228*n*68; death and burial 189; early life 96–97; *General Historie of Virginia* (1624) 183, 220*n*49; identified 8; incarceration 96, 97, 105; injured by powder burns 132, 133, 145, 151, 152, 154, 231*n*127, 231*n*132; Jamestown council and 104–6, 121, 122, 130, 163, 224*n*119; London Company and 125–26, 132, 133; *A Map of Virginia* (1612) 175, 220*n*49; New England coast explored by 188; Opechancanough and 112–15, 117, 190, 226*n*7, 226*n*9; Pocahontas and 15, 97, 104, 119–24, 128–33, 189, 228*n*69, 230*n*110, 231*n*123; Pocahontas's last meeting with 182–85, 231*n*116; Powhatan and 104, 123, 125–29, 131, 182–85, 229*n*72, 229*n*81; as president 152, 153; Ratcliffe and 106, 108–9, 121, 127–20, 130, 132, 136, 151, 154, 231*n*129; returns to England 134, 151, 155, 163; shortness 96, 108, 113–16; at Werowocomoco 117–20, 122–26; West and 153–54; writings 97, 118, 119, 125, 189
Smythe, Thomas 6, 13, 78–79, 91, 133, 135, 175, 188, 219*n*18; identified 8; Jamestown and 162, 166–67, 172, 188, 238*n*28
Smythe, Thomas "Customer" 8
sodomy 48, 106, 238*n*28
Somers, George 153, 158, 162, 178, 238*n*37; as admiral of Jamestown resupply fleet 135–37, 143; death 174, 239*n*39, 239*n*40; during Bermuda interlude 145–50; during wreck of *Sea Venture* 137–41, 143, 144; identified 9; on Jamestown council 163, 169; as principal of London Company 91, 92; returns to Bermuda 169–70, 173–74
Somers, Matthew 153, 162, 170, 173–74, 239*n*40
South Carolina 104, 218*n*12
Southern Sea 23, 36; *see also* Pacific Ocean

Spain 2, 19–21, 23, 26, 30, 48–49, 82, 97, 103, 119; Black Legend and 48; England's war with 6, 11, 13, 31–32, 45, 87; English privateers and 36, 39, 41, 45, 63, 196n20; fishing vessels from 43, 199n68; Native Americans and 48–49, 104; Netherlands vs. 31–38, 197–98n22, 202n10; New World explorations 22–23; Portugal and 19–20; relations with England 37, 41, 91, 193, 197n32, 199n50, 201n118; spies for 7, 136, 168, 225n133, 225n134, 231n121; as threat to England's American colonies 59, 65, 68, 73, 86, 105, 136, 168, 210n72; in Tidewater Virginia and Carolinas 102–3, 218n12; treasure fleets 52, 135, 202n13, 203n44, 207n12
Spanish Armada 6, 14, 72–74, 94–95, 202n11, 214n13, 215n22; defeat 3, 4, 67, 75–78, 164, 215n15, 215n16, 215n19; The Enterprise of England and 37, 66, 73
Spanish Inquisition 31, 33, 48
Spanish Main 48, 63
Spelman, Henry 235n22, 235n26, 236n27
Spenser, Edmund 46, 77, 88, 205n99
Spice Islands 33
spice trade and spices 17, 19, 20, 33
Spicer, Edward 79, 83–84
Squirrel 43, 204n76
Stafford, Edward 211n111
Starving Time (Jamestown) 6, 106, 154, 160, 241n34
Strachey, William 174, 181, 221n60, 223n115, 227n23, 227n24; Algonquin glossary 159, 175; earlier life and career 136–37; *The Historie of Travell Into Virginia Britania* 174, 175; identified 9; as Jamestown secretary 151, 169; journal 139, 142, 148, 161; *Laws, Divine, Morall and Martiall, &c.* 173, 174; Lost Colonists and 146, 191, 192; writings 174–75
Straits of Magellan 3, 22, 41, 198n37
Stuart, Arabella 186
Stuart, Henry, Lord Darnley 2
sugar 33, 34
Susan Constant 94–95, 103, 105, 134, 189
Susquehanna River 122
Swallow 153, 156, 157, 159, 166, 169
Syon House 182

Tachonekintaco 108, 131, 152, 225n145
Tappahannock, Virginia 115, 227n25
tar and pitch 128
Tatahcoope 236n33
The Tempest (Shakespeare) 15, 181
Tenochtotlan 62

Terceira 72
Terra Australis 22
Thames River 1, 46, 75, 76, 94, 185, 188, 219n27
Throckmorton, Elizabeth *see* Raleigh (Ralegh), Elizabeth Throckmorton
Tidewater Virginia: Algonquins 54, 60; drought in 99; map 100; Spanish in 103; *see also* Tsenacommacah
Tierra del Fuego 22, 198n37
Tilbury 75
tobacco 9, 10, 177, 186–88, 190, 219n31, 240n64, 240n65, 241n27
Todkill, Anas 190
Torporley, Nathaniel 46
Tower of London: Elizabeth imprisoned in 2 4; Pocahontas visits 182, 240n3; Raleigh imprisoned in 1, 2, 15, 87, 90, 186
trade: among Native Americans 56, 62, 160, 193, 236n28; for furs 22; with Native Americans 58–59, 70, 154–57, 175, 187, 211n92, 225n139, 230n100, 242n44
trade winds 20, 33, 57, 63, 197n6; Jamestown voyage and 134, 135, 139
Treaty of Joinville (1584) 206n7
Treaty of London (1604) 91
Treaty of Tordesillas (1494) 20, 21, 197n21
Trinidad 177
Triumph 213n139
A True Relation (Smith, 1608) 125
Tsenacommacah (Tidewater Virginia) 98–99, 107, 113, 116–17, 120, 123, 146, 168, 179, 184, 190; deforestation 187, 225n125; de Velasco's repatriation to 102–3, 223n106; map 100; pacification 170, 171; population 207n20, 221n63
Tyger 13, 58, 60, 196n20, 209n46; runs aground 57, 64, 80

Unity 153, 166
Uttamatomakkin 181–84
Uttamussak 116, 117, 227n30

Velasco, Don Luis de 102–3, 224n107
Venezuela 90
Venice 3, 17
Verazzano, Giovanni da 20, 198n28
Vespucci, Amerigo 20
Virgin Queen (Elizabeth I) 12, 25, 44, 49
Virginia 153, 156, 159, 165
Virginia Beach 70, 103
Virginia colony 12, 13–14, 171, 177, 190; governors 6, 9, 10, 166, 178; mortality in 187–88; naming 12, 44; patent for 46, 50, 64; purposes 51–52; Raleigh and 44, 46, 50, 66, 87

Virginia Company of London 7–10, 197n36, 215n43, 219n24, 234n60, 239n43; charter 91, 189; motives 14, 126, 219n26; Roanoke and 92–93

Wahunsenacawh (Powhatan) 15, 98, 221n57, 221n62, 222n82, 223n102, 225n138, 226n2, 235n13
Wainman, Ferdinando 169, 237n13
Waldo, Richard 163
Walsingham, Francis 65, 87, 196n18, 196n22, 209n49; Elizabeth and 12, 13, 45; identified 3
Wanchese 61, 63, 70, 103, 213n153; in England 50, 53, 58
Warner, Walter 46, 47
Washington, North Carolina 193
Waters, Robert 146, 150, 174
Watts, John 79, 215–16n43
Werowocomoco 108, 113, 128, 145, 156, 225n147, 229n77, 229n85; Newport at 130–31, 229n82; Smith at 117–20, 122–26, 183
West, Francis 150, 154, 169, 190, 229n77; beheads captives 157, 159; identified 8; sails for England 158, 164, 166, 236n30; Smith and 153–55
West, Thomas, Baron De La Warr 9, 153, 166, 172, 191, 237n1, 237n5, 237n13; Algonquin policy 167, 170, 175; arrives at Jamestown 169, 170, 189; as governor for life 168, 172; identified 8
West Africa 17, 139
West Country of England 14, 206n120; Raleigh and 41, 42–43, 204n86; seadogs 13, 14, 91
West Hundred 173
West Indies 5, 9, 56, 66, 104, 177, 232n11; privateers and 36, 51, 52
Westminster Abbey 91, 182

Westminster Palace 186
Weyhohomo 154, 223n106
Whitaker, Alexander: identified 8–9; Pocahontas and 8–9, 176
White, John 65, 212n134, 216n45, 216n48; Chesapeake Bay explored by 60, 70; death 85, 86; expedition 65, 66–72, 94; identified 6; Lost Colonists and 191; map by 192, 193–94; as member of Durham House, 51, 53; narrative 85–86; paintings by 51, 57, 60, 61, 64, 86; returns to England 71–72, 192, 214n165; Roanoke resupply effort 73, 78, 79–86
Whitehall Palace 11, 46, 181, 182
Wimble Shoals 83, 85
wine 33
Wingfield, Edward Maria 7, 104, 127, 151, 158, 219n17, 220n42, 224n121; identified 9; as Jamestown council president 105–7; London Company and 91–92, 95; Smith vs. 96, 111, 220n52
Wingfield, Richard 91–92
Wingina 54, 58, 59, 61; *see also* Pemisapan
Winne, Peter 163
Wococon (Wokokon) Island and Inlet 79, 80, 207n19, 209n47, 216n48, 216n49, 216n53
women 26; Algonquin 48, 56, 60, 101, 118, 157, 176; Jamestown and 106, 137, 144, 153, 172, 173, 187
Wowinchopunck 105, 107, 114, 115, 223n115
Wright, John 71
Wyatt, Francis 178; identified 9
Wyatt, Henry 178
Wyatt, Thomas 9, 24, 178, 199n51
Wyatt, Thomas (the poet) 178
Wyatt's Rebellion 9, 25, 199n51

Yeardley, George 178, 189; identified 10
York River 221n62, 225n147